Akron · Alamosa · Arvada · Aspen ·

Basalt · Battlement Mesa · Bennett · Bo

Broomfield · Brush · Buena Vista

Carbondale · Castle Rock · Cedaredge

The Colorado
Golf Bible

Colorado Springs · Commerce City · Cope · Copper Mountain
Cortez · Craig · Crested Butte · Crestone · Delta · Denver · Durango
Eads · Eagle · Eaton · Edwards · Elizabeth · Englewood · Erie · Estes Park
Evergreen · Falcon · Firestone · Flagler · Florence · Fort Collins · Fort
Lupton · Fort Morgan · Fowler · Fruita · Glenwood Springs · Golden
Granby · Grand Junction · Grand Lake · Greeley · Gunnison · Gypsum
· Haxtun · Highlands Ranch · Holyoke · Hugo · Ignacio · Julesburg ·
Keystone · Kirk · La Junta · La Veta · Lakewood · Lamar · Larkspur · Las
Animas · Lafayette · Leadville · Limon · Littleton · Longmont
Louisville · Loveland · Mancos · Meeker · Milliken · Monte Vista
Montrose · Monument · Morrison · New Castle · Niwot · Pagosa
Springs · Parker · **David R. Holland** · Ridgway · Rifle
· Rocky Ford · Salida · Sedalia · Silverthorne · Snowmass · South Fork
Springfield · Steamboat Springs · Sterling · Stratton · Telluride
Thornton · Trinidad · Vail · Walsenburg · Westcliffe · Westminster
Windsor · Winter Park · Wolcott · Woodland Park · Wray · Yuma

www.golfbibles.com

The Colorado Golf Bible
David R. Holland

Published by:

Fandango Publishing Company
Dallas, Texas USA
www.fandangopublishing.com
Please report errors and changes to: updates@golfbibles.com

Printed in the USA

Copyright © 2004

Editors: Regan Brown and Jason Stone
Design and layout: Mary Catherine Kozusko
Production Artist: Bryan Cox

   ISBN: 0-9724707-2-7
   Library of Congress Control Number: 2004105778

   First edition
   Printed and bound in the United States of America

The Golf Bible Phenomenon

Envision a guide to golf and travel that offers some erudition and discernment along with a totally practical approach to the wandering golfer's needs. The book would combine scrupulously researched listings of every place to golf, sleep, eat, and drink with the willingness to push the envelope for adventure.

Die-hard golf bums, occasional hacks, country club members, aspiring beginners, and even a broader readership that includes the budget-minded and those interested only in traveling the most obscure regions of their respective states, relish a Golf Bibles' wit and eagerness to explore the back roads, as well as its willingness to embrace the fact that golfers want value as well as variety, and that not every golfer wants or can afford the high-toned, ultimate links experience.

The Golf Bible series is more than a golf directory. It isn't just about where to play golf, but rather your guide to getting out there, period. Nothing equals pursuing the game of golf and being able to travel the open roads. "One of life's greatest joys is traveling and playing golf-wherever it may be." Go ahead. Step inside and find out how to make the most of your next golf adventure.

HELP US UPDATE

We've gone to a lot of effort to ensure that *The Colorado Golf Bible* is accurate and up-to-date. Inevitably, by the time we go to press some of the information in here will already be out of date. Future updates will not only ensure accuracy and inclusiveness, but continue to enhance the book's style and scope as well as develop content that might be lacking because of the vastness of the subject. If we've got it wrong or left something out, please let us know. We'll credit all contributions, and send a copy of the next edition (or any other Golf Bible you prefer) for the best letters. Please send all correspondence via email to updates@golfbibles.com, or to:

GOLF BIBLE UPDATES
P.O. BOX 88
WESTON, CO 81091

ACKNOWLEDGEMENTS

Dan Hogan, inductee Colorado Golf Hall of Fame and noteworthy Colorado golf historian. City of Denver Municipal Golf Courses, Gregg Blew, Ken Shearer and Tom Woodard. *Colorado AvidGolfer*, Jon Rizzi, Editor. Cherry Hills Country Club, Gene Neher, Heritage Committee. George E. Brown III, author of the book "Cherry Hills Country Club, 1922-1997". Kent Stephens, College Football Hall of Fame. University of Colorado athletic department. Mark Simpson, Dave Plati. Colorado Golf Association, Aaron Kellough, Dustin Jensen. Colorado Tourism Office. Convention and Visitor's Bureau web sites throughout Colorado. Chamber of Commerce, City, County web sites throughout Colorado. Special thanks to the Colorado Golf Hall of Fame.

Dedicated to every 10-handicapper who experiences elation with a 75 one day, felt a little cocky, and followed it up with a shank-infested 90 the next time out.

PHOTO CREDITS

Cover photos by Dick Durrance II, The Golf Club at Redlands Mesa*

David Snyder, Gene Neher-Arnold Palmer photo

Bob McIntyre, The Broadmoor photos

CU Sports Information Department, Hale Irwin and Dale Douglass photos

Special thanks to Dan Hogan and the Colorado Golf Hall of Fame

*DRINKER DURRANCE GRAPHICS

Internationally renowned photographer Dick Durrance II and his partner and wife, Susan G. Drinker, have teamed together to provide the world of golf with the ultimate solution to golf course photography—fully optimized digital images.

Combining the extensive skills honed from 37 years of professional work including a 7-year staff position at National Geographic and 20 years of corporate and advertising assignments, Dick has spent the past 10 years traveling the world's most beautifully crafted golf terrain. His list of clients include Troon Golf, for whom he works as their preferred photographer, the PGA TOUR, who commissioned him to photograph their TPC courses, and a wide assortment of individual courses.

Susan, a professional photographer for the past 22 years, brings both her unique photographic aesthetic and her masterful printing skills to the team. As a graduate student at the Art Institute of Boston, she embraced the magic of the darkroom, which she has now transferred to the new world of digital retouching. Her client list includes Marlboro, for whom she became the first woman to be offered an assignment, United Airlines, Fuji Film and Houghton Mifflin. She and Dick have worked together for the past 15 years, and have combined their talents in many areas, including the production of Dick's two most recent books, Golfers, published in 2000, and The PGA TOUR, a look behind the scenes, published in 2003.

With their combined talents, they bring what they term, Virtual Perfection, to the craft of golf course photography. Dick photographs the courses with a high-resolution digital camera, which provides greater control over the color saturation and contrast in the images. Sue then optimizes each image, removing unsightly objects, divots, and discolorations as well as enhancing skies, lakes and mountains.

Their final product represents all of the best that each course has to offer, images that capture the magic of the golfing experience.

CONTENTS

BEFORE YOU TEE UP: A GUIDE TO THIS GUIDE

Miller Barber said it best about travel and golf. "I'm happiest when I have a hotel room key in my pocket."

The luckiest people on earth are the ones who get to see the world because they love to travel and can afford to. Some suit-and-tie guys who are forced to travel and sit in excruciating meetings all day hate business travel. Little wonder.

But how about the ones who travel and play golf for their vacation? Lots of Coloradans ski in the winter, but some take off on a January day when there's snow on the ground and point the SUV westward—somewhere near old Route 66. Tomorrow they'll be playing golf in 70-degree weather in the desert of Arizona or on the Pacific Coast of California. Could life be any better?

Yes it can. You could be playing the perfect course on a 70-degree day in the glorious Rocky Mountains on July 4th.

This travel-golf guide book tells you where to go, which courses are must-plays, where to sleep, where to dine, and what other activities you can enjoy on a golf vacation in Colorado. This book wasn't meant to be pretty on your coffee table. It was written to be used. Throw it in the trunk next to your golf clubs. It doesn't matter if you spill a Fat Tire Ale on *The Colorado Golf Bible*; just dry it off and keep dreaming of golf in the Grand Valley at The Golf Club at Redlands Mesa.

Imagine passing through Trinidad on I-25 motoring home to Denver from an Albuquerque business trip. It's a glorious day, the sky is blue, the wind is calm, and you have some time on your hands. Pull out *The Colorado Golf Bible* and lo and behold—right here on the historic Mountain Branch of the Santa Fe Trail there's a little nine-hole golf course that many believe is the premier hidden gem of Rocky Mountain golf. Hmm, the book even has directions to the course.

Heck, even a non-golfer might enjoy the tidbits and history factoids about the old days of Colorado to be found in these pages. Several worthy Colorado groups and golfers are trying to preserve the history of golf in the state. *The Colorado Golf Bible* aims to do that as well.

The Colorado Golf Bible is more than a travel-golf book, informing readers about Colorado's history and serving as one of the state's most comprehensive travel guides even for the non-golfer. What other Rocky Mountain guidebooks offer travel information about remote locales such as Eads, Rifle, or Crestone? And unlike most books with a bottom line, you don't even have to read it all. Use it for reference the next time you're in Grand Junction or Delta or Cortez.

This book includes narratives of more than 240 golf courses, and we've tried to spice up the familiar golf jargon by telling you when a golf course has a claim to fame or if it has historical significance. After all, how many ways can you say "par-3 beauty, "Rocky Mountain vistas," or "prairie-links golf"?

We tried to dig up the true architects and dates—who designed the front nine, and who designed the back nine? Who came in years later and did extensive remodeling? But this is a nigh-impossible task—many times the pro or general manager didn't have the answer and couldn't refer us to someone who would know. For years and years, the pro at Salida said no one knew who designed the course, but someone recently decided to do the research and found the answer. Investigative work isn't easy.

Something this book isn't going to do is rank courses. That's a public relations job, and one way *Golf Digest* and *Golf Magazine* sell their product. Rankings are just opinions. And everyone has one. We will tell you when the above publications gave a high rank to a particular Colorado course. And we will tell you about the courses not to miss. We are however, presenting *Colorado AvidGolfer Magazine's* "Best of Colorado" article, which contains a ranking voted on by readers.

But who is to say you can't have just as much fun at Cattails Golf Course in Alamosa, paying a few dollars at 5 p.m., over a $225 round at Cordillera's Mountain Course with a forecaddie? Give me Alamosa any day.

The Colorado Golf Bible won't be listing any fax numbers, either. What good is that to someone on the road? Why do you need to know the name of the pro? By the time this is printed, they've moved on to another job. How does it help you when a so-called golf guidebook gives you a P.O. box? You can't plug that into your GPS system. And if you need to know what the dress code is, you need to go ask your mommy for a clothing allowance.

We do not list specific pricing for each course. Instead we will give you a price range. And if one of the courses on the I-70 westward corridor is overpriced, we will tell you so. Yep, The Broadmoor is pricey, but check the website frequently—they do offer specials from time to time. It's worth the money, even at full price.

We are listing country clubs, because from time to time you municipal golfers will get an invitation. And there are private clubs, like Sterling Country Club, that offer tee times to visitors with out having to be a member of a private club. Sure, there are places like Kissing Camels in Colorado Springs where they won't even let you in the gate. And remember, Sanctuary may be one of the most exclusive private clubs in the world, but you can play it—in a charity event. For a public-access golfer, a day on the fairways of Sanctuary is something he'll remember for the rest of his life.

Our aim was to make *The Colorado Golf Bible* the most comprehensive and interesting tour guide to Colorado golf available. To do that, we could use your input. This is only the first of many editions, a living, breathing organism that will keep evolving just as the game and our enjoyment of it has evolved. So please help us out. If you experience something that you enjoy on your golf travels, make a note of it and tell us. Maybe that Monster green-chili burrito you had at Pueblo's Walking Stick was the best ever. Or maybe you played the Rio Grande Club in South Fork and the Apple Dumpling Bed & Breakfast was world-class (we agree on that one). Jot these items down and e-mail us at feedback@coloradogolfbible.com.

Colorado offers an endless variety of golf experiences, many of which have never before been covered in detail. The typical layouts have been addressed, but no one knows about the hidden gems of the eastern plains. The Colorado golf experience is wide open. There are no limits to what you can experience.

We're going to provide you with information and inspiration, but what you do with that is the key. This book transcends any other guidebook because it will help you create your own ultimate golf experience. Fill up the ice chest, spread out the maps, throw the clubs in the back of the truck, and head down the road for your own Colorado golf adventure.

Now, turn the pages and start planning your next round of golf.

DAVID R. HOLLAND
APRIL 2004

COURSE PRICE LEGEND — Due to the constant fluctuation in green fee pricing, as well as the various rates one might pay based on a particular day of the week or time of day, the following price legend depicts an approximate green fee with cart during peak times. Note that these figures do not depict any sort of course rating, and are not official price guides to each facility, but are presented to give the reader the approximate cost to play with a cart.

$ = $1 TO $24
$$ = $25 TO $49
$$$ = $50 TO $74
$$$$ = $75 TO $100+

Walter Fairbanks swings away in 1904 at Denver Country Club.

COLORADO GOLF: A BRIEF HISTORY

The year was 1895. The City of Denver had already been around for about 25 years. The first professional football game was played, in Latrobe, Pennsylvania, between the Latrobe YMCA and the Jeannette Athletic Club. (Latrobe won the contest 12-0.). Wilhelm Rontgen discovered a type of radiation later known as X-Rays. W.G. Morgan invented volleyball. Buster Keaton, the American comedian, actor was born.

And golf came to Colorado.

1895   Overland Park Golf Course opens (it moved to another location in 1930).

1898   Patty Jewett Golf Course opens as the Town and Gown Club. Patty Jewett is the oldest course in Colorado in the same location.

1902   The grounds of Overland Park Golf Course serve as Denver's first auto racing strip, as well as the site of the first horse racing track.

1903   Pueblo Country Club opens.

1904   Denver Country Club opens.

1910   The grounds of Overland Park Golf Course became the site for Colorado's first air field.

1913   Bill Cody, a.k.a. Buffalo Bill, performs his final "Wild West Show" on the grounds of Overland Park.

1915   Trinidad Golf Course opens. The architect is unknown, but according to legend, Donald Ross or one of his crew worked or consulted on the course while also constructing Broadmoor East.

1915   The Colorado Golf Association is founded, headed by M.A. McLaughlin.

1915 - 1916   Frank Woodward of Denver serves as President of USGA.

1918   The Broadmoor East opens, designed by Donald Ross. He describes it as his best work to date – even better than the course now known as Pinehurst #2. It also claims to be the world's only championship course over 6,000 feet in elevation.

1923   Cherry Hills Country Club opens. Architect William S. Flynn is paid $4,500 to design the layout.

1926   Wellshire Country Club opens. Legendary architect Donald Ross is paid a reported $1.50 per hole for designing the course.

The trouble that most of us find with the modern matched sets of clubs is that they don't really seem to know any more about the game that the old ones did. —Robert Browning

1927 A member at Cherry Hills proposes filling in the moat around the 17th green because he is losing so many golf balls. A membership poll votes down the change, 59-3.

1932 From August to April of the next year, Cherry Hills' green fees are reduced from $3 to $1.50 on Wednesdays, weekends, and holidays and to $1 or other days.

1936 The City of Denver buys Wellshire for $60,000. The course name is changed to Wellshire Golf Club.

1937 Will Nicholson of Denver serves as President of the USGA from 1937 to 1941.

1937 From September 1937 to October 1938, new members at Cherry Hills don't even have to pay an initiation fee—just $15 a month.

1938 Ralph Guldahl wins the U.S. Open at Cherry Hills Country Club with a score of 284.

1941 Vic Ghezzi defeats Byron Nelson in the PGA Championship at Cherry Hills.

1946 Smiley Quick wins the USGA Public Links at Wellshire.

1947 Charles "Babe" Lind becomes the first native Coloradan to play in The Masters.

1948 Ben Hogan wins the Denver Open at Wellshire Golf Course.

1957 PGA Tour star Dow Finsterwald wins the Vardon Trophy (70.30 stroke average). He also makes his first Ryder Cup team and goes on to play on the 1959-61-63 teams. (He captained the 1977 Ryder Cup team.)

1958 Dow Finsterwald wins the PGA Championship by two strokes over Billy Casper at Llanerch CC in Ardmore, Pennsylvania, shooting 14-under-par. Starting with this tournament, the format of the PGA Championship is changed from match play to stroke play. He is selected PGA Tour Player of the Year.

1958 Tommy Jacobs, who was born in Denver, wins the Denver Centennial Open at Wellshire. Jacobs leads the entire tournament, which included Arnold Palmer.

1959 Jack Nicklaus wins the U.S. Amateur at Broadmoor East.

1959 Bill Wright of Seattle wins the U.S. Pub Links at Wellshire, becoming the first African-American to win a USGA event.

1959 Jim English of Denver is low amateur at the U.S. Open at Winged Foot.

1959 The Broadmoor's Barbara McIntire wins the U.S. Amateur in '59 and '60.

It's not altogether to your advantage while standing over a 5-iron shot to be thinking, "I've got to remember to get some Freon in the Toyota."—Dan Jenkins

PARK HILL G.C.
1948

BOB HOPE JOHN ROGERS

Macho poses from Bob Hope and John Rogers at Park Hill in 1948.

1960 Arnold Palmer wins the U.S. Open at Cherry Hills Country Club. He drives the par-4 first green, registers a birdie and a 65, and posts a 280 score.

1961 Dave Hill, Colorado Golf Hall of Famer, wins the Denver Open.

1962 USA wins the Curtis Cup at The Broadmoor, 8-1.

1962 Bob Goalby wins the Denver Open.

1962 Fire guts the restaurant at the Wellshire Clubhouse, causing $300,000 in damages.

1962 Arnold Palmer edges out best friend Dow Finsterwald for the 1962 Masters title.

1963 Chi Chi Rodriquez wins the Denver Open at Denver Country Club. The diminutive PGA Tour pro once served a stint as assistant pro at The Broadmoor.

1964 Bill Bisdorf secures the inaugural Colorado Open at Hiwan Golf Club. When he also wins in 1965 and 1967 he becomes the first three-time champion.

1967 Don January wins the PGA Championship at Columbine Country Club. Playing 7,436 yards, Columbine holds the distinction of being the longest course ever to host a PGA Championship.

1967 Bob Dickson wins the U.S. Amateur at The Broadmoor.

1972 Thirty minutes of golf instruction cost $8 at Cherry Hills. "A" caddies earn $5 an hour and "B" caddies take home $3.50.

1974 Boulder High grad Hale Irwin wins his first U.S. Open at Winged Foot Golf Club, Mamaroneck, New York.

1977 Paul Runyan is awarded the National PGA Horton Smith distinction. He served head pro at Green Gables Country Club from 1973 to 1982.

All those who drive thirty yards suppose themselves to be great putters. —Sir Walter Simpson

1977 The City of Denver issues a temporary order banning golf cart use at Wellshire, as part of a dispute with the concessionaire.

1978 Andy North wins U.S. Open at Cherry Hills with a 285.

1978 Legendary CU Buff volunteer golf coach Les Fowler dies. The Colorado Hall of Famer, born in 1949, coached Hale Irwin and Dale Douglass.

1979 Hale Irwin wins his second U.S. Open at Inverness Club in Toledo, Ohio.

1980 Larry Webb wins the Colorado Open at Hiwan. besting Bob Tway by two strokes.

1980 Will Nicholson Jr. serves as President of the USGA for two years.

1982 Cherry Hills resident Craig Stadler opens The Masters with a 75, but wins in a playoff with Dan Pohl.

1982 USA wins the Curtis Cup at Denver Country Club, 14 to 3.

1982 Juli Inkster wins her third U.S. Amateur, this one at The Broadmoor.

1983 Larry Webb wins the PGA Club Pro Championship at La Quinta in California.

1983 Jay Sigel defeats Randy Sonnier in the U.S. Mid-Amateur at Cherry Hills.

1985 Hubert Green wins the PGA Championship at Cherry Hills with a score of 278.

1986 The International makes its debut at Castle Pines Golf Club from a vision by Jack Vickers. His use of the modified Stableford system is a hit with the tour pros. Vickers' hospitality also is heralded throughout the PGA Tour.

1986 Fort Morgan's Dale Douglass wins U.S. Senior Open at Scioto, Ohio. He is a former golfer at CU.

1986 Bill Loeffler wins USGA Mid-Amateur at Annandale, Mississippi.

1986 The Broadmoor's Judy Bell captains the Curtis Cup team.

1987 Tom Woodard, Denver's Director of Golf, wins the first Colorado PGA Apprentice Championship and becomes a three-time champion with wins in 1988 and 1989.

1987 Colorado Golf Hall of Famer Bill Loeffler plays on the winning Walker Cup team.

I have a classic case of the yips. You know, people say it's all in your head, but it's not a mental thing with me. I have a physical problem. When I sign my name, sometimes the pen jumps and there's nothing I can do. There's a loose wire back there or something. There's nothing you can do.—Johnny Miller

1987   Eleven-year-old Tiger Woods competes in U.S. Junior Amateur at Sonnenalp Golf Club (formerly known as Singletree Golf Club).

1988   Yuma, Colorado native and CU grad Steve Jones wins the Colorado Open at Hiwan with a four-stroke victory over Bruce Summerhays.

1990   Phil Mickelson defeats Manny Zerman in the U.S. Amateur at Cherry Hills.

1990   Hale Irwin wins U.S. Open at Medinah C.C. in Medinah, Illinois.

1992   Bill Loeffler plays on U.S. Walker Cup Team.

1993   Jack Nicklaus wins the U.S. Senior Open at Cherry Hills with a score of 278.

1995   Annika Sorenstam wins the Women's U.S. Open at Broadmoor East.

1996   Steve Jones wins the U.S. Open at Oakland Hills C.C. in Birmingham, Mich.

1996   Jonathan Kaye of Boulder wins the Colorado Open at Inverness with a 269 score.

1996 - 1997   Judy Bell of Colorado Springs serves as President of the USGA.

1997   The Jim Engh-designed Sanctuary opens in Sedalia. *Golf Digest* names it Best New Private Course in the USA.

1998   Hale Irwin wins the U.S. Senior Open at Riviera C.C. in Pacific Palisades, CA.

1998   The Broadmoor hosts the PGA Cup Matches. USA PGA Club Pros defeat club pros from Great Britain and Ireland, 17-9.

1999   Mike McGetrick, who teaches Juli Inkster and other LPGA stars, is named National PGA Teacher of the Year.

2000   Hale Irwin wins the U.S. Senior Open at Saucon Valley C.C. in Bethlehem, Pennsylvania.

2000   Kaye Kessler, the first golf journalist to interview a young boy named Jack Nicklaus, receives the PGA's National Lifetime Achievement Award for Journalism.

2002   Derek Tolan, 16-year-old ThunderRidge High School golfer, qualifies for the U.S. Open at Bethpage Black. The USGA says Tolan is the first amateur in history to have played in the U.S. Open, the U.S. Public Links Championship, the U.S. Junior Amateur, and the U.S. Amateur in the same year, doing so between June and August, 2002. He signs to play for the Colorado Buffaloes.

2003   Craig Stadler wins on two tours back-to-back. He wins the Champions Tour Players Championship and the B.C. Open on the PGA Tour.

To break 90, mentally remove every pin and instead concentrate on hitting greens. Take dead aim at the center of each green. Do this from every distance outside 50 yards.—Jim McLean

2003 Colorado Open canceled for lack of sponsorship.

2003 Colorado PGA section opens historical display at the Bear Dance club-house.

2004 Colorado Golf Hall of Fame display opens at Riverdale Dunes.

2004 Denver-born Jonathan Kaye, who grew up playing at City Park, wins the FBR Open in Scottsdale, his second tour win.

2005 U.S. Women's Open scheduled for Cherry Hills.

Dan Hogan, Colorado Hall of Fame member and the state's leading golf historian.

COLORADO GOLF HALL OF FAME

THE COLORADO HALL OF FAME, founded in 1973, honors men and women who have made outstanding contributions to golf in Colorado. Preserving the history of Colorado golf is part of its mission. A board of directors evaluates men, women, amateurs, and professionals for selection. Selection criteria include playing ability and record (local, state, national); teaching ability and results (professionals only); administration and/or working within the game; promotion and staging.

MEMBERS INCLUDE:

Ralph "Rip" Arnold	Lawrence Bromfield	Howard Creel
Marcia Bailey	Phyllis Buchanan	Rick Dewitt
James Bailey	Jack Butler	Vivian Dorsey
Robert Baker	Richard Campbell	Dale Douglass
Judy Bell	Noble Chalfant	Ed Dudley
H.R. Berglund	Robert Clark	Larry Eaton
Joan Birkland	John Cochran	Jim English
Bill Bisdorf	Clayton Cole	Walter Fairbanks
Earl Brayer	Myran Craig	Katie Fiorella

The Broadmoor's Barbara McIntire (left) presents the 1976 Broadmoor Ladies Invitational Cup to Debbie Massey. Nancy Lopez finished second and Judy Bell (right) went on to serve as the USGA's first female president in 1996-97.

The harder I practice, the luckier I get.—Gary Player

Carol Flenniken
Dow Finsterwald
Les Fowler
John Gardner, II
Maggie Giesenhagen
Nathan Grimes
Jim Haines
John Hamer
Sally Hardwick
Ted Hart
Dorothy Heitler
Dave Hill
Dan Hogan
Bob Hold
Henry Hughes
Helen Hyman
Hale Irwin

William Jewett
Steve Jones
Charlie Keller
Robert Kirchner
Charles Kline
John Kraft
Patricia Lange
Charles "Babe" Lind
Bill Loeffler
Gary Longfellow
Bill Majure
Press Maxwell
Larry Mcatee
Barbara McIntire
M.A. McLaughlin
Paul McMullen
Bill Metier

Stanley Metsker
Janet Moore
Ralph W. Moore, Jr.
Ron Moore
N.C. Morris
Will F. Nicholson, Sr.
Will F. Nicholson, Jr.
Lew North
Tony Novitsky
Tom O'Hara
John Olive
Dick Phelps
Marion Pfluger
Phyllis Preuss
Paul Ransom
Pat Rea
John Rogers
Gene Root
Art Severson
Robert Shearer
Warren Simmons
Jordan Smith
Warren Smith
Raymond Stenzel
Nancy Roth Syms
J.D. Taylor
Thayer Tutt
Jack Vickers
Ralph Vranesic
Fred Wampler, Jr.
Larry Webb
Frank Woodward
Wilford Woody
Claude Wright
Starr Yelland
Babe Zaharias
Penny Zavichas
Oscar Zesch
Lynn Zmistowski

An excellent athlete, some claim Hale Irwin's best sport was baseball.

The man who runs from his office to the golf club, gulps a sandwich, belches and races to the first tee has no business howling in anguish when he puts his first two shots in the woods, then tops a 3-iron into the pond.—Tony Lema

THE COLORADO GOLF HALL OF FAME DISPLAY

R iverdale Dunes is home to the Colorado Golf Hall of Fame display, where you can view portraits of each inductee along with a narrative of their accomplishments.

John Edwards, publisher of *Colorado Golfer*, and Dan Hogan, an inductee into the Hall of Fame, head up the project. You can also read about all the inductees at www.golfhousecolorado.org/hof/html.

When *The Colorado Golf Bible* wanted to research the history of golf in the Centennial State, the name that kept coming up was Hogan, a soft-spoken, retired Burlington & Northern Railroad employee. Imagine who his favorite golfer was— Texan Ben Hogan.

Charles "Babe" Lind, one of the state's best all-time amateurs and member of the Colorado Golf Hall of Fame.

Hogan, a life-long resident of Denver, is no doubt, the leading authority on Colorado golf history. He not only contributed photos for *The Colorado Golf Bible*, but also helped with the historical timeline. Hogan attended and played golf at Regis High School and University. He also played in the British Amateur Championships of 1970 and 1977 and was local medalist as he qualified six times for the U.S. Public Links Championships. Hogan grew up caddying at Park Hill and City Park won the Denver Municipal Course title in1963, 1964 and 1969. He was City Park Club Champion 10 times.

The Colorado PGA Section also has a historical display in the clubhouse at Bear Dance.

Perhaps the most fatal beam of all that can float over your mental vision is the vision of a past hole played badly which you are filled with some insane notion of "making up for." The idea of "making up," by present extra exertions, for past deficiencies is one of the most deadly and besetting delusions that is prone to affect the golfing mind. Its results are inevitably ruinous.—Horace Hutchinson

COLORADO GOLF: OVERVIEW & ARCHITECTURE

I t's been said that people come to Colorado for the summers, but stay for the winters. But the opposite could just as easily be said. Colorado is perhaps America's most scenic state, with dramatic weather and climatic conditions to match any extreme it might offer in terms of geography. Ever since the great game got its start here in the closing years of the 19th century, there's rarely been a dull moment for golf in Colorado. Today golfers can play anything from old-school traditional to cutting-edge daily fee, but in terms of architecture, golf in Colorado has arrived in phases: traditional, public emphasis, daily fee, and trail-blazing.

THE TRADITIONAL YEARS: EARLY GOLF COURSE DESIGN

A Scotsman, Willie Campbell, laid out what is now Patty Jewett Golf Course in Colorado Springs in 1898—it's the third oldest course in continuous operation west of the Mississippi River.

The original Overland Park opened in 1895, but was moved in 1930—the credit for the design goes to W.H. Tucker Sr. and W.F. Bell. But golf really got rolling when people like Henry Hughes, William S. Flynn, and Donald Ross came to the state and presented stunning handiwork during the 1930s—a golden era for Colorado golf course design.

Father-son design tandems started with Henry T. Hughes and son Henry B. Hughes. Then came the Maxwells. Dad Perry, designer of Colonial Country Club in Fort Worth, died in 1952 and son Press, a member of the Colorado Golf Hall of Fame, moved to Colorado in 1958. J. (James) Press Maxwell lived in Morrison until his death in 2002. He was a pilot and colonel during World War II and designed or remodeled more than 20 courses in Colorado. His portfolio includes work at Applewood, Boulder CC, Cherry Hills, Hiwan, Inverness, Kissing Camels, Pinehurst, Rolling Hills, Vail, Columbine, Denver CC, Lakewood, and Patty Jewett. But he also has his name on Southern Hills in Tulsa and even a remodel at Augusta National.

So call the early days of Colorado golf architecture the traditional era. That pretty much lasted until the 1970s, when Dick Phelps took over and started a new phase of Colorado architecture that put an emphasis on affordable, public golf. A member of the Colorado Golf Hall of Fame, Phelps is still going strong today, and son Rick has already authored an award-winner, too—Devil's Thumb in Delta.

For an amateur, standing on the first hole of the Masters is the ultimate laxative.—Trevor Homer

DICK PHELPS AND COLORADO PUBLIC GOLF

"In 1967 Henry Hughes and Press Maxwell were slowing down a bit," said Phelps. "The opportunity was there for me. Those first public golf courses I designed, like Indian Tree, Foothills and at Fort Carson, were low budget. You could not move a lot of soil and those sites didn't have a lot of trees. The cost was around $500,000 and people probably refer to them today as 'plain Jane,' but we did what we could."

Dick has his name associated with 38 designs in Colorado and has composed more than 76 golf courses; he's consulted on at least 300 other golf-course projects. Phelps Design Group also has put a stamp on other Colorado courses with master and remodeling plans.

"I'm proud that we were able to provide fun, affordable golf for a lot of people," he said. "That's what we really need today. There is a current downturn in golf, because we are pricing the average guy out of golf—we need to provide golf for everyone."

The Phelps era has also includes other names in Colorado architecture. Frank Hummel, who designed Aspen Golf Club, Collindale, and the Air Force Academy's Silver Course, was born in La Junta. He has definitely put his own stamp on Colorado golf. Now 77, Hummel lives on Highland Hills Golf Course in Greeley and still plays golf a couple of times a week. He's retired, but says if offered a design job in his neighborhood he'd jump on it. Off the golf course he enjoys flying his Bonanza and travelling for fun, not for work.

Dick Phelps, the Father of Colorado public golf.

Modern Colorado architecture includes Robert Trent Jones Sr. and Jr., Tom Fazio, Jack Nicklaus, Arnold Palmer, Greg Norman, and Pete and Perry Dye. Yep, most of these designs are going to cost you big bucks to play. Perry Dye's

Never putt for a three-foot circle. If you aren't trying to hole every putt you have, you are going to lose to someone who is.—Dr. Bob Rotella

Green Valley Ranch is one new one that isn't overpriced.

Grand Junction-born Jay Morrish, who graduated from and taught at Colorado State University, had a hand in the design of Castle Pines when he worked for Mr. Nicklaus. He also put his mark on Sonnenalp Golf Club in Vail, Eagle Springs in Wolcott, and Grandote Peaks in La Veta. River Valley Ranch in Carbondale is his design alone and one of Colorado's Top Ten. Another proposed Morrish project, Ravenna near Roxborough State Park, is scheduled for 2004 construction.

JIM ENGH, COLORADO'S TRAIL-BLAZER

But the next generation is a trail-blazer. In 1998, *TravelGolf.com* called Jim Engh, a North Dakotan who set up shop in Castle Rock, the "Hottest Architect in America." Today, Engh is no longer hot—he's on fire.

Self-described as an architect who likes to push the envelope, Engh is winning awards for just about 100 percent of his projects. In 2002 he won *Golf Digest's* award for best new public upscale course—Tullymore Golf Club in Stanwood, Michigan. That means he's the only architect on the planet to have won in all three of *Golf Digest's* categories—Best New Affordable, Best New Upscale, and Best New Private.

Call it a Triple Play—his 1998 Sanctuary in Sedalia was Best New Private. His Redlands Mesa in Grand Junction was Best New Affordable in 2001. Other award-winners include Red Hawk Ridge in Castle Rock and Hawktree Golf Club in Bismarck, North Dakota. Columbia Point Golf Course in Richland, Washington is Engh's lone design that did not receive an award.

In 2003, Engh again was the big winner of *Golf Digest's* awards—The Club at Black Rock in Coeur d'Alene, Idaho was named Best New Private golf course in America and Engh was named the magazine's first-ever "Architect of the Year." And his brand-new Fossil Trace Golf Club, a Golden municipal, placed in the Best New Affordable category.

"It was a goal of mine to win all three *Golf Digest* categories," said Engh. "They started giving these awards in 1983 and I thought early in my career that if I could win one it would be an achievement of a lifetime. To get one in all three categories early in my career is just phenomenal. But you can't get caught up in designing a course with an award in mind. I try just to design the best course I can on every project."

Engh's upcoming projects include the Snowmass redesign that will open in 2004. Then there's Lakota Canyon Golf Club near Glenwood Springs in New Castle, set for a tentative 2004 opening. The Club at Pradera in Parker begins

---

*In tournament play, don't worry about things you cannot control, like the
wind or what other players are doing.*

seeding in 2004 and could open in 2005. Cañon City has an Engh project on the boards called Four Mile Ranch. In the summer of 2005 another Engh design, True North Golf Club in Harbor Springs, Michigan, will also probably be honored.

COLORADO GOLF TODAY

The purists call some of today's golf "eye candy." They accuse course designers of adding waterfalls, lakes with native rocks and cascading water, sandstone outcroppings encroaching putting surfaces, or great-looking bunkers that serve no strategic purpose—they just look good. Ignore those armchair critics. Sure, there are a few goofy Colorado mountain golf courses, but ask the question: "Are you having fun yet?" It's hard not to have fun playing golf in Colorado. And when you think about it, Colorado is God's eye candy.

But whoa! On the other extreme, minimalism is alive and well in Colorado. Tom Doak, author of world-ranked Pacific Dunes in Bandon, Oregon is working on Ballyneal, a sand-dune design in the eastern plains of Colorado near Holyoke. And he's also taking on a Castle Rock-area project called The Canyons right next door to Castle Pines. Both probably have tentative 2005 opening dates, depending on business stuff—financing and all that.

And there's that Phelps family again. Rick Phelps will unveil his 8,100-yard golf course in 2004—Antler Creek near Falcon. Also, Art Schaupeter, a Keith Foster protégé, will open his strategic layout called Highlands Meadows Golf Club in Windsor. He says it is somewhat like Foster's Buffalo Run (which he worked on) and a high-plains layout.

As I said—never a dull moment for golfers in Colorado.

Armed with ignorance, golfers shell out hundreds, sometimes thousands of dollars on new clubs, believing that their investment is going to help them play better. You can spend a million dollars, if your clubs don't fit, you're not going to play good golf.—Jonathan Abrahams

HIGHLIGHTS OF COLORADO-BASED ARCHITECTS*

DICK PHELPS

Bookcliff Country Club — Grand Junction
Cattail Creek Golf Course — Loveland
Cattails Golf Club — Alamosa (back nine)
Colorado Springs Country Club — Colorado Springs
Centennial Golf Club — Littleton
Coal Creek Golf Course — Louisville
Englewood Municipal Golf Course — Englewood
Foothills Golf Course — Denver
Fort Carson Cheyenne Shadows — Fort Carson
Grand Lake Golf Club — Grand Lake (back nine)
Indian Tree Golf Club — Arvada
Mariana Butte Golf Course — Loveland
Perry Park Country Club — Larkspur
Pine Creek Golf Club — Colorado Springs
Raccoon Creek Golf Course — Littleton
The Ranch Country Club — Westminster
Rifle Creek Golf Course — Rifle (back nine)
Springs Ranch Golf Club — Colorado Springs

RICK PHELPS

Broadlands Golf Club — Broomfield
Antelope Hills Golf Club — Bennett
Antler Creek Golf Club — Falcon
Devil's Thumb Golf Club — Delta

JIM ENGH

The Club at Pradera — Parker
Fossil Trace Golf Club — Golden
Four Mile Ranch — Cañon City
Lakota Canyon Golf Club — New Castle
Red Hawk Ridge Golf Course — Castle Rock
Sanctuary — Sedalia
Snowmass Club — Snowmass

I'm very tightly wound. All that jabbering is a pressure valve. I couldn't do without it.—Lee Trevino

PRESS MAXWELL

Applewood Golf Course — Golden
Boulder Country Club — Boulder
Cherokee Ridge Golf Course — Colorado Springs
Conquistador Golf Course — Cortez
Hiwan Golf Club — Evergreen
Inverness Golf Club — Englewood
Kissing Camels Club — Colorado Springs
Lake Valley Golf Club — Longmont
Pinehurst Country Club — Denver
Rolling Hills Country Club — Golden
Saddle Rock Golf Course — Aurora
South Suburban Golf Course — Littleton
Woodmoor Pines Country Club — Monument

FRANK HUMMEL

Aspen Golf Club — Aspen
Collindale Golf Course — Fort Collins
The Courses at Hyland Hills — Westminster
Air Force Academy Silver Course — Air Force Academy
Highland Hills Golf Course — Greeley
Bunker Hill Country Club — Brush
Cedar Ridges Golf Course — Rangely
Fox Hill Country Club — Longmont
Gleneagle Golf Club — Colorado Springs
Hillcrest Golf Club — Durango
Hollydot Golf Course — Colorado City
Southridge Golf Club — Fort Collins
Twin Peaks Golf Course — Longmont
West Woods Golf Club — Arvada
Wray Country Club — Wray

PERRY DYE

Green Valley Ranch Golf Club — Aurora
Copper Creek Golf Club — Copper Mountain (with Pete Dye)
Riverdale Dunes and Knolls — Brighton (with Pete Dye)
(*NOT INCLUSIVE)

Real men don't use old balls on water holes.—Colorado rancher

Colorado Golf Association & the Colorado Women's Golf Association

Dating back to the early 1900s, both the CGA and the CWGA were founded to promote and preserve the best interests and the true spirit of the game of golf in Colorado. Each organization comprises individual golfers and the member clubs to which they belong. The CGA consists of over 250 golf clubs of amateur men and juniors, totaling over 46,000 memberships. The CWGA serves amateur women golfers throughout the state, benefiting approximately 19,000 women and over 270 member clubs.

To become a member, golfers must obtain an official USGA Handicap Index within the state of Colorado. Member clubs exist at most Colorado golf courses, and several non-real-estate leagues exist for those who enjoy playing at different facilities with their organized group. Members receive quarterly newsletters and the association's course directory, Colorado Golf, which lists phone numbers, addresses, and course rating information to assist with the handicap service. Members also receive eligibility to participate in state championships, handicap support, hole-in-one certificates, and the helpful assistance of the customer support office staff.

FOR MORE INFORMATION on the amateur golf associations of Colorado, visit the following:
- www.golfhousecolorado.org
- CGA office at 800-228-4675
- CWGA office at 800-392-2942

The Colorado Section PGA

One of the best things any golfer can do to improve their game is to consult with a PGA Professional. The Colorado PGA, founded in 1957 and the 31st of 41 Sections of the Professional Golfers' Association of America, is comprised of 750 members and includes the state of Colorado, Eastern Wyoming, and Western South Dakota. At over 240 facilities throughout the section, the members are the primary representatives of golf in local communities.

Membership involves the completion of an extensive training curriculum, known as the PGA Professional Golf Management program. In addition to passing the playing ability test (PAT), the three level program is designed to allow apprentices to gain on the job work experience and understand all areas of golf

---

There's nothing worse for your putting than dwelling on the putts you've missed. Develop a long-term memory of your made putts and a short-term memory of your missed putts.—Dr. Bob Rotella

course operations.

In 1997, the Colorado PGA Foundation was formed to administer the charitable and philanthropic affairs of golf professionals. Through its various programs and events, the Foundation's primary goal is to "impact the game of life through the game of golf – to bring together professionals and amateurs in a fraternity of caring and sharing, whose mission is to help the needy and foster the finest values of the game of golf". Over the years, the Foundation affairs have promoted the growth of junior golf, implemented scholarship programs, supported the minority and underprivileged youth in Colorado, continued the development of the Colorado PGA Historical Center, and contributed to various allied charitable organizations.

In March of 2003, the Section offices moved to the new Golf Club at Bear Dance in Larkspur and introduced the Colorado PGA Historical Center in the same facility. An outstanding facility, the impressive collection of memorabilia and photographs highlights the achievements of the 45-year history of the Colorado PGA.

COLORADO PGA
6630 BEAR DANCE ROAD, 2ND FLOOR
LARKSPUR, CO 80118
888-987-2742
WWW.COLORADOPGA.COM

Colorado Junior Golf Association

E stablished in 1984, the Colorado Junior Golf Association is the youth tournament program of the Colorado Golf Association. Their mission is "to promote and preserve the best interests and the true spirit of the game of golf in Colorado for juniors". By conducting competitive events, publishing newsletters, and conducting clinics, the CJGA strives to teach "the life values of sportsmanship, honesty, self-discipline, integrity, and competitive spirit". By working with Colorado golf clubs, golf courses, and PGA and LPGA professionals, the non-profit organization creates opportunities to cultivate their philosophies and prove that participation in the game develops character while having fun.

If one has not learned enough of golf by the time he steps on to the first tee,
then he has run out of time.—Bobby Jones

Bob Hope uses some body English to try and wiggle this putt in at The Broadmoor, home to some of the trickiest greens on the planet.

BEST OF
COLORADO GOLF

I n determining the "Best Of Colorado Golf," *Colorado AvidGolfer* inserted ballots into its September 2003 issue. More than 1,000 readers responded, and the results were tabulated independently of the magazine staff and appeared in the Spring 2004 issue. In addition to publishing "Readers' Choice" Awards, the editors of *Colorado AvidGolfer* also added "Staff Picks" to add more ballast to the selection.

BEST NEW COURSE
1. Fossil Trace
2. Vista Ridge
3. Red Sky Ranch (Norman Course)

Test your game in a real-life Jurassic Park. The experience of the par-five twelfth hole, with its cliff setting, protruding limestone fins and fossil remnants, is alone worth the price of admission.

BEST FRONT RANGE COURSE
1. The Ridge at Castle Pines North
2. The Golf Club at Bear Dance
3. Arrowhead Golf Club
4. Buffalo Run Golf Club
5. Green Valley Ranch Golf Club

What do you get when you cross an inspired Tom Weiskopf-designed course, scenic meadow, forest and mountain terrain and world-class service? You get a daily-fee golf experience that sits atop all others on the Front Range.

Few pleasures on earth match the feeling that comes from making a loud bodily-function noise just as a guy is about to putt. —Dave Barry

BEST MOUNTAIN COURSE
1. The Raven
2. Breckenridge Golf Club
3. Pole Creek Golf Club
4. Keystone River Course
5. Cordillera Resort

The Raven soars above Colorado's mountain golf meccas with dramatic elevation changes, soul-stirring vistas, impeccable conditioning and a strategic design that demands shotmaking excellence.

BEST RESORT COURSE
1. The Broadmoor
2. Omni Interocken
3. The Inverness
4. Keystone River Course
5. Cordillera Resort

Both courses at The Broadmoor have hosted national championships. Jack Nicklaus won his first major here. So did Annika Sorenstam. The courses Donald Ross and Robert Trent Jones, Sr. have captivated – and tormented – VIPs from around the world for more than 75 years.

BEST OVERALL COURSE
1. The Ridge at Castle Pines North
2. The Raven
3. Redlands Mesa
4. The Golf Club at Bear Dance
5. Riverdale Dunes

Hole for hole, shot for shot, The Ridge comes out on top. The wooded holes on the back nine remind you why you live in Colorado in the first place. The tee shot at eighteen is one of the best in golf.

Sometimes in a drive to improve your game, you can lose the intuitive, imaginative, target-oriented attitude to a mechanical, swing-oriented approach. Be sure to be playful, imaginative, and instinctive on the golf course. —Dr. Bob Rotella

BEST COURSE ($100+)

1. The Ridge at Castle Pines North
2. The Raven
3. The Broadmoor
4. Arrowhead Golf Club
5. Red Sky Ranch

You know the old saying, "you get what you pay for." When it comes to golf courses, that's not always true. But the staff at The Ridge covers the details that make it worth top dollar. When only the best will do…

BEST COURSE ($50 - $99)

1. The Golf Club at Bear Dance
2. Redlands Mesa
3. Red Hawk Ridge
4. Vista Ridge
5. The Heritage at Eagle Bend

With its dense woods, rolling terrain and demanding design, The Golf Club at Bear Dance is reminiscent of Castle Pines Golf Club, site of The International. But a tee time at Bear Dance is much easier to come by (and easier on the wallet).

BEST COURSE (UNDER $50)

1. Riverdale Dunes
2. Fox Hollow
3. Green Valley Ranch
4. Walking Stick
5. (tie) Buffalo Run, Heritage at Westmoor, Murphy Creek

Colorado may have the best collection of inexpensive golf courses in the country. None is better than the links-inspired Riverdale Dunes. You may not smell the sea here, but you will feel the wind. The course plays differently every day—so it never gets old.

STAFF PICK: Devil's Thumb, Delta: Set in a remote moonscape on the Western Slope, this Rick Phelps track has won national acclaim. Low-profile tees and greens help the course blend in perfectly, and plenty of risk-reward options keep it interesting.

When warming up before a round, make the last shot you hit on the practice tee the same as the first shot you have to hit on the course.—Ken Venturi

AUTHOR'S PICK: Trinidad Golf Course and Cattails in Alamosa. These two are absolute fun and dirt cheap. Play Trinidad early in the morning, soaking up the vistas of the Sangres and Spanish Peaks. Then motor over to Alamosa for twilight golf on the banks of the Rio Grande and in the shadows of 14,000-foot Mount Blanca.

BEST COURSE VALUE

1. Green Valley Ranch
2. Fox Hollow
3. Heritage at Westmoor
4. Buffalo Run
5. Murphy Creek

You want bang for your buck? Head out to Green Valley Ranch. The layout is superb—the unexpected wetland holes are unlike any others on the Front Range. This is private club quality at a price anyone would love.

BEST OVERALL EXPERIENCE

1. The Raven
2. The Ridge at Castle Pines North
3. Redlands Mesa
4. (tie) The Golf Club at Bear Dance, The Broadmoor

The Raven exhilarates and delights golfers with its pristine location and its humbling views. The staff treats you like royalty, and the course is maintained like a garden. Who could ask for more?

STAFF PICK: The Broadmoor. A trip to The Broadmoor is a trip to another era of elegance, grace and luxury. Treat yourself. You'll be glad you did.

AUTHOR'S PICK: Nothing compares to the history and luxury of The Broadmoor in Colorado. In fact, people around the world have said this is the ultimate in a travel golf vacation.

MOST UNDERRATED COURSE

1. The Heritage at Westmoor
2. Green Valley Ranch
3. The Golf Club at Bear Dance
4. Buffalo Run
5. King's Deer

Practice in ways that build confidence. —Dr. Bob Rotella

HERE'S A RIDDLE: Can a category winner be classified as "underrated"? You won't underrate The Heritage at Westmoor once you've played this modern classic by the design team of Michael Hurdzan and Dana Fry.

MOST SCENIC COURSE

1. Arrowhead
2. The Raven
3. (tie) The Golf Club at Bear Dance, Redlands Mesa
4. Pole Creek

Arrowhead could win this category on a national basis. That's what 500-foot sandstone spires, sweeping city and mountain views and serene water features will do for a golf course.

STAFF PICK: River Valley Ranch, Carbondale. The Crystal River and the towering Mount Sopris will keep your shutter finger busy even though the course demands your full attention.

MOST DIFFICULT COURSE

1. The Golf Club at Bear Dance
2. Breckenridge Golf Club
3. Legacy Ridge Golf Club
4. Red Sky Ranch (Norman Course)
5. Vista Ridge

Think the tee shots are tough at Bear Dance? They are. Think the approach shots are tough? You're right. But just wait until you get to the greens. This Bear may dance, but don't fool yourself into believing it's tamed.

BEST COURSE TO HOLD A CORPORATE EVENT

1. Omni Interlocken
2. The Inverness
3. The Ridge at Castle Pines North
4. Arrowhead
5. Sanctuary

The Omni Interlocken is built for business. Twenty-seven holes mean that an event won't choke the pace. An excellent business hotel is on-site and wired to the tournament center. And the course is enjoyable for golfers of all skill levels.

Tension in the arm muscles ruins golf swings, most often promoting a slice. Almost anything that causes a golfer to squeeze his club harder will ruin his game; conversely, almost anything that causes a golfer to ease up on his death grip will improve his accuracy and length. Hence, beer. —David Owen

STAFF PICK: Vista Ridge. The staff at Vista Ridge treats every event like it's the biggest event. And the on-cart leaderboard system is a thrill for all players.

BEST COURSE TO BRING OUT-OF-STATERS
1. Arrowhead
2. The Golf Club at Bear Dance
3. The Ridge at Castle Pines North
4. The Raven
5. Redlands Mesa

No matter where your guests live, they've never seen anything like Arrowhead before. Warning: Their visits may increase in frequency once they do.

STAFF PICK: Fossil Trace. Unless your out-of-state friends have grown tired of courses where they can view triceratops tracks and fossilized ferns.

BEST COURSE FOR BUSINESS ENTERTAINING
1. The Ridge at Castle Pines North
2. Omni Interlocken
3. The Inverness
4. Arrowhead
5. The Raven

It's just a short hop from downtown or the Tech Center, but The Ridge is a world away. Your clients will know you care enough to host them in style.

STAFF PICK: The Inverness. A fine hotel, a top restaurant and a fun and interesting golf course, all just a stone's throw away from the Lear jets idling at Centennial Airport.

BEST "HIDDEN GEM" COURSE
1. Mariana Butte (Loveland)
2. Devil's Thumb (Delta)
3. Grandote Peaks (La Veta)
4. Fairway Pines (Ridgway)
5. Pelican Lakes (Windsor)

A moderate infusion of alcohol can have the same effect on the muscles of golfers that it is said to have on the inhibitions of attractive strangers in bars. That is why golfers sometimes refer to alcoholic beverages as "swing oil."—David Owen

You may need a roadmap to get to this foothills gem on the western edge of Loveland. It's worth it. This little course has it all – interesting holes, mountains, rivers. After playing it, you'll remember the way.

STAFF PICK: Saddleback, Firestone. No course has ever done more with less than Saddleback. You won't see the beauty of Saddleback at first glance, but you will at first round.

AUTHOR'S PICK: Grandote Peaks is boondocks golf at its very best. Hidden Gem? Just drive into the parking lot on a weekday morning, you might see five cars. Two of those are probably staff members.

BEST EGO-BOOSTER COURSE
1. Park Hill
2. Overland
3. Lake Arbor
4. Aurora Hills
5. Kennedy

Sometimes you just need a little TLC. When your game has got you down, a round on the friendly fairways and gentle greens of Park Hill will cheer you up.

MOST COVETED PRIVATE COURSE INVITATION
1. Castle Pines Golf Club
2. Sanctuary
3. Cherry Hills
4. Denver
5. Hiwan

It's a great part of golf, playing a course the pros play. And if you get that invitation, you can finally taste one of those famous milkshakes.

STAFF PICK: Cherry Creek Country Club. We hear that the Nicklaus design team has done great work. This year, maybe we'll get a chance to see for ourselves.

On the first tee, a golfer must expect only two things of himself: to have fun, and to focus his mind properly on every shot.—Dr. Bob Rotella

BEST MAINTAINED
1. The Ridge at Castle Pines North
2. The Broadmoor
3. The Raven
4. Green Valley Ranch
5. The Heritage at Westmoor

You may feel bad for taking a divot out of these fairways, but really, it's okay. And the only truer greens around are on pool tables.

AUTHOR'S BEST OF COLORADO CLUB-FITTING
Dimension Z Golf, Inc. Don Ingermann once headed the Ben Hogan Company. He's here in Colorado to pass along his expertise to you. If you have never owned a set of custom-fitted clubs, the time is now. Log on to www.dimensionz.com or call them at 888-271-1889 or 303-403-8344.

BEST PACE OF PLAY
1. Fox Hollow
2. The Raven
3. (tie) Buffalo Run, The Ridge at Castle Pines North, Green Valley Ranch

With twenty-seven holes and good sight lines on all three nines, it's a pleasure to play at Fox Hollow. Golf shouldn't take all day, and here it doesn't.

BEST WALKER'S COURSE
1. City Park
2. Wellshire
3. Meadow Hills
4. Flatirons
5. Park Hill

City Park is a classic walker's course—greens and tees are close together, and you pass the halfway house several times to take advantage of free refills on soda.

Let us consider the equipment we have to use. A more ill designed set of implements could hardly have been created. Yet we descend upon each new model with cries of glee, drooling over the gleaming heads. —Chris Plumbridge

MOST FEMALE-FRIENDLY COURSE
1. Fox Hollow
2. Green Valley Ranch
3. Links at Highlands Ranch, Highlands Ranch
4. Red Hawk Ridge
5. South Suburban

With a name like that… But seriously, Fox Hollow offers multiple tee boxes, a nice clubhouse and easy tee times (with one nine reserved for nine-hole play each day) to win with the ladies.

MOST FAMILY-FRIENDLY COURSE
1. Kennedy
2. South Suburban
3. Hyland Hills, Westminster
4. Foothills, Lakewood
5. Heritage at Westmoor

The family that plays together stays together, and Kennedy can make it happen. The par-3 course is a great way to introduce kids to the game. And the fun center adjacent to the lighted driving range keeps everyone happy.

BEST OPENING HOLE
1. Fossil Trace
2. Keystone River Course
3. The Raven
4. River Valley Ranch
5. Bear Dance

Bomb one off the elevated tee, hang a left at the old kiln in the middle of the fairway and leave yourself a nice approach between the cottonwoods on the right and the bunkers on the left. That's how to cover the 600 yards of the opener at Fossil Trace.

STAFF PICK: Green Valley Ranch. From the back tees, you need about 220 just to carry the wetlands and reach the crown of the fairway. Then it's a mid-iron to a skyline green where an invisible wind is always lurking. Good luck!

There is only one Michael Jordan. He is very talented, but what sets him apart is his attitude of consistently striving for improvement and his consistent competitive focus. — Dr. Bob Rotella

AUTHOR'S PICK: Rio Grande Club in South Fork. The journey begins with an 80-foot tee-shot drop to the No. 1 fairway, with a stone wall complete with chimney-rock formations running down the entire right side.

BEST FINISHING HOLE
1. Green Valley Ranch
2. Red Hawk Ridge
3. The Ridge at Castle Pines North
4. Buffalo Run
5. The Heritage at Westmoor

A gambler's delight. Big-hitters can flirt with trouble on the right and have a chance to get home in two. Short-knockers can play safe and wedge it close to exact their revenge. Trouble on every shot. A great finish to a great course.

STAFF PICK: Vista Ridge. Tee off to a plateau fairway that bends slightly right around a massive bunker complex. Then take your best shot at an angled green protected by water front and right and by sand left. A par wins a lot of matches here.

AUTHOR'S PICK: Any and every course No. 18 by Jim Engh.

TOUGHEST HOLE
1. Saddle Rock #10
2. Green Valley Ranch #18
3. Raoon Creek #17
4. Legacy Ridge #16
5. Flatirons #16

Start with a 225-yard carry off the tee. Sprinkle in an angled fairway, with protected wetlands to the left and a steep hill covered with deep grass on the right. Add a pinch of elevation to the green, and sand to taste. That's the recipe for one tough golf hole.

STAFF PICK: Murphy Creek #12. At 509 yards (par four!) from the back tee, this one looks tough on paper. It's much tougher than that. The tee shot is uphill, cutting off as much of the gulch as you dare. Then it's a long-iron to a peninsula green. Ouch!

Go to the practice green and try to make some four-foot putts, the kind that you're probably missing on the golf course. If you can make the four-footers on the practice green but not on the course, then your problem isn't your stroke.—Dr. Bob Rotella

TOUGHEST GREENS

1. The Golf Club at Bear Dance
2. The Broadmoor
3. South Suburban
4. Arrowhead
5. Keystone Ranch Course

Remember, they renovated several of the greens after the first year of play to make them less severe. That should take the sting out of one of those three-putts, at least.

STAFF PICK: The Broadmoor. Everything breaks away from the Will Rogers Shrine. What's that? That means it will break UPHILL? We didn't believe it, either. We do now.

BEST PRACTICE FACILITY

1. Murphy Creek
2. Omni Interlocken
3. (tie) Green Valley Ranch, Vista Ridge
4. The Ridge at Castle Pines North

The range at Murphy Creek is so large that you can adjust your hitting direction to accommodate any wind direction. An outstanding short game area lets you practice all the shots. The putting green is near the first tee. Does a perfect practice area make for perfect golf? Find out for yourself.

BEST PRO SHOP

1. The Broadmoor
2. The Ridge at Castle Pines North
3. The Raven
4. Heritage at Westmoor
5. Buffalo Run

When only the finest will do, turn to The Broadmoor. The golf shop features history books, artwork, an extensive selection of golf attire and surprisingly deep inventory of junior golf equipment. And that Broadmoor logo just makes it all a little better.

The test of a great golfer is his ability to recover from a bad start.—P.G. Wodehouse

BEST 19TH HOLE
1. The Ridge at Castle Pines North
2. Fox Hollow
3. Buffalo Run
4. (tie) Arrowhead, Heritage at Westmoor

The Ridge provides the perfect apres-golf experience. A stone patio overlooks the eighteenth green. If it gets cool, move in to sit by the fireplace or cozy up to the rustic bar. This 19th hole makes even your bad rounds feel good.

AUTHOR'S PICK: Patty Jewett in Colorado Springs. Cold beer, freshly made sandwiches and a view of Pikes Peak.

BEST JUNIOR PROGRAM
1. (tie) Indian Tree, Arvada; Park Hill
2. South Suburban
3. Englewood, Englewood
4. Flatirons, Boulder

Indian Tree has tirelessly promoted junior golf for decades, and its summer programs have won national recognition. Park Hill's efforts have been so highly regarded that Tiger Woods staged a clinic there. Golf grows because of programs like these.

BEST ON-COURSE BEVERAGE SERVICE
1. Fox Hollow
2. Heritage at Westmoor
3. The Raven
4. Kennedy
5. Vista Ridge

The folks at Fox Hollow know how to get the cart to you at just the right time. The staff is trained in golf etiquette, and the carts are well stocked with all you'll need to replenish and finish.

BEST GOLF COURSE FOOD
1. Vista Ridge
2. The Ridge at Castle Pines North
3. Buffalo Run
4. (tie) Legacy Ridge, Fox Hollow

Surround yourself with players who challenge you to get better.—Dr. Bob Rotella

Non-golfers actually come to Vista Ridge just for the food. This isn't just a 'dogs and burgers shack. It's a full menu and top-notch service, all with a golf course view.

BEST INSTRUCTOR/GOLF SCHOOL

1. McGetrick Golf Academy at Green Valley Ranch
2. Rick Smith Golf Institute
3. GolfTec
4. Bogart Golf

Mike McGetrick has put champions in the winner's circle while putting Colorado on the map for golf instruction. His coaching instills confidence, and his equipment is state-of-the-art. If you're looking for more game, you'll find it here.

AUTHOR'S PICK:for Best Club Fitting: Founder Don Ingermann and son Brad make Dimenzion Z the best in Colorado. Dimension Z Golf, Inc., 14700 W. 66th Place, Suite #9, Arvada, CO 80004. (888) 271-1889 or (303) 403-8344.

AUTHOR'S BEST OF COLORADO GOLF PUBLICATIONS

COLORADO AVIDGOLFER MAGAZINE — Simply put, this is the state's best golf publication. First-class all the way. Pick up a free copy at many pro shops in Colorado and check out www.coloradoavidgolfer.com.

TRAVELGOLF.COM — With 2 million hits per month, the travel golf stories about Colorado that appear within these pages are read by more people world-wide than any other publication.

ROCKIESGOLF.COM, the very first publication under the *TravelGolf.com* corporate flag, now emphasizes Canadian Rockies, but still has some Colorado travel golf stories.

GOLFVIEWS MAGAZINE – Great photography and color ads in a funky size and format. Check out www.golfviews.com.

COLORADO GOLF MAGAZINE — Again, classy photography, beautiful glossy layout in a publication published four times a year. Check out www.coloradogolf.com.

COLORADO GOLFER — This black and white newsprint tabloid presents excellent Colorado Golf Association and PGA Section tournament coverage and is the champion for smaller-budget golf courses throughout the state. No web site.

Tommy Bolt points his club down the No. 1 fairway at Pueblo Country Club. He was in town for a 1958 exhibition. PCC celebrated its 100th Anniversary in 2003.

DENVER

DENVER

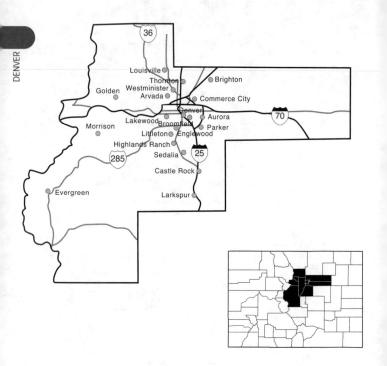

Denver Mileage

	Arvada	Aurora	Brighton	Broomfield	Castle Rock	Centenniel	Commerce City	Denver	Englewood	Evergreen	Golden	Highlands Ranch	Lakewood	Larkspur	Littleton	Louisville	Morrison	Parker	Sedalia	Thornton	Westminster
Arvada		17	20	10	37	17	9	15	18	29	6	29	6	47	18	12	32	31	9	14	7
Aurora	17		24	22	27	17	8	14	29	26	21	37	21	60	24	26	16	32	16	14
Brighton	20	24		19	30	16	9	8	23	33	20	42	27	50	19	31	16	44	16
Broomfield	10	22	19		24	30	16	12	18	23	18	27	13	55	19	2	45	37	9
Castle Rock	37	27	50	24		24	23	22	46	32	10	10	32	10	35	57	40	25	9	6
Centenniel	17	17	16	30	24		16	10	9	25	18	7	13	50	8	27	20	19	19
Commerce City	9	8	9	16	23	16		9	15	24	26	21	35	50	16	8	26	36	18
Denver	15	14	8	12	22	10	9		8	26	20	15	10	42	13	13	22	33	19
Englewood	18	29	23	18	46	9	15	8		34	18	7	17	38	11	24	26	7	18
Evergreen	29	26	33	23	32	25	24	26	34		12	24	13	56	25	29	10	41	27
Golden	6	21	20	18	10	18	26	20	18	12		34	9	50	13	13	31	35	18
Highlands Ranch	29	37	42	27	10	7	21	15	7	24	34		24	38	11	9	35	26	30
Lakewood	6	21	27	13	32	13	35	10	17	13	9	24		42	13	35	27	15
Larkspur	47	60	50	55	10	50	50	42	38	56	50	38	42		35	57	45	48	47
Littleton	18	24	19	19	35	8	16	13	11	25	13	11	13	35		27	24	14	20
Louisville	12	26	31	2	57	27	8	13	24	29	13	9	35	57	27		25	8
Morrison	32	16	16	45	40	20	26	22	26	41	14	35	27	45	14	25		30	20
Parker	31	32	44	37	41	23	36	33	26	41	31	26	27	48	19	30		25	23	20
Sedalia	9	16	16	36	11	19	14	7	33	14	36	14	31	30	25	32
Thornton	14	16	9	9	35	19	15	10	11	27	14	8	33	32
Westminster	7	14	16	6	36	19	6	15	18	27	18	30	20	6

Mount Evans is a crystal-clear image framed perfectly down a lush blue-grass fairway. The Rocky Mountains are suspended in a cloudless Denver early-morning sky. It's another perfect September day in Colorado—warm, sunny, and void of wind. For a golfer, experiencing a day like this at Cherry Hills Country Club makes it even more perfect.

There's no way to stand on the first tee at Cherry Hills without thinking about Arnold Palmer. This is the exact spot where, in 1960, Palmer drove the first green, made birdie, and went on to win and post a 65 during the final round of the U.S. Open.

Gene Neher, a pivotal cog in Cherry Hills' Heritage Committee, enjoys reliving the moment. He was a marshal that day, standing right beside the No. 1 green.

"Conditions were firm and fast," Neher remembers "There's a swale just in front of the green that normally has five inches of thick bluegrass in it. But on this day Palmer's drive landed short of the swale and bounced hard over it, running on to the green."

No doubt it is the most talked-about drive in Colorado golf history. But what does Neher consider the second most important event that happened on the famous fairways of Cherry Hills?

"Probably Jack Nicklaus winning the 1993 Senior Open here," Neher said. And with a twinkle in his eyes, Neher started remembering what happened just after the tournament.

"One of the neatest things we have here is a display case in the entrance to the clubhouse with memorabilia from Palmer's 1960 win. Well, I wanted one of Jack's clubs to display and I had asked club president Howard Alexander to take care of that task."

As Nicklaus and Alexander made a beeline through the clubhouse at the end of the day, Neher was there, tugging on Alexander's sleeve to remind him of his assigned duty. Alexander finally asked, "Jack could we have your 3 wood to display in the clubhouse?" Nicklaus stopped and peered at Alexander's bald head. "Howard, you have more chance of growing hair than ever getting that 3 wood."

That might be the only time someone said no to Cherry Hills. This special place has an entire room dedicated to Dwight D. Eisenhower, who frequently played here. Members use the room for drinking coffee and playing cards, but you'll find letters from the president, a scorecard, his set of irons, and the last golf ball he ever hit on the grounds—a Spalding Dot.

Through the years Cherry Hills has felt very comfortable with William Flynn's 1922 design. There have been very few cosmetic changes over time, but one amusing change happened before the 1993 U.S. Senior Open. Palmer was

Gene Neher of Cherry Hills' Heritage Committee shows Arnold Palmer the plaque that's on the first tee at the elite Denver country club. It reads: Arnold Palmer, 1960 U.S. Open Champion. Palmer drove this green in the final round scoring 65 for a 280 total and victory.

invited back as a courtesy before the championship and played a round with Warren Smith Jr., head pro from 1963 to 1990 and a member of the Colorado Golf Hall of Fame. Smith asked Palmer before the round to make some mental notes as he played and perhaps, suggest some changes.

Guess what change Mr. Palmer suggested? "Why don't we make a championship tee box at No. 1, increasing the yardage?" Arnie's suggestion stretched the hole back to 404 yards—the yardage on his famous drive was 346.

"Under my breath I was talking to myself," Neher recalled. "I was thinking that Arnie didn't want anyone else ever driving No. 1 during a championship event at Cherry Hills."

Next up on the championship docket for Cherry Hills is the 2005 Women's U.S. Open. Over the years it has hosted the U.S. Open titles in 1938, 1960, and 1978. Two PGA Championships have been staged here, in 1941 and 1985. Also the 1976 U.S. Senior Amateur, the 1983 U.S. Mid-Amateur and the 1990 U.S. Amateur.

Assuredly there are many other golf courses in the Denver Region that share a special place in Colorado golf archives. Loaded with money and surrounded by suburbia, there's enough golf in the Denver region to keep even the most determined golfer busy for months.

Why am I using a new putter? Because the old one didn't float too well.— Craig Stadler, 1993 U.S. Open

ARVADA

Elev. 5,340 Pop. 104,000

DENVER

Named for Hiram Arvada Hoskin, Arvada dates back to 1850 when Lewis Ralston made Colorado's first documented gold find while camping near the confluence of Ralston Creek and Clear Creek. Several of the prospectors settled the area and began farming, but Arvada didn't officially become a city until 1904. The town is located just northwest of Denver, with 76 parks and a total of 135 miles of trails that link downtown to the foothills. Arvada also celebrates a Harvest Festival, is home to Red Rocks Community College, and boasts 81 golf holes at four quality public courses.

INDIAN TREE GOLF COURSE

THE GOLF This popular golf complex recently received an influx of cash to enlarge the clubhouse and install artificial turf on the heavily used driving range. Indian Tree offers a 9-hole, par-3 course in addition to its 18-holer. Water hazards dot the rolling terrain, coming into play on seven holes, and narrow fairways roll to elevated, contoured greens.

The signature hole is No. 13, a 210-yard par 3 that requires a tee shot over water to an elevated green.

THE DETAILS 303-403-2541. 7555 Wadsworth Blvd. Arvada, CO 80003.
- Dick Phelps, 1969. 18 holes. Par 70. Blue - 6,723 (70.7/119). White - 6,308 (68.9/114). Women's - 6,308 (74.7/135). Red - 5,880 (72/129). Price - $$.
- Par 3 Course. 9 holes. Par 27.

GETTING THERE Located about 3 miles north of I-70 on N. Wadsworth Blvd. The course is on the west side of Wadsworth.

LAKE ARBOR GOLF COURSE

THE GOLF Located in the busy neighborhood of Wadsworth and 86th Street, Lake Arbor is a fun place to learn the game—it measures a short 5,865 yards at a par 70. The course's calling card is its excellent putting surfaces.

Water holes, fairways bordered by trees, and friendly 300-yard par 4s make this an ego booster for the accomplished golfer, but No. 16 will challenge you at 420 yards with a bunker guarding the green on the left.

Never break your putter and driver in the same round or you're dead.—Tommy Bolt

THE DETAILS 720-898-7360. 8600 Wadsworth Blvd., Arvada, CO 80003.

- www.lakearborgolf.com
- Gordon Revsink, 1972. 18 holes. Par 70. Blue - 5,865 (66.5/109). White - 5,655 (65.5/106). Pink - 5,579 (70.2/121). Red - 4,856 (66.3/113). Price - $$.

GETTING THERE From I-70 take Wadsworth north to 87th Ave. The course is a half block east of Wadsworth behind a small group of storefronts that face Wadsworth.

STONEY CREEK GOLF COURSE

THE GOLF An executive course with water on every hole except one, Stoney Creek's Tim Root-designed layout has a links feel, with tiny targets to help you hone in your iron game. The best hole is No. 2, a 125-yarder with a creek that bends around the sides to the back of a long, narrow green. The elevation drops 20 feet from tee to green.

Stoney Creek is also an easy walk, playing only 3,800 or so yards from the tips.

THE DETAILS 303-431-9268. 13939 West 96th Ave., Arvada, CO 80005.
- Tim Root, 1998. 9 holes. Par 30. Back - 3,806 (57.2/86). Middle - 3,656 (56.6/83). Forward - 2,706 (53.2/91). Price - $.

GETTING THERE Take Hwy. 36 to 104th and go west until it turns into Church Ranch Blvd. Go past Wadsworth, where Church turns into 100th Ave. It dead-ends at Alkire; turn left and find 96th. Turn right and follow 96th Ave. to the course.

WEST WOODS GOLF CLUB

THE GOLF The 27-hole West Woods is classic Dick Phelps golf: Difficult doglegs, fairways with shrinking landing areas, creeks, views of Table Mountain, and a layout that offers a challenge for good players while also being fair to the average hack.

The Sleeping Indian and Cottonwood nines were built first, with the Silo nine added later. Some think Cottonwood would be better named Lakes, since all nine holes see water.

Every shot counts. The three-foot putt is just as important as the 300-yard drive.—Henry Cotton

Cottonwood's No. 12 is the signature hole, a par 3 playing through a grove of cottonwoods with bunkers guarding the green and water on the left. The finale on Cottonwood is a par-5, 512-yarder that makes the big hitter think—water is left and right of the fairway. Thread the needle and you might get home in two.

THE DETAILS 720-898-7370. 6655 Quaker St., Arvada, CO 80007.

- www.westwoodsgolf.com.
- Dick Phelps, 1994. Silo 9 designed by Rick Phelps, 1998. 27 holes. Par 72. Price - $$.
- Sleeping Indian/Cottonwood: Black - 6,896 (72.8/135). White - 6,335 (70/126). Plum - 5,626 (66.7/119). Women's White - 6,335 (76.2/141). Women's Plum - 5,621 (72.1/129). Women's Teal - 5,197 (69.8/126).
- Cottonwood/Silo: Black - 6,690 (71.6/130). White - 6,197 (69.2/124). Plum - 5,508 (65.6/115). Women's White - 6,197 (75.9/140). Women's Plum - 5,508 (72/129). Women's Teal - 5,114 (69.9/123).
- Silo/Sleeping Indian: Black - 6,654 (71.4/131). White - 6,188 (69.4/124). Plum - 5,478 (66.1/113). Women's White - 6,197 (75.7/144). Women's Plum - 5,454 (71.5/130). Women's Teal - 5,074 (69.5/124).

GETTING THERE From I-70 take Ward Rd. north to Ralston Rd. (64th Ave). Turn left (west) and follow 64th west to Quaker St. and turn right. The entrance to the clubhouse is on the left.

ARVADA NOTES

Arvada's **Historic Olde Town** is the place to start after-golf excursions, and the best cold beer locale is the **Cheshire Cat Brewery** (303-431-9000), billed as "Brewpub, Freehouse, and Home Away From Home". The menu features sandwiches and such, and their unique ales are served in a handsomely restored 1891 brick house. During the summer the **Olde Town Farmers Market** at the corner of Olde Wadsworth and West 57th Ave. is worth touring, and the best spot for lodging is the **On Golden Pond B&B** (303-424-2296), a secluded getaway just minutes from the **Arvada Center for Performing Arts**.

Don't praise your own good shots. Leave that function to your partner, who if a good sport, will not be slow in performing it.— Harry Vardon

AURORA

Elev. 5,342 Pop. 276,000

Donald Fletcher had a dream to expand Denver east in 1891 from the downtown Capitol Hill area. Originally called Fletcher, Aurora is now the second largest city in the Denver Metro area and the third largest city in the state.

Expansion didn't hit Aurora until 1921 when the military put the town on the map. During World War I, the Army decided to build a hospital to treat the wounded. Many had been affected by mustard gas and tuberculosis and Colorado's climate was known for its healing effects of lung ailments. So Aurora was chosen as the site of Fitzsimons Army Hospital in 1921.

Fitzsimons eventually closed down, but the good news was the emergence of the Fitzsimons Golf Course into the golf portfolio of this modern suburb of Denver.

AURORA HILLS GOLF COURSE

THE GOLF Aurora's first public golf course, 9-hole Aurora Hills, was no doubt a stepping stone to what is now a very impressive collection of golf options in the Denver Metro area.

As with all Aurora golf courses, residents get a price break by purchasing a golf card, and on this layout they see tree-lined fairways with generous landing areas and large greens. The signature hole is No. 10, a par-5, 545-yard dogleg right with water framing the fairway.

Colorado Hall of Famer Paul McMullen served as the head pro here until his retirement in 1991.

THE DETAILS 303-364-6111. 50 S. Peoria St., Aurora, CO 80012.
- www.golfaurora.com
- Henry Hughes, 1969. 9 holes. Par 36. Blue - 6,735, (70.1/115). White - 6,446 (68.8/112). Red - 5,919 (71.5/120). Price - $.

GETTING THERE Exit I-225 at Alameda Ave. and head west. At Peoria St. (about 1 mile) turn right (north). The entrance is on the east side of the street just north of Alameda Ave.

CENTRE HILLS GOLF COURSE

THE GOLF Tune up your game at this Dick Phelps-designed par-3 course, which offers a lighted training center with putting and chipping greens for after-hours

---

Never needle, harass or poke fun at a playing partner who's on the edge of despair.— Doug Sanders

golf practice. This is a great place for a beginner to get started, and anyone can sharpen their short-game skills here.

The ninth is the best hole: a 150-yarder with water on the right side that runs through the middle of the fairway.

THE DETAILS 303-343-4935. 16300 E. Centre Tech Pkwy., Aurora, CO 80011.
- www.golfaurora.com
- Dick Phelps, 1989. 9 holes. Par 27. 1,305 yards. Price - $.

GETTING THERE From I-225, head east on 6th Ave. past Chambers Rd. and turn right at the first traffic light (Centre Tech Pkwy.). Proceed to the course, which is next to the Community College of Aurora.

CHERRY CREEK COUNTRY CLUB

THE GOLF Cherry Creek Country Club, designed by Jack Nicklaus and his son Jack II, is Denver's first new private golf country club in 20 years. Located on a 210-acre site off East Iliff Avenue just west of Parker Road, it's a reconstruction of the old Los Verdes Country Club, which opened in the 1960s.

Los Verdes owner Stacey Hart picked the Nicklaus duo expecting greatness, and the designers obligingly introduced something never before seen in Colorado—Dominant Plus Creeping Bentgrass in the fairways. More than 320 mature trees were transplanted to enhance the course, which has eight lakes, stream crossings, and a double-ended driving range.

No. 17 is a signature-caliber hole. It's 208 yards from the back with a carry over Cherry Creek. Anything short and right is dead. A huge waste area defines another par 3, the 187-yard No. 3.

Hart plans to limit the number of Cherry Creek memberships to 445 with the initial membership fee at $50,000. Besides the Nicklaus course, the facility includes a full-service spa and fitness center. The former Los Verdes club hosted 50,000 rounds a year during its busiest time.

THE DETAILS 303-755-0711. 9200 E. Iliff Ave., Aurora, CO 80231.
- www.cherrycreekcountryclub.com
- Jack Nicklaus, Jack Nicklaus II, 2002. 18 holes. Par 72. Black - 7,316 (74.6/133). Gold - 6,900 (72.7/131). Blue - 6,413 (70.4/129). White - 5,820 (67.3/118). Women's Blue - 6,413 (76.4/151). Women's White - 5,820 (72.9/143). Red - 4,992 (68.1/123). Private club, members and guests only. Price - $$$$.

In choosing a partner, always pick the optimist. —Tony Lema

GETTING THERE Take I-25 to Evans. Go east to I-225 to Iliff, then west on Iliff 2.5 miles to course.

FITZSIMONS GOLF COURSE

THE GOLF Fitzsimons offers another chance to stroll the storied fairways where General Dwight D. Eisenhower once walked. The course opened with just three sand greens in 1918 before expanding over the years. The course is located next to the now-defunct Fitzsimons Medical Center, where President Eisenhower recovered after suffering a heart attack at Cherry Hills Country Club.

MSgt. Orville Moody served as the pro here while he was on active duty and he still holds the course record of 63, set in 1958. Moody recorded 11 birdies that day, becoming the All-Military Champion, and he went on to win the 1969 U.S. Open. Moody returned to Fitzsimons in later years to conduct clinics.

One of Fitzsimons' memorable holes is No. 8, a 486-yard par 5 with a dogleg right and bunkers guarding both sides of the fairway. Water must be negotiated to reach the green, which is bunkered on both sides.

THE DETAILS 303-364-8125. 2323 Scranton St., Aurora, CO 80010.
- www.golfaurora.com
- Army Corps of Engineers, 1939-46. 18 holes. Par 72. Blue - 6,530 (69.5/119). White - 6,294 (68.4/115). Red - 5,914 (73.3/130). Price - $$.

GETTING THERE Take Colfax from I-225 and head west into the old Fitzsimons Medical Center complex. Or exit I-70 south at Peoria and find Montview Blvd., and turn left onto the base at Montview.

HEATHER GARDENS GOLF COURSE

THE GOLF Rumored to be one of the best executive courses in the western United States, Heather Gardens features undulating greens that are difficult to read, water hazards on four holes, and out-of-bounds impacting play on every hole. Note the emerging trees on the dogleg 275-yard fifth hole, where big hitters are tempted to just angle it toward the hole for an easy birdie opportunity.

THE DETAILS 303-751-2390. 2888 S. Heather Gardens Way, Aurora, CO 80014.
- Dick Phelps, 1973. 9-hole executive course. Par 32. Blue - 2,461 (62.2/114). White - 2,277 (62.2/112). Red - 2,006 (66/110). Price-$.

Golf puts a man's character on the anvil and his richest qualities—
patience, poise, restraint—to the flame. —Billy Casper

GETTING THERE Exit I-225 at Parker Rd. and go southeast to Vaughn Way. Turn left at the stoplight and proceed to Heather Gardens Way. Turn left on Heather Gardens Way and follow it to the course entrance on the right.

HEATHER RIDGE COUNTRY CLUB

THE GOLF Bowling-alley-narrow fairways that lead to small, undulating greens, combined with out-of-bounds and water on six holes, make Heather Ridge challenging—tough enough to host the Denver Open in 1989.

No. 7 is the best hole: a 506-yard, par 5 with sand traps and out-of-bounds. The club allows for reciprocal play for holders of the American Golf Card and guests of the Aurora DoubleTree Hotel.

THE DETAILS 303-755-3550. 13521 E. Iliff Ave., Aurora, CO 80014.
- Dick Phelps, 1973. 18 holes. Par 70. Black - 6,095 (69.1/ 116). White - 5,727 (67.3/114). Red - 5,204 (70.6/124). Semi-private club. Price - $$.

GETTING THERE Take Iliff Ave. from I-225 west one block to the course.

HERITAGE EAGLE BEND GOLF & COUNTRY CLUB

THE GOLF An Arthur Hills-designed layout that rolls through hilly terrain with some elevation changes, Heritage Eagle Bend opened in 2000 near the Denver Tech Center. Like many of Hill's designs, this one offers plenty of challenge, with 62 strategically placed bunkers, lakes, streams, and a beefed-up 7,105-yard route that meanders through a golf community.

Avoid the tall, snake-infested rough and focus on course management. The beauty of the course is the scenic canyon vistas and a back nine that is loaded with water. Even with the homes, the rugged land and mountain views give the course the character of a more remote layout.

The signature hole is No. 15, a 194-yard par 3 downhill to a small green protected by bunkers.

A large practice facility with chipping area, putting green, and 36 natural grass teeing stations awaits the golfer who enjoys grinding it out during practice sessions.

The club offers a "preferred players" membership without expensive initiation fee or monthly dues.

THE DETAILS 303-400-6700. 23155 East Heritage Pkwy., Aurora, CO, 80016.

"When practicing pick the club that gives you the most trouble, not the one that gives you the most satisfaction." —Harry Vardon

- www.heritageeaglebend.com
- Arthur Hills, 2000. 18 holes. Par 72. Gold - 7,105 (71.9/129). Blue - 6,603 (69.6/119). White - 5,798 (65.5/109). Green - 5,045 (68.8/118). Price - $$$.

GETTING THERE Take E-470 to the Gartrell Rd. exit. Go south on Gartrell Rd. about a half-mile and take a right on East Heritage Pkwy.

MEADOW HILLS GOLF COURSE

THE GOLF A 1950s-style traditional route that features tree-lined fairways, large lakes, lush greens, and manicured grounds, Colorado favorite Meadow Hills received a 3-1/2 star rating from *Golf Digest* and is the annual host for the Aurora City Amateur Tournament.

The course requires accuracy from the tees. No. 18, a 401-yard par-4 dogleg left, involves a drive over water, then an uphill second to a two-tiered green with out-of-bounds left and right.

THE DETAILS 303-690-2500. 3609 South Dawson Aurora, CO 80014.
- www.golfaurora.com
- Henry Hughes, 1957. 18 holes. Par 70. Blue - 6,492 (70.5/133). White - 6,122 (68.9/128). Red - 5,417 (70.2/120). Price - $.

GETTING THERE From I-225 take Parker Rd. south to Hampden Ave. and turn left. At Dawson turn right, and the entrance is two blocks down on the right.

MIRA VISTA GOLF COURSE

THE GOLF Once home for the airmen of Lowry Air Force Base, Mira Vista Golf Course was designed by architect Robert Baldock and is owned by the Colorado Golf Association and Colorado Women's Golf Association. Both associations made the course their home until 2003.

Offering mountain views and scenes of downtown, this is another course with tree-lined fairways and undulating bentgrass greens. Mira Vista also makes a great place to practice, with a reasonable monthly fee, lighted driving range, putting green, chipping area, practice bunker, and a teaching pro on staff. Mira Vista is another drought success story. The course had no water from September to May 2003, but after reseeding in April, the water came back on and conditions are now normal and lush.

Mira Vista hosts a program called Open Fairways, which provides urban youths access to the great game of golf.

THE DETAILS 303-340-1520. 10110 East Golfer's Way, Aurora, CO 80010.
- www.miravistagolf.com
- Robert Baldock, 1972. 18 holes. Par 72. Blue - 6,872 (71.7/130). White - 6,574 (70/122). Gold - 6,240 (68.7/120). Red - 6,018 (73/124). Price - $$.

GETTING THERE From Denver, take I-225 north and exit on 6th Ave. Turn left and find 1st. Ave., then turn right and look for the course.

MURPHY CREEK GOLF COURSE

THE GOLF Most travel golfers love Colorado for the mountain golf, but Murphy Creek is a high plains award-winner near the Denver International Airport that opened in the summer of 2000. Originally named The Homestead at Murphy Creek, the Ken Kavanaugh layout rolls away from the farm-style clubhouse to a total of 7,456 yards from the tips.

And while the fairways are generous, there are more than 80 deep bunkers, including the huge sand waste expanse on the par-3, 205-yard No. 5.

Wiry, thick Canadian fescue, sometimes cut at five inches, surrounds the bunkers, and some of these hazards are right in the middle of the wide fairways.

Be sure to spend some time in the clubhouse, dine in Murphy's Tavern, and view the other buildings. The 1920s farmhouse decor includes white siding with steep-pitched green roofs. The cart barn is a replica of a real barn and the range-ball machine is located in a silo. Former alfalfa fields are littered with old, rusting farm equipment, a horse-drawn wagon, and even an original barn.

You might feel like an Eastern Plains farmhand as you aim your golf cart down dusty roads with only faded barn-wood signs pointing the way to the next hole and rusty signs signaling tee box numbers. Watch for the one that says: "Royal Melbourne, 5,767 miles."

THE DETAILS 303-361-7300. 1700 S. Old Tom Morris Rd., Aurora, CO 80018.
- www.golfaurora.com
- Ken Kavanaugh, 2000. 18 holes. Par 72. Black - 7,456 (74.6/131). Blue - 6,878 (71.6/128). White - 6,451 (69.8/122). Gold - 5,977 (67.5/116). Gold - 5,977 (72.5/125). Red - 5,335 (68.7/120). Price - $$.

My philosophy? Practice, practice, practice—and win.—Babe Didrikson Zaharias

SADDLE ROCK GOLF COURSE

THE GOLF With the surprising duo of Murphy Creek and Saddle Rock Golf Course both receiving *Golf Digest* honors, Aurora became the only city in the country to have two separate facilities make the magazine's elite "Best New Courses" list.

Saddle Rock, designed by Dick Phelps in 1997, is another prairie-links style track dotted by large native areas and plenty of wildlife. Piney Creek and Saddle Rock Gulch move through the back nine, which features large, undulating greens, hilly terrain, cactus, yucca, wild grasses, and even a few pines.

The 17th, a double-dogleg par 5 that rambles 585 yards, is a strict test. Water comes into play on both sides of the fairway and the green is two-tiered.

Host of the Colorado Open for three years, Saddle Rock is a modern design with lots of trouble. Missed fairways result in difficult shots from native grasses —that is, if you can find your ball. Be prepared to use every club in the bag because you must think your way around this course. The pros found the greens particular demanding, but putts roll true.

Note the elevated tee box holes that allow golfers to pick out a distant mountain peak as a target.

THE DETAILS 303-699-3939. 21705 East Arapahoe Rd., Aurora, CO 80016.
- www.golfaurora.com
- Dick Phelps, 1997. 18 holes. Par 72. Black - 7,351 (74.4/135). Blue - 6,907 (72.2/132). White - 6,358 (70/126). Gold - 5,757 (67.3/112). Red - 5,444 (70.9/126). Price - $$.

GETTING THERE Take I-25 to Arapaho Rd. and go east nine miles to Liverpool St. Follow the signs to the course.

SPRINGHILL GOLF COURSE

THE GOLF Springhill's slogan, "Your Best Hole-in-One Chance," stems from the fact that this executive course has 10 par-3 holes. The course is located in a rural area highlighted by open space and horse properties along Sand Creek. Water guards the green on both sides of the No. 4 signature hole, a 530-yard par 5. Hugging the left side of the fairway here is rewarded with an easier approach.

THE DETAILS 303-739-6854. 800 Telluride St., Aurora, CO 80011.
- www.golfaurora.com

Golf is a game of finding what works, losing it, and finding it again. Ken Venturi

- Dick Phelps, 1973. 18 holes. Par 64. White - 4,999 (66.4/105). Red - 4,651 (64.6/100). Price - $.

GETTING THERE Exit I-225 at 6th Ave. and head east for just over 2 miles to Telluride St. Turn left and go north to the course on the right.

VALLEY COUNTRY CLUB

THE GOLF Revered for its walkability, VCC features narrow fairways that are lined with pines, firs, and willows, along with nasty rough that causes problems for wayward tee shots.

Designed in 1956 by William Bell, the course has water hazards that come into play on six holes and a compact, old-style track. It's scenic, requires strategy, and offers some of the best bentgrass greens in town. An oilman from New Mexico donated many of the trees that line the fairways.

Track veterans consider No. 10, a 421-yard par 4, their favorite hole. The tee shot must carry Cherry Creek to a valley, then there's out-of-bounds left and water right. The large green is protected by bunkers on each side.

THE DETAILS 303-690-6377. 14601 Country Club Drive, Aurora, CO 80016.
- William Bell, 1956. 18 holes. Par 72. Blue - 6,866 (71.7/133). White - 6,508 (70.1/125). Black - 5,871 (74.4/134). Red - 5,387 (71.2/126). Private - Members and guests only. Price - $$$.

GETTING THERE Exit I-25 at Arapahoe Rd. Go east on Arapahoe for 4 miles to Jordan. Take a left onto Jordan, follow it for about half a mile, and the course is on the right.

AURORA NOTES

Golf might be the biggest claim to fame for this large city, which has the benefit of being close to Denver's amenities and all of the features of a modern suburb. However one of the Denver area is greatest secrets rests in an Aurora strip mall, near a nail salon and tattoo parlor. **Bender's Brat Haus** (303-344-2648) is famous locally and lines back up out the door during lunchtime. The links are sold to-go, and it's recommended to order with "cheese". In the evenings head to the boonies east of town and look for the funky **Emil-Lene's Sirloin House** (303-366-6674), where the parking lot requires a 4-wheel drive and an old tree grows in the middle of the dining room where great steaks are served. For lodging look to affordable chains like the **Best Western Gateway Inn**

At least he can't cheat on his score—because all you have to do is look back down the fairway and count the wounded.—Bob Hope

& Suites (866-748-4800), **Doubletree Hotel** (303-337-2800), or the **Radisson** (303-695-1700).

BRIGHTON

Elev. 4,982 Pop. 20,905

An Eastern Plains city located on the banks of the South Platte River, Brighton lies 22 miles northeast of downtown Denver. The small-town atmosphere meets agriculture here with the Murray Maize Maze. This outdoor corn maze off Havana Road is designed in the shape of a bear and two wolves, covers 15 acres of corn, and has four miles of trails. The city also invites outdoor lovers to Barr Lake State Park, a good place to view wildlife, bike, boat, fish, and ride horses. Unique for a Colorado town of 20,000, Brighton offers three public 18-hole golf courses.

BOX ELDER CREEK GOLF COURSE

THE GOLF Box Elder Creek has expanded to 18 holes with a new nine, designed by Redstone Golf.

Routed around Box Elder Creek, the course features large greens, generous landing areas, bunches of bunkers, and few trees in a links-like layout. No. 6, a 443-yard par 4 that goes uphill, has out-of-bounds and a drop-off on the right side of the putting surface.

The contrasts from the old nine to the new one add variety. The back nine is more of a target test. No. 17 requires a fade through a narrow chute of cottonwoods; since it's only 350 yards, many hit an iron to keep it in play. The finale is 636 yards and is a definite three-shot hole.

Perplexed golfers were entertained over the 2003 Labor Day weekend when a stray emu named Betty Lou showed up at the course. Betty Lou escaped from Wendy's Rescue, a nonprofit animal rescue organization, and was also joined by a friend named Big Bird. Luckily, neither cared about picking up golf balls, just chasing them. One of the owners, Cannon Shippy, said a large pen will be constructed near the windmill and the birds will become mascots of the course.

THE DETAILS 303-659-7177. 32000 E. 144th Ave., Brighton, CO 80601.
- Redstone Golf, 1999. 18 holes. Par 72. New back nine not rated. Blue / Gold - 6,606 (71.0/122). White/Blue - 6,099 (68.5/116). White/Blue - 6,099 (73.9/130). Red/White - 5,612 (71.1/124). Price - $.

I was three over: one over a house, one over a patio, and one over a swimming pool.—George Brett

GETTING THERE Take I-76 north to Bromley Lane. Head 6 miles east to Lanewood, then go 1 mile south to course.

RIVERDALE DUNES

THE GOLF Pot bunkers, railroad ties, mounds, water, and the South Platte River combine here to create the Denver Metro area version of Ireland. Designed by Pete and Perry Dye, this Colorado Top Ten daily-fee course is walkable and void of houses—a definite must-play.

Supposedly Pete Dye's first public course west of the Mississippi, Riverdale Dunes is a combination of Scottish links style and stadium golf. The course is known for its pristine conditions and is next door to Riverdale's first course, Riverdale Knolls.

No. 11, a 544-yard par 5 where your risk may cause disaster, might be one of the state's most difficult holes. At about 275 yards out the fairway narrows with water right and tall native grass left. Nail it long and down the middle and you still might have an uneven lie. Hit a long iron, play it safe, and you might have a flat lie, making that second shot easier. Still, water guards the right side of the green on the third shot.

Take note of No. 7, a tight hole with water all down the left side. No. 8 is a fun, short par 3 with a shallow and tiered green.

The course has hosted the 1993 U.S. Public Links Championship, as well as the 1996 and 1997 Nike Colorado Classics.

THE DETAILS 303-659-6700. 13300 Riverdale Rd., Brighton, CO 80601.
- www.riverdalegolf.com
- Pete and Perry Dye, 1985. 18 holes. Par 72. Gold - 7,027 (72.1/129). Blue - 6,364 (68.8/120). White - 5,830 (66.3/113). Red - 4,903 (67.6/123). Price - $$.

GETTING THERE Take I-25 to exit 223 (120th Ave.) and go east to Colorado Blvd. Turn north and go to 128th Ave., turn east and proceed to Riverdale Rd. Turn north to the clubhouse.

RIVERDALE KNOLLS

THE GOLF A traditional park-style layout that is sliced by canals, The Knolls is famous for challenging, elevated greens that are easy to three-putt. There are plenty of other hazards and trees, and a round here requires consistent course

Successful competitors want to win. Head cases want to win at all costs.—Nancy Lopez

management, but this is a good course to walk and makes for an enjoyable after-noon on the links.

The canal is in view of the drive on No. 13, a 569-yarder. Another good par 5 is No. 7 at 528 yards. In old-style golf fashion, it allows the approach to be run on the green.

The details 303-659-6700. 13300 Riverdale Rd., Brighton, CO 80601.
- www.riverdalegolf.com
- Henry B. Hughes, 1965. 18 holes. Par 71. Blue - 6,771 (71.1/123). White - 6,365 (69.6/119). Red - 5,891 (72.3/126). Price - $.

Getting there Take I-25 to exit 223 (120th Ave.) and go east to Colorado Blvd. Turn north and go to 128th Ave. Turn east and proceed to Riverdale Rd. Turn north to the clubhouse.

BRIGHTON NOTES

Brighton's **Comfort Inn** (303-654-1400) is the most clean and affordable place to stay, and La Placita (303-659-7782) and **Wingman's** (303-655-1449) are more than adequate for post-round golf outings. However if you're headed outside of town to a B&B and a grill is handy, first stop at **Dale's Exotic Game Meats** (800-289-9453), one of the largest distributors of game meats in the U.S. Rattlesnake, alligator, and the famous canned Jackelope Stew are all available. Holed up business travelers looking for exercise enjoy the **Brighton Recreation Center,** complete with a weight room, swimming pool, and a gym.

BROOMFIELD

Elev. 5,420 Pop. 38,272

Broomfield is a booming town on the technology corridor just 20 minutes from Denver and 10 minutes from Boulder. Luxury lodging and golf are avail-able at the 300-acre Omni Interlocken Resort, which shares the Interlocken Advanced Technology Park with companies such as Corporate Express, Level 3 Communications, and Sun Microsystems. A hotel shuttle transports golfers to the 27-hole golf course, and the surrounding area also boasts three more cours-es and more than 15 miles of scenic trails for hiking, jogging, and biking.

If there is doubt in your mind over a golf shot, how can your muscles know what they are expected to do?—Harvey Penick

BROADLANDS GOLF COURSE

THE GOLF Strategy, says Rick Phelps, is the key to toppling your opponent at Broadlands Golf Course, a 7,263-yard muni that spreads across 177 acres.

The course features wide fairways, water hazards, and subtle features. Some hazards are only detectable from certain sides of a fairway and some greens are more receptive from the correct ball position. Watch out for sloped fairways that funnel golf balls toward trouble. Views include the foothills, a running stream, 11 lakes, and challenging sand traps.

The greens are huge and easy to three-putt. Phelps recommends taking chances off the tee, because the wide fairways can handle big draws and big fades. Water comes into play on 11 of 18 holes, and the peninsula green on the second can spell a watery grave. Also look for waterfalls between the 9th and 18th holes.

After playing, enjoy the 7,000-square-foot clubhouse, which sits atop the highest knoll on the property. The Broadlands also has a complete practice facility with a driving range, practice putting green, chipping green, and practice bunker.

THE DETAILS 303-466-8285. 4380 West 144th Ave., Broomfield, CO 80020.
- www.broadlandsgolf.com
- Rick Phelps, 1999. 18 holes. Par 72. Gold - 7,263. (72.9/125). Blue - 6,691 (70/122). White - 6,034 (67/114). Red - 5,348 (68.4/118). Price - $$.

GETTING THERE To get there, take I-25 north out of Denver to 120th Ave. Go west on 120th to Lowell Ave. Take Lowell north to 144th Ave. and proceed west about 400 yards.

EAGLE TRACE GOLF CLUB

THE GOLF Eagle Trace offers Rocky Mountain views, a challenging but fair Dick Phelps design, five lakes, huge native cottonwoods, 65 bunkers, and quality bentgrass greens. The 518-yard, par-5 No. 6 is one of the better holes.

In addition to the recent lengthening of the course, other updates brought in 200 tons of new sand for the bunkers and 100 newly planted aspens. Tee boxes have been landscaped with ornamental grasses and flowers, and a natural grass practice tee has been added to the driving range.

DENVER

THE DETAILS 303-466-3322. 1200 Clubhouse Dr., Broomfield, CO 80020.
- www.eagletracegolfclub.com
- Dick Phelps, 1963. 18 holes. Par 72. Gold - 6,742 (71.1./23). Black - 6,119 (69.4/118). Silver - 5,346 (64.8/112). Women's Black - 6,119 (74.1/141). Women's Silver - 5,380 (69.9/128). Price - $$.

GETTING THERE Take I-25 to exit 223 (120th Ave.) north from Denver. Turn west on 120th Ave. and follow it to Main St. in Broomfield. Turn right (north) and follow Main St. to the Eagle Golf Club on the right. The entrance to the club is through the housing development just north of the holes visible from Main St.

GREENWAY PARK GOLF COURSE

THE GOLF At 9-hole Greenway golfers face few trees, but water and sand force accuracy on this par-3 track. The 109-yard No. 4 hole requires a wedge over trees to hit the green. The 93-yard sixth is the easiest hole—it's flat, while most of the course is more rolling.

THE DETAILS 303-466-3729. 110 Greenway Drive, Broomfield, CO 80020.
- Architect unknown, 1971. 9 holes. Par 27. 1,074 yards. Price - $.

GETTING THERE Take I-25, turn west on 120th Ave. to Lamar, then drive south to Greenway Dr.

OMNI INTERLOCKEN RESORT

THE GOLF Home of Sun Microsystems' annual John Elway Celebrity Classic, Interlocken features three nines built in 1999 by David Graham and Gary Panks. A year-round resort with inspiring vistas of the Rockies between Denver and Boulder, this club's layout rolls over 300 acres that have been enhanced with some 3,000 newly planted trees. The bent greens are superb, with only subtle tiering. The wide fairways allow hacks to hit big from the tee.

The brawniest hole is No. 4 on the Vista nine. A par 5 at 565 yards, it plays long and uphill and is usually against the breeze heading up to the course's highest point. Native grass right makes wayward shots disappear, and a bunker right of the green spells trouble (15 feet below ground level).

Aside from Vista No. 4 there are some reachable par 5s, and a fun 325-yard par 4 that is driveable for the straight, long hitter. Enjoy the 12-acre practice

---

In 1987, Judy Bell, long associated with The Broadmoor, became the first woman ever to be elected to the Executive Committee of the United States Golf Association.

facility with driving range, multi-tiered putting greens, and chipping greens that are located south of the clubhouse, which includes Fairways Restaurant and Bar.

In one Elway classic, with the greens running 12-plus on the Stimpmeter, former major-leaguer Rick Rhoden carded nine birdies and an eagle on his way to 36 points in one day in his Stableford scoring system victory.

THE DETAILS 303-464-9000. 800 Eldorado Blvd., Broomfield, CO 80021.
- www.elwaycelebrityclassic.com, www.omnihotels.com
- David Graham, Gary Panks, 1999. 27 holes. Par 72. Price - $$$
- Eldorado/Vista: Black - 6,957 (72.4/139). Gold - 6,538 (70.5/133). Blue - 6,099 (68.4/125). White - 5,618 (70.9/139). Red - 5,181 (69.5/127).
- Sunshine/Eldorado: Black - 6,955 (72.5/135). Gold - 6,552 (70.5/129). Blue - 6,122 (69/122). White - 5,701 (67.4/114). Red - 5,220 (70/130).
- Vista/Sunshine: Black - 7,040 (72.9/139). Gold - 6,622 (71/132). Blue - 6,131 (68.6/126). White - 5,655 (67.1/119). Red - 5,157 (69.3/128).

GETTING THERE From I-25 travel west of Hwy. 36 to the Interlocken Loop. Go south almost a mile to Eldorado Blvd. and turn right. The clubhouse is on the left.

BROOMFIELD NOTES

Relax after golf at the Omni Interlocken clubhouse grill known as **Fairways**, and the **Meritage Restaurant and Tap Room** are available as well. In Broomfield, **Roosters Bar & Patio** (303-465-2070) is preferred for its patio, and the **Flatiron Crossings** shopping center and entertainment complex is nearby, with more than 200 retail shops, restaurants, and cafes surrounded by over 30 acres of parks, streams, and trails. One great spot in the mall is **Gordon Biersch Brewing** (720-887-2991), which only serves German-style lagers. Steak lovers should try the **Hoffbrau Grill & Bar** (303-422-7755) in nearby Westminster at 88th and Wadsworth.

CASTLE ROCK

Elev. 6,202 Pop. 20,225

Some say the massive, flat-topped rock formation that sits 29 miles south of Denver on I-25 looks like a European castle, while others can see a face in the stone. When prospector David Kellogg passed through this area in 1858, he and a couple of friends climbed the huge rock. Upon reaching the top, they celebrated their achievement with a volley of gunfire and a christening. The forma-

---

Colorado Golf Hall of Famer Judy Bell was a member of the 1960 and 1962
United States Curtis Cup teams and served as captain in 1986.

tion they named Castle Rock has served as a navigational point for Native Americans, early settlers, today's modern traveler, and countless rock climbers who scale it each year. Today an extensive trail system surrounds the town of Castle Rock, and recreation areas like Castlewood Canyon State Park and the Pike National Forest are just miles away.

The big rock also serves as the perfect target on the tough par-4 No. 10 hole at Castle Pines Golf Club, which is home of The International, one of the PGA Tour's most coveted stops.

CASTLE PINES GOLF CLUB

THE GOLF This stunning, tough Jack Nicklaus layout is known the world over for the scenes televised each August from The International, the PGA Tour stop that uses the modified Stableford system of scoring. Opened in 1981, Castle Pines is another of the upper-echelon Denver private layouts that cater to the elite of the metro area; it's 22 miles south of Cherry Hills Country Club. Situated in the foothills at 7,500 feet, the course offers stunning Rocky Mountain scenes, sandstone rock formations, ponderosa pines, scrub oak, pristine conditioning, wiry rough, and a tough walk for the pros. It rolls up and down over countless hills throughout the 7,503 yards.

The generous fairways often lull competent golfers to sleep, but the approaches are attention-grabbers. Nicklaus doesn't let you nap—miss the approach and you are in trouble.

The opening hole is a birdie chance. The 644-yard dogleg left features a 180-foot drop from tee to green with a spectacular view of the Rockies. This one begs for 400-yard drives from the pros, but is the longest hole on the PGA Tour and offers a second shot from a downhill lie for shoter hitters.

No. 9 is another long 458-yard, par-4 aesthetic walk, but requires an accurate tee shot to avoid a series of ponds and waterfalls that line the right side. The approach is semi-blind with a 5- or 6-iron to a green that slopes back to front. Staying below the hole is imperative.

The real test all the pros talk about is No. 10, a 485-yard par 4 that requires an approach shot sometimes measuring more than 200 yards over water to the green. This hole has ruined many rounds in the tournament.

Golf Digest has been dropping Castle Pines in its "America's 100 Greatest Courses" rankings, but the course still makes the list. It's now ranked No. 74, while neighbor Sanctuary is No. 89. Cherry Hills Country Club is the only other Colorado course on the list at No. 25.

The guy on the bulldozer for Tom Doak at Pacific Dunes in Bandon, Oregon was Jim Urbina, who lives in Denver. He also shaped the award-winning Texas Tech golf course.

THE DETAILS 303-688-6000. 303-688-6022. 1000 Hummingbird Lane, Castle Rock, CO 80104.
- www.golfintl.com
- Jack Nicklaus, 1981. 18 holes. Par 72. International - 7,594 (77.4/155). One Bird - 7,381 (76.4/153). Two Bird - 6,753 (72.7/148). Three Bird - 5,971 (73.7/141). Four Bird - 5,427 (71.1/131). Private, invitation only. Price - $$$$.

GETTING THERE Take I-25 south to Happy Canyon exit and go west for 1 mile to the Castle Pines guard house. Turn right and follow the signs to the course.

THE COUNTRY CLUB AT CASTLE PINES

THE GOLF Situated on a bluff high above the older Castle Pines Golf Club, The Country Club at Castle Pines offers such incredible views of the panoramic foothills, sandstone rock outcroppings, towering pines, and Rocky Mountains that you will want to want forget golf and gawk instead. Even Mr. Nicklaus, who routed it with no two holes running parallel, advised, "Forget about your score, just enjoy the scenery."

The Colorado mountain-lodge-style clubhouse overlooks the course from a 300-foot rock ledge and gives members a luxurious perch for discussing and imbibing after a round.

Cut from a forest of ponderosa pines, scrub oak, and rock, this is one hilly golf course. No. 5 is muscular at 659 yards and presents a divided fairway.

The opener is the best chance for birdie. It's a downhill par 5 and only 530 yards. A scenic cliff is on the left as it plays into the beautiful foothills of the Castle Pines area.

THE DETAILS 303-688-6400. 6400 Country Club Drive, Castle Rock, CO 80108.
- Jack Nicklaus, 1986. 18 holes. Par 72. Back - 7,143 (73.7/141). Middle - 6,579 (71.3/129). Forward - 6,101 (68.7/127). Ladies - 5,385 (71.7/128). Private, members and guests only. Price - $$$.

GETTING THERE Take I-25 south to the Happy Canyon exit and go west for 1 mile to the Castle Pines guard house. Turn right and follow the signs to the course.

Colorado Golf Hall of Famer Marcia Bailey, as a determined competitor, dominated women's golf in the state as a two-time winner of the Denver Women's Invitation Golf Championship (1963, 1967) and four-time winner of the Colorado Women's Golf Association Match Play Championship (1963, 1965, 1966, 1967).

PLUM CREEK GOLF & COUNTRY CLUB

THE GOLF Pete Dye designed the Plum Creek Golf and Country Club in the 1980s as a TPC Stadium Course, and it had some early drama as a Senior PGA Tour stop that attracted Arnold Palmer, Lee Trevino, Chi Chi Rodriquez, Gary Player, and Sam Snead.

Today, Plum Creek strives to serve as a steward of the land. The superintendent actively works to preserve water and reduce use of pesticides. In fact, the decision to build a target layout helps save water in time of drought.

The course has PGA-style rough and bentgrass fairways and greens. Water hazards add to the beauty, coming into play on holes 16, 17, and 18. Railroad ties and pot bunkers are evident throughout the course, but multiple tees make it playable for many skill levels.

Watch out for water on the signature hole, No. 16, a par 4 of 416 yards. There's a slight bend to the fairway as a lake routes all the way to the green, which is surrounded by water. A strong headwind also makes this hole more difficult.

The 33,000-square-foot clubhouse is a focal point for the members with a formal dining room that overlooks the 18th hole and the front range. There's also a casual bar and grill, tennis courts, and an aquatic complex that includes an outdoor swimming pool and jacuzzi.

THE DETAILS 303-688-2611. 331 Players Club Drive, Castle Rock, CO 80104.
- www.plumcreekgolfandcc.com
- Pete Dye, 1984. 18 holes. Par 72. Black - 7,118 (73.6/137). Blue - 6,583 (70.7/132). White - 5,907 (67.7/121). Red - 4,973 (67/116). Private club, reciprocal play accepted. Price - $$$.

GETTING THERE Take I-25 to exit 181 in Castle Rock, then go east a half-mile to a four-way stop sign and the Plum Creek Blvd. and waterfall entrance. Turn right and go south for about one mile.

THE RIDGE AT CASTLE PINES NORTH

THE GOLF The Ridge at Castle Pines North, a Troon Golf-managed facility that was purchased by LPGA tour star Grace Park and her family, is considered to be Colorado's premier upscale public-access golf course. Since opening in July 1997, the Tom Weiskopf design has won awards from just about every golf publication—both statewide and national.

Colorado Golf Hall of Famer James Bailey, longtime club pro, won the PGA's Horton Smith Award in 1976. This award honors the golf professional who has made the most significant contribution to the PGA National Education Program.

Golf Magazine honored The Ridge as one of its Top 10 New Courses in its first year of operation, and it's currently ranked No. 66 on its Top 100 You Can Play List. The Tom Weiskopf design has also been recognized by *RockiesGolf.com* and other publications as the No. 1 upscale public facility in Colorado. Surely Weiskopf was a prophet a few years ago when he predicted that "the best golf courses since the 1930s will be built in the 1990s." The Ridge helps make his prophecy a reality.

Located within minutes of Sanctuary and Castle Pines Golf Club, the course shares the same outstanding topography—front-range foothill scenes that include sandstone rock formations, gambel oaks, ponderosa pines, many varieties of wildlife, and majestic looks at the Rocky Mountains. The Ridge left lots of room for the environment—it's arranged in two huge loops with natural space in between. The wildlife corridors and gaps were left on the course to make way for migrating elk herds.

The course displays two contrasting nines. The front nine is wide open and plays through scrub oak and pines. Then the back nine traverses sandstone ridges with some tight, Ponderosa pine-framed holes. Some of the holes seem to have two faces. From the tee box one might see wide open fairways with generous landing areas, then on the approach face diabolical golf shots into elevated greens surrounded by deep bunkers. The greens are difficult bentgrass with lots of contours and multi-tiered.

No. 18's tee box is scenic. From the tips the golfer sees sandstone monoliths and a gully, but it's only a carry of 170 yards.

As is typical with award-winners, every hole is an attention-getter with a myriad of fun challenges. Glancing up from the fairway of No. 8, golfers enjoy the view from "The Ridge"—south to 14,110-foot Pikes Peak and to Devil's Head and Mt. Evans in the west. Northward, downtown Denver is in view.

The Ridge Restaurant serves breakfast, lunch, and dinner, and attracts lots of non-golfers in for the view and outside patio seating.

THE DETAILS 303-688-0100. 1414 Castle Pines Pkwy., Castle Rock, CO 80104.
- www.theridgecpn.com
- Tom Weiskopf, 1997. 18 holes. Par 71. Black - 6,939 (71.8/143). Gold - 6,368 (69.2/131). Silver - 5,875 (66.9/123). Jade - 4,895 (67.4/122). Price - $$$$.

GETTING THERE From downtown Denver, head south on I-25 to Exit 188 (Castle Pines Pkwy.), turn right and go west 2 miles until you see the clubhouse on the left side of the road.

Jonathan Kaye, winner of the 2004 FBR Open in Scottsdale, was born in Denver in 1970 and grew up playing at City Park. It was his second tour victory. Kaye also played for the CU Buffs.

RED HAWK RIDGE GOLF COURSE

THE GOLF Jim Engh remembers the day when he walked members of the USGA up to the tee-box perch of hole 15 and told them it was a 528-yard par 4. He got a few goofy looks in return. Maybe the push-the-envelope architect had pushed a little too much.

"The altitude is 6,400 feet, there's a wind at your back, and it's downhill— why can't a good player hit it 400 yards?" Goofy looks turned to looks of understanding. "Shoot, at this altitude and with a multitude of downhill holes, you would have to make every course 8,000 yards," Engh told them.

Award-winning architect Engh, who has an office just minutes from Red Hawk Ridge, won awards for this one, too. When the course opened in 1999 it was named No. 7 Best New Affordable Golf Course by *Golf Digest* and *GolfWeek* ranked it No. 19 on its America's 30 Best Municipals list.

Red Hawk Ridge is a dream course that gathers sweeping views of the front range from its high points, rocky buttes, thick native grasses, and scrub oak teeming with wildlife. It features wide fairways with big landing areas framed by large grassy moguls, bunkers, greenside lakes bumped against sand and stacked rock, and massive contoured bentgrass greens with tough, thick collars.

The City of Castle Rock wanted a fun course, and that's what Engh gave them. Golfers enjoy the trio of par 3s on the back nine and the three par 5s. Why that combination? Engh took city administrators to a high ridgeline that defined the back nine and pointed to placement of the holes. As Engh's vision became clear to the administrators, light bulbs went off in their heads—fun!

Standing on the tee of the course's No. 14 signature hole, a 210-yard par 3 downhill, you can see Long's Peak and Rocky Mountain National Park in the distance, along with Pikes Peak to the south. The wind sweeps over your shoulder as your shot flies high and drops 75 feet to the green's surface. Picking the right club is a task.

THE DETAILS 720-733-3500. 2156 Red Hawk Ridge Drive, Castle Rock, CO 80104.
- www.redhawkridge.com
- Jim Engh, 1999. 18 holes. Par 72. Black - 6,872 (71.6/129). Gold - 6,276 (69/118). Blue - 5,923 (71.1/119). Red - 4,636 (67.5/107). Price - $$$.

GETTING THERE From I-25 take the Wolfensberger exit and turn. Next turn right onto Red Hawk Dr., and go about another quarter mile. The course is on the left.

The Golf Club at Redlands Mesa, a public daily-fee course, is No. 4 on Golf Digest's list of best Colorado courses. Those ahead are private clubs—Cherry Hills, Castle Pines, and Sanctuary.

CASTLE ROCK NOTES

Thousands come here every day for the **Prime Outlets at Castle Rock** stores, and many chain restaurants surround the 100-plus name-brand stores. The **Best Western Inn & Suites** (303-814-8800) is a short walk away and offers golf packages to area courses. The **Rockyard Brewing Company** (303-814-9273), set in a ski lodge atmosphere, is the oldest brewpub in town, and The **Old Stone Church Restaurant** (303-688-9000) is set in an 1888 Catholic church and is a memorable experience. Also consider The **Castle Café** (303-814-2233), the former Keystone Hotel that hosted wild brawls and inebriated cowboys that supposedly rode their horses through the bar. The café specializes in pan-fried chicken, steaks, and fish. Each summer the city hosts a 100-mile bike tour around Colorado, called the **Elephant Rock**, that begins and ends in Castle Rock.

CENTENNIAL   ELEV. 5,390 POP. 103,000

Centennial, Colorado's newest city and the largest newly incorporated city in America, proudly graces the pages of *The Colorado Golf Bible* by technicality—residents voted to incorporate on September 12, 2000, and this little slice of Denver suburbia officially became a city on February 7, 2001. Now the local golf course, which boasts a 9-hole par 3 route in addition to its normal 18, lists a Centennial address.

SOUTH SUBURBAN GOLF COURSE

THE GOLF Dick Phelps' South Suburban layout includes Dry Creek, trees, water, and hills as obstacles, and the sloping greens present issues every now and then. Most locals like the 587-yard par-5 fifth. The drive carries Dry Creek past trees to the top of a hill. The play is to lay up right of the bunker and then play the blind shot over the hill to a mild left dogleg. The green is elevated with a bunker in back.

South Suburban includes an 18-hole regulation course and a 9-hole par-3 course for those who are just beginning or for players wishing to sharpen their short game skills. The South Suburban Recreation District is a three-time National Gold Medal Winner for Excellence in Park and Recreation Management.

THE DETAILS 303-770-5508. 7900 South Colorado Blvd, Centennial, CO 80122.

Rick Dewitt, Regis High grad and member of the Colorado Golf Hall of fame was featured as one of the nation's top amateurs in the May 4, 2002 issue of Golf Week *and in a 2000 USGA Golf Journal.*

- Dick Phelps, 1973. 18 holes. Par 72. Blue - 6,698 (70.1/122). White - 6,318 (68.4/116). Women's White - 6,263 (74.6/133). Women's Gold - 5,638 (71.4/126). Women's Red - 5,274 (69.2/122). Price - $.
- Nine-hole par-3 course. Par 27. Price - $.

GETTING THERE Located west of I-25 on S. Colorado Blvd. between Dry Creek Road and County Line Road.

CENTENNIAL NOTES

The first reader of *The Colorado Golf Bible* who can recommend a non-chain eating establishment with a Centennial address will receive a new box of Titleist Pro V1s. But as chains go, **Maggiano's** (303-858-1405) is a good bet for sit-down Italian food and red wine to wash the shanks away. Centennial's neighbor is Littleton (Page 107), which is a bigger slice of suburbia with even more golf and extra-curricular activities.

COMMERCE CITY   Elev. 5,166 Pop. 20,991

Commerce City was incorporated when the small communities of Dupont, Adams Heights, Derby, Irondale, and Rose Hill were combined in 1952. The gold rush brought the first settlers here a hundred years earlier; and now the area is dotted by wheat fields, stock yards, and hotbeds where young plants are born in winter.

Commerce City has the state's largest Memorial Day parade, and the immediate area serves as a gateway to the Rocky Mountain National Wildlife Refuge, Barr Lake State Park, and the Prairie Gateway area. All of these attractions offer trails, open spaces, and wildlife preserves. But the open spaces of most interest to the golfer should be the outstanding Buffalo Run Golf Course.

BUFFALO RUN GOLF COURSE

THE GOLF The Keith Foster-designed Buffalo Run Golf Course is a must-play prairie-links gem that will test your game. It can be ghoulish because of its mounding, undulating fairways, 65 deep sand traps, streams and lakes that bump fairways, and large contoured greens that are closely cropped around the fringes.

From the tips the course rolls 7,411 yards and presents a multitude of risk/reward challenges. On the front side, No. 4 is a beauty: an uphill par 3 that

---

Collindale Golf Course in Fort Collins opened a new $2.65 million clubhouse in 2003. It features Colorado lodge architecture.

features a rock-strewn stream down the right side and a marshy, cattail-laden right side that gobbles up errant strokes.

On the back No. 14 stands out—an interesting 259-yard par-4—as does the 207-yard, par-3 17th. Water is left and wraps to the back of the green, which is shaped like an upside-down L. The hole plays downhill, so picking the right club is tough. If you bail out right, there's still a scary chip back with water looming on the other side of the green.

Foster describes the course as a link to British Isles golf with Rocky Mountain views. Buffalo Run's amenities are first-class, too, from its clubhouse and restaurant to the great practice facilities.

Buffalo Run has hosted U.S. Open qualifiers, Colorado Open qualifiers, and PGA Sectional events, and it will be the host of the 2004 Denver Open.

THE DETAILS 303-289-1500. 15700 E. 112th Ave., Commerce City, CO 80022.
- www.golfexperience.com/buffalorun
- Keith Foster, 1996. 18 holes. Par 72. Black - 7,411 (74.3/129). Gold - 7,016 (72.6/128). Blue - 6,499 (70/122). White - 6,113 (68.3/117). Women's White - 6,115 (74.2/128). Women's Red - 5,227 (68.8/117). Price - $$.

GETTING THERE Exit I-76 at 120th Ave. (exit 16) and drive east on 120th about a half-mile to Chambers Rd. Turn right (south) and go one mile to 112th Ave. Turn left (east) and go a half-mile to course.

COMMERCE CITY NOTES

Denver looms nearby with all of its glorious eateries and entertainment options, but the **Bison Grill** (303-289-7700) or the **Butcher Block** (303-289-2055) are excellent local options for post-round eats. Places like the **Penn Motel** (303-287-7366), **Super A Motel** (303-288-6389) or **Triple A Motel** (303-296-3333) are all available for very affordably overnight excursions.

DENVER

Elev. 5,280 Pop. 554,636

Colorado's capital was established by a party of prospectors on November 22, 1858, after a gold discovery at the confluence of Cherry Creek and the South Platte River. An 1859 mass migration of more than 100,000 souls prompted the U.S. government to establish Colorado Territory in 1861. Denver has been cow

---

LPGA Tour player Jill McGill is a graduate of Cherry Creek High School.

town, oil and gas town, telecommunications town, and brew town since then.

Today Denver itself has half a million folks, but the sports-crazed metro area bulges to 2.1 million. Situated on high plains at the eastern base of the Rocky Mountains, the weather is dry and cool and the sun shines 300 days a year, warmed by Chinook winds, making golf possible all year when snow is absent on the fairways. And the golf is superb, with numerous upscale facilities open to the public at amazingly affordable prices.

BEAR CREEK GOLF CLUB

THE GOLF A prominent all-male facility known for some of the most impressive greens in Colorado, Bear Creek was designed by Arnold Palmer and Ed Seay, who must have been angry at something when they routed this one. It's penal, hilly, strategic, and you must be heroic to tame it. Some of the undulating, slick greens have three tiers, but the conditions are magnificent and there's nothing better than snaking in a putt that breaks three times on its way to the hole.

No. 16 is a great hole, requiring a long iron approach into a peninsula green. In fact, just driving it into position on this hole—through a narrow fairway with trees lining both sides—is an accomplishment.

THE DETAILS 303-980-8700. 12201 Morrison Rd., Denver, CO 80228.
* Arnold Palmer, Ed Seay, 1985. 18 holes. Par 72. Black - 7,221 (74.3/146). Blue - 6,891 (73.3/141). White - 6,489 (71.4/129). Gold - 5,698 (66.9/115). Private course, men only, members and guests; reciprocal play tee time must be made by professional. Price - $$$$.

GETTING THERE Take 6th Ave. west from downtown to Kipling and go south on Kipling to Morrison Road West for 1.5 miles. Turn right at Wright Way and proceed to the course.

CITY PARK GOLF COURSE

THE GOLF Dating back to 1919, historic City Park is a classic—one of the longest courses in the country when it first opened, and the long-time favorite of downtown businessmen. Views of the Denver skyline greet golfers, old trees line the fairways, and small sloping greens and unusual bunkering make this a fun test for anyone.

Surrounded by the Denver Zoo, museum, and parks, the golf course has lots of foot traffic; legend has it that "ball burglary" has been a hobby for years of

---

Englewood resident and PGA Tour pro Mark Wiebe won the 1989 Colorado Open. His son Gunner caddied for him in 2003 at The International.

those just hoofing it through this layout, which was the City Park Dairy Farm before its grand opening.

Jim Thorpe, Babe Zaharias, and recent PGA Tour winner Jonathan Kaye have all spent time on this course. Kaye was involved in the junior golf program here, and his hardware is on display in the clubhouse's impressive trophy collection.

Historical recaps of City of Denver municipals are here, too, thanks to Ken Shearer, who calls City Park "home of heroes, hustlers, and hard luck." Shearer and Director of Golf Tom Woodard agree that golfers have been coming here for more than 40 years to engage in a Friday Skins Game. No doubt Woodard has participated—he owns the course record at 61 and has been playing the course since he was a kid.

City Park's architect is unknown, but this gem was recently polished up with a 7,000-square-foot clubhouse that opened in 2002, a pro shop and restaurant, and a new irrigation system with 1.5-acre lake.

Today, City Park is also home to a First Tee facility, a four-hole course for beginners. The kids can also get six hours of golf instruction for only $30.

After playing 18 holes, travel golfers might feel inspired to visit the Denver Zoo and the Denver Museum of Natural History, conveniently located across the street from City Park Golf Course.

THE DETAILS 303-295-2096. 2500 York St., Denver, CO 80205.
- www.cityofdenvergolf.com
- 1919. 18 holes. Par 72. Gold - 6,740 (70.6/122). Blue - 6,470 (69.2/121). White - 6,095 (687.4/117). Red - 5,639 (70.5/119). Price - $.

An old-school chipping clinic at City Park Golf Course

Englewood resident Craig Stadler caddied for his son Kevin in the 2002 Colorado Open at Sonnenalp. Kevin, who played golf at the University of Southern California, won the event, his first as a professional.

The "fellas" at Denver Country Club

GETTING THERE Take Colorado Blvd. to 30th Ave., head west to York, and the new clubhouse is on the left side.

DENVER COUNTRY CLUB

THE GOLF When the 46th Trans-Mississippi Championship came to Denver Country Club in 1946, Denver's Charles "Babe" Lind made a shot that has gone down in Centennial State history.

Lind was in the semi-finals facing Dallas' Jack Munger and the match was all-square coming to the 18th. Both players hit approach shots into greenside bunkers. Munger's sand blast came to rest 15 feet from the cup, but Lind, known as a short-game master, blasted one that landed softly and dropped in the hole to win the match.

Former Denver Broncos running back Terrell Davis, MVP of Super Bowl XXXII, sports a 22 handicap and favors Heritage Eagle Bend Golf & Country Club in Aurora.

Skee Riegel won the title the next day, but the shot is still remembered. Lind even donated the wedge, a 1930 Wilson Top Notch, to the Colorado Golf Hall of Fame.

Denver Country Club has long been known as a shot-makers course. Today's big hitters need to ponder if they have enough discipline to keep the driver in the bag. Can you avoid the many mature trees on one of the state's oldest courses? Can you stay out of Cherry Creek and the lakes that taunt you on 11 holes?

If so, then you might just tame this old-timer and be able to envision a walk back into time. From the scenic tee of the 184-yard, par-3 fifth hole, stroke it solid over a pond and don't get distracted by the Denver skyline as a backdrop.

THE DETAILS 303-733-2444. 1700 E. First Ave., Denver, CO 80218.

- J. Foulis, 1902. Remodels: W. Flynn, H. Coulis, B. Diddle, Arnold Palmer, Ed Seay, Bill Coore. 18 holes. Par 71. Blue - 6,806 (72.6/137). White - 6,388 (70.8/133). Gold - 6,142 (70/130). Red - 5,935 (73.5/137). Orange - 5,826 (72.9/136). Private: members and guests only. Price - $$$$.

GETTING THERE From I-25 exit at University Blvd. and drive north 3 miles to First Ave. Turn left and proceed to Gilpin and the entrance to the country club.

FOOTHILLS GOLF COURSE

THE GOLF The Foothills complex is a Dick Phelps undertaking that includes a championship 18-hole course, a par 3, 9-hole course, and an Executive 9. Mature trees, bunkers, water, testy rough and subtle contours on the greens define this bargain.

On the championship layout No. 6 is considered the signature hole. This 542-yard par 5 requires a tee shot over a pond while the second shot must clear an irrigation ditch with out-of-bounds on the left. Another good test is No. 16, a 551-yard par 5. The fairway is generous and bends left with creek left and rough right. The creek weaves back in front of the green 100 yards from the green.

THE DETAILS 303-409-2400. 3901 S. Carr St. Denver, CO 80235.

- Dick Phelps, 1971. 18 holes. Par 72. Blue - 6,795 (71.6/122). White - 6,365 (69.6/117). Women's White 6,314 (74.5/133). Women's Red - 5,841 (71.9/127). Price - $$.

Colorado Avalanche captain Joe Sakic cards a 5.5 index and is a member of the men's only Bear Creek Golf Club in Denver. He hosts an annual charity event called the Sakic Classic.

- Foothills Executive 9: Dick Phelps, 1992. Par 31. Blue/Gold - 4,283 (60.2/94). White/Blue - 3,903 (59.5/90). Women's Blue/Gold - 4,283 (63.2/103). Women's White/Blue - 3,903 (60.7/100). Women's Red/White - 3,493 (58.3/96). Price - $.
- Foothills Par-3 Course: Dick Phelps, 1971. Par 27. 1,175 yards. Price - $.

GETTING THERE Exit West Hampden Avenue at Wadsworth Blvd., going south. Turn west on the Frontage Road and go to South Carr St. Turn left (watch for sign) and proceed to course parking lot.

GREEN GABLES COUNTRY CLUB

THE GOLF Green Gables is a prime example of an old, traditional Denver country club—a classic, lush parkland layout that was built in 1929. The rolling, wooded site was once owned by Cripple Creek silver baron Verger Reed, who had a summer estate here. Green Gables Realty bought the estate in 1928 for $75,000 and built the country club. Reed's colonial manor house was converted into the clubhouse, surrounded by 140 acres of manicured beauty along dusty Morrison Road, which led to the silver camps of the Colorado Rockies.

Green Gables was so popular that it hosted President Dwight D. Eisenhower in September 1955, when he stopped to play golf and attend a dinner in his honor.

In 2003 Arthur Hills and staff were hired to update the course. Hills' remodeling goals included adding strategy to the layout, increasing the back tee distance to 6,951 and the forward tees to 5,171 yards, creating one or two signature holes, and increasing its standing in the Denver rankings. The team was also asked to revitalize the creek, which was eroding, and to remove some 300 trees (elm, cottonwood, conifer, maple) that had squeezed the layout and suffocated some holes. Some of the trees were transplanted into more strategic locations.

Hills' staff also updated the push-up greens, which were mostly flat with bunkers left and right. After years of top dressing, the drainage had deteriorated. All of the greens were redone with modern technology and the bunkers were reconstructed.

Green Gables superintendent John Madden worked previously at famous Winged Foot before coming to Green Gables. Two-time PGA Championship winner Paul Runyan made his home here in the 1970s and early 1980s, serving as golf professional and instructor. Born in Hot Springs, Arkansas, Runyan won a total of nine PGA Tour events in 1933.

Denver Broncos quarterback Jake Plummer sports a 10 handicap and is a member at Southern Dunes Golf Club in Scottsdale and The Club at Black Rock, Jim Engh's new design in Coeur d'Alene, Idaho.

DENVER

THE DETAILS 303-985-1525. 6800 West Jewell Ave., Denver, CO 80232.
- www.greengablescc.org
- Front nine, William Tucker, 1929. Back nine, James L. Haines. Remodel - Arthur Hills, 2003. 18 holes. Par 71. Blue - 6,707 (71.1/ 128). White - 6,329 (69.3/124). Gold - 6,062 (68.0/120). Women's White - 6,329 (75.4/141). Women's Gold - 6,062 (73.9/138). Women's Red - 5,600 (71.7/125). Members and guests only, no reciprocal play. Price - $$$.

GETTING THERE The Green Gables entrance is located on West Jewell Ave. between South Sheridan Blvd. and South Wadsworth Blvd.

GREEN VALLEY RANCH GOLF CLUB

THE GOLF The plains prairies east of Denver near the airport don't generally stimulate exciting visions of outstanding golf. However, Green Valley Ranch is a huge, pleasing surprise—just like its DIA neighbor Murphy Creek.

Perry Dye's gem, 12 years in the making, is big, bold prairie golf at 7,241 yards, and unique because it's an oasis. The drive to the course is all prairie, then suddenly there's a wall of old cottonwoods and wetlands. Six holes are sculpted around the protected native areas and offer strategic shots. No. 10, a 417-yard par 4, is encircled by dense growth. Then other holes present open prairie tests running along a ridge.

Green Valley is a true test of your approach shot—the fairways are wide and inviting, but trouble lurks if the approach isn't on target. End your day with a monolithic big-boy hole of 643 yards—if you par it, then celebrate.

Green Valley Ranch hosted the Denver Open in 2003, won by Boyd Summerhays, nephew of Senior Tour player Bruce Summerhays. It was the first time the tournament had been held since 1963. Green Valley is also scheduled to host the 2004 Colorado Open.

This great course is affordable and should not be overlooked.

THE DETAILS 303-371-3131. 4900 Himalaya Rd., Denver, CO 80249.
- www.gvrgolf.com
- Perry Dye, 2001. 18 holes. Par 72. Black - 7,241 (72.7/131). Blue - 6,682 (71.2/123). Gold - 6,208 (68.8/116). Green - 5,670 (66.4/107). Gold - 6,208 (74.4/144). Women's Green - 5,670 (71.7/134). Women's White - 4,992 (68.2/119). Price - $$.

Les Fowler, Colorado Golf Hall of Famer, was the 1954 Colorado Match Play Champion and runner-up three other times. He was a volunteer University of Colorado golf coach from 1948-1977. His top pupils were Hale Irwin and Dale Douglass.

GETTING THERE Take I-70 east to Pena Blvd. north then exit at 48th Ave. and drive east about a mile past Tower Rd. Turn left at the fire station (Himalaya Rd.) and look for the golf course.

HARVARD GULCH GOLF COURSE

THE GOLF Sporty Harvard Gulch offers a fun, 9-hole par-3 course in South Denver. You can breeze around it in an hour, sharpening short-game skills when on a tight business schedule. Novices gain experience here striking shots to small, bunkered greens over scenic, watered hazards, and hopefully miss the stately trees that make Harvard Gulch a fun place to learn the game.

The land used for the course was once the Colorado State Children's Home, which was a hot political issue for sure. The city assumed the 63 acres where 17,000 orphans passed through its doors from 1902 to 1982, while the Colorado State Children's Home moved to a 156-acre spot near the old Stapleton International Airport.

THE DETAILS 303-698-4078. 660 Iliff, Denver, CO 80212.
- www.cityofdenvergolf.com
- Charles "Babe" Lind, 1982. 9 holes. Par 27. Price - $.

GETTING THERE From I-25 south take the Broadway exit and head south. Find Iliff, and drive 6 blocks east to the course.

JOHN F. KENNEDY GOLF COURSE

THE GOLF Mounding, risk-reward options, strategic bunkers, lakes bumped up to greens—that sums up the 27 holes of Kennedy, which also has a 9-hole par-3 course.

The West and East nines are open, but have mature trees to dodge. The Creek nine has more trees, Cherry Creek, and large greens with mild contours. The property covers 150 acres just below the Cherry Creek Dam in southeast Denver.

The panoramic mountain views encompass the front range, Mount Meeker, and Long's Peak. Practice facilities include a driving range with large tees and target greens, a chipping green with practice bunker, and a 5,000-square-foot undulating putting green. Kennedy offers the state-of-the-art Callaway club-fitting system and takes club trade-ins.

In April 1964, the Denver City Council voted to change the course's name

U.S. Open champ Steve Jones was all-state track, basketball, and golf at Yuma High School.

from Cherry Creek Golf Course to honor President John F. Kennedy. And in 2003 the East Nine's name was changed to the Charles "Babe" Lind Nine in honor of Lind, who served nearly 30 years as Denver's first Director of Golf. Lind was in the first group named to the Colorado Golf Hall of Fame in 1973.

THE DETAILS 303-755-0105. 10500 E. Hampden Ave., Aurora, CO 80014.
- www.cityofdenvergolf.com.
- Henry Hughes, Dick Phelps 1963. 18 holes, Par 71.
- West/East: Blue - 7,009 (71.9/116). White 6,777 (70.7/114). Women?s White - 6,777 (76.6/135). Women?s Red - 6,405 (74.6/126).
- West/Creek: Men - Blue - 6,753 (71/122). White - 6,376 (69.2/114). Women?s White - 6,376 (75.2/140). Women?s Red - 5,721 (72/125).
- East/Creek: Blue - 6,868 (71.7/126). White - 6,499 (69.9/119). Women?s White - 6,499 (76/142). Women?s Red - 5,726 (72.2/124).
- 9 Hole Course: West - 3,455, Par 36. East - 3,580, Par 36. Creek - 3,304, Par 35.
- Par 3 Course: 1,219 yards, Par 27.

GETTING THERE From I-225 take the Yosemite exit north to Hampden and go east approximately 1 mile. The golf course is on the right. From 1-25 take the Hampden exit and go east approximately 4 miles.

MOUNTAIN VIEW GOLF CLUB

THE GOLF Water defines three holes on this 9-hole course, which features a moderate amount of trees along with flat terrain and greens. Placement is key on the first hole, a 358-yard par-4 dogleg right with water lining the right side. No. 8 is also a solid hole, with out-of-bounds left and water right making the 536-yard par 5 difficult to reach in two. The green is small and flat, creating good opportunities for a one-putt once you get it on.

THE DETAILS 303-694-3012. 5091 South Quebec St., Denver, CO 80237.
- Architect unknown, 1983. 9 holes. Par 33. Blue - 4,697 (61.9/101). Red - 4,034 (63/100). Price - $.

GETTING THERE The course is just off I-25 and Bellview. Exit west on Bellview and travel to Quebec St.

In 2003, Omni Interlocken's Steve Irwin, son of Hale, won the Colorado Golf Association Mid-Amateur at the Roaring Fork Club.

OVERLAND GOLF COURSE

THE GOLF The first golf course built in Colorado was called Overland Country Club. Contrived in the middle of a horse track around 1893 to 1895, that course was later moved, making Colorado Spring's Patty Jewett Golf Course (1898) the oldest course in Colorado operating continuously from the same location.

The city purchased Overland Park in 1919 and in 1930 the race track and the original golf course were demolished and a new nine holes constructed. Overland was expanded to 18 holes in 1957. The property bordered the South Platte River and on June 16, 1965, the course was flooded and 16 holes were completely rebuilt.

Today's Overland Golf Course is traditional golf set along the Platte River Valley. It features small, flat greens and its rolling fairways are lined with tall old oak trees, cottonwoods, and Colorado evergreens. Purists love the old-school feel of this experience and must deal with risk/reward opportunities, mounding, bunkers, green-side lakes, and streams.

Jackie Hartman tees off in the Park Hill Invitational in 1942 against Charles "Babe" Lind, who won the event.

Four Denver investors, Tim Kratz, Bill Martin, Timber Notestine and Tony Pasquini, have purchased 3,000 acres next door to the world-famous Sand Hills in Nebraska and have plans for a new world-class golf course.

DENVER

THE DETAILS 303-777-7331. 1801 South Huron, Denver, CO 80223.
- www.cityofdenvergolf.com
- 1895, W.H. Tucker Sr. & W.F. Bell. 18 holes. Par 72. Blue - 6,676 (69.6/118). White - 6,496 (68.5/113). Red - 6,097 (73.2/129). Price - $.

GETTING THERE At Evans and Santa Fe drive half mile west, then turn north on Huron and follow the bend left on Jewel. The clubhouse is on the left side.

PARK HILL GOLF CLUB

THE GOLF Just 10 miles from downtown, this well-conditioned course is a scenic ego-booster with its abundance of wildlife, mature trees, and a lake that comes into play on two holes. The Denver skyline and mountains are in view from the tee box of No. 12, a 331-yard par 4 that bends right and is guarded by bunkers.

Noble Chalfant, a member of the Colorado Golf Hall of Fame, helped build Park Hill Golf Club in 1930 and became assistant pro in 1938. It was here he was instrumental in the Park Hill Invitational and was a frequent playing partner of Babe Didrickson Zaharias and her husband George.

Chalfant had a storied career outside of Park Hill, too, starting as a caddy at City Park in 1924. He later worked at the University of Iowa after getting Park Hill growing, worked for the Denver Post, gave that up to replace Ky Lafoon as pro at Grand Junction in 1939, came back to Park Hill as head pro in 1950-1954, then to Denver Country Club 1955-1966.

THE DETAILS 303-333-5411. 4141 East 35th Ave., Denver, CO 80207.
- Clark Hamilton, 1930. 18 holes. Par 71. Blue - 6,675 (70/123). White 6,385 (68.6/118). Red - 5,811 (70.1/116). Price - $.

GETTING THERE Take I-70 to Colorado Blvd., exit south and go 1 mile to 35th Ave. Turn left and proceed to Park Hill.

PINEHURST COUNTRY CLUB

THE GOLF A Press Maxwell course is a treasure in today's golf architecture world, and this one is golden. Pinehurst's 18-hole track is called the Maxwell Course—a 6,802-yard par 70 that's offered in conjunction with a 9-hole, par-3 layout known as the Pflueger Course.

Both courses were routed through rolling terrain with subtle, undulating greens that are difficult to read. Mature trees are plentiful and can alter shots.

Overland Park's first site was also where Rufus Clark grew the state's first potatoes in 1862.

Wellshire's classic Tudor-styled clubhouse opened in 1927. Two greats of the game put their mark on this historic golf course – Donald Ross designed it and Ben Hogan won the 1948 Denver Open here.

The Maxwell Course has three lakes that come into view on five holes. Pflueger's strength is that it's a great place to polish the short game.

THE DETAILS 303-985-1559. 6255 West Quincy, Denver, CO 80235.
- Press Maxwell, 1960. 18-hole Maxwell Course. Par 70. Blue - 6,802 (71.5/129). White - 6,244 (68.8/126). White - 6,325 (75.5/136). Red - 5,714 (72.2/124). Price - $$$.
- Pflueger Course: 9 holes. Par 36 Blue - 5,812 (66.6/113). White - 5,495 (70.122). Red - 5,393 (64.6/109). Price - $$$.

GETTING THERE From the West Hampden Ave. exit, go south on Sheridan Blvd., then west on Quincy. The course entrance is on the north side.

WELLSHIRE GOLF COURSE

THE GOLF Two greats in golf history put their mark on Wellshire Golf Course. Donald Ross designed it in 1926 and Ben Hogan won the Denver Open here in 1948. Amazingly, Ross charged $1.50 per hole to design this classic, just one of the historical tidbits that makes a visit to Wellshire worthwhile.

Ross' construction boss on the project, Henry Hughes, went on to become famous in Colorado golf course architecture. Hughes was retained as Wellshire's "first greenskeeper," as they called them in those days.

Golf course architecture aficionados claim that Wellshire would still be nationally ranked if its course length wasn't so short at 6,541 yards. Clearly, this

Park Hill's Noble Chalfant co-founded in 1957 the 31st Section of the PGA of America with Gene Root. He was also a president of the Colorado Chapter of the PGA Rocky Mountain Section at one time.

classic course was built to stand the test of time. Arnold Palmer once said that Wellshire's No. 7 was Colorado's toughest hole.

Wellshire winds through mature trees just minutes from downtown, and locals have tabbed holes 12 through 14 as their own version of Amen Corner. Certainly the Ross signature is a draw—65,000 rounds a year are played here and it's difficult to get on during weekends.

Typical of Ross designs, Wellshire has risk/reward opportunities, beefy mounding, difficult bunkers, green-side lakes, and streams. And there are doglegs that force shaped shots. But the greens are much more fair than Ross' famous crowned ones found at Pinehurst No. 2.

One of Wellshire's earliest brochures touted the 417-yard par 4 as "a good place to wreck a score." The hole plays from an elevated tee over a gully and up a rise. Weak drives leave poor views of the approach shot to the green (directional flag will help you arrive at the green), which is over a second gully to a bunker-guarded green that has a bench running through its middle, creating deceptive slopes.

Water wreaks havoc as well, with Denver's Highline Canal cutting through the property. The unusual driving range points golfers into Wellshire's irrigation lake, which was built by the Skeel family when the land was a working farm. The Skeel family farmhouse first served as the clubhouse; a magnificent Tudor-style clubhouse opened in 1927, making Wellshire Country Club one of the fanciest in the country. The total cost for golf course and clubhouse was $300,000, but after a bankruptcy brought on by the Great Depression, the City of Denver purchased Wellshire for $60,000 in 1936. The course's name was changed to Wellshire Golf Club; today it's known as Wellshire Golf Course.

In 1948 the three-day Denver Open had a first prize of $2,150 and Gen. Dwight D. Eisenhower was in the gallery. But Ben Hogan didn't even collect the check. He finished his round in early afternoon and headed for the train station, assuming he hadn't won. While waiting for his train to Salt Lake City, Hogan was told of his victory, but he didn't have time to return to Wellshire and pocket the money. It was his sixth straight win on tour. Local sportswriters were less than impressed with Hogan, who was reported as unfriendly and uncooperative when it came to talking about his round.

All this national publicity gave Wellshire a reputation to uphold. It hosted the 21st USGA Amateur Public Links Championship in July 1946 and another one 13 years later. On July 13, 2001, Wellshire celebrated its 75th anniversary with a tournament and festivities.

Wellshire has come a long way since golfers in the 1940s had to hitchhike to get here—the streetcars didn't come to the course back then, and many of the

---

Colorado Golf Hall of Famer Dale Douglass of Fort Morgan is one of only five players to have played in more than 500 Champions Tour events.

streets were still dirt roads. Today golfers and folks wanting to dine at the upscale Wellshire Inn still flock to this historic spot in Colorado golf lore.

THE DETAILS 303-757-1352. 3333 South Colorado Blvd., Denver, CO 80222.
- www.cityofdenvergolf.com
- Donald Ross, 1926. 18 holes. Par 71. Black - 6,541 (71.3/127) Blue - 6,498 (71.1/129). White - 6,232 (70/127). Red - 5,720 (71.2/129). Price - $.

GETTING THERE Take I-25 to Hampden and head west to Colorado Blvd. Turn right on Colorado, and the entrance for the clubhouse is on the left-hand side.

WILLIS CASE GOLF COURSE

THE GOLF Willis Case Golf Course sits on the hill across from Inspiration Point Park—a monument to the golden era of golf, and one of Denver's golf treasures. Just seven minutes northwest of downtown Denver, this 18-hole beauty displays a panorama of the Rocky Mountains from the first tee.

The design skirts through mature trees, with narrow, sloping fairways and small, subtle greens. Some holes are well-bunkered, requiring accurate approaches.

Golf has been played at this site for a while—the Interlochen Golf Club was organized here in 1902. In 1906 the city acquired the land for Berkeley Park—land that is now the southern half of Willis Case, occupied by I-70 and Berkeley Lake.

In 1924, the Shriners of the El Jebel Temple became involved. They used insurance money from their burned-down temple to buy the 9-hole golf course of the failing Interlochen Club. The other nine holes became known as Berkeley Park. Eventually a man named Willis Case helped the city acquire the land with a $113,000 donation. The course was renamed Willis Case in 1936.

Legend has it that the wealthy Mr. Case, a successful real estate man, was murdered on the grounds by a woman he had been courting. She was convinced he was not going to marry her and she gunned him down. In his pocket was a marriage license.

Willis Case has also just added a First Tee course for beginners.

Dow Finsterwald Jr., is the head professional at Colonial Country Club in Fort Worth. He graduated from Cheyenne Mountain High in Colorado Springs while his famous father was director of golf at The Broadmoor.

DENVER

THE DETAILS 303-455-9801. 4999 Vrain St., Denver, CO 80212.
- www.cityofdenvergolf.com
- El Jebel/City of Denver, 1928. 18 holes. Par 72. Blue - 6,364 (68.9/114). Red - 6,103 (73.2/126). Price - $.

GETTING THERE Take I-70 west to the Lowell-Tennyson exit. Go north on Lowell and turn left at the stop light on 50th Ave., then proceed to Vrain.

WINDSOR GARDENS GOLF COURSE

THE GOLF A good walking par-3 course with trees and slightly rolling terrain, Windsor Gardens offers the chance to sharpen up your short game and enjoy a casual, quick round of golf. The longest hole is No. 9, a 198-yarder, which requires a carry of water that fronts the slightly elevated green.

THE DETAILS 303-366-3133. 595 South Clinton, Denver, CO 80231.
- Henry Hughes, 1965. 9 holes. Par 27. 1,062 yards. Price - $.

GETTING THERE From the I-25 exit head west on 6th Ave. Follow 6th to Havana

Berkeley Park Municipal Golf Course with the Flatirons in the background. This is a June 1934 WPA photo. Berkeley later became Willis Case Golf Course.

Peter Coors, grandson of beer maker Adolph Coors, has golf memberships at Augusta National, Castle Pines Golf Club, Denver Country Club and Rolling Hills Country Club.

and turn left, then head south to Alameda. Turn right and proceed about a half-mile to Clinton on the left.

DENVER NOTES

Colorado's Capital city offers everything for the traveling golfer, and while it's wise to plan your trips around where you'll be playing, the downtown area is the recommended home base for golf visits. Lower downtown, known as **LoDo**, is a 20-block area where the city was born and has been reborn as the place for restaurants, clubs, shops, and galleries. What better way to spend a summer day than to work in 18 or 36 holes and mosey into LoDo and all it has to offer before and after a Rockies baseball game at Coors Field? And while there are numerous downtown drinking establishments worth mentioning, the liveliest area is around Coors Field, with countless sports bars and places to dine. The Breckenridge Brewery (303-297-3644) and the state's first brewpub, the Wynkoop Brewing Co. (303-297-2700) head the pack and serve excellent brewpub items. **Duffy's Shamrock** is another good watering hole with solid Southern-style fares. Teddy Roosevelt was the first President to overnight at the **Brown Palace** (800-321-2599, www.brownpalace.com), Denver's most famous hotel. He came to hunt bear in the Rockies and his Bull Moose Party fund-raiser cost a mere $10 to attend. Oxygen masks must have been needed—1,500 cigars were in the room that night. **The Palace Arms** is a classy restaurant in the hotel, and features outstanding game specialties like venison and buffalo and a legendary wine list that approaches 1,000. Also downtown find the **16th Street Mall**, which has many shopping areas and places to relax. Other lodging choices include the **Capitol Hill B&B** (303-839-5221), the historic **Queen Anne B&B** (303-296-6666), which faces a quiet park and the **Hotel Monaco** (303-296-1717) is another excellent choice. And don't forget the largest hotel in Colorado, the **Adam's Mark** (303-893-3333, www.adamsmark.com), or the Doubletree (303-321-3333, www.doubletree.com), **Embassy Suites Downtown** (303-297-8888 or www.esdendt.com), or **Hyatt Regency Denver Downtown** (303-295-1234, www.denverregency.hyatt.com). As for dining, Denver's reputation as a Western-themed steak and potatoes mecca has become more refined in recent years, with many south-western-styled options in addition to the upscale Rocky Mountain cuisines. Look for *Westword*, a free weekly that serves as a great starting point when looking for dining options in the Mile High City. For breakfast find **Racine's** (303-595-0418) south of downtown, and for lunch look to **Wolfe's Barbecue** (303-831-1500) or the **20th Street Café** (303-295-9041). The oldest restaurant in town is The **Buckhorn Exchange** (303-534-9505), a great place to get into the spirit of the city. The walls are coated with stuffed trophies, they serve tasty game dishes like rattlesnake and alligator tail, and the upstairs saloon plays live folk and cowboy music. Above the famous

---

Denver Country Club hosted the 1982 Curtis Cup.

Tattered Cover Bookstore (303-322-7727) you'll find the stylish **Fourth Story Restaurant & Bar** (303-322-1824), with an extensive wine list and eclectic atmosphere.

ENGLEWOOD

ELEV. 5,369 POP. 31,727

DENVER

Ute tribesmen once drank from the creek that runs through the now-historic fairways of Cherry Hills Country Club. A hundred yards away, buffalo and antelope roamed, and eventually William Green Russell, who found a gold nugget in Little Dry Creek, established a gold mining camp. Thus was the birth of Englewood.

In 1860, Thomas Skerritt, an Irish immigrant and the so-called Father of Englewood, filed a homestead of 640 acres and became the first white settler in the area. Englewood was first called Orchard Place, for its bountiful orchards, but in 1903, the town decided to change its name and incorporate as Englewood.

Cherry Hills way back in 1940.

The University of Colorado at Colorado Springs has a PGA Management program, one of only five such schools west of the Mississippi.

Englewood is located close to two major reservoirs offering sailing, boating, water skiing, and swimming. The Rocky Mountains loom west just an hour's drive away, and there's a helluva lot of golf—five total facilities highlighted by the Inverness resort course and the famous Cherry Hills CC.

CHERRY HILLS COUNTRY CLUB

THE GOLF The most storied tournament golf course in Colorado history, Cherry Hills Country Club has hosted the U.S. Open three times (1938, 1960, and 1978), and the Women's U.S. Open is scheduled for the historic site June 23 to 26, 2005. Cherry Hills is ranked No. 1 in Colorado and No. 21 in the U.S. by *Golf Digest.*

In 1960 Arnold Palmer drove the first hole, kick-starting him to six birdies in the first seven holes. He was seven strokes behind the leader before that magical string, and recorded 30 on the front nine and 65 for the round to capture his only U.S. Open Championship. He had to fight off Ben Hogan and a college kid named Jack Nicklaus that day, and Hogan was nipping at his heels until his approach on No. 17 spun back into the lake. A commemorative plaque reminds players today about Palmer driving the par-4 first hole.

Ralph Guldahl won that first U.S. Open at Cherry Hills in 1938 on a layout that also offers a 9-hole, par-3 course. The pros today face small, fast greens and mature trees lining its storied fairways. The par-5 No. 18 is the signature hole, and members also consider it the toughest at 491 yards.

The par-3 layout is known as the Rip Arnold Course, and it features sand bunkers surrounding every one of its undulating greens.

THE DETAILS 303-761-9900. 4125 South University, Englewood, CO 80110.
- www.chcc.com
- William Flynn, 1922. 18 holes. Par 72. Gold - 7,160 (74.3/140). Blue - 6,872 (73.1/136). White - 6,481 (71.2/134). Red - 5,851 (74.2/142). Private club, no reciprocal play. Members and guests only. Price - $$$$.

GETTING THERE Drive I-25 to Hampden Ave. exit and go west for 2 miles to University. Go south 1 mile to the clubhouse entrance.

ENGLEWOOD GOLF COURSE

THE GOLF The South Platte River serves as a buffer between the two nines of this manageable track, where golfers should take advantage of the par-5 No. 15, a

---

Colorado Golf Hall of Famer Dale Douglass of Fort Morgan is 18th on the all-time Champions Tour money list, winning 11 events.

500-yarder that's reachable in two.

Englewood is also a major practice venue. The complex includes an indoor learning center, lighted grass driving range, over 50 grass hitting stations, two putting greens, and two chipping greens with practice sand bunkers. Also check out the par-3 course designed by Perry Dye.

Be sure to call about specials, which sometimes include five holes for five bucks just before sunset.

THE DETAILS 303-762-2670. 2101 W. Oxford Ave., Englewood, CO 80110.
- Dick Phelps, 1983. 18 holes. Par 72. Blue - 6,836 (71.4/122). White - 6,484 (69.7/119). Red - 5,737 (66.2/105). Women's Gold - 5,961 (73.3/133). Women's Red - 5,737 (71.9/128). Price - $.
- Perry Dye-designed par-3 course. Price - $.

GETTING THERE Take Sante Fe Blvd. to Oxford Ave. and turn west. Proceed to the golf course on the right.

GLENMOOR COUNTRY CLUB

THE GOLF Pete Dye's 1985 Glenmoor CC is typical of his style—target holes, links style, minimal trees, and well-guarded greens. At only 6,621 yards, accuracy is more critical than distance.

The par-4 No. 7 is 416 yards and bends left into rolling land with water on the left and marshy cattails on the right. Either of these hazards could mean double digits. The most entertaining hole is the driveable par 4 No. 10 (297 yards). Bunkers guard it, but you can still hit the shot of your life and have a short eagle putt.

THE DETAILS 303-781-0400. 110 Glenmoor Drive, Englewood, CO 80110.
- www.glenmoorcountryclub.org
- Pete Dye, 1985. 18 holes. Par 71. Gold - 6,621 (71.3/134). Blue - 6,284 (69.7/131). White - 5,907 (68/126). Women's White - 5,730 (73/138). Red - 5,377 (71.3/31). Women's Green - 4,887 (68/119). Members and guests only. Price - $$$.

GETTING THERE Go west on Bellview off of I-25 for 2 miles to Glenmoor Dr. and turn right.

Colorado Buffs basketball coach Ricardo Patton is a single-digit handicapper with memberships at Bear Creek Golf Club, Boulder Country Club, and Fox Hill Country Club.

INVERNESS HOTEL & CONFERENCE CENTER

THE GOLF Inverness is too young to have hosted Teddy Roosevelt or Dwight D. Eisenhower, but Bill Clinton has played golf and stayed in this modern hotel and conference center. A traditional layout designed by Press Maxwell, who lived in Colorado until his death in 2002, Inverness hosted the Colorado Open from 1992-97, serving up a sneaky, tough route for the pros. The front views from the hotel are breath-taking mountain vistas, and the back opens onto the verdant carpet of this championship golf course.

Cottonwood Creek runs through the property, and the course was almost named for the creek. But Inverness was a more traditional moniker, taking the roots of golf into consideration.

It's also a place where former Head Pro Tom Babb greeted a rookie quarterback named John Elway who was looking for some golf instruction. Babb must be a decent teacher, because Elway is a near-scratch golfer in addition to being a NFL Hall of Famer.

Built in 1974, the Inverness layout features bentgrass greens, a plethora of bunkers, and water hazards that come into play on 12 holes. It is open 365 days a year and sometimes boasts play on 270-plus days of the year.

The par threes are most challenging, especially from the back tees. Three stretch out more than 200 yards and the 15th is 192 yards. No. 11 is a picturesque 211-yarder that has a lake in front. No. 3 is also guarded by water on the right and measures 211 yards. No. 8 doesn't have water, but it's 201 yards uphill and against the prevailing southerly breeze. No. 15 also has water carry.

Average hacks have to lay up on No. 2, a par-5 562-yarder. There's a creek short of the green. No. 13, a 418-yard par 4, has a water carry from the tee to a dogleg-left fairway, and then another carry over water just in front of the green, which is guarded on the left by a huge cottonwood tree.

Golf packages are available via the hotel, which has 302 deluxe guest rooms and 26 suites. Rooms overlook either the golf course or the mountains. Guests can choose from the ample dining opportunities at the upscale The Swan and The Garden Terrace or relax at The Fireside Lounge, The Pub, or The Golf Grille.

THE DETAILS 303-397-7878. 866-260-9475. 200 Inverness Drive West, Englewood, CO 80112.
- www.invernesshotel.com
- Press Maxwell, 1974. 18 holes. Par 70. Blue - 6,818 (71.3/131). White -

---

The bronze trophy given to the Colorado Open champion was modeled after Colorado Golf Hall of Famer Bill Loeffler's swing.

6,396 (69.5/128). Gold - 5,701 (66.3/117). Red - 4,924 (68.2/127). Members, hotel guests only. Price - $$$$.

GETTING THERE Exit I-25 at Dry Creek Rd. and go east to Inverness Drive West. Turn south on Inverness Dr. and follow the signs to the course.

MERIDIAN GOLF CLUB

THE GOLF Jack Nicklaus-designed Meridian is void of trees, but has some bite due to the tall native grasses lining each hole, along with water (eight holes). The signature hole is No. 7, a par-4 379-yarder that is beautiful. The course offers three regulation practice holes in addition to the 18 designed by Nicklaus.

One of the easier holes is No. 10, a short 359-yard par 4 with only a few greenside bunkers to get in the way. Nos. 12 and 15 stand out because of the double greens, where an approach into the wrong level could mean at least a three-putt.

THE DETAILS 303-799-4043. 9742 South Meridian Blvd., Englewood, CO 80112.
- www.meridiangolfclub.com
- Jack Nicklaus, 1986. 18 holes. Par 72. Gold - 7,243 (73.3/139). Black - 6,896 (71.7/136). Blue - 6,432 (69.6/132). White - 5,983 (67.5/126). Red - 5,362 (71.2/127). Private club, reciprocal play if pro makes reservation. Price - $$$.

GETTING THERE Take I-25 south to Lincoln and go left to the second light, Havana. Turn left and go about 150 yards, where the road forks. Turn right on Meridian, which runs into the course.

ENGLEWOOD NOTES

Base your golf time in Englewood from the **Inverness Hotel & Conference Center** (800-832-9053), where you can package lodging and golf in luxurious accommodations and take advantage of the five well-rounded dining options. The **Hilton Denver Tech South** (303-779-6161), which is also convenient to Fiddlers Green Amphitheater and **Park Meadows Mall**, is another solid option. Everything suburbia has to offer can be found in Englewood, where chain restaurants, outdoor shops (REI, Orvis, etc.), bookstores, upscale restaurants, and neighborhood pubs abound.

When Ben Hogan won the 1948 Denver Open at Wellshire it was his sixth consecutive victory.

EVERGREEN

ELEV. 7,500 POP. 40,602

French pioneer Jerome De Risse founded Evergreen in the 1860s, settling on a ranch that included forested land on the hillsides and meadows on either side of Bear Creek.

But things began to change in 1926 when the construction of the Troutdale Hotel transformed the town into a nationally renowned resort frequented by movie stars like Clark Gable and wealthy bluebloods from the eastern aristocracy. With such big names coming to visit, the Evergreen Golf Club soon became a haven for wealthy vacationers who danced to the music of the big bands at Troutdale.

In 1919 the city of Denver acquired the 420-acre Jerome De Risse Ranch by condemnation for $25,000. In 1926 Troutdale Hotel and Realty Company deeded the City and County of Denver 17.867 acres, stipulating that Denver always maintain a golf course on the tract. Today Evergreen offers residents the best of both worlds—country living that's close enough to the big city for cultural excursions.

EVERGREEN GOLF COURSE

THE GOLF In its early days Evergreen Golf Club was a symbol of the old world aristocracy. However, the course is now part of the city of Denver's golf portfolio and offers a much more toned-down experience.

Located on the shores of Evergreen Lake west of downtown at an elevation of 7,100 feet, the course has awe-inspiring views. Uneven lies confound flatland golfers, and there are plenty of wooded and out-of-bounds areas that suck in stray shots.

Evergreen's first nine was completed in 1925 and then in 1983-84, Denver golf legend Charles "Babe" Lind decided to retool the original sand-green course. Upwards of $1 million was appropriated for the upgrading of the golf course, and Kennedy Golf Course builder Jack Neavill was selected as construction superintendent for the Evergreen Project.

The route plays to a par 69 at only 4,877 yards, and Lind said the new course was "so easy it was tough." The historic course has character throughout with buildings like the 1926 log-cabin clubhouse, which doubles as an impromptu lightning shelter during storms.

THE DETAILS 303-674-6351. 29614 Upper Bear Creek Rd., Evergreen, CO 80439.

Colorado Golf Hall of Famer Dale Douglass of Fort Morgan is the son of the late Hal Douglass, former Fort Morgan golf pro.

- www.evergreengc.com
- Unknown architect, 1927. Charles Lind, redesign 1984. 18 holes. Par 69. Blue - 4,877 (62.4/111). Red - 4,494 (64.4/118). Price - $.

GETTING THERE Take Interstate 70 to the Evergreen Pkwy. / El Rancho exit (Hwy. 74). Travel south on Hwy. 74 about 7 miles. Exit at the north shore of Evergreen Lake onto upper Bear Ceek Rd. The course is half a mile west from the exit.

HIWAN GOLF CLUB

THE GOLF This beautiful mountain course, only a short drive from Denver, hosted the Colorado Open for 28 years, a run that ended in 1992. Al Geiberger, Dave Hill, Willie Wood, Mark Wiebe, and Steve Jones were title holders, and low amateurs included Peter Jacobsen, Bob Tway, Corey Pavin, Steve Elkington, Mark Hayes, and Phil Mickelson.

The pros always respected the greens of Hiwan, some of which seem to defy gravity—appearing to be uphill when they actually slope downward. At 7,000 feet there is a generous 15 percent distance boost, but staying below the hole is imperative to negate three-putts.

Craig Hospital benefited from the first Colorado Open played in 1964 at Hiwan. Then the CU Cancer Center became the beneficiary. After 1992 the tournament moved to Saddle Rock, Inverness, and back to the mountains in Edwards at Sonnenalp before its cancellation in 2003 because of a lack of sponsorship.

Hiwan is private, but one of those must-plays if you have connections in the country club scene.

THE DETAILS 303-674-3369. 30671 Clubhouse Lane, Evergreen, CO 80439.

- www.hiwan.com
- Press Maxwell, 1962. 18 holes. Par 70. Blue - 6,961 (73.1/139). White - 6,479 (71.2/131). Gold - 6,015 (69.9/128). Women's White - 6,479 (76.6/151). Women's Gold - 6,015 (74.0/146). Women's Red - 5,507 (71.1/139). Private club. Price - $$$$.

GETTING THERE Take I-70 to the Evergreen exit (exit 252). Follow the road through Bergen Park, then take Hwy. 74 toward Evergreen. Turn left at the entrance to Hiwan and follow the road to the clubhouse.

The Colorado Women's Golf Association was formed on March 14, 1916, by a group of eight women.

EVERGREEN NOTES

Evergreen boasts some charm with an arts scene (Evergreen Artists Association), lively restaurants, and bustling shops like **Village Gourmet** (303-670-0717), a local fixture with gourmet foods and Colorado specialties. One place to hang out is **Little Bear** (303-674-9991), where burgers, beer, local music, and national acts sometimes appear. Another great spot is the historic **El Rancho Restaurant** (303-526-0661). Denver Mountain Parks were purchased in the early 1900s by the city and county of Denver, and several of them are located in the Evergreen area, perfect picnicking and enjoying summer evenings. **Bears Inn B&B** (303-670-1205) and **Highland Haven Creekside Inn** (303-674-3577) are worthy overnight options.

GOLDEN

ELEV. 5,674 POP. 17,159

The historic foothills community of Golden is the I-70 gateway into the mountains—home of the Colorado School of Mines, the Coors Brewery, and numerous museums.

The first inhabitants were the Arapahoe and Plains Indians. Kit Carson, Louis Vasquez, and Major Stephen Long were early explorers who helped put the area on the map. In 1843 a man by the name of Rufus Sage camped on the banks of Clear Creek and guzzled the icy water from the melting snowpack that rushed out of the mountains and onto the plains. He saw gold flakes in the stream, but he was a hunter and didn't want to waste his time bobbing for gold.

David Wall, however, settled here in 1858, obtained land, laid out a two-acre garden, and irrigated it with water from the creek. By the next year he was selling goods to folks like George Jackson, who discovered gold in the canyons of Chicago Creek early in 1859.

APPLEWOOD GOLF CLUB

THE GOLF Owned by the Coors Brewing Company, the former Rolling Hills Country Club was designed by Press Maxwell. The course has foothills scenery, bentgrass greens, lots of wildlife, and is convenient to the brewery—a unique 19th-hole option.

The signature hole is No. 9, a par 3 of 178 yards over water. The tee, which is perched high above the course, offers spectacular panoramic views of the course layout and the mountains.

Colorado Golf Hall of Famer Rip Arnold was a full-time assistant pro at Denver Country Club in 1932 and along with John Rogers played on the winter tour of the PGA Tour.

THE DETAILS 303-279-3003. 14001 W. 32nd Ave., Golden, CO 80401
- Press Maxwell, 1961. 18 holes. Par 71. Black - 6,145 (68/114). Silver - 5,992 (67.4/112). Front - 5,374 (69/118). Price - $$.

GETTING THERE Take I-70 to Exit 264 (Youngfield & 32nd Ave.). Turn west onto 32nd Ave., and the course is 1 mile down on the right.

FOSSIL TRACE GOLF CLUB

THE GOLF It took 13 years of government red tape, but when travel golfers see Fossil Trace Golf Club for the first time all will be forgotten. Golden's long-awaited municipal is a bonus for public golf in the Denver Metro area and another example of the first-rate municipal courses being built today.

Jim Engh routed this one in the shadows of Table Mountain, and it only takes one stroke to see the history of this land. The chimney of a brick kiln was left standing in the middle of the fairway on the par-5 No. 1, right in sightline of your second stroke.

The par-5 12th is highlighted by the 20-foot tall pillars of sandstone positioned in the fairway, a reminder of the property's quarry history—clay mining equipment remains on the site where 64 million years ago fossils of bird tracks, palm fronds, leaves, and triceratops footprints were cemented in time. A split-rail fence near the green leads you to the viewing area for the fossils.

The course is loaded with 10-foot-deep squiggly bunkers, circled by muscular mounds and thick rough. Avoid the pot bunkers and take advantage of the one punchbowl green. Throughout the round you'll also encounter a couple of low-lying collection areas behind putting surfaces and the ever-present Engh trademark—steep banks covered with rough should you over-club.

THE DETAILS 303-277-8750. 3050 Illinois St., Golden, CO 80401.
- www.fossiltrace.com
- 2003, Jim Engh, 2003. 18 holes. Par 72. Black - 6,831 (71.8/138). Blue - 6,241 (69/130) White - 5,559 (66.4/114). Price - $$.

GETTING THERE From I-70 take the 32nd Ave. exit. Follow 32nd Ave. west 1 mile to Kendrick. Turn south on Kendrick up the hill and right to the entrance of the club.

Colorado Golf Hall of Famer Rip Arnold was hired as head pro at Cherry Hills in 1939. He was a personal friend of President Eisenhower and most always joined "Ike" when he played at Cherry Hills.

ROLLING HILLS COUNTRY CLUB

THE GOLF Another gem created by Press Maxwell, this layout is famous for the mountain holes built into the side of South Table Mountain only 20 minutes from downtown Denver. After the course opened in 1961, Coors offered the membership a better piece of land, so a new course was built in 1967 and the old course became today's Applewood.

Rolling Hills has been updated through the years by the Phelps designers; recent upgrades involved the rework of four greens. "Every time we have remodeled here, we have tried to keep its original Maxwell flavor," said Rick Phelps. "So you can truly say this is still his design."

The four greens were toned down, giving them more pin locations. "This is just a good challenge every day, a shot-maker's course and you never get tired of playing it," said pro Jeff Seltz. "We call Maxwell's greens 'potato chips' because they roll and dip and can be level on the sides."

Go for birdie on the 520-yard par-5 No. 1. It is downhill, the wind is at your back, and approach shots can be bumped on. Water comes into play on 15 holes, the most prominent being the par-3, 214-yard No. 17, where a massive water carry is required.

Rolling Hills was credited with the No. 1 junior program in the state by the Colorado Section of the PGA. It has hosted an LPGA tourney, U.S. Open qualifiers, and Mid-Am qualifiers; the Women's Stroke Play Championship was held here in 2003.

THE DETAILS 303-279-7858. 15707 West 26th Ave., Golden, CO 80401.
- www.rhillscc.org
- Press Maxwell, 1967. Dick & Rick Phelps, several updates. 18 holes. Par 71. Blue - 6,972 (72.3/138). White - 6,452 (69.6/130). Red - 5,675 (72.5/128). Green - 5,255 (71.4/129). Private club, reciprocal play when pro makes reservation. Price - $$$.

GETTING THERE From I-70 take the 32nd Ave. exit. Follow 32nd Ave. west 1 mile to Kendrick. Turn south on Kendrick up the hill and right to the entrance of the club.

GOLDEN NOTES

In Golden be sure to explore the history of the Old West as well as the cultural arts of the New West. Visit **Buffalo Bill's Museum**, then take a tour of the **Coors Brewery**

Colorado Golf Hall of Famer Rip Arnold promoted war bonds during World War II and arranged an exhibition match with Bing Crosby playing against Bob Hope and John Rogers. Another exhibition included Babe Zaharias.

(303-277-2337) the largest single-site beer maker in the world. Tours run every day except Sunday and holidays. Just minutes from Golden, on I-70 heading uphill, are Lookout Mountain and Buffalo Bill Cody's grave. Buffalo Bill lived his final days in Denver after serving as a Pony Express rider, a buffalo hunter, and ultimately, the world's greatest showman. Lodging options here include the **Courtyard by Marriott** (303-271-0776) and the **Dove Inn B&B** (303-278-2209), however **The Golden Hotel** (303-279-0100) offers **Coburn's Restaurant** along with affordable accommodations. The same goes for the **Table Mountain Inn**, which offers the **Mesa Bar & Grill** (303-271-0110) for American specialties prepared southwestern style. In fact most of Golden's restaurants are filling and affordable. Kenrow's has a breakfast buffet for around $3 and is one of the town's most popular bars, with live music on the weekends.

HIGHLANDS RANCH ELEV. 5,389 POP. 70,931

Arapahoe Indians originally inhabited these parts, and the Spanish came through in the 1500s. In 1859, a potato farmer named Rufus H. Clark bought the 160-acre homestead that is the site of today's Highlands Ranch Golf Club. As his wealth grew he became a philanthropist and gave money to the victims of the great Chicago fire. He later donated 80 acres of land and $500 to a Methodist college, which eventually became the University of Denver at University Park. He also donated money and land that became Jewell Park and later Overland Park.

Lawrence Phipps, Jr. owned a 23,000-acre tract here from 1937 until 1976, when the Mission Viejo Company purchased the land and began to develop it. Residents moved into the Highlands Ranch development in 1981, and golf appeared soon thereafter.

HIGHLANDS RANCH GOLF CLUB

THE GOLF Marcy Gulch, rolling hills, and broad, smooth-rolling bentgrass greens define the Hale Irwin-designed Highlands Ranch Golf Club, which opened in 1998. The brawny expanse measures 7,080 yards at par 72. Some holes play open in a parkland style while other skirt the gulch with lots of trees.

Go for the green on the short, 292-yard, par-4 No. 6, but hit it accurately because it is uphill and a bunker lies right of the flat, narrow green. No. 17 is dif-

---

Aspen Glen used some historical materials in the building of its clubhouse. Some bricks came from the on-site 1885 Sievers Ranch, including antique corrugated metal roofing and aged cabin wood. The back nine uses land from the 1895 Diamond A Ranch.

ficult, a par 3 of 200 yards with trouble in the form of a lateral hazard and out-of-bounds.

After your round relax in The Grill at Highlands Ranch Golf Club, where you can enjoy a wide variety of selections and the views of the city, golf course, and mountains. The club is also home of the Dave Pelz and Nicklaus-Flick golf schools.

THE DETAILS 303-471-0000. 9000 Creekside Way, Highlands Ranch, CO.
- www.highlandsranchgolf.com
- Hale Irwin, 1998. 18 holes. Par 72. Black - 7,080 (72.9/126). Blue - 6,606 (70.5/124). White - 6,231 (68.9/119). Red - 5,288 (68.9/119). Price - $$$.

GETTING THERE Take Santa Fe Drive south to C-470. Go east to Lucent and turn right (south), then proceed to Town Center Dr. Turn right (west) and take Creekside north to the course.

THE LINKS AT HIGHLANDS RANCH

THE GOLF With great views of the mountains, The Links is a par 62, Dick Phelps-designed executive course that places a premium on accuracy with eight par 4s and ten par 3s.

Try to find birdie time on No. 8—it's 414 yards, but the green receives shots in a friendly way if you miss the bunkers. No. 17 is a 201-yard par 3 with no room for error. Water hugs the green on the left side and there's a bunker on the right wing.

THE DETAILS 303-470-9292. 5815 E. Gleneagles Village Pkwy., Highlands Ranch, CO 80126.
- Dick Phelps, 1985. 18 holes. Par 62. Blue - 4,576 (60.9/98). White - 3,992 (58.1/91). Red - 3,337 (57.6/94). Price - $$.

GETTING THERE Take C-470 to Quebec and drive south. Turn right on Gleneagles Village Pkwy., veer to the left, and proceed through the stop sign to the Links on the right.

"I never pick signature holes on my courses. Catamount is a prime example of why—there are a lot of holes I really like, so I prefer to let those who play it pick their own personal favorite."—Tom Weiskopf on Steamboat Springs' Catamount Ranch and Club

HIGHLANDS RANCH NOTES

Find a wee bit of Scotland in Highlands Ranch at the **Colorado Scottish Festival** (www.scottishgames.org) and **Rocky Mountain Highland Games** at the Highland Heritage Park each fall. Dine at **Bisetti's Italian Restaurant** (720-344-9530) or **Dewey's Food & Spirits** (720-348-0101). Lodging bets include **Comfort Suites** (303-770-5400) or the **Fairfield Inn Denver South** (303-290-6700). Nearby **Park Meadows Mall** has something for everyone.

LAKEWOOD

ELEV. 5,450 POP. 144,126

The Lakewood area was used by prospectors dating back to the gold rush days, but wasn't incorporated until June 24, 1969. A walking tour of the city, funded in part by a State Historical Fund grant award from the Colorado Historical Society, provides an easy, user-friendly way to learn more about local history and the Belmar Park area. Golf in Lakewood comes in the form of the venerable, Donald Ross-designed Lakewood Country Club and the immensely popular Fox Hollow golf complex.

FOX HOLLOW GOLF CLUB

THE GOLF Fox Hollow Golf Club is one of the most popular 27 holes of golf in the Denver Metro area, with three distinct nines to provide variety.

Denis Griffiths' 1993 layout is a nature hike—the course is located in the City of Lakewood's wild and wide-open Bear Creek Lake Park, a beautiful 2,600-acre setting right on the edge of town.

The Canyon Nine has dramatic elevation changes as it climbs from the clubhouse along Coyote Gulch to an isolated ridge then comes sweeping back down through the rugged canyon areas. No. 6 is a scenic, 200-yard par 3 with trees framing the green over a ravine. The 7th presents another ravine carry that forces you to dodge a creek on its 384-yard journey.

The Meadow Nine rambles along Bear Creek and past some of the oldest and most spectacular trees in the park. Huge cottonwoods come into play here.

The Links Nine travels along the face of Bear Creek Dam and presents a links style. With a layout set against a sweeping vista of the Rocky Mountain foothills rising in the west, this nine reminds the golfer of Scotland.

The Raven Golf Club at Three Peaks had formerly been Eagles Nest, a Dick Phelps design that struggled. They built nine holes in 1986, but when the original developer died in a plane crash construction stopped. Finally the back nine opened in 1989.

DENVER

Golf Digest picked the Canyon/Meadow combination as No. 2 among the Best New Courses in 1994. It was also rated No. 24 in *Golf Digest's* America's Top 75 affordable courses. Fox Hollow is also a national Environmental Steward Award winner. The course was one of the first golf courses in the country to be completely handicapped-accessible and has hosted two annual tournaments of the Association of Disabled American Golfers.

For a quick change of pace after a round of golf, Bear Creek Lake Park offers opportunities for hiking, fishing, camping, archery, boating, and much more. Horseback riding is also available.

THE DETAILS 303-986-7888. 13410 Morrison Road., Lakewood, CO 80228.
- www.golffoxhollow.com
- Denis Griffiths, 1993. 27 holes. Price - $$.
- Canyon-Meadow: Blue - 6,562 (70.9/131). White --5,982 (68.9/125). Red - 5,094 (64.6/115). Women's White - 5,982 (73.3/137). Women's White - 5,746 (72.2/133). Women's Red - 5,094 (67.9/122). Women's Gold - 4,450 (64.4/112). Par 71.
- Meadow-Links: Black - 6,888 (72/131). Blue - 6,639 (71/129). White - 6,181 (69.3/124). Men's Red - 5,356 (65.2/114). Women's White - 6,181 (74.7/136). Women's Red - 5,356 (69.7/123). Women's Gold - 4,812 (66.5/116). Par 71.
- Links-Canyon: Black - 7,030 (72.9/132). Blue - 6,745 (71.8/129). White - 6,347 (70.1/126). Men's Red - 5,392 (66/116). Women's White - 6,315 (75.6/135). Women's Red - 5,392 (69.8/123). Women's Gold - 4,802 (66.7/114). Par 72.

GETTING THERE From Interstate C-470, take the Morrison Rd. exit and go approximately 3 miles east. For golfers arriving on Kipling, find Fox Hollow a half-mile west of Kipling on Morrison Rd. The course is on the south side of the street.

THE HOMESTEAD AT FOX HOLLOW

THE GOLF What do you do when you have one of the most popular complexes in town and a little acreage, but not enough for a bruising 7,000-yard course? You build an executive course that would please the most discerning golfer.

The Homestead at Fox Hollow opened in 2002, designed by Denis Griffiths. His inspiration came from Scotland, where he had just collaborated on the incredibly popular new St. Andrews Bay; Sam Torrance and Bruce Devlin both

---

Former British Open champion Tom Lehman and designer Dana Fry competed in a nine-hole skins game at the grand opening of The Raven Golf Club at Three Peaks in Silverthorne in 2000. Guess who won? Fry defeated Lehman.

have their names there on two new 18s not far from The Old Course.

The Homestead has 200 feet of elevation changes, pot bunkers, rye grass, tall tan fescue, eyebrows with rough edges, and a Scottish feel. A new clubhouse also enhances the layout—it's done in ranch style with outlying buildings taking on a barn look, complete with rough-cut lumber.

Measuring at 5,100 yards, The Homestead is still a challenge, with hole names that include "Death Valley" and "Lookout Point." In the distance you can see Red Rocks Amphitheater and the Denver skyline, while homestead accents like old wagons, windmills, and sunken wooden yardage markers indicate this was once a working farm.

THE DETAILS 720-963-5181. 11500 West. Hampden Ave., Lakewood, CO 80227.
- Dennis Griffiths, 2002. 18 holes. Par 65. Black - 5,048 (62.6/110). Blue - 4,735 (65.8/114). Silver - 4,378 (63.6/109). Red - 3,845 (60.8/106). Price - $$.

GETTING THERE Take Hampden west to the Kipling exit. Turn north on Kipling and turn west immediately on the frontage road. Go west and the road ends at the clubhouse.

LAKEWOOD COUNTRY CLUB

THE GOLF One of three Donald Ross courses in Colorado (Tom Bendelow also gets some design credit), Lakewood is a traditional and difficult course—one that members seldom tire of even after hundreds or thousands of rounds. The course has always had a reputation for having some of the best golfers in Denver, making it friendly to golfers looking to wager on their golf game.

The signature hole is the 454-yard par-4 No. 4, which doglegs right; the green slopes right to left. Unless you really nail your drive, the approach could be somewhat blind to a green that sits below the fairway. The green is difficult to read and has a steep back-to-front tilt.

Gil Hanse, known as one of the country's up-and-coming traditional golf-course architects, redid the bunkers from 1994 to 1999. The course measures 6,699 yards from the championship tees at par 71.

Lakewood is rich in golf history and lore. The course hosted a match-play game back in 1913 that would have made even Tiger Woods turn his head and become spell-bound.

Just before the historic 1913 U.S. Open at Brookline, won by caddy Francis Ouimet, two superstars of the British Isles toured the U.S., challenging the best

---

Sterling Country Club's Labor Day Tournament is the longest consecutive running competition in Colorado at 75 years.

DENVER

players of the best golf courses in America. That duo was Harry Vardon and Ted Ray, and on that day at Lakewood Country Club, they played against one of the best match-play champions Colorado has ever had—M.A. McLaughlin, a member of the Colorado Golf Hall of Fame.

Babe Zaharais and Doug Sanders were once members. Charlie Coe, a famous amateur golfer, won the Trans-Mississippi here in 1952, and the 65th Women's Amateur Championships were held here in 1965

THE DETAILS 303-233-0503. 6800 West 10th Ave., Lakewood, CO 80215.
- www.lakewoodcountryclub.net
- Donald Ross, Tom Bendelow, 1908. Gil Hanse, restoration, 1994-1999. 18 holes. Par 71. Blue - 6,699 (71.9/136). White - 6,370 (70.8). Red - 5,755 (73.8/146). Price - $$.

GETTING THERE Take 5th Ave. west to Wadsworth. Go north to 10th Ave. and look for the course.

LAKEWOOD NOTES

Shop till you drop at **Colorado Mills** on West Colfax Ave., where the food court has just about everything you need. Cruise Colfax Avenue, America's longest continuous street—some 40 miles long with loads of territory for exploring during non-golf time. Places to stay include the **Courtyard by Marriott Denver Southwest** (303-985-9696) and **Sheraton Denver West-Lakewood** (888-625-5144), both very close to Golden's new **Fossil Trace Golf Club.**

LARKSPUR

ELEV. 6,200 POP. 234

Larkspur is nestled among a spectacular area that includes towering ponderosa pines, sandstone ridges, and red-rock formations. Its claim to fame is that it hosts the summer Colorado Renaissance Festival. In the summer of 2002 the whole area was threatened by the devastating Hayman Fire, but was mostly spared. Just outside Larkspur and against the foothills, Perry Park Country Club's fairways meander through the rock formations and Sentinel Rock, once the site of a stagecoach stop, juts nearly 300 feet above the fairways. One of Colorado's best new daily-fee courses, The Golf Club at Bear Dance, is also nearby.

Golfers from 12 different states, including as far away as California, Minnesota and Florida come to Trinidad Golf Course for its Labor Day Tournament, which is the second longest running tournament in the state at 62 years.

THE GOLF CLUB AT BEAR DANCE

THE GOLF Just south of Castle Rock in an area known as Douglas Park, a retired Frontier Airlines pilot named Gene Taylor bought some land and dreamed of building a golf course. Taylor first visited the acreage in 1982 and his vision for a golf course came true in 2002, when The Golf Club at Bear Dance opened. The course was designed by a trio of golf pros introduced to Taylor by architect Rick Phelps.

Bear Dance is one of the best new courses in Colorado. It's a big boys golf challenge—the pro tees measure 7,661 yards, and the next set of tees plays a healthy 7,213 yards. Phelps actually did the initial routing, and the trio of pros mapped out changes on holes 11, 12, 13, 17, and 18.

The name Bear Dance comes from a sacred Native American ritual, and the Colorado PGA Section liked the area so much they chose it as a permanent home. In the spring of 2003, the 15,000-square-foot clubhouse opened and the 750-member Colorado PGA Section moved into new offices, including a large area to showcase Colorado memorabilia. Visitors are welcome to come by and discover the history of Centennial State golf.

The golf course, which has the Parview GPS system on the carts, has elevation changes of 600 feet and a stern slope of 141. A gauntlet of flashed bunkers with white sand dot the layout, and prominent mounding, twisting fairways, and eight ponds cause problems.

No. 9, named Iron Byron, is a 502-yard par 4, playing uphill through a tree chute and over a huge ravine. Average golfers accept bogeys with a smile here, since it's difficult to avoid the huge ponderosa pine guarding the right fairway boundary.

Enjoy the views of Pikes Peak, Raspberry Butte, Devil's Head, Dawson Butte, Larkspur Butte, and the snow-capped Continental Divide, since the soothing serenity helps the three-putts go down easier.

The club has received awards from *Golf Digest*, *Golf Magazine*, and *Colorado AvidGolfer*.

THE DETAILS 303-681-4653. 6630 Bear Dance Rd., Larkspur, CO 80118.
- www.thegolfclubatbeardance.com
- Rick Phelps, Dennis Hogan, Stuart Bruening, Corey Aurand, 2002. 18 holes. Par 72. Green - 7,213 (74/141). Black - 6,799 (72/137). Blue - 6,315 (69.8/128). Gold - 4,987 (69/124). Price - $$$.

GETTING THERE From Denver take I-25 south to Castle Rock (exit 181). Turn

---

Gary Player claims to be the most traveled athlete in history with 12 million air miles. His signature design Sumo Golf Village in Florence opened in 2003.

right and proceed south on the frontage road for approximately 5 miles. Turn right at Tomah Rd., then left at Bear Dance Rd. and proceed 3 miles to the clubhouse.

PERRY PARK COUNTRY CLUB

THE GOLF The summer of 2002 brought the massive Hayman Fire so close to the Perry Park Country Club that residents were told to evacuate. Fortunately the awesome landscape, nestled among spectacular red-rock formations and surrounded by towering ponderosa pines, was saved from the fires.

Designed by Dick Phelps in 1969, this wild west beauty is just outside Larkspur. Fairways are set against the foothills and exalted ochre monoliths tower into blue skies, serving as geological lessons for city folks who rarely see such grandeur. Sentinel Rock, said to be the site of a stagecoach stop, climbs 300 feet above the fairways.

The course has hosted numerous Colorado Golf Association tournaments. The clubhouse, named Manor House, is a relic from the 1890s where members relax, have lunch, and enjoy the view of Lake Wauconda.

THE DETAILS 303-681-3305. 7047 Perry Park Blvd., Larkspur, CO 80118.
* www.perryparkcc.com
* Dick Phelps, 1969. 18 holes. Par 72. Blue - 6,938 (72.3/134). White - 6,580 (70.7/128). Red - 5,740 (72/129). Private club, reciprocal play accepted when made by club pro. Price - $$$$.

GETTING THERE Take I-25 south from Denver to exit 173. Drive south on Spruce Mountain Rd. for about 1.5 miles to Perry Park Ave. Turn right and head 8 miles to the entrance.

LARKSPUR NOTES

The **Best Western Inn & Suites** (303-814-8800) of Castle Rock has golf packages for Bear Dance, Red Hawk Ridge, and The Ridge at Castle Pines North. It is a short walk away from the **Prime Outlets** and numerous restaurants. Larkspur hosts the **Colorado Renaissance Festival,** an annual medieval theme park rich in music, entertainment, games, and food. It's held on the weekends from July to August, and is a great place to people-watch on a clear summer evening.

Members come from all over the country when invited to join Castle Pines Golf Club. Only about 33 percent are from Colorado.

LITTLETON

Elev. 5,390 Pop. 40,340

Like many of the cities that emerged near Denver, Littleton was born from the discovery of gold in 1859. Prospectors came, followed by merchants and farmers who provided the goods needed to live. As Denver began to grow, ditches were constructed to carry water to farms in this semi-arid land. One of the engineers hired to design this system was Richard Sullivan Little of New Hampshire. Thus Littleton was named.

The Little family also helped build the Rough and Ready Flour Mill in 1867, and a solid city base began to emerge. Agriculture remained the town's lifeblood and the city continued to evolve. Chatfield Reservoir, constructed in 1972, draws thousands each year for recreation.

ARROWHEAD GOLF CLUB

THE GOLF Golf on the Red Rocks is awesome—dedicated travel golfers could wander the planet for 100 years and never find a more incredible setting for a golf course. Geologists say it took 300 million years for the slanted, jagged cerise rocks here to form. It took Robert Trent Jones Jr. a fraction of that time to design this course. Located in Roxborough State Park just south of Denver, it's one of the most photographed golf courses in the world. The cathedral-like conglomerate rocks and the rolling terrain make it unbelievably unique—a must-play course if there ever was one.

Opened in 1974, the Arrowhead Golf Club features profound elevation changes, quick greens, abundant wildlife, and one of the most picturesque par-3 holes in the state. No. 13 is 174 yards downhill and the shot is framed by the red-rock protrusions and a lake behind the hole that is protected by two bunkers in the front.

The Denver skyline is visible from the par-3, 199-yard No. 3. Take note of the left side of the green, nestled among the rocks. The best birdie chance is the par-5 No. 18, playing 543 yards; it's reachable in two, with a somewhat flat green. Another par 5, the 454-yard 6th, is also reachable in two shots.

Arrowhead is booked heavily for corporate events, so call before making the drive. The clubhouse, which replaced one that burned down, is popular for events; the Roxborough Room, accommodating up to 150 people, has floor-to-ceiling windows on three sides that offer panoramic views of the course and the rocks. The On the Rocks Bar & Grill is a great post-golf spot and perfect for golf events.

Fort Collins' Collindale Golf Course opened a lodge-styled clubhouse in 2003. The 14,683-square foot building cost $2.65 million, replacing a 32-year-old structure.

The land's recent history is interesting—early settlers laboriously plowed the meadows between the rocks, built irrigation ditches, and planted crops. During Prohibition, the remoteness made for an ideal whiskey-running locale because of the hiding places among the rocks. Prostitution arrived as well, with a house of ill repute completing the scene for a time.

THE DETAILS 303-973-9614. 10850 W. Sundown Trail, Littleton, CO 80125.
- Robert Trent Jones, Jr. 1972. 18 holes, Par 70. Gold - 6,662 (71.5/134). Black - 6,229 (69.6/126). Forward - 5,437 (71.2/128). Price - $$$$.

GETTING THERE From Denver take I-25 south to C-470. Head west on C-470 to Santa Fe Drive, then south to Titan Rd. Turn right (west) on Titan Rd. and travel about 7 miles (look for signs). From Colorado Springs take Hwy. 85 at Castle Rock and go north until you see the sign for Roxborough State Park. Head west (the red rocks are visible from the highway).

CENTENNIAL GOLF & TENNIS CLUB

THE GOLF Located in the heart of Littleton, this executive course is owned by South Suburban Parks and Recreation and is known for having some of the best greens in Colorado. The course is flat, but out-of-bounds, bunkers, and trees create tight driving areas. The route challenges with two par 5s, five par 4s, and eleven par 3s.

After play try the Centennial Grill, a full-service restaurant and bar that makes a great place to review the round.

THE DETAILS 303-794-5838. 5800 South Federal Blvd., Littleton, CO 80123.
- Dick Phelps, 1987. 18 holes. Par 63. Blue - 4,708 (61.6/99). White - 4,270 (59.6/94). Red - 3,466 (58.9/95). Price - $$.

GETTING THERE Take Santa Fe Dr. to West Bowles Ave. Drive west on Bowles to Federal Blvd. and turn right to the course.

COLUMBINE COUNTRY CLUB

THE GOLF Lanky Texan Don January will always remember Columbine Country Club, site of the 1967 PGA Championship. He defeated fellow Texan Don Massengale here by two strokes for his biggest career victory.

Still holding the record as the longest course to host a PGA championship,

The Mike McGetrick Golf Academy at Green Valley Ranch spans 4,500-square feet, featuring private tee areas and three indoor-outdoor heated hitting bays. McGetrick, 1999 National PGA Teach of the Year, tutors Juli Inkster, Meg Mallon, and Laurie Meten.

Columbine was set up at 7,436 yards for that 1967 major. They finished the regulation 72 holes in 7-under-par 281, one stroke ahead of Jack Nicklaus and Dan Sikes.

Columbine, ranked No. 11 in Colorado by *Golf Digest*, is a traditional course that would fit in a midwestern city. However CCC offers Rocky Mountain views, the South Platte River, mature cottonwood trees, verdant fairways, and tough bluegrass rough. The greens are true bentgrass rollers and mostly flat, but the course presents golfers with some side-hill lies and it is sneaky tough.

No. 4 is the signature hole, a 426-yard (middle tees), par-4 challenge that requires shots over water on both the drive and the approach. The par 3s on the front side are 200 yards long. And when faced with the shorter par 4s like Nos. 5, 6, 11, and 18, it's not necessarily possible to overpower them. Play for placement and avoid the hazards.

THE DETAILS 303-794-6333. 17 Fairway Lane, Littleton, CO 80123
- Henry Hughes, 1956. 18 holes. Par 72. Black - 7,179 (73.8/134). Blue - 6,743 (72/130). White - 6,246 (69.8/122). Red - 5,777 (72.3/130). Gold - 5,286 (69.6/125). Members and guests, reciprocal play accepted when pro makes reservation. Price - $$$.

GETTING THERE Take South Sante Fe Drive to Bowles Ave. and head west. Turn south on Middlefield Rd. The entrance is on the east side of the road.

DEER CREEK GOLF CLUB AT MEADOW RANCH

THE GOLF Deer Creek Golf Club offers the chance to play a Colorado course designed by Scott Miller—an architect based in Arizona. Views include the rugged mountain terrain of the Dakota Hogback just off C-470. Once known as an American Golf-managed disaster, the course is finally out from under a much-maligned situation.

The course has a links look with natural grass, perilous water hazards, and environmental areas maintained in their natural state. Holes No. 6 through 13 run along the highway and turn west, then northwest along Kipling. Thankfully for the golfer, tall berms stop some of the traffic sights and sounds.

Staying in the fairway is especially important on this course, since it's often difficult to determine the proper line to the hole. No. 7 is a 199-yard par-3 tester that plays across wetlands to an island-like area.

THE DETAILS 303-978-1800. 8135 Shaffer Pkwy., Littleton, CO 80127.
- www.golfexperience.com/deercreek

Sanctuary's Dave and Gail Liniger are true ambassadors for Colorado. Charity events at the exclusive private club raised more than $5 million in 2003 and total $18 million since the course opened in 1997.

- Scott Miller, 2000. 18 holes. Par 72. Black - 6,989 (72.8/136). Gold - 6,432 (70.1/123). Silver - 5,734 (71.9/137). Green - 4,829 (67.4/126). Price - $$.

GETTING THERE From the Denver Tech Center take I-25 to the C470 exit, then west for about 10 miles to the Kipling exit. Drive north for about a half-mile to Chatfield, then head west for a half-mile and turn left on Schaffer Pkwy.

LONE TREE GOLF CLUB & HOTEL

THE GOLF Lone Tree is a different kind of resort, first built as a private country club in 1985 then purchased by the South Suburban Parks & Recreation in 1991 and opened to the public. Golfers here enjoy spectacular views and thought-provoking play on this Arnold Palmer-designed course.

The view from the No. 15 tee box—the highest point on the course—is notable. It's a 369-yard par 4 with a view of downtown and the Rocky Mountains to the west.

Located near the I-25 Denver Tech and Inverness Business Parks area, Lone Tree has a 45,000-square-foot clubhouse that includes 15 luxury guest suites, pool, tennis, cafe, pro shop, and a fitness area.

THE DETAILS 303-799-9940. 9808 Sunningdale Blvd., Littleton, CO 80124.
- Arnold Palmer, 1985. 18 holes. Par 72. Gold - 7,039 (72.6/133). Blue - 6,486 (70/125). White - 6,045 (67.8/117). Red - 5,340 (69.4/121). Price - $$.

GETTING THERE From I-25, exit Lincoln, and head west 2 miles to Lone Tree Pkwy. Turn right and find the first intersection (Sunningdale Blvd.). Turn right on Sunningdale and follow it into the hotel parking lot.

THE MEADOWS GOLF COURSE

THE GOLF Watch out for the deep ravine that cuts across the front nine on this target-styled layout—it's a natural ditch that makes beginners squirm. The course runs up against the foothills and there are numerous side-hill lies to conquer, along with bunkers and water hazards.

No. 7, a par 5 of 572 yards, involves a ravine left and out-of-bounds. The second shot has bunkers in the sightline and the ravine is just in front of the green protected by large bunkers.

We could make this into an 8,000-yard course in a matter of minutes. All we would need is a weed eater.— Jack Nicklaus at Cordillera's Summit Course.

THE DETAILS 303-972-8831. 6937 South Simms, Littleton, CO 80127.

- Dick Phelps, Brad Benz, 1984. 18 holes. Par 72. Gold - 7,011 (72.2/135). Blue - 6,558 (69.8/132). White - 6,112 (67.5/127). Women's White - 6,112 (73.8/131). Women's Special Red - 5,505 (70/126). Women's Red - 5,437 (69.6/125). Price - $.

GETTING THERE From C-470 take Ken Caryl east to Simms St. Turn north on Simms and drive approximately 1.5 miles to the entrance of the course.

RACCOON CREEK GOLF COURSE

THE GOLF Raccoon Creek has a grander history than just being named for the creek that rolls through this golf course. Known as the Grant Ranch, the land once belonged to former Colorado governor James Benton Grant, who grew up in the deep South and brought traditions of hunting and shooting with him in the late 1870s.

The Grant Ranch has been active as a working ranch and enjoyed by the family for riding and equestrian competitions. During World War II it was a breeding center for the U.S. Army Remount Service, providing stud services. Granville, one of the ranch stallions, ran in the 1936 Kentucky Derby. The sporting history of the Grant Ranch goes back over a century and continues with great golf today.

No. 11, a par 5 at 531 yards, is the signature hole. Drive it straight through a chute of trees into the doglegs right, then deal with the creek that crosses in front of the green and protects the right side. No. 10, a 375-yard par 4, is vulnerable to big hitters and has even been aced.

The Grove, located at Raccoon Creek, offers breakfast and lunch service with views of the historic grounds nestled in the Rocky Mountain foothills.

THE DETAILS 303-932-0199. 7301 West Bowles Ave., Littleton, CO 80123.

- www.raccooncreek.com
- Dick Phelps, 1983. 18 holes. Par 72. Blue - 7,045 (73.3/131). White - 6,517 (71.3/126). Gold - 5,830 (67.7/120). Red - 5,130 (68.2/125). Price - $$.

GETTING THERE Take I-25 south, exit at Bowles Ave., and go west to the course on the right.

A good putter can get the ball in the hole with an old shoe if he must. Any putter you pick up, unless it's been sloppily built or damaged, is going to be a much better instrument for rolling a ball than an old shoe.—Dr. Bob Rotella

LITTLETON NOTES

Littleton is home to the South Platte River and the Chatfield Reservoir, so consider excursions around these locales. South Platte Park is jammed between housing developments and a shopping center, but offers a bit of solitude, and the best place to load up on picnic goods is **Tony's Meats and Specialty Foods** (303-770-7024), which has several locations around town. Spend the night at the **Denver Marriott South** (303-925-0004), just five minutes from Park Meadows Mall. Meals can be found at **Baja Fresh** (303-730-1466), **Beau Jo's** (303-694-9898), and **Cafe Rio** (303-721-9433) among many others.

LOUISVILLE

Elev. 5,337 Pop. 18,937

Incorporated in 1882, Louisville lies in Boulder County about six miles east of Boulder and 25 miles northwest of Denver. Coal miners played a big part in the beginning of Louisville and a Miners Memorial statue stands in front of City Hall. In August 1877, the Welch Mine opened and Louis Nawatny began farming. The next year he registered the name Louisville after himself.

Unlike miners in many Colorado coal camps, the workers here lived in town and weren't beholden to a company. During the peak coal-producing years of 1907 to 1909, Boulder and Weld counties were rich with coal, with 12 mines in operation. Coal use slowed following World War II and the last mine closed in 1952.

Golfers who find themselves in Louisville will spend time at the appropriately named Coal Creek Golf Course.

COAL CREEK GOLF COURSE

THE GOLF With views of the Flatiron Mountains from the fairways, this Dick Phelps design features flat terrain and out-of-bounds on seven holes. The front nine has a links-style layout with an abundance of water. The back nine has sensational elevation changes and bunkers to avoid. Coal Creek and a number of lakes are in view from many areas.

Two holes stand out, both on the back side. No. 13 is a good birdie opportunity at 410 yards straightaway and a flat green. The par 4 No. 16 plays 388 yards straight downhill, a unique hole for this flat course.

When I'm on a golf course and it starts to rain and lightning, I hold up my one iron, 'cause I know even God can't hit a one iron.—Lee Trevino

DENVER

THE DETAILS 303-666-7888. 585 W. Dillon Rd., Louisville, CO 80027.

- www.coalcreekgolf.com
- Dick Phelps, 1989. 18 holes. Par 72. Gold - 6,921 (72.4/136). Blue - 6,593 (71.1/131). White - 6,009 (68.5/121). Red - 5,120 (67.3/118). Price - $$.

GETTING THERE. From Denver, take I-25 north to Hwy. 36. Take Hwy. 36 west to the Superior/Louisville exit. Go east on Dillon Rd. for 2 blocks to the course entrance.

LOUISVILLE NOTES

The **Louisville Historical Museum** (303-665-9048), which occupies two historic buildings constructed between 1904 and 1908, tells the story of early-day Louisville and its coal mining heritage. Take your pick of chain restaurants, or find The **Blue Parrot** (303-666-0677) on Main Street, famous for spaghetti and other Italian dishes. On 75th and Arapahoe, **KT's BBQ** (303-661-9429) is the best lunch option before heading out of town, but if you're intent on killing time in Louisville, wander towards **The Huckleberry** (303-666-8020), which is housed in two old buildings on the National Historic Register and might be one of the most popular breakfast spots in the Denver-Boulder area (steak and eggs). Weekenders should stay at the **Courtyard by Marriott** (303-604-0007).

MORRISON

Elev. 5,800 Pop. 427

Morrison may be tiny, but the drive into this scenic little hamlet is spectacular—an entrance that must be seen to be believed. It's as if the Dakota Hogback formation, which runs through this neck of the rocky western Denver suburbs, parted and invited folks in.

In the beginning this place was called Mt. Morrison. Then, in 1872 a group of Denver businessmen, headed by Colorado Governor John Evans, incorporated the Denver and South Park Railway. This narrow-gauge railroad came west from the Platte River to Morrison and the plan was to extend it into South Park and up into mining high country. The railroad ignited growth, carrying stone from Morrison's quarries into Denver.

In addition to the railroad, Bear Creek played an important role in the town's development—it provided water for Denver, Englewood, and Morrison.

Red Rocks Park is a major draw today, and golfers with access to the impres-

---

I like to play in the low 70's. If it gets any hotter than that I'll stay in the bar! —Bob Hope

sive Red Rocks Country Club enjoy partaking of its pleasures before roaming into charming Morrison for refreshments.

RED ROCKS COUNTRY CLUB

THE GOLF Red Rocks Country Club was blessed with the red-rock beauty that runs through this western part of the foothills. Geologists claim the formations were created by erosion of "steep monoclinal sedimentary sections that resulted in a series of three major hogbacks and strike valleys, exposing highly scenic dipping plates, spires, and monoliths." The formations are red because of iron minerals oxidation.

These exalted geological wonders run on a line from Red Rocks Park past Morrison to Arrowhead Golf Club near Littleton, then to the Larkspur area and Perry Park Country Club and all the way down to the Garden of the Gods in Colorado Springs. Routing golf courses through this sort of terrain creates an awesome links experience.

The Red Rocks course is hilly with uneven lies, water on half the holes, and fast greens. A whale-shaped red rock sprouts from the lake behind the green on the par-4 No. 16, a 354-yard dogleg right uphill. Don't let the scenery distract you, because this is the quickest green on the course.

And you can play here even though it's a private club. The club has a unique "Member For a Day" program that invites non-member golfers to come out and play. The offer includes use of all the other club facilities, such as the driving range, the private hiking trails, the pool, the catch-and-release trout pond, the private dining room, or the Lookout Grill where you can enjoy an al fresco meal. The Member for a Day fee is credited to your account should you become a member.

THE DETAILS 303-697-4438. 16235 West Belleview Ave., Morrison, CO 80465.
- www.redrockscountryclub.com
- Jefferson, 1968. 18 holes. Par 72. Blue - 6,609 (72/132). White - 6,198 (70.2/126). Gold - 5,524 (66.7/120). Red - 4,864 (67.3/119). Private club, guests welcome. Price - $$$.

GETTING THERE From C-470, exit at Quincy Rd. Turn and continue south until you reach a three-way stop sign at Belleview. Turn right (west) on Belleview Ave. and travel for 1.5 miles. Red Rocks Country Club is on the right side just over the hill.

I had enough controversy as a player, so I try to stay away from design controversy.—Tom Weiskopf

MORRISON NOTES

There's not all that much to Morrison, but check the schedule for the **Red Rocks Park Amphitheatre**, one of the most unique venues for live music in the world. The perfect golf weekend might involve a round at the RRCC, followed by a Gonzales Steak at **The Fort** (303-697-4771), and an evening listing to live music in the park. The Fort serves exotic game in a replica of Bent's Old Fort, which is actually located hundreds of miles away on the plains of eastern Colorado near La Junta on the Santa Fe Trail. The famous restaurant, home to real Colorado "food", has great character and once hosted world leaders in town for the Denver Summit in the 1980s. **The Morrison Inn** (303-697-6650) offers solid Mexican food and great margaritas.

PARKER

Elev. 5,870 Pop. 23,558

Parker began in 1860 as a stagecoach stop named Twenty-Mile House, located 20 miles from the origination point of the Butterfield stage line at the Denver intersection of Colorado Blvd. and Colfax Ave. While Parker still retains some small-town flavor, it is one of the country's fastest-growing cities. And where there's growth, there's golf, as evidenced by Parker's three quality golf facilities.

CANTERBERRY GOLF COURSE

THE GOLF Canterberry, one of the rare chances to play a Jeff Brauer-designed course in Colorado, has experienced a rebirth with an influx of money and attention. When the course opened in 1996 with 200 feet of elevation changes and its views of Pikes Peak and Long's Peak, it made *Golf Digest*'s list of "Best New Affordable Courses."

Routed through arroyos and ravines in rolling hills, the layout has accents of Scotland. Thick rough, long carries, and front-range views make this a must-play. No. 14, a par 3 at 165 yards, is a beauty over water and bunkers.

By 2004 Canterberry will have a brand-new 10,000-square-foot clubhouse that will serve as a gathering place for the community.

THE DETAILS 303-840-3100. 11400 Canterberry Pkwy., Parker, CO 80138.
- Jeff Brauer, 1996. 18 holes. Par 72. Black - 7,178 (73.4/142). Gold - 6,719 (71/132). Blue - 6,320 (69.1/124). White - 5,384 (69.8/126). Price - $$$.

Golf is a game where guts, stick-to-itiveness and blind devotion will always net you absolutely nothing but an ulcer. —Tommy Bolt

GETTING THERE From I-25 take Lincoln Ave. (exit 193) east to Parker Rd. (about 5 miles). At Parker Rd. turn right (south) to Main St. Next turn left (east) and follow Main St. about 2 miles to Canterberry Pkwy. Turn right and follow it to the course.

THE PINERY COUNTRY CLUB

THE GOLF The Pinery has three nines with rolling terrain, few trees, tough native-grass rough, and narrow fairways. The Lake-Valley combination is the best, mostly due to the Lake's No. 8, a 207-yarder to a volcano-like green set on top of a shaved-off hill.

THE DETAILS 303-841-2850. 6900 Pinery Pkwy., Parker, CO 80134.
- David Bingham, 1972. 27 holes. Par 72. Private club, reciprocal play accepted when reservation made by pro. Price - $$.
- Mountain-Lake 18: Black - 6,784 (71.9/135). Blue - 6,488 (70.4/128). White - 6,131 (68.5/122). Red - 5,449 (70.0/122).
- Lake-Valley 18: Black - 6,897 (72.3/135). Blue - 6,557 (70.6/128). White - 6,235 (69.6/121). Red - 5,503 (70.7/122).
- Valley-Mountain 18: Black - 6,957 (72.2/137). Blue - 6,677 (70.8/131). White - 6,266 (69/125). Red - 5,766 (71.9/128).

GETTING THERE Go south on Parker Rd. to Pinery Pkwy. (south of Parker).

THE CLUB AT PRADERA

THE GOLF Jim Engh loves Irish golf—he was thinking of Ballybunion when he designed this new private layout in rugged open prairie dotted with canyons and valleys. Engh loves modern golf, too, so The Club at Pradera will blend both styles when it opens in 2004, but beware of quirky blind shots and pot bunkers.

Situated on a 1,500-acre hillside in Douglas County, The Club at Pradera promises an upscale lifestyle complete with a 23,000-square-foot clubhouse, fitness center, tennis courts, lounge, and indoor and outdoor dining.

No. 15 should be a favorite hole because the golfer sees Pikes Peak on the tee looking down toward Colorado Springs. It's a 189-yard par-3 gem carved into a hillside—a great golf hole with distinctive proportions and a linear green matching the natural contours. A small pond in front of the green contains wetlands and cattails.

Golf and sex are the only two things you can enjoy without being good at either of 'em! —Jimmy Demaret

THE DETAILS 303-851-2425. 5350 Rhyolite Way, Parker, CO 80134.

- www.clubatpradera.com
- Jim Engh, 2004. 18 holes. Par 72. Championship - 7,306. Back - 6,547. Middle - 5,780. Front - 5,021. Private club set to open in 2004. Not yet rated.

GETTING THERE Take Founders Pkwy. from near the Castle Rock Outlet Stores; head east and connect to Crowfoot Valley Rd., then to Pradera Pkwy. From Parker come down Parker Rd. south, take a right on Stroh Rd., and connect on Crowfoot Valley Rd. to Pradera Pkwy.

PARKER NOTES

Stop by the **Mountain Man Fruit & Nut Co.** (303-841-4041) to pick up goodies for the road or gifts for those back home (beef jerky, trail mix, dried fruits, etc.). **Aurelio's** (303-805-4744) is a long, one-room joint with simple décor and fabulous meals served with jazz music in the background; pizza is their specialty. **Cherry Creek State Park**, next door to Parker, is a good place to swim, enjoy the beach, jet ski, cycle, camp, and ride horses. Lodging is best had at the **Hilton Garden Inn Denver South** (303-824-1550).

SEDALIA

Elev. 5,860 Pop. 211

Sedalia is located on a dusty stretch of Highway 85 between Littleton and Castle Rock. Fur trappers and Ute and Arapahoe Indians once roamed the Plum Creeks area here, but no permanent settlement occurred until D.C. Oakes started a lumber mill on West Plum Creek. Oakes started shipping the finished lumber to Denver by horse-drawn wagon, and Sedalia evolved into a cattle holding area after the Civil War.

By 1900, with old crank-box telephones in town, Sedalia became a stop for travelers going to and from Denver and Colorado Springs. Moonshiners were frequent during Prohibition, giving the town a pinch of lusty allure, but today it's still just a bump in the road that people pass through on their way to outstanding golf.

Today's Sedalia is surrounded by some of the more scenic golf courses in Colorado. The red rocks of Arrowhead Golf Club are minutes away, as are Sanctuary and Castle Pines—two of the elite golf clubs in the U.S.

The best golf courses built since the 1930s were built in the 1990s and are to come in 2000 and beyond.—Tom Weiskopf

SANCTUARY

THE GOLF This is the most coveted round of golf in Colorado. Don't bother calling for a tee time or asking for a membership package. This is an unusual, stunning masterpiece with two members—Dave and Gail Liniger, the RE/MAX co-founders.

You can play the course in one of the Linigers' charity events—but the price tag is $1,500 or more. The club hosted only 6,900 rounds in 2002, with $14.5 million raised for charities. But if you can't afford that, just drive to Leigh Daniels Park, bring a picnic basket and binoculars, and enjoy the awesome view of the golf course from the ridge picnic tables

Only four holes play uphill on this Jim Engh-designed course; overall, the day involves a downhill journey of more than 850 vertical feet. Three cascading waterfalls have been integrated into play, with the largest providing 6,600 gallons per minute recirculating at the par-3 14th hole. The five tee boxes are named Rattlesnake, Elk, Bear, Mountain Lion, and Fox. Rattlesnake plays 7,076, par 72, and Fox comes in at 4,676.

Each Rattlesnake tee box climbs to the top of a pedestal. These scenic platforms provide 360-degree panoramic views of ponderosa pines, yellowing scrub oak stands, sandstone formations, and trophy-trout ponds. If you're lucky enough to be around in early morning or late evening, you might hear the bugling of the rutting elk.

The first tee is the highest elevation on the layout, with an awesome view of the front range west and a 200-foot vertical drop. Just a smooth, easy swing of a 3-wood can result in a 280-yard drive because of the dramatic drop to the fairway. This 604-yard beauty is an award-winner—one of America's greatest golf holes and one of the best par 5s in Colorado.

The 27,000-square-foot clubhouse opened in June 2003 situated on the land's highest point, taking advantage of the beauty of the Colorado foothills.

In October 2003, the Cherokee Ranch wildfire almost crippled Sanctuary, burning right up to the edge of No. 2 and working its way inside the course boundary. The maintenance crew turned on the irrigation system and worked to fight the fire. Still, a couple of beautiful ponderosa pines and a stand of scrub oak were lost.

Golf Digest ranks Sanctuary No. 3 in Colorado and named it America's best new private golf course in 1997.

The harder you work, the luckier you get.—Gary Player

THE DETAILS 303-224-2860. 7549 Daniels Park Rd., Sedalia, CO 80135.

- Jim Engh, 1997. 18 holes. Par 72. Rattlesnake - 7,076 (73.1/147). Elk - 6,380 (70.8/131). Bear - 6,001 (69.3/124). Mountain Lion - 5,445 (66.8/117). Fox - 4,676 (67/119). Play by invitation only, except charity events. Price - $$$$.

GETTING THERE From I-25 take Castle Pines Pkwy. west 2.5 miles to Daniels Park Rd. Turn right, and you'll see a huge gate on the left. The public can't enter "heaven's gates," but keep going straight to Daniels Park and you can see the course on the ridge line high above the course.

SEDALIA NOTES

The privileged with access to Sanctuary enjoy post-round festivities at the club and its new clubhouse. But in case a day at Sanctuary precedes weekend family time, the **Lost Valley Dude Ranch** (www.lostvalleyranch.com, 303-647-2311) might be the best way to see the Rocky Mountains on horseback, with more than 26,000 acres of the **Pike National Forest** available for exploration. Well-marked trails follow old logging roads, traverse wooded ridge tops, and wind through stands of shimmering aspens. South Denver metro area residents know about **Gabriel's** (303-688-2323), a highly rated Italian restaurant with an extensive wine list.

THORNTON

Elev. 5,342 Pop. 82,384

This northern suburb of Denver is hardly recognizable from the view atop speedy I-25, but golfers eventually find themselves here, enjoying time at the Thorncreek GC and looking for things to do after golf. Everything suburbia has to offer is in Thornton, and downtown Denver is just a short drive away, however one unique local summer tradition is to enjoy the free evening concerts sponsored by Thornton's Community Service Department. Scheduled in the town's various charming parks, R&B, bluegrass, and reggae fill the clear, cool, Colorado air—not a bad way to spend a summer night in Thornton.

THORNCREEK GOLF COURSE

THE GOLF Rolling hills, water hazards, diabolic bunkers, and moderately contoured greens defined this 7,124-yard, par-72 Baxter Spann design.

Host to Nike Tour and U.S. Open qualifying events, Thorncreek is a chal-

---

I'm in the woods so much I can tell you which plants are edible.—Lee Trevino

lenging layout that proudly displays all of the typical design characteristics of the award-winning Finger, Dye, and Spann firm.

Thorncreek's No. 4, a 228-yard par 3, is one of the meanest holes, with water and two bunkers on the left side and two more bunkers behind the green. A large grass bunker catches bail-out shots to the right.

THE DETAILS 303-450-7055. 13555 North Washington, Thornton, CO 80241.
- www.americangolf.com
- Baxter Spann, 1992. 18 holes. Par 72. Green - 7,124 (74/131). Gold - 6,698 (72.8/126). Black - 6,335 (70.8/125). Silver - 5,547 (72.2/130). Price - $$.

GETTING THERE Take I-25 to the 120th St. exit and go east to Washington. On Washington go north, 1.5 miles to the course entrance on the left.

THORNTON NOTES

Head for the **Extra Point Restaurant & Sports Bar** (303-452-9353) after a round of golf to watch the Broncos, Rockies, Nuggets, or Avalanche, or consider the Original **Chubby's Mexican Food** (303-287-4250) when yearning for south-of-the-border fare. For lodging look to the **Radisson North Denver Graystone Castle** (800-422-7699).

WESTMINSTER

Elev. 5,280 Pop. 100,940

The discovery of gold on Little Dry Creek in 1858 encouraged pioneers to settle in Colorado rather than continue on to California. Pleasant DeSpain was the first permanent settler to build in Westminster, and in 1870 he established 160 acres of farmland near what is now the intersection of 76th Avenue and Lowell Boulevard. Buffalo and antelope roamed the surrounding countryside back then, and gradually the area became known for its apple and cherry orchards and grain production. Those days are long gone—Denver's expansion has bulged Westminster into suburbia, bringing four golf courses along with the growth.

I know I'm getting better at golf because I'm hitting fewer spectators.—Gerald Ford, part-time Vail resident

THE COURSES AT HYLAND HILLS

THE GOLF A longtime favorite of Denver-area golfers, Hyland Hills has received *Golf Digest's* 4-star ranking and has long been considered in one of the top 20 courses in Colorado. When it opened in 1965—before the current golf-course building boom—Hyland Hills was definitely a new star on the golf scene in Denver. It may have slipped down from the top shelf, but it remains one of the state's hidden gems and a must-play course.

Hyland Hills' golf offerings include the 18-hole Gold Course, the 9-hole regulation Blue Course, two par-3 9-hole courses, a lighted practice facility with four target greens, and an 18,000-square-foot practice putting green. The Gold Course features three peninsula greens, hilly terrain, and seven ponds that come into play on 11 holes.

In June 1990 the U.S. Women's Public Links Championship was played here on the Gold Course. Cathy Mockett won the match play title entered by 920 golfers from all over America.

Another thing that makes Hyland Hills different is a golf cart designed for golfers with limited physical abilities. The new cart was donated by the U. S. Golf Association and is distributed by Golf for Fun in Englewood. The cart features hand controls and a swivel seat that enables golfers to make long shots and putts without ever leaving the cart.

THE DETAILS 303-428-6526. 9650 N. Sheridan Blvd., Westminster, CO 80030.
- www.hylandhills.org
- Frank Hummel, 1965. 18 holes. Par 72. Gold - 7,021 (72/138). Blue - 6,693 (70.2/125). White - 6,171 (67.8/116). Red - 5,654 (71.8/131). Price - $$.
- Hyland Hills also includes a 9-hole course, a 7-hole par-3 layout and a 9-hole par-3 course in addition to the 18-hole course.

GETTING THERE From Hwy. 36 west, take the Sheridan Blvd exit and turn right. When you come to 96th Ave. turn right and the road dead ends at the club.

LEGACY RIDGE GOLF COURSE

THE GOLF Rolling prairie, wetlands abundant with wildlife, cottonwoods, and panoramic views of the Rocky Mountains are on display at the Arthur Hills-designed Legacy Ridge Golf Course. The 7,251-yard route has been lauded for environmental sensitivity and *Golf Magazine* selected it as one of Colorado's Top

---

I don't fear death... but I sure do hate those three footers for par.—Chi Chi Rodriquez

10 public golf courses when it opened in 1994. It has also hosted the LPGA Futures Tour.

THE DETAILS 303-438-8997. 10801 Legacy Ridge Pkwy., Westminster, CO 80031.

- Arthur Hills, 1994. 18 holes. Par 72. Black - 7,251 (74/144). Blue - 6,765 (71.9/137). White - 6,073 (69.3/120). Red - 5,409 (70.6/122). Price - $$.

GETTING THERE From I-25, take Hwy. 36 west to the 104th Ave. exit and go east approximately 1 mile.

DENVER

THE HERITAGE GOLF COURSE AT WESTMOOR

THE GOLF Heritage, a younger sibling of Legacy Ridge, was designed to be less intimidating, but still retains the views, wetland bird sanctuaries, natural prairie grasses, and groups of cottonwoods like the other course. Audubon International was so impressed that it designated Heritage at Westmoor as the second Certified Audubon International Signature Sanctuary in Colorado, and the 40th in the world.

Designed by the award-winning firm of Michael Hurdzan and Dana Fry, Heritage has wide fairways, large greens, and multiple tees stretching out to a hefty 7,420 yards. The tricky pin placements and forced carries are challenging. One pleasing aesthetic is that the open spaces adjacent to the course are abundant with three-foot-high wheat.

A full-service restaurant and banquet room are available, complete with great views of the Flatirons and the 18th hole.

THE DETAILS 303-469-2974. 10555 Westmoor Drive, Westminster, CO 80021.

- Michael Hurdzan, Dana Fry, 1999. 18 holes. Par 72. Gold - 7,420 (74.3/132). Black - 6,798 (71.3/126). Blue - 6,319 (69.1/121). White - 5,801 (66.8/109). Women's Blue - 6,319 (75.4/141). Women's White - 5,801 (72.5/134). Women's Red - 5,200 (69.1/123). Price - $$.

GETTING THERE From I-25 take Hwy. 36 west to the Hwy. 121 (Wadsworth) exit. Drive south on Wadsworth to 108th and head west to Westmoor Dr. Drive north on Westmoor to the course.

The Lord answers my prayers everywhere except on the course. —Rev. Billy Graham

THE RANCH COUNTRY CLUB

THE GOLF Members say this Dick Phelps design, which features rolling terrain and scenic mountain vistas, has continued to mature and improve since it opened in 1974. Small greens that slope from back to front add to the difficulty, and there are plenty of trees, water, bunkers, and out-of-bounds to put a dent in a good score. A creek runs down the right side of No. 3—a par-5, 591-yarder—but it is reachable in two.

All told, the layout has the perfect combination: playable for the novice and challenging for the low-handicapper. Women and juniors benefit from their own programs here, along with a driving range, putting green, chipping green, and member tournaments.

THE DETAILS 303-466-2111. 11887 Tejon St., Westminster, CO 80234.
- www.theranchcc.com
- Dick Phelps, 1974. 18 holes. Par 71. Blue - 6,628 (70.2/129). White - 6,278 (68.7/123). Red - 5,478 (70.6/133). Private club, reciprocal play accepted. Price - $$$.

GETTING THERE From I-25 take 120th St. west to Tejon and turn left into the club. Look for the large white bubble that is the indoor tennis facility.

WESTMINSTER NOTES

The Westminster City Center area, located near U.S. 36 and Sheridan Blvd., has one of Colorado's largest concentration of retail stores. More than 300 stores, including a number of large department stores, are clustered in and around the **Westminster Mall.** Westminster is also home to the Westminster Promenade, an outdoor pedestrian village, as well as numerous hotel and convention facilities, a variety of restaurants and cafes, walking trails, and a zoo. Westminster's history is on display at the **Bowles House Museum** and buildings that are on the National Register of Historical Places. Stay at the **La Quinta Inn Denver North** (303-252-9800) or try the **La Quinta** (303-425-9099) at the Westminster Mall.

SOUTH CENTRAL

SOUTH CENTRAL

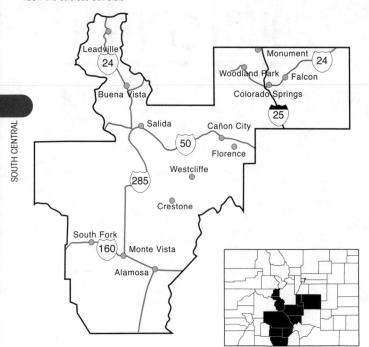

South Central Mileage

	Alamosa	Buena Vista	Cañon City	Colorado Springs	Crestone	Falcon	Florence	Leadville	Monte Vista	Monument	Salida	South Fork	Westcliffe	Woodland Park
Alamosa		99	160	164	39	184	154	137	17	184	82	45	133	192
Buena Vista			83	91	60	117	91	38	97	110	27	115	81	72
Cañon City				46	105	63	9	121	137	65	56	154	46	64
Colorado Springs					157	18	40	129	181	20	102	210	77	20
Crestone						177	114	150	56	176	49	40	94	176
Falcon							57	147	181	34	129	225	94	58
Florence								129	145	60	65	163	138	58
Leadville									135	147	65	153	119	110
Monte Vista										201	81	29	135	169
Monument											121	230	97	38
Salida												97	54	98
South Fork													152	186
Westcliffe														95
Woodland Park														

South Central Colorado is a cornucopia of some of the world's biggest, highest, tallest, oldest and most popular tourist attractions, in addition to being one of the state's most overlooked golf frontiers. Yet visitors to the region unfortunately focus only on Colorado Springs, often ignoring the opportunity to branch out and discover the myriad of other attractions. For those determined to really dig in and experience South Central Colorado, the region is a vagabond's reward—especially when it comes to golf.

Yet no trip to South Central Colorado would be complete without Colorado Springs, where golfers could spend weeks playing golf at different courses. The historic Patty Jewett Golf Course opened in 1898 and is Colorado's oldest golf course still in its original locale.

The classic, stately Broadmoor resort is home to the Donald Ross-designed East Course where Jack Nicklaus won his first major—the 1959 U.S. Amateur.

Head into the Rio Grande National Forest on State Road 149 toward Creede and visit Wheeler Geologic Natural Area. It's a hike or a long and bumpy four-wheel-drive journey here, but the remote site has volcanic tuff sculpted into a photographer's dream.

Continue to Creede and explore its mining history before traveling 30 more miles to Thirty-Mile Campground, a place where my Boy Scout troop from West Texas fell in love with Colorado and trekked off on 50-mile hikes through the Weminuche Wilderness. Fish in the Rio Grande Reservoir and just lay back, soaking up the back country.

Or you could follow Highway 24 through Salida and Buena Vista to Leadville, where Mount Massive Golf Course is the USA's second highest golf course at 9,680 feet. It combines sky-scraping heights and golf. On your left on most of the journey are the Collegiate Peaks, each with a name of a college. This Sawatch Range also parallels, for many miles, the whitewater rafters' paradise known as the Arkansas River.

Country and western songs have been written about a truck trying to negotiate Wolf Creek Pass, a harrowing, twisting ribbon of pavement on Highway 160 that leads you into hidden golf destinations at South Fork, Monte Vista, and Alamosa continuing to La Veta in Colorado's South East region. It's also minutes from Wolf Creek Ski Area, which annually gets more snow than any other Colorado ski resort.

One ideal road trip for golf, fishing, hiking, camping, and natural-wonder gazing would start in Alamosa at Cattails Golf Course and continue to the new Rio Grande Club, beside the trout-filled Rio Grande River.

Finally, the climate of the South Central region is ideal for golf, offering more than 300 days of sunshine per year. Blue skies, below-average humidity, reason-

Two things that ain't long for this world—dogs that chase cars and professional golfers who chip for pars.—Lee Trevino

able heat, and refreshingly cool summer evenings all make the golf experience worthwhile from April to October.

At The Broadmoor sometime around 1943, Fred Corcoran was collecting celebrity items for an auction to benefit American soldiers in Europe. Bing Crosby gave the shirt off his back.

Give me golf clubs, fresh air and a beautiful partner, and you can keep my golf clubs and the fresh air.—Jack Benny

ALAMOSA

ELEV. 7,544 POP. 7,960

Alamosa, whose name means "cottonwood grove" in Spanish, is the largest city in the world's largest high-mountain valley, the San Luis Valley. It can be bitterly cold here (30 below zero) in the winter as frigid air sits in the bottoms and doesn't move out until a quick-moving cold front pushes through. Strangely, if it starts snowing the temperature generally warms up.

But the summers in this old railroad town are perfect for golf—clear skies, bright sunshine, and 70-degree afternoons are plentiful. The Rio Grande River rolls through the town, which is surrounded by the Sangre de Cristo range on the east and the San Juan Mountains to the west.

Cattails' stacked sod bunkers.

The Great Sand Dunes National Park, 32 miles northeast of Alamosa and Colorado's largest sandbox, is constantly shifting and changing with dunes as tall as 700 feet. This geologic wonder, along with the charming Cattails Golf Club, make the Alamosa area a worthy golf road-trip destination.

CATTAILS GOLF CLUB

THE GOLF The serenity of the back nine of Cattails Golf Club is best experienced as the sun is setting, casting a reddish hue on 14,000-foot Mount Blanca. Deer wander through the fairways, a red fox trots along seeking his prey, and countless birds can be heard along the cottonwood-lined Rio Grande River nearby.

This truly hidden gem started out as an old-fashioned 9-holer famous for its volcano-like first green and a devilish seventh hole. No. 7 requires a strong drive into a dogleg-right fairway that is lined by tall cottonwoods, followed by an approach guarded by marshy cattails. If you don't bomb one out past the fairway bend, you aren't going to par this one.

In 1991 Dick Phelps came to town and created a beguiling back nine that includes river wetlands and lots of solitude. The driver isn't necessary on sever-

The only reason I played golf was so that I could afford to go hunting and fishing.—Sam Snead

al holes, and the recommended play is a 3-wood placed for position. No. 10 is a par 5 that requires a big fade off the tee. The final three holes all can be played safely with an iron from the tee, and the tricky No. 17 will surprise you when you come within sight of the green. Stacked-sod bunkers were added in 2003.

THE DETAILS 719-589-9515. 6615 North River Rd., Alamosa, CO 81101.
- www.AlamosaGolf.com
- Dick Phelps, back nine, 1992. 18 holes. Par 71. Black - 6,530 (71.9/130). Blue - 6,002 (69.8/121). Women's Blue - 6,002 (72.6/135). Women's Green - 5,542 (69.9/129). Red - 5,112 (67.6/121). Price - $$.

GETTING THERE From Hwy. 160 east of town, take the first right after crossing the Rio Grande River. Go to State Street, turn right (north), and find the course.

ALAMOSA NOTES

After seeing the **Great Sand Dunes** look for **Mosca Pass**, a historic route that was once a toll road. Stop and check out the deserted historic landmark of Sharp's Trading Post, a two-story adobe that once served as a hotel and trading post. The scenic **Los Caminos Antiguos Byway** passes Alamosa on its way to Antonito, where you can take the Cumbres and Toltec Scenic Railroad (www.cumbrestoltec.com) to Chama, New Mexico. Nearby Fort Garland is another quick post-golf adventure, now a simple farm community that was once commanded in the 1860s by Kit Carson. In Alamosa stay at the **Cottonwood Inn** (719-589-3882), a B & B that offers golf packages. Also consider the **Best Western** (800-459-5123) or the **Great Sand Dunes Lodge** (719-378-2900) at the entrance to the dunes. And for dining avoid the chains and find the **True Grits Steakhouse** (719-589-9954), the **Hideaway Steakhouse** (719-589-4444), or **Taqueria Cavillo** (719-587-5500), where you can dig into a chicken Santa Fe burrito and ponder the fact that Jack Dempsey, the son of a poor timber and mining family from Manassa (just south of Alamosa), was born here in 1895 and began boxing in area saloons under the name of "Kid Blackie."

BUENA VISTA
ELEV 7,599 POP. 2,195

The small town of Buena Vista, nestled at the base of the Collegiate and Sawatch Mountain Ranges, is named for its "good view." Spanish speakers shudder when they hear the locals pronounce it "Buna Vista." This Upper Arkansas River Valley was once home to the Ute Indians; when Lt. Zebulon Pike passed

Selecting a stroke is like selecting a wife. To each his own. —Ben Hogan through in 1806, he found a community of 3,000 Utes. Miners and ranchers soon arrived, and with 36 saloons the city became rowdy and unruly enough that the district government sent a hanging judge to town.

Today Buena Vista serves as a jumping-off point to some of the best river rafting in Colorado. Brown's Canyon, eight miles south, is known as a whitewater capital. The Collegiate Peaks Range to the west has the most concentrated number of peaks above 14,000 feet in Colorado. Here the outdoorsman can choose from a plethora of hiking and mountain-bike trails, while the history-minded tourist can explore countless ghost towns. Buena Vista is also home to many natural hot springs.

COLLEGIATE PEAKS GOLF CLUB

THE GOLF Cottonwood Creek snakes through this 9-holer, which also involves houses and out-of-bounds lining the fairways. Think your way around the water on the par-5 No. 5, an interesting hole because it's only 480 yards and you can get home in two for birdie. No. 4 is a good warm-up for the fifth with 392 yards of fairway lined by a creek on the left that eventually slides in front of the green.

THE DETAILS 719-395-8189. 28775 Fairway Drive, Buena Vista, CO 81211.
- Dick Phelps, Jeff Brauer, 1978. 9 holes. Par 36. Women's Red/Yellow - 5,547 (70.3/128). Women's White/Blue - 6,161 (73.9/135). Men's White/Blue - 6,165 (67.7/118). Price - $.

GETTING THERE Take Hwy. 285 to Buena Vista. Turn right at the stop light in town and then look for signs on the right side of the street.

BUENA VISTA NOTES

Buena Vista can be bustling on a Friday afternoon, with tourists passing through and the locals preparing for weekend fun. **Bongo Billy's** (719-395-2634) has outstanding High Country Coffees and serves sandwiches. Three solid options for a meal are the **Buffalo Bar & Grill** (719-395-6472), **Jan's Restaurant** (719-395-6140), or the eclectic **First Street Café** (719-539-4759), which is in nearby Salida's old red light district and serves great Mexican dishes and breakfast. Consider a stay at the nearby **Nordic Inn B&B** (719-486-1830, www.twinlakesnordicinn.com), an authentic National Historic Site that was formerly a stagecoach stop and brothel. It's located in the heart of the San Isabel National Forest country at the base of Mt. Elbert, Colorado's high-

---

This hole right here can have a par of anything you want it to be. Yesterday it was a par 47—and I birdied the sucker.—Willie Nelson

est peak, in historic Twin Lakes. In Buena Vista consider southwestern-styled **The Adobe Inn** (719-395-6340), which is also next to **Casa Del Sol** (719-395-8810), the perfect place for chips, homemade salsa, and extremely cold Mexican beers. Aside from golf, mountain bikers enjoy the **Midland Railroad Grade** and **Colorado Trails**, and scenic driving is available via a 19-mile stretch of US 24 from Trout Creek Pass southwest to Frenchman's Creek north of Buena Vista (The Highway of the Fourteeners). Fish trips are organized out of **ArkAnglers** (719-395-1796), a friendly little fly shop.

CAÑON CITY

ELEV 5,332 POP. 15,431

The mountains that surround Cañon City generally protect the area from harsh weather, which made it the ideal camping area for the Ute Indians and home of roaming dinosaurs. Hollywood movies have been filmed here but nature created the biggest tourist draw, the Royal Gorge, which lies eight miles west of town. The Arkansas River cut this huge chasm, which today is spanned by the world's highest suspension bridge (1,053 feet above the rambling river). In 1999, for the first time in 30 years, tourists were able to travel through the breath-taking Royal Gorge by rail aboard the Cañon City and Royal Gorge Railroad.

SHADOW HILLS GOLF CLUB

THE GOLF Located in the piñon and foothills south of town, Shadow Hills is an interesting semi-private club that features rolling terrain, tight fairways, small greens, plenty of bunkers, and lots of water.

The front nine was built by committee in 1959, and Keith Foster came along in 1998 to add another nine. Recently the members added a $1.2 million clubhouse and eight-foot-wide concrete cart paths. They also plan to lengthen the par-70, 6,172-yard layout, but it's still a tough course that includes an uphill, 600-yard, par-5 sixth hole.

Because of the moderate climate, golf is available year-round and the course hosts many tournaments. Duffer's Holiday partners people from all over the country in a member-guest format. In June there's a Couples Tournament known statewide. Then in October the Shadow Hills Pro-Am benefits muscular dystrophy and teams two pros with three members. The highest-scoring pro on one team switches teams each day. Club pros from as far away as Arizona join in on the fun for charity.

Putting affects the nerves more than anything. I would actually get nauseated over three-footers…—Byron Nelson

Anyone outside Freemont County can play the golf course if they call one day in advance, subject to tee time availability.

THE DETAILS 719-275-0603. 1232 County Rd. 143, Cañon City, CO 81212.
- www.golfshadowhills.com
- Members-designed front nine, 1959. Keith Foster, back nine, 1998. 18 holes. Par 70. Semi-private, non-member play allowed. Blue - 6,172 (69.3/121). White - 5,672 (67.8/111). Women's White - 5,618 (71.1/123). Women's Red - 4,849 (66.9/116). Price - $$.

GETTING THERE From Hwy. 50 find 9th St. Drive south on 9th to Elm and head west on Elm to Oak Creek Grade (Fremont County Rd. 143). Next drive south 2 miles to the course.

CAÑON CITY NOTES

The **Royal Gorge Park** (www.royalgorgebridge.com, 888-333-5597) was completed in 1929 after five months of construction without a single fatality. The 4,200 wires in the suspension cables were pulled across the gorge one at a time. All the steel was manufactured at Colorado Fuel & Iron in Pueblo. Combine golf time with tours of the Royal Gorge and time enjoying world-class rafting and fishing in the Arkansas River. **Royal Gorge Anglers** (719-269-3474) can help organize trips and provide gear. Stay at the cozy **Cañon Inn** (800-525-7727, www.canoninn.com), now a **Quality Inn & Suites**; John Wayne, Goldie Hawn, George Segal, and others have stayed here while making films in the area. The **St. Cloud Hotel** (719-276-2000) was built in the old mining town of Silver Cliff, and it is comfortable and affordable. The best Italian food in southern Colorado is served at **Merlino's Belvedere** (719-275-5558), and steaks and salmon are served at the **St. Cloud Bar and Grille** inside the St. Cloud hotel. The middle of town has a few inexpensive Mexican restaurants and neighborhood bars. The **Owl Cigar Store** is an institution, a local watering hole that serves burgers, with hunting trophies on the wall and a few pool tables.

COLORADO SPRINGS ELEV 6,008 POP. 360,890

Colorado Springs is a modern, growing city that offers anything and everything you might hope to find in a place to have fun. In fact, one might argue

---

Someone once said that No. 11, a 411-yard par-4 is a grown-up hole. This hole plays into the prevailing wind with both distance and accuracy demanded. Keep a close eye on the wind, because there is a wetlands crossing 190 yards from the green. The approach is lengthy with Gypsum Creek meandering along the right side.—Chris Woolery, Cotton Ranch Golf Club

that the city has expanded too much in recent years, losing some of its small-town charm. Originally developed as a weekend getaway destination in the 1870s, the spirit of the city became so high-toned that it earned the nickname of "Little London." Today the city sprawls for miles along I-25 with 14,000-foot-plus Pikes Peak's looming large and the incredible red sandstone rocks of the Garden of the Gods and historic Manitou Springs also nearby. Old Colorado City is loaded with 1800s-era architecture, so the city is not totally void of historic charm; especially when it comes to golf, with the world-famous Broadmoor resort heading a slew of impressive golf options.

APPLETREE GOLF COURSE

THE GOLF Appletree isn't a flashy course, but it's an affordable place to enjoy the typical mountain views of the region. The design is mostly flat with moderate-sized greens, sporadic bunkering, and water on seven holes.

The back side offers two of the best holes. No. 12 is a short par-5 birdie opportunity of 459 yards. It doglegs left, allowing aggressive tee shots over the trees to cut the corner. No. 18 is a par-5 498-yarder, with water on the second shot to an elevated green and a few bunkers.

THE DETAILS 719-382-3649. 10150 Rolling Ridge Rd., Colorado Springs, CO 80925.

- Lee Trevino, 1973. 18 holes. Par 72. Blue - 6,407 (69.9/120). White - 6,108 (68.9/116). Red - 4,920 (67.4/120). Price - $.

GETTING THERE Take I-25 to exit 135 or Academy Blvd. Go east to Hwy. 85-87 and turn right 3 miles to Fontaine. Turn left and drive 5 miles to Marksheffel. Turn right and go one mile to Peaceful Valley. Turn left and head to Rolling Ridge and the course.

THE BROADMOOR EAST COURSE

THE GOLF One of the world's premier golf resort destinations, the historic Broadmoor is a must-play for any serious travel golfer.

When Donald Ross finished work on Broadmoor East in 1918, he claimed it was his best work to date, topping a famous little course he had finished in North Carolina now named Pinehurst No. 2. Jack Nicklaus won his first major here—the 1959 U.S. Amateur—as a 19-year-old. Annika Sorenstam won her

I'm proud that we were able to provide fun, affordable golf for a lot of people,. That's what we really need today. There is a current downturn in golf, because we are pricing the average guy out of golf—we need to provide golf for everyone.—Dick Phelps

first major here—the 1995 U.S. Women's Open. And Babe Zaharias won three Broadmoor Women's Invitationals in 1945, 1946, and 1947. This is the same 3,000-acre resort where Dwight D. Eisenhower and Gerald Ford played golf often. Industry leader L.B. Maytag was once president of the golf club and J.C. Penney visited here.

Broadmoor East isn't the same as when Ross left it, but the charm is still present, especially in the amazing greens. Three-putts are common, and it's not surprising to witness a playing partner roll a putt completely off the green during the course of a round.

Unlike Pinehurst No. 2, where the greens are shaped like an upside-down saucer and can cause some good shots to roll off the green, these greens are more fair when it comes to receiving a shot. However, they are extremely fast, playing just under the 11 Stimp meter reading registered during the 1995 U.S. Women's Open.

Even if you know ahead of time that the greens break away from the Will Rogers Shrine on Cheyenne Mountain, you're still going to shake your head in confusion over how these putts roll. A putt may look straight but end up breaking a foot. First-timers tend to end the day frustrated and mumbling at how much trouble the slick surfaces cause.

Get your camera out for Nos. 9 and 18—both classic holes with water guarding the greens. No. 9 is a 540-yard, par 5 with The Broadmoor framed through a chute of trees. A draw produces the best result, since the fairway slants to the right. With a prevailing southerly breeze, hitting the green in two is possible. No. 18 is the consummate finishing hole—a 415-yard, par 4 that doglegs slightly right.

Long-time PGA Tour player Dow Finsterwald served as Director of Golf here 30 years (1963-1993) and is a Colorado Golf Hall of Fame inductee. In 1957 he won the Vardon Trophy for lowest stroke average on tour and played on the Ryder Cup team. He also won the PGA Championship the following year.

The Broadmoor submitted a bid for the 2008 U.S. Senior Open for the East Course. The preliminary selection committee visited the course for a second time in November 2003 and the course is one of five in the final competition to secure the bid.

THE DETAILS 719-577-5790. 1 Lake Circle, Colorado Springs, CO 80906.
- www.broadmoor.com
- Donald Ross, 1918. 18 holes. Par 72. Blue - 7,112 (72/125). White - 6,525 (67.9/120). Gold - 5,982 (67.4/117). Red - 5,800 (73.2/139). Price - $$$$.

The best new golf course to open this century in Colorado (Redlands Mesa) was not designed by Nicklaus or Palmer or Dye or Fazio or Jones. It was designed by Jim Engh.—RockiesGolf.com, 2001

Bob McIntyre: A Golf Photographers' Diary

Imagine being the chief photographer for The Broadmoor for more than 50 years. Bob McIntyre's lens, which became a Nikon D-1x digital five years ago, has captured six presidents, numerous world rulers, and a plethora of celebrities.

Presidents Dwight D. Eisenhower and Gerald Ford were probably the most photographed presidents, because both loved Colorado golf and The Broadmoor. But the elder Bush, Nixon, Kennedy, Ford, and Reagan have also visited the historic Colorado Springs resort.

Here are some moments McIntyre remembers best:

During the 1953 NCAA Tournament he took a picture of Thayer Tutt, president of The Broadmoor Golf Club, and Ted Payseur, head of the NCAA, standing on the steps of the golf club. Payseur told Tutt they needed to toughen up the course by making the fairways narrower and growing thicker rough. Instead of growing it longer, McIntyre said, The Broadmoor staff decided to mow everything close. "The Broadmoor courses are about putting," McIntyre said.

A good example of that was when McIntyre overhead Mark O'Meara, Fred Couples, and several others one day talking about how easy it was to four-putt if you got on the uphill side of a hole. And there was the day he heard this remark on the first tee: "That gal will never be a great golfer because of that swing." The gal being critiqued was LPGA Hall of Famer Nancy Lopez.

McIntyre even got to take Jack Nicklaus fishing. It was during the 1959 U.S. Amateur, Nicklaus' first major championship victory. "I took Jack and his father to the Rosemont Reservoir, a fishing spot for hotel guests. I explained to them that it wasn't really the right time of the day for fishing (it was 1 p.m. to 3 p.m.), but if we trolled we would have more luck. They both caught their limit and Jack went on to win the title by chipping in on the 18th against Charlie Coe," McIntyre said.

Probably one of McIntyre's fondest memories was of Bob Hope. "Twenty-four years ago, Bob Hope was playing and allowed me a couple of holes to shoot his picture. I got a good shot of him on the green with lots of body English. That night I gave him a print and for the next 24 years I got a Christmas card from Bob," McIntyre recalled.

The public is saying Redlands Mesa is spectacular, scenic, canyon golf with some of the best shot values they have ever played. It's challenging, but fair, and it includes some of the most unique design characteristics ever used on a golf course.—Michael Somma, Redlands Mesa general manager

GETTING THERE From I-25, take exit 138 and follow Circle Dr. west toward the foothills. It's 3 miles to the hotel from the interstate.

THE BROADMOOR MOUNTAIN COURSE

THE GOLF Arnold Palmer and Ed Seay routed the 18-hole Mountain Course back in 1976. But unfortunately, shifting, unstable earth destroyed nine holes of the Mountain layout, and for some time only nine holes were open for play. Then in 2002 the course closed because of the severe drought.

Future plans include a complete remodeling of all 18 holes by Nicklaus Design, slated at 7,500 yards from the tips and tentatively scheduled for a 2006 opening.

"We think it will be player-friendly," said Russ Miller, head pro. "There won't be any blind shots and there will be generous landing areas off the tees. Green designs aren't final, but they won't be as difficult as you find on the East and West Courses."

THE BROADMOOR WEST COURSE

THE GOLF Many believe the Broadmoor West, designed by Robert Trent Jones, Sr. in 1965, is the most difficult course on the resort. While not quite as nostalgic as the East Course, the West side hosted the PGA Cup Matches in 1998 and still has great character.

Long and narrow, playing to a par 72 at 7,083 yards, the layout is spectacular from the start. There's nothing quite as peaceful as heading down No. 1 with a morning red hue on Cheyenne Mountain. The waterfall on this par-4, 372-yard hole makes some purists cringe, but is noteworthy for its beauty.

No. 11 is a longtime favorite: a par 3 that plays 229 yards and drops 100 feet. The hole is surrounded by trees and a lake front and left. Since the green is 30 yards deep and tilts to the water, the preferred play is to aim to the right side of the green and hope for a good kick towards the pin.

The blue spruce and Douglas firs towering over the course have seen it all. Bob Hope and Bing Crosby played here frequently, and Broadmoor's long-time photographer Bob McIntyre snapped a famous pose of Jackie Gleason here: left hand with cigarette on hip, right hand and weight supported by a 2-iron, Gleason looked down the fairway, impatiently waiting for the green to clear. His foursome on that day included Buddy Hackett, Flip Wilson, and head pro Ed Dudley, who also served as the winter pro at Augusta National.

If you watch a game, it's fun. If you play it, it's recreation. If you work at it, it's golf.—Bob Hope

This classic pose shows Jackie Gleason glaring down the fairway in 1962 at The Broadmoor.

THE DETAILS 719-577-5790. 1 Lake Circle, Colorado Springs, CO 80906.
- www.broadmoor.com
- Robert Trent Jones, Sr., 1965. 18 holes. Par 72. Black - 7,083 (73.1/126). Blue - 6,930 (72.4/124). White - 6,461 (69.5/120). Gold - 5,723 (66.9/114) Red - 5,507 (71.7/139). Price - $$$$.

GETTING THERE From I-25 take exit 138 and follow Circle Dr. west toward the foothills. It's 3 miles to the hotel from the interstate

---

When I first viewed the Redlands Mesa site I had that same excitement that I did at Sanctuary, which I considered a once-in-a-lifetime opportunity. But Redlands Mesa was my second chance at the same kind of opportunity. It's a great site with boulders the size of houses. Every time I visit this location I shake my head—it's kind of a moonscape on rolling terrain with large mesas and valleys.—Jim Engh

CHEROKEE RIDGE GOLF CLUB

THE GOLF Press Maxwell designed Cherokee Ridge back in the early 1970s. This no-frills 9-holer is easy to walk and features very little water, few trees, and flat greens with subtle contours. No. 4, a 154-yard par 3, is a solid hole with a large, kidney-shaped green and bunkers.

THE DETAILS 719-597-2637. 1850 Tuskequee Place, Colorado Springs, CO 80915.

- Press Maxwell, 1971. 9 holes. Par 36. White/Blue - 6,427 (68.5/110). Blue/Red - 5,938 (72.9/130). Price - $.

GETTING THERE From I-25 take Exit 149 and Woodmen east to Powers. Turn right on Palmer Park. Turn left and at the top of the hill look for the golf course entrance.

COLORADO SPRINGS COUNTRY CLUB

THE GOLF Known for average rounds under 4 hours, the CSCC is a traditional, 1950s-era, member-designed layout that has been modified by Dick Phelps over the years. Water hazards are not predominant, although the par-3 No. 12 hole makes good use of a handsome water feature.

THE DETAILS 719-473-1782. 3333 Templeton Gap Road, Colorado Springs, CO 80907.

- Members, 1957. Dick Phelps, remodels. 18 holes. Par 71. Black - 6,957 (71.9/129). Blue - 6,708 (71.1/127). White - 6,429 (69.6/124). Women's White - 6,476 (75.7/135). Women's Yellow - 5,410 (69.8/122). Women's Red - 5,861 (72.3/127). Private, but reciprocal play is allowed. Price - $$$.

GETTING THERE In Colorado Springs exit I-25 at Fillmore St. Go east about 4 miles to Union and turn left. Proceed north to Templeton Gap Rd., then turn right to the entrance of the club.

I think Grand Junction golfers are just overwhelmed by the vision of Jim Engh placing the holes the way he did. Life-long residents looked at that land as a dried-up desert. I found the golf course an incredible challenge, with the scenery most distracting, and I kept thinking what a masterful job the designer did crafting this course in craggy rocks and through rugged terrain.—Debbie Kovalik, Executive Director of the Grand Junction Visitor and Convention Bureau, from RockiesGolf.com

THE COUNTRY CLUB OF COLORADO

THE GOLF Best known as Pete Dye's first Colorado layout, this 1973 gem was a mystery for years. The club had its membership, but most of the resort play came from folks attending conferences during weekdays. Weekend visitors found the resort deserted, a result of poor marketing. In 1985 the name changed to Cheyenne Mountain Conference Resort. Finally, new ownership took over in 2002 and focused on improving the course's reputation with the traveling golfer.

These days the resort has it all—300 rooms, a variety of dining options, tennis courts, squash and racquetball courts; two restaurants, a lounge and a pub, health and fitness center, and a 35-acre recreation lake (the course's back nine plays around it) for water sports such as windsurfing, canoeing, sailing, and trout fishing. The only sand beach in Colorado Springs is here, too, and it bustles on weekends.

Set in the historic foothills of Cheyenne Mountain, the course layout circles the lake, known as Curr Reservoir. Slick greens that run as high as 12.5 on the Stimpmeter and water carries have long given this course a tough reputation.

In the 1970s a special salt-resistant grass was developed here because of a problem in one area with the salinity of the soil.

No. 14 is the consummate Dye risk-reward par 4. Playing 354 yards and packaged around the lake, the hole tempts aggressive golfers to cut the hole short by clearing much of the water. No. 17 can ruin a round—it's a scary 187-yard par 3, with water along the right. Going at the flag on 17 requires a full carry of the water.

THE DETAILS 719-538-4095. 125 E. Clubhouse Drive Colorado Springs, CO 80906.
- www.cheyennemountain.com
- Pete Dye, 1973. 18 holes. Par 71. Blue - 7,030 (72.4/138). White - 6,477 (69.6/129). Gold - 5,825 (66.9/114). Women's White - 6,477 (75.8/139). Women's Gold - 5,921 (72.6/132). Women's Red - 5,273 (68.7/125). Resort guests, members, reciprocal privileges. Price - $$$.

GETTING THERE Exit I-25 at Tejon (exit 140B) and follow the signs to Colorado Route 115 south. Drive south 2 miles to Cheyenne Mountain Blvd. and take the Clubhouse Dr. exit to the golf course entrance.

Antler Creek is wide open with sandy soil and no wetlands but it has two sand arroyos that will come into play. I think this course will have a wind-blown look with bunkers like Murphy Creek that have ragged edges and tall grass surrounding them.—Rick Phelps on the new 8,100-yard course in Falcon

SOUTH CENTRAL

EISENHOWER BLUE GOLF COURSE

THE GOLF The Colorado Springs area retirees and fortunate airmen have one of the best bargains in the state—a historic Robert Trent Jones, Sr. track that is consistently ranked as one of Colorado's Top Ten courses. President Dwight D. Eisenhower hit the ceremonial first tee shot to open the course in 1963, and his driver is on display in the pro shop today.

Similar to The Broadmoor's terrain, the Blue rolls through the foothills with fairways lined by ponderosa pines and scrub oak. There are bunkers scattered across the flat land, but it's difficult to find a straight putt. Wild turkeys and deer also frequent the course.

Active duty, reserve, retired military, and civilian employee ID card holders can play two of the best golf courses in the DOD, and guests can also play when accompanied by a card holder.

In July of 1963, former President Eisenhower personally dedicated the Blue Course by hitting the ceremonial first shot off the number one tee.

THE DETAILS 719-333-2606. USAF Academy, Bldg. 3170, 125 E. Clubhouse Drive, USAFA, CO 80840.
- www.usafa.af.mil
- Robert Trent Jones, Sr., 1963. 18 holes. Par 72. Black - 7,291 (74.2/137). Blue - 6,966 (72.6/134). White - 6,516 (70.5/128). Senior's Red - 6,091 (68.2/120). Red - 6,049 (73.4/135). Men's Gold - 5,559 (65.3/115). Women's Gold - 5,559 (71/125). Price $. Military, DOD and guests. Fees depend on rank. Guest fees are $66.

EISENHOWER SILVER GOLF COURSE

THE GOLF In 1976 Frank Hummel designed the Silver Course, which plays shorter than the Blue but is similar in difficulty because of the slick greens and uneven lies. Water comes into play on four holes.

The strength of Devil's Thumb is the site itself. This is such an odd place for Colorado, but it is beautiful. The northeast view brings in the Adobe Hills, which reminds me of the surface of moon, but is just a combination of the terrain that made it interesting to me. It's one of the truest desert-style courses you will find in Colorado.—Rick Phelps on Devil's Thumb in Delta

No. 15 is a solid birdie opportunity, playing 356 yards downhill with a wide-open fairway and a green that slopes from front to back. No. 17 is the signature hole, playing downhill 211 yards to a narrow green with water left and sand right. While it looks like an easy target, it's a frustrating golf shot.

If you are a first-time guest, don't miss a trip to the Air Force Academy's Visitor Center after your round. More than 1.4 million visitors come each year to see the huge, scenic grounds, which teem with wildlife, and the inspiring Cadet Chapel. On many days you can glance up and see cadets circling the grounds, taking glider training.

THE DETAILS 719-333-2606. USAF Academy, Bldg. 3170, 125 E. Clubhouse Drive, USAFA, CO 80840.

- www.usafa.af.mil
- Frank Hummel, 1976. 18 holes. Par 72. Blue - 6,510 (70.5/121). White - 6,003 (68/116). Men's Gold - 5,167 (63.5/105). Women's White - 5,997 (72.8/128). Men's Red - 5,469 (65.1/107). Women's Red - 5,469 (69.8/125). Women's Gold - 5,167 (67.8/124). Price - $. Military, DOD, and guests. Fees depend on rank. Guest fees are $66.

GETTING THERE From I-25 take exit 156 (USAF Academy North entrance) west-bound. After passing through the North Gate, proceed to the intersection at the B-52 display and turn left (south) onto Stadium Blvd. Proceed to the first inter-section and turn right onto Cadet Loop. At the next intersection turn left to the golf course. First-time visitors should ask for directions—the AFA is a huge facility.

FORT CARSON GOLF CLUB

THE GOLF Set in the shadow of Cheyenne Mountain, the Fort Carson Golf Course (a.k.a. Cheyenne Shadows) is a fun, 18-hole championship layout, home to a proud group of soldiers—Fort Carson was instrumental in the liberation of Iraq. Soldiers and civilians can play here all year, and the course hosts frequent tournaments.

Recently FCGC upgraded its facility, spending hundreds of thousands of dollars on a new irrigation system, new cart paths, additional tees, 300 new trees that are 15-30 feet tall, additional water hazards, and a GPS system for the carts.

THE DETAILS 719-526-4122. Bldg. 7800, Titus Blvd., Fort Carson, CO 80913.

- Dick Phelps, 1971. 18 holes. Par 72. Blue - 6,959 (72.3/129). White -

---

Colorado Golf Hall of Famer Bill Majure, Director of Golf at The Country Club of Colorado, led the U.S. Open at Oakmont Hills after the first round in 1991. "My 73 led the first round and in the second round I got it to 2-under after 13 holes," Majure said. "A double bogey at 15 was end of that dream."

6,585 (70.7/126). Women's White - 6,585 (76.2/134). Women's Red - 5,791 (71.8/125). Military course open to public. Tee times taken on weekends - call three days in advance after 11 a.m. Price - $$.

GETTING THERE The clubhouse and pro shop are located on Titus Blvd. near Evans Army Community Hospital. From I-25 and Academy Blvd. (Exit 135), go 2 miles west to Hwy. 115, then head south past Fort Carson (gate 1 to gate 5). Turn left and drive about a half-mile to the course on the left.

GLENEAGLE GOLF CLUB

THE GOLF Gleneagle is a traditional layout with winding hills, blind shots, and scenic views of Pikes Peak and the Air Force Academy. Located at Colorado Springs' highest elevation in the Gleneagle subdivision just north of town, it has been a private club but is currently open to the public. In 2003 new ownership assumed management, which means that the club could become exclusive again.

Frank Hummel's 1972 design is long, difficult, and known for having some of the best bentgrass greens in the state. The greens vary in size and many are severely undulating. The 458-hard No. 10 hole, listed as a par 4 from the tips, doglegs right into the fairway and leaves you with a blind approach to the green.

THE DETAILS 719-488-0900. 345 Mission Hill Way, Colorado Springs, CO 80921.

* Frank Hummel, 1972. 18 holes. Par 72. Gold - 7,276 (73.9/128). Blue - 7,129 (73.4/125). White - 6,734 (71.8/119). Red - 5,600 (71.1/126). Women's Green - 5,269 (69.2/122). Price - $$.

GETTING THERE Take I-25 to exit 156A (Gleneagle Dr.). Go east for a half-mile and turn left onto Gleneagle Dr. Proceed to the four-way stop and turn right to continue on Gleneagle Dr. Follow this to Mission Hills Way and turn left to the course.

KISSING CAMELS GOLF CLUB

THE GOLF When Press Maxwell arrived on this flat mesa overlooking The Garden of the Gods in 1961, it was treeless, but with an unforgettable view. The

---

A special salt-resistant grass was developed at the Country Club of Colorado in the 1970s. Because there was a problem in one area with the salinity of the soil, superintendent Stan Metzger worked with University of Colorado to develop the salt-resistant grass that the Scotts Company has on the market today.

backdrop was Pikes Peak and a spectacular red-rock formation known as Kissing Camels.

Maxwell's original 18-hole layout included Austrian and piñon pine, numerous doglegs and bunkers, and open fairways that rolled to contoured bentgrass greens. Then in 1996 Denver-based architect Mark Rathert, who trained under Robert Trent Jones, Jr. and has received recent acclaim with his Boulder Creek course in Las Vegas, came in for a remodel and additional nine. Rathert basically remodeled the entire place, routing the nines back to the clubhouse while retaining some of the existing holes to keep as much of Maxwell's original design as possible.

These days the first trees that were planted are upwards of 40 feet tall, and the areas with smaller trees indicate where the newest holes were constructed toward the north end of the mesa along a scenic bluff. Rathert's remodeling of the bunkers utilized new technology, and he tried to give each a little more of a flared look. The original Maxwell greens, which Rathert calls "Maxwell rolls," are more elevated now, and many of them have bumps and humps.

Note that Kissing Camels is a totally exclusive, private club—the gates will keep you out unless you're a resident, and the 27-hole complex doesn't allow reciprocal play.

THE DETAILS 719-632-5541. 4500 Kissing Camels Drive, Colorado Springs, CO 80904.

- Press Maxwell, 1961. Mark Rathert, remodel, rerouting, nine-hole addition, 1996. 27 holes. Par 72. Private. No reciprocal play allowed. Price - $$$.
- North/West Course: Blue - 6,951 (71.3/123). White - 6,504 (69.3/118). Men's Red - 6,084 (67.2/114). Men's Yellow - 5,331 (63.6/105). Women's Red - 6,009 (73.3/134). Women's Orange - 5,735 (71.6/130). Women's Yellow - 5,257 (69.1/123).
- West/South Course: Blue - 6,879 (71.1/124). White - 6,484 (69.2/120). Women's Red - 6,012 (73.1/133). Women's Orange - 5,634 (70.7/129). Women's Yellow - 5,235 (68.5/124). Men's Red - 6,033 (67/113). Men's Yellow - 5,277 (63.2/102).
- South/North Course: Blue - 6,910 (71.2/125). White - 6,442 (68.9/121). Men's Red - 5,993 (66.6/114). Women's Red - 5,927 (72.8/133). Women's Orange - 5,681 (71.1/130). Women's Yellow - 5,138 (68/124). Men's Yellow - 5,106 (62.4/102).

Simply the most spectacular golf course I have ever seen!—Gary McCord on Jim Engh's Sanctuary

GETTING THERE From I-25 in Colorado Springs, exit at Fillmore St. and head west 1.5 miles to Mesa Dr. Turn right and go a half-mile to the guard gate.

PATTY JEWETT GOLF COURSE

THE GOLF The Patty Jewett GC first opened in 1898 and is the oldest Colorado golf course still in its original location. Colorado Springs was an upscale summer escape for the elites of East Coast industry back in those days and golfers needed a place to play. It was first known as the private Town and Gown Club, but it went bankrupt and was purchased by a group headed by William Jewett, who was a good friend of Colorado Springs founder, Gen. William Jackson Palmer. Jewett eventually bought out all of the other partners. When he decided to give the property to the city he stipulated that it would be called Patty Jewett, after his wife, and that the land would always be used as a golf course.

Patty Jewett, the third oldest course west of the Mississippi, is a friendly place to play even today, and has been a junior training ground for decades thanks to the leadership of former pro Paul Ransom. You never know who you might see here. Rocco Mediate might be on the practice putting green—his nephew is in one of the junior programs here, as are Mark Calcavecchia's nephew and niece and Mark Wiebe's son, Gunner.

The layout, which also has a 9-hole course, offers an awesome view of Pikes Peak and regularly hosts the Pikes Peak Amateur Tournament (won by Hale Irwin in 1965).

Willie Campbell, a flashy Scot who also laid out The Country Club at Brookline, Mass., site of the 1999 Ryder Cup, designed the course. Features include uneven fairway boundaries guarded by thick, nasty rough, loads of strategically placed, dogleg guarding trees, and water hazards that cross the fairways in the perfect spots, forcing golfers to contemplate every shot.

However, the layout is not exactly like it was back in 1898. "There were other holes in play that you can still see remnants of, but it is easier to say the original course consisted of the front nine and the nine-hole course. Renovations were implemented in 1967 and they are most easily recognized by the drastically undulating greens," says Dal Lockwood, Director of Golf for the Colorado Springs municipals.

The Phelps Golf Course Design crew have implemented some minor renovations to restore some of the original greenside bunkers and return others to their original depth. Finally, you can't go wrong with post-golf time at the Patty Jewett Bar & Grill, a great spot for burgers and beer with a spectacular view of Pikes Peak.

It is special in the Pebble Beach sense.—Tom Cushman, San Diego Union Tribune about Jim Engh's Sanctuary

THE DETAILS 719-385-6950. 900 East Española, Colorado Springs, CO 80907.
- www.springsgov.com
- Willie Campbell, 1898. Numerous Phelps Design remodels. 18 holes. Par 72. Black - 6,928 (72/129). Blue - 6,535 (70.4/124). White - 6,183 (68.4/121). Gold - 5,758 (66.5/113). Women's White - 6,183 (74.2/128). Women's Gold - 5,758 (71.7/128). Price - $.
- Patty Jewett Nine: 9 holes. Par 36. White/Blue - 6,166 (67.5/113). Women's White/Blue - 6,193 (73.8/131). Women's Gold/White - 5,907 (72.1/127). Price - $.

GETTING THERE From I-25 take the Nevada exit off I-25, then head east on Española to the golf course.

PINE CREEK GOLF CLUB

THE GOLF The Dick Phelps-designed Pine Creek is demanding and tight, with small targets, lots of tall, unforgiving native grass, and a creek that bisects the front nine, forcing carries. The back nine is a bit more lenient and has far less trouble as it opens up with views of the Air Force Academy. The course routes through 200 acres in the Pine Creek Valley.

Fifteen of the 18 holes involve natural grasslands and creek beds that come into play. No. 1 is a good indication of what's ahead, since the hole is sliced by a creek and forces a target drive.

THE DETAILS 719-594-9999. 9850 Divot Trail, Colorado Springs, CO 80920.
- www.pinecreek.com
- Dick Phelps, 1987. 18 holes. Par 72. Gold - 7,050 (72.6/139). Blue - 6,579 (70.4/132). White - 6,040 (68/123). Women's White - 6,040 (74.1/129). Women's Red - 5,351 (70.2/122). Price - $$$.

GETTING THERE Take I-25 to the Briargate Parkway (exit 151). Go east to Chapel Hills Dr., turn left, and follow the subdivision signs to the clubhouse.

SAND CREEK GOLF COURSE

THE GOLF This executive 9-hole course features two par 4s and seven par 3s. Seven of the holes cross back and forth across a dry, sandy creek bed. The rough is high and the greens roll true. No. 3, a 130-yarder, has out-of-bounds behind the green and involves a carry of Sand Creek to an elevated green.

Sanctuary is an unbelievable testimony to Jim Engh's architectural skills.
—Peter Kostis CBS Golf Analyst, PGA Tour Professional

THE DETAILS 719-597-5489. 6865 Galley Road, Colorado Springs, CO 80915.

- Mark Fontana, 1993. 9 holes. Par 29. Men's - 1,653. Women's - 1,326. Price - $.

GETTING THERE Take the Woodmen Rd. exit from I-25. Go east on Woodmen for 6 miles to Powers and turn east for 9 more miles. Turn left on Gallery, and the course is on the right.

SILVER SPRUCE GOLF COURSE

THE GOLF There's a golf tournament in the Air Force called the Corona, a long-time tradition that travels from base to base. Seasoned veterans of Silver Spruce Golf Course say when the tournament comes to Peterson Air Force Base there are more stars on the fairways than in the sky—meaning that lots of generals take part in the festivities.

The golf course was born because of Bing Crosby and Bob Hope, who played a benefit at The Broadmoor and some of the money raised went to Peterson AFB to build a driving range. Later, nine holes were added and in the 1970s nine more were built.

Silver Spruce is fairly flat, with mildly contoured greens and nine holes that have out-of-bounds. Four holes have water and there are minimal bunkers. No. 3, a 207-yard par 3, has a narrow green that slopes from back to front—a tough hole to put one close.

THE DETAILS 719-556-7414. 401 Glasgow, Bldg. #1054 Peterson AFB, CO 80914.

- Dick Phelps, back nine, 1974. 18 holes. Par 72. Blue - 6,833 (71.4/124). White - 6,476 (69.5/122). Women's White - 6,476 (75.6/135). Women's Yellow - 5,601 (70.7/126). Women's Red - 6,092 (73.2/129). Military, DOD rates depend on rank. Guests allowed when accompanied by DOD cardholder. Price - $.

GETTING THERE Exit I-25 at Woodmen Rd. (exit 149) and go east about 6 miles to Powers Blvd. Turn right (south) and drive 7 miles to Platte Ave. (Hwy. 24). Turn left and go 1 mile to the Peterson AFB guard gate. Follow the signs to the course on the east side of base.

My design philosophy has taken a lot from early American golf architects such as Perry Maxwell and Donald Ross. I like Alister MacKenzie's flair. Ross, especially was about building substance—strategy—into his courses. He was very aware of the importance of making courses beautiful, but substance was his first priority.—Tripp Davis, who designed Grand Elk with Craig Stadler

SPRINGS RANCH GOLF CLUB

THE GOLF Opened in 1997, Springs Ranch is a links course with desert-like waste bunkers and natural borders along Sand Creek, which serves as a hazard. With Pikes Peak in the foreground, the downhill, par-3, 170-yard 16th hole is one you will remember. Take less club and avoid flying the green, where trouble lurks in the form of a bunker and steep slope.

THE DETAILS 719-573-4863. 3525 Tutt Boulevard, Colorado Springs, CO 80922.

- www.springsranch.com
- Dick Phelps, 1998. 18 holes. Par 72. Silver - 7,092 (72.6/132). Maroon - 6,661 (71.3/125). Green - 5,555 (65.8/107). Men's Sand - 6,054 (68.4/116).Women's Sand - 6,054 (72.8/127). Women's Green - 5,555 (70.5/119).Women's Brown - 5,014 (67.2/112). Price - $$.

GETTING THERE Exit I-25 at Woodmen Rd. (exit 149) and drive east about 6 miles. Turn right on Powers Blvd., go 4 miles, and turn left (east) on North Carefree. Turn right (south) on Tutt Blvd.

VALLEY HI GOLF COURSE

THE GOLF Situated just south of the heart of the city, with typical Cheyenne Mountain and Pikes Peak views, Valley Hi offers flat terrain and wide-open fairways, with well-placed bunkers and lakes that add to the challenge. The course opened in 1956 and was purchased by the city of Colorado Springs in 1975. Regulars say the quality greens are the course's calling card.

THE DETAILS 719-385-6911. 610 Chelton Road, Colorado Springs, CO 80910.

- Henry Hughes, 1956. Dick Phelps, 1983, remodel. 18 holes. Par 72. Black - 6,890 (71.7/118). Blue - 6,437 (69.6/114). Men's Sandstone - 5,616 (65.9/105). Men's Green - 5,153 (63.8/102). Women's Black - 6,890 (78.4/139). Women's Blue - 6,437 (74.8/129). Women's Sandstone - 5,616 (70/120). Women's Green - 5,153 (67.3/116). Price - $$.

GETTING THERE Take I-25 south to exit 139 (Hwy 24 bypass) and turn left on Chelton Rd. The course is on the left.

Our members are thrilled because they love the diversity and the views. They think it is very manageable from tee-to-green, but this course is defined by the difficult greens. I've seen plenty of good players exit No. 18 mumbling to themselves about three putts.—Chris Lai, on the Fazio Course at Red Sky Ranch

VINEYARD GOLF CLUB

THE GOLF Unusual in that it's located on the grounds of a winery and wine tasting room, the Vineyard Golf Club includes 110 acres of land, the Pikes Peak Winery, a restaurant, and even a cabin for overnight excursions. The cabin rents for $125 per night and includes golf.

The course is nestled among cottonwood trees alongside Fountain Creek. No. 1 is a par-5 563-yarder with a double dogleg. No. 7 tees from a chute of trees and doglegs a little right toward the green 330 yards away.

THE DETAILS 719-226-2466. 3819 Janitell Road, Colorado Springs, CO 80906.
- www.ppvineyardgolf.com
- Mark Rathert, 1999. 9 holes. Par 37. Men's Blue/Burgundy - 6,629 (70.7/125). Men's White/Blue - 6,143 (68.6/116). Women's Red/White - 5,660 (70.4/122). Price - $.

GETTING THERE I-25 to the South Circle exit. Head east about a half-mile to Janitell Road. Turn right and look for the course.

COLORADO SPRINGS NOTES

The **Broadmoor** (800-634-7711) is the first option for the serious travel golfer, offering every possible amenity, and the **Charles Court** or **Stratta's** for dining. Just up the hill is the **Cheyenne Mountain Zoo** (www.cmzoo.org, 719-633-9925), the highest in the USA at 6,800 feet and perfect for families waiting on Dad to finish his round. At nearby Manitou Springs, Teddy Roosevelt slept at the **Red Crags B&B** (www.redcrags.com, 800-721-2248,) while visiting an ex-Rough Rider friend. **The Cliff House** (www.the-cliffhouse.com, 888-212-7000) at Pikes Peak, built in the winter of 1873, has been open to guests longer than Colorado has been a state. Clark Gable bunked there. The **Cliff House Dining Room** is a winner of AAA's Four Diamonds Award and the wine list exceeds 550 selections. And the elegant **Adam's Mark Antlers Hotel** (www.antlers.com, 719-473-5600, 800-444-2326) in the heart of downtown actually pre-dates The Broadmoor. The hamburgers at **Conway's Red Top** (719-329-1445) are amazing, and **Steaksmith** (719-596-9300), **Margarita at Pine Creek** (719-598-8667) or **Jose Muldoon's** (719-636-2311) on the Acacia Park square also offer solid dining options. Summer weekend nights should be focused around **Tejon Street**, where you can bar-hop and people-watch to take your mind off the day's golf round.

Back in the late 1800s, Colorado Springs was a pretty ritzy summer home for the elites of East Coast industry—thus, the need for a golf course in the west. You can still see the wealth of those old days in the immense Victorian and Queen Anne homes in the downtown areas of Colorado Springs. In 1898, the location of Patty Jewett would have been in the boondocks plains, a mile or so out of the city. Today it is central town.—Steve Collins of Austin, TX

One of Old Colorado City's best bars is **Meadow Muffins** (719-633-0583), which serves interesting munchies (Jiffy burger) along with pool tables and live music. And one of the most famous towns in the area is **Cripple Creek**, an old gold-mining establishment that sits next to an extinct volcano crater in the boondocks region on the backside of Pikes Peak. Gaming is alive here just like in the saloon days.

CRESTONE

ELEV 8,200 POP. 200

At 14,165 feet, Kit Carson Peak looms over this tiny hamlet nestled in the pines on the eastern edge of the San Luis Valley. Secluded Crestone was part of the historic 100,000-acre Baca Grande Land Grant, which extended 40 miles north of Alamosa on Colorado Highway 17. Today the area is home to spiritual centers espousing a wide range of doctrines and disciplines. The high point of a narrow ridge on the northwest collar of Carson Mountain was renamed Challenger Point to honor the astronauts of the ill-fated Challenger mission. Golf in Crestone comes in the form of a 9-hole executive course, which is also named after the Challenger mission.

CHALLENGER GOLF CLUB

THE GOLF Formerly known as Baca Grande Los Cumbres Golf Course, this scenic layout is a favorite of golf road-trippers because it's uncrowded and surrounded by three 14,000-foot mountain peaks. Jim Barnes routed the course in the 1970s with four par 4s and five par 3s.

Located four miles west of town, the course is adjacent to the White Eagle Village Conference Retreat Center and Inn—a solid option for a weekend golf getaway.

THE DETAILS 719-256-4856. 4905 County Road T, Crestone, CO 81131.
- Jim Barnes, 1974. 9-hole executive course. Par 31. Women's Red/White - 3,632 (58.7/97). White/Blue - 4,121 (58.5/98). Price - $.

GETTING THERE Take Hwy. 285 south to Hwy. 17, then drive south to the town of Moffatt. Next head east on County Road T, 8 miles to the course.

Back in the 1960s and 1970s there were more rounds per year played at Patty Jewett than any course in the west. Of course that was before the days of the golf boom and buildup of courses in Arizona.— Loren Lutz, Colorado Springs

CRESTONE NOTES

This is an ideal home base for visits to the **Great Sand Dunes National Park** and some of the area hot springs. Revisit the 1960s at the **Crestone International Hostel** (719-256-4153) or stay at the **Silver Star Bed & Breakfast** (719-256-4686). Dining options include the **Desert Sage Restaurant** (719-256-4402) or the **On The Way Cafe** (719-256-5177), in nearby Moffat, UFO watching has been popular (www.ufowatchtower.com) since November 29, 1997, when four people in Crestone spotted "unusual multi-colored lights" in the sky about 20 miles northwest of town. There's even a Center for the Study of Extraterrestrial Intelligence (www.cseti.org) if your curiosity gets the better of you.

FALCON

ELEV 6,000 POP. Not available

The urban sprawl of Colorado Springs has found its way to the small community of Falcon, located just 12 miles to the northeast in an area of sand ridges and arroyos that straddle the south side of the Palmer Divide. Two residential projects are under construction: the Woodmen Hills development and the Meridian Ranch project, which will include more than 3,000 home sites, a recreational center, and a golf course.

ANTLER CREEK GOLF CLUB

THE GOLF Scheduled for a summer 2004 opening, the Rick Phelps-designed Antler Creek Golf Club will be the longest golf course in Colorado at a whopping 8,100 yards. Although the flat land around Falcon is considered part of the plains, Antler Creek will surprise many with its drastic elevation changes.

Six sets of tees will give golfers of varying skills options as they play into a wide-open course that routes around two sand arroyos. Picture a sandy, windblown prairie with no wetlands and ragged bunkers surrounded by tall native grasses.

Phelps has hinted that the first three holes might be the most challenging risk/reward opening holes in Colorado. A ravine will split the par-5 first hole. No. 2 is a short dogleg right, with hazards lining the entire right side. The par 4 No. 3 will play downwind, but goes uphill an incredible 510 yards. The greens are designed to have a good variety of contoured and flat bentgrass.

Rick Phelps said his dad Dick and uncle, who both grew up in Colorado Springs, played Patty Jewett many times during the 1950s and 1960s. "Sadly, many of the course's bunkers were removed during that era. It happened all over the USA under the blanket excuse of speeding up play," Phelps said.

THE DETAILS Opening summer of 2004.

- Rick Phelps, 2004. 18 holes. Par 72. Not yet rated. Opening set for July 1, 2004.

FALCON NOTES

Fast-food shops and chains are sprouting up as the community grows, but the recommended post-golf excursion involves a trip back into Colorado Springs for nightlife.

FLORENCE

ELEV 5,191 POP. 3,653

Not far from Pueblo, Florence is a pretty little town with views of Pikes Peak and the Wet Mountains. It's known as the home of one of the highest-security federal prisons in the U.S. The town was named after the daughter of settler James McCandless, who came west with European settlers and liked this scenic area near the rambling Arkansas River that was home to the Ute, Sioux, and Arapahoe Indians. As pioneers pushed west, some decided to settle in Florence rather than trying to cross the Royal Gorge. Wayfarers plan excursions to Florence to experience The Sumo Golf Village, explore the Victorian-style buildings that house antique shops, and have dinner at the interesting Sunny's Seafood & Steakhouse.

THE SUMO GOLF VILLAGE

THE GOLF The charismatic Gary Player arrived here one bright October day, looked around, and took a big breath of clean Colorado air. "You know, you people who live here are in a one-percent category of the whole world," he said.

"You have this wonderful view, which reminds me of my ranch in South Africa, no pollution, and you have a great lifestyle with food on the table three times a day. You should be thankful every day of the year," he said.

The Sumo Golf Village is a Player signature layout and a complete remake of the old 9-hole Bear Paw track. The 7,196-yard, par 72 traverses native arroyos that originally served as the hunting grounds of area locals. Sumo isn't a links course, but Player refers to it as "linksy," and he said his team tried to blend the layout in with the desert.

The Keystone Ranch Course is a true test of traditional golf, and it is a test of shot making. To score you must be humble and pay attention to the shot making because there are some very strategic placements. It is narrow and there is not much room for error on the front nine. The back nine is much more forgiving, and you can attack the pins on most of the greens.—Steve Corneillier

THE DETAILS 719-784-4000. 2960 Siloam Rd., Florence, CO 81226.

- www.sumovillage.com
- Gary Player, 2003. 18 holes. Par 72. Black - 7,196. Gold - 6,859. Blue - 6,540. White - 6,119. Red - 5,472. Not yet rated. Price - $$.

GETTING THERE Take I-25 to Hwy. 50 west and find Hwy. 67 south. Turn right at Hardee's, drive over the railroad tracks, and head left on Siloam Rd. to the course.

FLORENCE NOTES

Take advantage of the proximity of the Arkansas River, which runs along the edge of Florence and provides launching points for rafting trips, fishing, and scenic hiking. Several scenic mountain trails nearby are perfect for hiking, horseback riding, and rock climbing. Summertime views of the Monarch Ski Resort are available just a 1.5-hour drive to the west at the top of Monarch Pass. Weekenders should stay at the **Cañon Inn** in Cañon City (www.canoninn.com, 719-275-8676, 800-525-7727), or head over to Pueblo which offers hundreds of activities for the tourists. As mentioned in the introduction to Florence, **Sunny's Seafood and Steakhouse** (719-784-1984) has solid food and service in several relaxing dining rooms.

LEADVILLE

ELEV. 10,152 POP. 2,821

Located on the Top of the Rockies Byway, Leadville has the highest elevation of any incorporated city in America and is an extremely cold place in the winter. More than 20,000 macho mining men once called Leadville home during the Wild West's silver boom. For today's wandering golfers Leadville is a must-stop—a charming town built around a National Historic Landmark District, with blocks of Victorian architecture and the highest 9-hole golf course in the USA.

MOUNT MASSIVE GOLF COURSE

THE GOLF Situated at 9,680 feet with stunning views of Mount Elbert's 14,433-foot peaks, the Mount Massive Golf Course competes with Copper Mountain's Copper Creek GC (18 holes at 9,700 feet) as one of the highest courses any-

---

Take a slower back swing so you don't get winded up here. But really, people find that they need one to two clubs less here because we are higher than 99.9 percent of the courses they have ever played. Factor in the super low humidity and you'll be hitting some 150-yard pitching wedge shots.—Steve Corneillier on the Keystone Ranch and River Courses

where. The design features wide-open fairways for holes 1 and 9, but the rest of the layout narrows down as it rolls in and out of the forest.

The par-3 second hole is a favorite, playing straight uphill to the green, offering a blind tee shot, rare for a par 3 hole. Golfers must climb the log tower next to the tee box to make sure the green is clear. The 506-yard, par-5 No. 6, which heads straight for Mount Massive, is another favorite hole.

THE DETAILS 719-486-2176. 259 County Road 5, Leadville, CO 80461.

- Adolph Kuss, 1939. 9 holes. Par 36. Blue/Black - 6,170 (66.7/112). White/Blue - 5,685 (64.2/104). Men's Red/White - 4,958 (61/95). Women's Red/White - 4,958 (64.4/110). Price - $.

GETTING THERE Take I-70 to Hwy. 91 south to Leadville. The course is west of Leadville via 6th street and CR 4 (Turquoise Lake Rd.).

LEADVILLE NOTES

A trip to Leadville for golf could not be complete without quality beer-drinking time at the **Boomtown Brewpub** (719-486-8297), labeled the "Best Cheap Buzz" in America by *Men's Journal* magazine. Housed in a late 1800s church, you'll achieve a relaxing post-golf buzz quickly at this altitude by sampling the refreshing Mineral Belt Pale Ale and other English-style ales. The historic **Delaware Hotel** (www.delawarehotel.com, 800-748-2004) offers golf packages for Mount Massive. Other overnight options include the **Apple Blossom Inn** (800-982-9279), also on the historic registers, or the elegant **Ice Palace Inn B&B** (800-754-2840), which is built with lumber salvaged from Leadville's old Ice Palace. The mining heritage is on display at the **National Mining Hall of Fame Museum** and the **Healy House & Dexter Cabin State Museum**, a three-story Victorian boarding house. The **Colorado Trail** provides easy access to miles of hiking and mountain biking trails. The route traverses Lake County and provides access to the cabins of the Tenth Mountain Division Ski Hut system. This was a training site for World War II ski paratroopers. The ski area later became Ski Cooper. **Callaway's** (719-486-1418) is in the Delaware Hotel, specializing in steaks and seafood. The popular **Grill Bar and Café** (719-486-9930) is the most lively joint in town, and the **Golden Burro Café & Lounge** (719-486-1239) is a solid bet anytime, but especially for an early morning breakfast. The most unique dining experience involves a little effort though. Find the Piney Creek Nordic Center at Ski Cooper and mountain bike or jeep for the 1-mile trail to the **Tennessee Pass Cookhouse** (719-486-8114), an upscale restaurant that requires reservations.

When Louis L'Amour, the western novelist, visited Durango, he stayed at the historic Strater Hotel, where you can still book a room. Old-timers say he always asked for the room directly above the Diamond Belle Saloon, Room 222, because the honky-tonk music helped set the mood for his novels of the Old West. Some say a good part of his Sackett's novels were written at the Strater Hotel.

MONTE VISTA

ELEV. 7,663 POP. 4,529

Monte Vista, Spanish for "mountain view," is a quiet little San Luis Valley town and headquarters for the Rio Grande National Forest. In the spring and fall the migration of sandhill cranes is a real treat to watch. Eleven buildings made from locally quarried rhyolite add charm to the downtown scene, and the warm summer days and cool nights here make Monte Vista perfect for growing potatoes, alfalfa, and Coors barley - as well as an ideal spot for a remote Colorado golf excursion.

SOUTH CENTRAL

MONTE VISTA COUNTRY CLUB

THE GOLF This 9-hole course is modest and uncrowded—an excellent place to learn the game or work in some quick rounds. The fairways are narrow and tree-lined and the greens are small and fast. A few holes provide the opportunity to really let it rip—especially the signature 446-yard par 4 No. 4 that plays narrow and straight into a multi-tiered green.

THE DETAILS 719-852-4906. 101 Country Club Drive, Monte Vista, CO 81144.
- James Newman, 1928. 9 holes. Par 35. White/Blue - 6,053 (66.7/111). Women's White/Blue - 6,019 (72.7/113). Women's Red/White - 5,536 (39.7/126). Price - $.

GETTING THERE In Monte Vista, drive 5 blocks west of Hwy. 285, then north on Dunham St. until you find Country Club Dr.

MONTE VISTA NOTES

Play golf in the morning, have lunch at **JB's Burger & Fries** (719-852-2272), grab a Colorado-brewed six-pack, then head to the **Monte Vista Wildlife Refuge** or **Alamosa National Wildlife Refuge** and watch the sandhill crane's leap and bow to attract their mates. **Restaurante Dos Rios** (719-852-0969) is a cantina-like joint north of town, and the **Victorian Restaurant** serves meals in the lobby of the historic **Monte Villa Inn** (719-852-5166). Check out the bullet-ridden hardwood bar for evening cocktails. Monte Vista also offers a slice of Americana you can't find any other place in the world. **The Best Western Movie Manor Motor Inn** (719-852-5921) is

---

Most people think holes 14-17 are as pretty as any stretch of holes anywhere. I only use my driver about four times during a round here, so it doesn't really play that long. Put the driver away, but you will use all your other clubs during a round. Keep the ball below the hole by all means—the greens can be slick.
—David Zalbowitz, The Glacier Club, Durango

the only movie motel on the planet. Your room faces the drive-in screen and sound is piped in. Mountain bikers head to the trails of **Cat Creek** 13 miles south of town.

MONUMENT

ELEV 6,961 POP. 1,971

Monument Hill is famous as one of Colorado's iciest spots. Natives speed along I-25 through Monument without even thinking—it's just a dot in the road on the 47-mile route between Colorado Springs and Denver. Situated atop the Palmer Divide at 7,200 feet, with Palmer Lake, Larkspur, Gleneagle, Woodmoor, and Black Forest all in this Tri-Lakes area, Monument has grown from a quiet pioneer town of ranchers and farmers into one of the strongest growth corridors in Colorado.

KING'S DEER GOLF CLUB

THE GOLF Originally known as The Divide at King's Deer, this Ric Buckton design is a prairie-links beauty routed through the tall, native grasses east of town. In the distance you can see ponderosa pines and Pikes Peak, but the course is basically treeless.

The tall grass defines this layout, and it's imperative to keep the ball in the fairway to manage the course. Otherwise the thick grass will twist and turn the clubhead, making it impossible to traverse the numerous forced carries, which look longer than they actually are.

The par 3s seem like islands surrounded by the nasty high grass.

On the front No. 3 stands out, a 455-yarder from the tips that offers a 180-yard forced carry on the approach. The most difficult hole on the back might be No. 14, a 569-yard, par 5 that also involves a forced carry.

The Pentcross bent greens are excellent and make for a challenging, but fun day of putting. Uphill putts should be stroked solidly, as you'll discover on No. 9, where the green is severely sloped even though it doesn't appear to be.

THE DETAILS 719-481-1518. 19255 Royal Troon Drive, Monument, CO 80132.
- www.kingsdeergolfclub.com
- Ric Buckton, Redstone, 1999. 18 holes. Par 71. Gold - 6,828 (72/136). Blue - 6,285 (70.1/126). White - 5,710 (67.9/118). Red - 5,054 (68.2/123). Price - $$$.

Nature is on display here. The course uses the valley, the Rio Grande, Alder Creek and climbs on the back nine into the aspens and pines and borders the Rio Grande National Forest.—Todd Small, Rio Grande Club in South Fork

GETTING THERE From Colorado Springs take C-105 from I-25 and head east to Roller Coaster Rd., then turn left. From Denver take County Line Rd. and head east, then turn right on Roller Coaster Rd.

WOODMOOR PINES COUNTRY CLUB

THE GOLF An extremely challenging track, Woodmoor Pines forces accurate tee shots into the narrow, ponderosa pine-lined fairways. However, getting it into the short grass doesn't guarantee success, since the postage-stamp greens are tough targets—especially with the hilly terrain causing uneven lies. Four ponds come into play on six holes.

No. 12 is the signature hole, a 413-yarder that bends right with out-of-bounds left and a pond and trees on the right. Picking the right line is imperative, otherwise the trees will block your view of the green on the approach.

THE DETAILS 719-481-2266. 18945 Pebble Beach Way, Monument, CO 80132.
- Press Maxwell, 1969. 18 holes. Par 72. Black - 6,734 (72.7/138). Blue - 6,396 (71.6/133). White - 6,019 (69.9/129). Women's Blue - 6,396 (75.4/142). Women's White - 6,037 (73.3/138). Women's Red - 5,640 (70.9/132). Women's Gold - 5,355 (69.4/128). Reciprocal play allowed. Price - $$$.

GETTING THERE Take I-25 to exit 163, and head east 1 mile before turning south on Furrow Rd. Follow Furrow for a half-mile and then turn west on Woodmoor Dr. The course is 1 mile down the road.

MONUMENT NOTES

Colorado Springs is very close, and Denver isn't much farther to the north, but there are a few worthy spots to check out in Monument. **Serranos Coffee Company** (719-481-9445) and the **Coffee Cup Café** (719-488-0663) are great early morning spots to hit before golf. Or before hitting the road post-round, sit down at the **La Casa Fiesta Restaurant** (719-481-1234). Overnight options include **Falcon Inn Resort** (719-481-3000) and **Rogers Inn** (719-488-4355), both clean, affordable options.

Even though the fairways are wide, they narrow closer to the greens. It's the toughest second-shot course I've ever played.—Fal Wood, Dalton Ranch, Durango

SALIDA

ELEV. 7,080 POP. 5,504

Salida is set amidst a land of flowing water and large cattle ranches. Originally settled by the Utes, it is the seat of Chaffee County and the crossroads for three main highways: US 24, 50, and 285. Explorers, miners, railroad builders, farmers, and ranchers arrived here in the 1870s; legend tells the tale of the railroad hub growing rapidly once a madam named Laura Evans established her house of ill repute, a place that amazingly survived until around 1950. As headquarters for the Arkansas River Valley State Park and home to a 1920s-era 9-hole golf course, Salida is a notable weekend golf destination.

SALIDA GOLF CLUB

THE GOLF Magnificent views of the Collegiate Peaks and the Sangre de Cristos prevail over this flat mountain course, which features tight fairways and small, fast greens. Eight of nine holes involve water, since the course routes around an irrigation ditch.

The 315-yard No. 4 is the best hole, requiring that you avoid a huge tree in the middle of the fairway. Clearing the tree isn't the only challenge, since the green is framed by water on each side.

Interestingly, for years no one knew the name of the course's 1926 architect. However, locals recently determined that Emmett Killian, a former employee of The Broadmoor, actually built the course.

THE DETAILS 719-539-1060. 404 Grant Street, Salida, CO 81201.
- Emmett Killian, 1926. 9 holes. Par 35. White/Blue - 6,256 (68.5/121). Red/White - 5,547 (65.1/109). Gold/Red - 4,921 (62/99). Women's White/Blue - 6,360 (74.7/131). Women's Red/White - 5,547 (70/122). Women's Gold/Red - 4,921 (66/114). Price - $.

GETTING THERE Take Hwy. 50 to Salida, and turn north at the Salida hot springs pool. Turn right on Poncha Blvd., then left on Grant Street and go to the clubhouse.

The 308-yard 17th reminded me a great deal of the 18th at Pebble Beach, if shortened to a par 4, because of the Animas River running down the left side. Ken Dye has designed and built a course not only of great beauty, but of considerable excitement. In short, every hole was unique and well thought out.
— unknown visitor to Dalton Ranch, Durango

SALIDA NOTES

Be sure to take a walking tour of downtown Salida to soak up the local history. The town thrived as a division point for the Denver & Rio Grande Railroad for 70-plus years, but frequent fires meant constant rebuilding. Eventually the Salida Fire Blocks district was created—the city fathers ruled that all downtown buildings had to be made of brick. Today it's a charming historic district that's on the National Registry of Historic Places. Spend the night at the **Piñon & Sage B&B** (719-539-3227), a restored Victorian home just a short walk from downtown, or the 1882 **River Run Inn** (800-385-6925), a good spot for fishing along the Arkansas river. The most famous Salida eatery is the **First Street Café** (719-539-4759), an especially pleasing Mexican dining experience in the old red light district that should proceed rowdy weekend time at the **Victoria Hotel and Tavern** (719-539-4819). Rafting excursions can be planned through **River Runners** (800-525-2081), one of the largest outfitters in the state. Another great outfitter is **Browner's Fly Shop** (800-826-6505), the best option for gearing up for trips on the Arkansas River and into the backcountry. In September, an excellent time to visit for golf, Salida restaurants populate Riverside Park for the **Taste of Salida**, complete with live entertainment and samplings from local wineries and brewpubs. The **Mountain Spirit Winery** (719-539-7848) west of town offers tastings and tours.

SOUTH FORK

ELEV 8,250 POP. 670

A remote town located where the South Fork of the Rio Grande joins the main body of the Rio Grande, South Fork has been a logging and lumbering community since the late 1880s. Over the years it has evolved into a popular tourist destination: the headwaters of the famous river are less than an hour away, and the spot between South Fork and Del Norte is one of the best opportunities for trophy trout in Colorado. The Wolf Creek Ski Resort is nearby, but for more than 100 years the only thing missing from this outdoors haven was golf. This problem was solved in 2001 with the opening of the Rio Grande Club. It's a long way from the Denver area, but anyone who makes the 4-hour drive here and plays the Rio Grande Club will become hooked. Nature, solitude, great views, and world-class golf make this a must-play destination.

Dalton Ranch in Durango is open mid-March through November 1, but it doesn't close because of snow and cold. It closes because the elk, up to 1,000 of them, descend on the golf course at the first indication of hunting season. The staff has to protect the golf course by fencing the greens and laying tarps on them.

RIO GRANDE CLUB

THE GOLF As the twentieth century drew to a close, developers cleared the long-horns off the Bar BR Ranch and Redstone's Ric Buckton went to work placing fairways along the Rio Grande River and up in the higher terrain that borders the Rio Grande National Forest and Alder Creek.

Buckton's design measures 7,155 from the tips and has 7.5 miles of cart path winding through towering ponderosa pines, scrub oak, and aspens. The layout offers Rio Grande River access for fishing and outstanding views at every turn.

No. 1 involves an 80-foot tee-shot drop to the fairway and a stone wall complete with chimney-rock formation running down the entire right side. The next few holes are traditional golf in an open meadow, passing only wetlands and ponds before reaching the stretch of Rio Grande that's part of the club. Holes 3 through 8 dance along the spectacular river.

The par-3, 193-yard No. 6 is a favorite, requiring a forced carry over the rambling waters. The 14th might be the best photo opportunity, with Alder Creek encircling the green 207 yards away. The par-5 ender plays 572 yards downhill. The green is guarded by a 2.5-acre lake and it is tough to hit if you draw a downhill lie.

The San Juan Mountains provide the backdrop for the massive, log-cabin styled clubhouse, which includes a dining room and lounge, spa and fitness facilities, conference rooms, business center, pro shop and locker rooms, and anything else you might expect out of one of Colorado's best golf facilities.

Golf Digest named the Rio Grande Club as No. 6 on its list of Best New Upscale Public Courses for 2003, even though it actually opened nine holes in 2001.

THE DETAILS 719-873-1995. 0285 Rio Grande Trail, South Fork, CO 81154.
- www.riograndeclub.com
- Ric Buckton, Redstone, 2001. 18 holes. Par 72. Black - 7,155 (72.1/133). White - 6,433 (69.4/125). Gold - 5,872 (67.1/117). Red - 5,367 (NR). Private, but currently open to the public. Price - $$$.

GETTING THERE Take Hwy. 160 from either Pagosa Springs or Del Norte. In the middle of South Fork turn right on Hwy. 149 toward Creede. Go 1 mile, and just across the Rio Grande River, turn right and drive 1 mile. Next to the BAR BR red barn is a clubhouse sign; the clubhouse is up the hill.

I first came to Vail in 1968 to do golf clinics with Dick Hauserman and it was just a small town and the Vail Valley area was sparsely populated. We think this golf course will do wonders for Eagle—it's very important for the public golfers to have a place in this area.—Arnold Palmer on his Eagle Ranch design

SOUTH CENTRAL

SOUTH FORK NOTES

Laid-back and free of traffic jams, South Fork is loaded with summer recreational opportunities including fishing, hiking, camping, biking, and everything else imaginable. The **Silver Thread Scenic Byway** begins at South Fork, continues through Wagon Wheel Gap and Creede, and ends at Lake City. The byway goes through the Rio Grande National Forests and you can see parts of the LaGarita, Weminuche, and Powderhorn Wilderness areas. Just up the road toward Creede is one of the most impressive geological wonders in the world—**Wheeler Geological Area**. Teddy Roosevelt thought the place was so special he asked the founding fathers of the National Park Service and Forest Service to always keep it remote. Pre-round flapjacks are served at the **Hungry Logger** (719-873-5504), and there is also a lunch and dinner menu. High-toned types head towards the **Chalet Swiss** (719-873-1100) for wine, cheese fondue, and international and Alpine cuisine; however the rowdy **Croaker's Saloon** caters to the roving golfer with pool tables, live music, and cold, cold beers. Don't miss a stay at the incredible **Apple Dumpling B&B Inn** (www.appledumplingbandb.com, 888-873-7583)—nestled against Beaver Mountain just 200 yards from the Rio Grande National Forest, the inn offers packages for golf, fishing, and much more. And the **Arbor House Inn B&B** (888-830-4642) overlooks the South Fork of the Rio Grande and is across from the Chalet Swiss restaurant.

WESTCLIFFE

ELEV 8,000 POP 453

Westcliffe started out as a railroad town not far from Silver Cliff, which was a booming mining town when the Denver and Rio Grande Railroad arrived. The miners came to Custer County in the early 1870s looking for gold, but found mostly silver in the Rosita and Querida area, east of Westcliffe in the Wet Mountains. At one point, Silver Cliff was the third-largest town in Colorado; today the area is dotted with ghost towns and abandoned mines. Sandwiched between the San Isabel and Rio Grande National Forests, Westcliffe is remote, beautiful, relatively unknown, and boondocks excursion.

ST. ANDREWS AT WESTCLIFFE

THE GOLF A "primitive" golf experience (someone once said that cows and realtors outnumber residents here), St. Andrews at Westcliffe is a 9-holer that's famous for its extremely small greens and spectacular views of the Sangre de Cristo Mountains. The drought of 2002 destroyed the greens, but the replant-

---

Jay Morrish, born in Grand Junction, was instrumental in the design of Castle Pines Golf Club while working on Jack Nicklaus' design team.

ing was such a success that the whole town had a celebration. Aside from the extra carry due to altitude, expect big, crazy bounces on the baked-out fairways.

Originally built by a wealthy golfer who wanted the course for his buddies to play, the course was purchased recently by Craig Walker, who has ambitions of expanding the route to 18 holes.

THE DETAILS 719-783-9410. 800 Copper Gulch Road, Westcliffe, CO 81252.
  • John Manson, 1989. 9 holes. Par 35. White/Blue - 5,488 (65/119). Women's White/Blue - 5,507 (71/133). Red/White - 4,947 (68/126) Price - $.

GETTING THERE In Westcliffe go 3 miles north on Hwy. 69 and turn right on Copper Gulch Rd.

WESTCLIFFE NOTES

Plan your golf trip here around "Jazz in the Sangres"—a music festival that takes place in Westcliffe every summer, and drive the **Frontier Pathways Scenic & Historic Byway** on your way to Westcliffe and discover an old frontier zone that marks travels of Native Americans, Spanish, French, and American territories. The Utes arrived first, followed by European explorers, ranchers, traders, trappers, homesteaders, and prospectors. Despite the limited summer hours for some of the restaurants, Westcliffe has an impressive array of dining options for such a small town. Sit-down meals can be found at **The Alpine Lodge** (719-783-2660), which also has rustic two-bedroom cabins, the **Oak Creek Grade General Store & Steakhouse** (719-783-2245), or **Morgan's** (719-783-3399), which has a wall of windows overlooking the mountains. Nearby lies the town of Rosita and the **Letter Drop Inn** (719-783-9430), a cozy spot that serves wild game. Other than The Alpine Lodge, look for accommodations at the **Main Street Inn B&B** (877-783-4006).

WOODLAND PARK

ELEV 8,465 POP. 6,953

Known as The City Above the Clouds, Woodland Park is 18 miles from Colorado Springs on the way to Cripple Creek. It was born in 1891 along a broad, high plateau at the junction of Ute Pass, and has a spectacular "backside"

Castle Pines is one of the top three courses on tour condition-wise. I love playing Jack Nicklaus golf courses, so I love this course and I think he is a great designer. Even at this altitude, the 7,500 yards can still play short, but it ranks with Muirfield and Augusta as the courses in top condition on the tour. Year in and year out the greens are great.—Ernie Els on Castle Pines Golf Club

view of Pikes Peak. Take it slow up here at the 8,465-foot altitude and enjoy the stunning views of the Pike National Forest.

SHINING MOUNTAIN GOLF CLUB

THE GOLF Formerly known as Woodland Park Fujiki Golf & Country Club, the name and ownership changed in 2001, jump-starting a transformation that has stunned those familiar with the course. Narrow fairways, thick natural rough, mountainous terrain, along with water on 12 holes, all harass struggling hacks.

Water and wind make the par-3 No. 17 one of the more difficult par 3s, shrinking the target 170 yards out.

Log Gulch runs across six holes on the front nine, which also involves wetlands and bunkers. The back nine has lots of elevation challenges and is a tough walk.

THE DETAILS 719-687-7587. 100 Lucky Lady Drive, Woodland Park, CO 80866.
- John Harbottle, 1995. 18 holes. Par 72. Black - 6,614 (71.2/135). Blue - 6,359 (70.7/131). White - 6,026 (69.1/126). Women's White - 6,099 (74.3/141). Red - 5,336 (69.6/126). Price - $$.

GETTING THERE From I-25 and US 24 (exit 141) take Hwy. 24 west to Woodland Park. Turn right onto Hwy. 67 (toward Deckers) and follow it north through town. The course is on the left near the outskirts of town.

WOODLAND PARK NOTES

Woodland Park has amenities, but weekenders should play golf at Shining Mountain and head to the town of **Cripple Creek**,—"The World's Greatest Gold Camp" that is home to several historic hotels and casinos and a National Historic District. In town though, overnight options include **Woodland Inn Bed & Breakfast** (719-687-8209) or **Country Inn** (719-687-6277). Locals will point you towards **Grandmother's Kitchen** (719-687-3118) for a home-style meal.

Trinidad-born artist Paul Milosevich is famous for golf art and did portraits of Ben Hogan, Nancy Lopez and Ben Crenshaw and the team portrait for the 1999 Ryder Cup.

SOUTHWEST

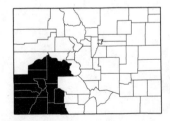

SOUTHWEST

Southwest Mileage

	Cedaredge	Cortez	Crested Butte	Delta	Durango	Gunnison	Ignacio	Mancos	Montrose	Pagosa Springs	Ridgeway
Cedaredge											
Cortez	188										
Crested Butte	80	227									
Delta	16	157	113								
Durango	151	45	199	129							
Gunnison	108	200	27	86	171						
Ignacio	174	68	222	152	27	194					
Mancos	186	10	233	164	35	206	58				
Montrose	44	135	92	22	107	64	130	142			
Pagosa Springs	211	105	221	189	60	194	51	95	96		
Ridgway	70	110	117	48	81	90	104	116	26	141	
Telluride	106	74	153	84	118	126	141	79	62	178	36

The true outdoorsman wants to get as far away from the big city as possible. Here in southwest Colorado happiness is a 50-mile hike in the Weminuche Wilderness munching on a deviled ham or dried-beef sandwich while taking on this ultimate challenge. Here on a lonely stretch of trail above the Continental Divide, where there is no Wal-Mart Super Center. You won't find a bag drop or a player's assistant to take care of your backpack.

A trail map, compass, and experienced guide are imperative since it's easy to get lost out here. After 50 miles on this trail a welcome sight comes into view—the massive Vallecito Lake—and you know your hike is almost done. Tonight you will dine in luxury in Durango. Tomorrow your vacation turns to golf at Dalton Ranch, Hillcrest, or the Glacier Club at Tamarron.

Organized civilizations have lived in Southwest Colorado for more than 1,000 years. The Anasazi, who built the amazing cliff dwellings at Mesa Verde National Park, wanted to live here forever. These farmers thrived until a drought probably caused them to scatter. Even the recent wildfires in the park couldn't destroy what these Native Americans built centuries ago.

Tourists from all over the world come to Southwest Colorado to explore mining ghost towns high in the San Juan Mountains on 4X4 vehicles. They come to look down into the Black Canyon of the Gunnison National Monument. They scale the Grand Mesa, the world's largest and highest flat-top mountain, and they find a region rich in Victorian architecture, western history, and Native American cultures. And they come to soak in the hot springs and ski at Crested Butte, Telluride, or Purgatory.

Durango, Gunnison, Telluride, Cortez, Pagosa Springs, or even Montrose make good home bases for exploring the area. Dalton Ranch and The Glacier Club at Tamarron in the Durango area are definite highlights. Press Maxwell's 1945 Conquistador Golf Course in Cortez is an old-school municipal, The Club at Crested Butte is upscale, pricey, and scenic, and Delta's Devil's Thumb is award-winning and strategic. Expensive and quirky golf can be found in Telluride and a no-frills experience awaits at Pagosa Springs Golf Club. And Ridgway's Fairway Pines is also a hidden gem.

Two high-profile projects are underway in the Southwest region. The Bridges at Black Canyon is a Steve Nicklaus design in Montrose. And the world's first synthetic turf 18-hole course is in the works in Mancos at Echo Basin Guest Ranch.

Southwest Colorado has golf, gold-medal fishing, rafting, hiking, horseback riding, four national forests, seven scenic byways, five major hot springs areas, three wilderness areas, one national monument and seven state parks and recreation areas. To get a sense of the terrain, take the Alpine Loop Back Country

Byway: 65 miles of spectacular scenery including glacial valleys, two 12,000-foot passes with the ghosts of mining days littered along historic, rugged pathways. Revisit the boom days of the late 1800s in rented 4-wheel-drive vehicles in Silverton, Ouray, or Lake City.

Another fun drive that captures the essence of the region is the 51-mile tour of the Grand Mesa area. It follows Colorado Highway 65 to I-70 between Mesa and Cedaredge going west along the Lands End Road (FDR 100) and across the top of Grand Mesa.

Don't miss the San Juan Skyway, either, through the San Juan National Forest, the Uncompahgre, Wilson, and Sneffels Range areas. The Silver Thread Scenic Byway goes through Creede, Lake City, and South Fork. And most of all, explore the Trail of the Ancients—it includes the Four Corners Monument and visits to all the ancient history that surrounds Mesa Verde National Park.

And if you are heading west from Four Corners it's only a short drive to Monument Valley, the spectacular land that straddles the Arizona and Utah state lines. Here, countless silver screen cowboys like John Wayne filmed dozens of shoot-`em-ups.

SOUTHWEST

CEDAREDGE

ELEV. 6,200 POP. 1,854

Cedaredge, Eckert, Cory, Austin and Orchard City make up this scenic area—known as the Surface Creek Valley—at the foot of The Grand Mesa with the San Juans lingering south. Tourists roll through for an area known as Pioneer Town, a cluster of turn-of-the-century buildings that provide a sense of what life was like for the pioneers of this area.

Golfers wandering this remote locale will run into a great little golf course on the sunny side of Grand Mesa—the 18-hole Deer Creek Village Golf Club.

DEER CREEK VILLAGE GOLF CLUB

THE GOLF Deer Creek serves up two distinct nines and four sets of tees at an elevation of 6,000 feet. Trees, water, and creek carries highlight the round in this master-planned golf community surrounded by fruit orchards and the foothills of the Grand Mesa. In years past the Colorado Golf Association has played its Western Chapter Championship here, and it's been home to the Colorado Women's Brassie Championship.

Deer Creek first opened as a 9-hole course with the creek dominating the route. Later the back nine was unveiled with elevation changes, scrub-oak-lined fairways, and water hazards. Most locals like No. 12, a 511-yard par five that rolls downhill with water cascading down the left side. Low handicappers must decide if they can carry the creek and go for it in two, while average hacks need to play it safe short of the water.

Landscaped berms help shield the golfer from the housing—a real plus in a course built among new houses.

THE DETAILS 970-856-7781. 500 S.E. Jay Avenue, Cedaredge, CO 81413.
- www.deercreekvillage-golf.com
- Bryan Coker, 1992. 18 holes. Par 72. Blue - 6,418 (70.1/128). White - 6,004 (68.3/123). Gold - 5,494 (65.9/114). Red - 5,077 (68.4/122). Price - $.

GETTING THERE Travel east 4 miles on Hwy. 92 out of Delta. Turn north on Hwy. 65 and go 11 miles to Jay Avenue, south of town.

The site for the Beaver Creek Golf Course can be described as dramatic and rugged Rocky Mountain terrain. While compact in size when compared with most golf course sites, the property presented an opportunity to create a strategic shot maker's golf course based upon precision and accuracy.—Robert Trent Jones Jr., on Beaver Creek Golf Club

SOUTHWEST

CEDAREDGE NOTES

The Divot overlooks the golf course and has patio dining, and other local eateries include **Berardi's** (970-856-7782) and **New Ponderosa** on Main Street. For lodging consider the **Howard Johnson Express Inn** (888-855-2700), which offers golf packages for Deer Creek Village Golf Club, or the **Cedar'sedge Llamas B&B** (970-856-6836) with its impressive 100-mile views. The **Grand Mesa Scenic Byway** (State Highway 65), leads from the valley to the top of Grand Mesa, the world's largest flat-top mountain. The Byway climbs from 5,000 feet to about 10,000 feet. Opportunities for fishing, hiking, sight-seeing, photography, and camping abound. In the fall hunters visit and in winter there's plenty of sledding, cross-country skiers, snowmobiling, and ice fishing. Lastly, the **Stoney Mesa Winery** (970-856-9463, www.stoneymesa.com) is set around an 1880s homestead and is one of the highest-altitude wineries in the U.S.

CORTEZ

ELEV. 6,201 POP. 7,977

Cortez, once called "Tsaya-toh" or rock-water by the Navajos for its spring, is one of the most unique Colorado outposts—not far from the Four Corners area and nine miles east of Mesa Verde National Park where the amazing Anasazi ruins were discovered. This part of Colorado is special, a rural ranching area influenced by archaeology and ancient spirits. As many as 100,000 Anasazi may have lived in the area, residing in unbelievable cliff-side homes that astound tourists. Thankfully golfers passing through can work in rounds at the Conquistador Golf Club while touring this amazing region.

CONQUISTADOR GOLF CLUB

THE GOLF Like the Four Corners area, Conquistador presents views of La Plata Peak, Mesa Verde, and Sleeping Ute Mountain. Located just 40 miles west of Durango, the Conquistador Golf Course is considered by many a traditional gem with flat fairways, trees, medium-sized greens, and testy water hazards. You'll notice that putts generally break toward the Mesa Verde range. Short approach shots aren't guaranteed to roll up to the green, as most of the putting surfaces are slightly raised.

Locals brag about its length, the quality roll of the bentgrass, and the fact that Notah Begay won his first tournament here—a junior event when he was seven.

I don't think it's the length of Broadmoor East, but it is the priority of hitting the greens in the right spots. Normally long is bad and short is good. The general rule is to keep the ball on the front part of the green with the flagstick between you and Cheyenne Mountain and you will have an easier putt.—Director of Golf Russ Miller of The Broadmoor

No. 3 stands out with a 203-yard carry over water to a green that is a small cigar-shaped target (more wide than deep), but this is a course full of quality holes.

THE DETAILS 970-565-9208. 2018 North Dolores, Cortez, CO 81321.
- Press Maxwell, 1945. 18 holes. Par 72. Gold - 6,963 (71.1/116). Blue - 6,637 (69.5/113). White - 6,207 (67.5/108). Red - 5,420 (69.3/121). Price - $.

GETTING THERE Take Hwy. 160 from Durango to Cortez. Turn right at North Dolores Road, and follow it 1 mile to the course (on right).

CORTEZ NOTES

Francisca's (970-565-4093) is a drop-in spot with outstanding enchiladas and homemade tortillas, the perfect warm-up for a visit to the popular **Main Street Brewery** (970-564-9112). **Nero's** (970-565-7366) serves solid Italian food, and **Homesteaders** (970-565-6253) is a popular breakfast place with traditional Western dishes for dinner. However, the best place to eat in Cortez is the **Dry Dock Restaurant** (970-564-9404), which specializes in seafood. **The Travelodge** (970-565-7778) is affordable and welcomes pets, but the unique **Kelly's Place B&B** (970-565-3125, www.kellyplace.com) has more character, including archaeological sites and ruins on the property, as well as horseback rides. And if post-round excursions lead to **Mesa Verde National Park**, consider the **Far View Lodge** (970-533-7731), the only lodging in the park and the starting point for tours of the ruins. Active types can take advantage of the terrain and mountain bike their rears off all throughout the Four Corners region. The slickrock canyon country and the prehistoric locales provide miles and miles of great trails.

CRESTED BUTTE   ELEV. 8,855 POP. 1,529

The Slate River runs here in this old mining town that is the closest thing to Switzerland in the U.S., completely surrounded by scenic wilderness and something travel writers recognized about this region back in the 1860s. The town is in the boondocks, and that's why tourists liked it once railroads and automobiles made it accessible. Today they come to fish, hike, camp, hang glide, enjoy the hot springs, gaze at the towering peaks, ride horses, mountain bike, ski in win-

---

The first permanent structure in Denver was a saloon.

ter, and play golf in summer. Crested Butte is the birthplace of mountain biking and is home of the Fat Tire Bike Week, the oldest bike festival in the world. The town is surrounded by mountain bike trails over scenic passes and is loaded with four-wheel-drive roads to old ghost towns.

THE CLUB AT CRESTED BUTTE

THE GOLF Originally named Skyland Country Club and designed by Robert Trent Jones Jr., this difficult course opened in 1984 and became known for its remote, back-country feel, with 12,162-foot Mount Crested Butte and its towering gray peaks dominating the landscape. The Elk Mountains, Mount Baldy, and Mount Bellview provide more spectacular views. The design features over 80 cloverleaf bunkers accented against tall native grasses, and the route is flat on the front nine, but becomes a bit more mountainous with elevation changes on the back.

The signature hole is the par-4 No. 13, significant because of its 9,003-foot elevation tee box. The hole rolls 450+ yards and you'll be able to see every inch of it from the tee, as drives hang in the air for eternities before they fall into the fairway lined by tall grass on the right and a series of bunkers on the left.

Recently investors spent more than $1 million on capital improvements to the clubhouse, maintenance facility, driving range, and golf course.

THE DETAILS 970-349-6131. 385 Country Club Drive, Crested Butte, CO 81224.
- www.theclubatcrestedbutte.com
- Robert Trent Jones, Jr., 1984. 18 holes. Par 72. Black - 7,208 (73.0/133). Blue - 6,635 (70.4/126). White - 6,355 (68.8/120). Women's White - 6,368 (75.0/145). Red - 5,702 (71.3/135). Price - $$$$.

GETTING THERE Located 28 miles north of Gunnison on Hwy. 135. Watch for the golf course sign and turn right (west), 2 miles south of Crested Butte.

CRESTED BUTTE NOTES

Soak up the character of the town by exploring Elk Avenue, Crested Butte's main street, where you'll find quaint shops, all kinds of restaurants and bars, and leads for how to go about planning your fishing, hiking, mountain biking, four-wheel drive ghost town adventures. Early morning coffee and huevos rancheros make the ideal pre-golf routine at the **Paradise Café** (970-349-6233). After golf look to the **Wooden Nickel** (970-349-6350), Crested Butte's oldest bar and meeting place, where elk tenderloin is a spe-

Many people don't know that we had a head pro once, Ed Dudley, who spent his summers here and winters as head pro at Augusta National.—Russ Miller, The Broadmoor.

cialty. And **Donita's Cantina** (970-349-6674) is a long-standing Butte tradition, along with the **Idle Spur and Crested Butte Brewery & Pub** (970-349-5026). The town also boasts the more high-toned **Le Bosquet** (970-349-5808) and **Bacchanale** (970-349-5257), both dining traditions since the 1970s. The newer **Buffalo Grille & Saloon** (970-349-9699) is upscale, healthy, and delicious. Golfers are best-served lodging-wise by staying in town instead of out on the slopes. **Cristiana Guesthaus B&B** (800-824-7899) is a cozy place to stay with a lobby that includes a stone fireplace and outdoor hot tub with mountain views. The **Elk Mountain Lodge** (970-349-7533), **Purple Mountain Lodge** (970-349-5888; gourmet breakfasts), and the **Old Town Inn** (970-349-6184) are all affordable and comfortable.

DELTA

ELEV. 4,953 POP. 6,400

Situated at the confluence of the Uncompahgre and Gunnison Rivers, desert-like Delta has a mild, dry climate and is surrounded by plateaus, mountains, rivers, orchards, and ranches.

Settled in 1830 by a French trapper who built a fort, Delta's countless recreational opportunities include open trails through spectacular country, best experienced via horseback or by hiking. Situated on the Western Slope of the Great Divide of the Rocky Mountains near the Sweitzer State Recreation Area, Needle Rock, and the Black Canyon of the Gunnison, this area is an outdoorsman's dream. Hunting and fishing have long been popular pastimes, and the opening of the Devil's Thumb Golf Course has created an off-the-beaten path locale for wayfaring golfers.

DEVIL'S THUMB GOLF COURSE

THE GOLF Award-winning Devil's Thumb Golf Course is no-frills golf at its best. Designer Rick Phelps says its strength is the site and the strategy that is built into the design.

It has been called a 7,176-yard moonscape, and in 2002 *Golf Digest* named the course its No. 2 Best New Affordable Public Golf Course in America. Devil's Thumb was an instant hidden gem mainly because of its off-the-beaten-path location, 41 miles down U.S. 50 from Grand Junction and Interstate 70. With spectacular views of the San Juan and West Elk Mountains and the Grand Mesa, this new layout is still waiting to be discovered.

Golfers need to think before immediately recognizing correct landing areas from the tees. No. 9, a par 4 of 436 yards, might be the best example. Two fair-

---

When John Elway arrived in Denver to play quarterback for the Broncos he asked Inverness' Tom Babb for help with his game. Babb also hosted Bill Clinton for a round of golf.

way bunkers protect the sides of the fairway that bends to the right. Drives too far right could find a pond; however, a fade puts you in the best position to execute the approach, which must carry the stream that fronts the green.

Devil's Thumb's beauty is unique, and not typical of other scenic Colorado tracks. The northeast view displays the Adobe Hills, which resemble the moon's surface. All told, this might be one of the truest desert-style courses you'll find in Colorado. In the Spring of 2004, an old-fashioned barn-raising was held by locals to begin construction on the new clubhouse.

THE DETAILS 970-874-6262. 968 1560 Drive, Delta, CO 81416.
- Rick Phelps, 2001. 18 holes. Par 72. Black - 7,176 (72.6/126). Gold - 6,750 (70.4/124). Blue - 6,190 (67.6/123). Silver - 5,686 (65.6/112). Green - 5,180 (69.1/109). Price - $$.

GETTING THERE Take Hwy. 50 south to Delta. Take 1575 north 2 miles to 1560, then go west one mile.

DELTA NOTES

Delta has two dining options of note: **The Stockyard** (970-874-4222) is a popular place for breakfast, and the **Fireside Inn** (970-874-4413) offers steaks and is the best spot for a night on the town. **Golf packages** are available for Devil's Thumb at the **Holiday Inn** (970-243-6790). Overnighters can also look to the **Escalante Guest Ranch** (970-874-4121, www.escalanteranch.com), which has remote cabins, a guest house, and plenty of places to fish, hike, canoe, hunt, and take in the wildlife scene. Dinosaurs once roamed here at the **Dry Mesa Quarry**, a spot that some refer to as one of the world's most significant paleological sites. And **Fort Uncompahgre** (970-874-8349) was built in the early 1800s by fur trader Antione Robidoux, and offers an interesting look back at the old days.

DURANGO
ELEV. 6,523 POP. 13,922

In 1879 the railroad town of Durango was designed to be the most modern city in Colorado. Signs of progress began to appear everywhere in the late 1880s and early 1890s, including the four-story brick Strater Hotel, electric lights with a home-owned electric company, telephones, an electric trolley, and the Newman Building, a three-story structure with an electric elevator. Surrounded

---

Golda Meir, future Israeli prime minister, attended Denver's North High School.

by the San Juan Mountains, reddish, sandstone bluffs, and boasting a thriving Main Street and a National Register Historic District, today's bustling Durango has a macho feel—a frontier western town created by the railroad with lots of character.

Durango is truly a year-round place to play. You can ski in the winter at Purgatory and do just about everything else in the summer: fly fish, take jeep tours, hike, mountain bike, take glider rides, go rafting, play tennis, go for a horseback ride, or play golf at one or all of Durango's three outstanding courses.

DALTON RANCH GOLF CLUB

THE GOLF Located six miles north of Durango, Dalton Ranch was designed by Ken Dye, who utilized the red cliffs of the surrounding San Juan Mountains, the Animas River, and the course-side Durango & Silverton Narrow Gauge Railroad to create an impressive golf experience.

Dye, whose firm Finger, Dye and Spann of Houston also authored New Mexico gems Paa-Ko Ridge and Piñon Hills, moved 800,000 cubic yards of dirt and created abundant mounds spread throughout the course. Typical of Dye courses, many greens are elevated and have significant drops to the bunkers, a tough challenge for approach shots.

Afternoon rounds are highlighted by the sunset glowing off the cliffs and the Animas River. The par-5 16th hole displays this scene, and is the perfect warm-up for the final two holes. Finish the day with a 308-yarder at No. 17 that bends for a nice draw along the river, then play precise on the 18th, a 408-yard beauty. Too much of a hook on 18 finds the river, while too much slice finds a question-mark-shaped lake that surrounds the right side of the green and continues behind it.

In the summer of 2002 the Missionary Ridge and Valley fires rolled through 70,000 acres of surrounding forest; one national news photo showed a Dalton Ranch mower rolling down the fairway with smoke and flames visible in the distance over his shoulder.

THE DETAILS 970-247-8774. 589 County Road 252, Durango, CO 81301.
- www.daltonranch.com
- Ken Dye, 1993. 18 holes. Par 72. Black - 6,934 (72.2/132). Gold - 6,394 (69.7/122). Silver - 5,982 (67.6/115). White - 5,539 (71.1/133). Price - $$$.

Douglas Fairbanks was expelled from Denver's East High before becoming one of the most famous silent movie stars of all time.

GETTING THERE From Durango, take Hwy. 550 north for 6 miles, and find the course sign on the right side of the road.

THE GLACIER CLUB AT TAMARRON

THE GOLF Originally named The Cliffs at Tamarron, this majestic setting is surrounded by the towering Hermosa Cliffs rising 3,000 feet in the blue southwestern Colorado sky. Since the resort is also 1,300 feet above Durango, the temperatures are 10 degrees cooler than the city, 18 miles away.

Tamarron Properties recently purchased the 750-acre resort, formerly owned by Sheraton. All the hotel rooms are perched on a cliff facing the layout and sport huge picture windows that urge you to pull up a chair with a cold beverage and observe the scenery and golf.

Troon Golf manages the golf operation, which includes a brand-new Todd Schoeder-designed Glacier Nine set to open in the summer of 2004 along with a new 20,000-square-foot clubhouse. The original nines are now called the Cliffs Nine and Hermosa Nine. The Glacier Nine will be totally private, but resort guests can still play the original layout.

The scenery is spectacular, with the San Juan National Forest, gambel oaks, ponderosa pines, bluegrass fairways, and strategic lakes and bunkers. The new nine has six pine-lined fairways followed by three final holes that feature neck-straining views of the cliffs, just east of the original layout.

The original 18 begins with a 200-yard layup, then the fairway drops through a natural area. A lake guards the left and a massive bunker collects anything short. The view from behind the lake is an impressive site and worth the time for a photo.

No. 7 is known as "Cliffhanger" and rolls a long 440 yards. A precise draw about 225 yards out is ideal for position at the end of a cliff looking down at the hole. Anything less than perfect gives you a blind approach, making this the most controversial hole on the layout.

Note that the original 18 is set for retooling, including new irrigation system, new cart paths, revamped bunkers, and landscaping. A new practice facility is also on the drawing board.

THE DETAILS 970-382-6700. 40292 U.S. Hwy. 550, Durango, CO 81301.
- www.theglacierclub.com; www.lodgeattamarron.com
- Arthur Hills, 1975. 18 holes. Par 72. Gold - 6,885 (73.3/144). Silver - 6,330 (70.8/139). Red - 5,334 (70.6/124). Price - $$$$.
- New Glacier 9, Todd Schoeder of Design Workshop, Denver, 2004. Private 9, no resort guests.

The Colorado Rockies opened on April 9, 1993 before 80,277 fans, the most to ever witness an opening game in baseball history.

GETTING THERE From Durango, take Hwy. 550 north for 18 miles to the course and resort, and look for the entrance on the right side of the highway.

HILLCREST GOLF CLUB

THE GOLF The Hillcrest Golf Club is located on a small mesa just next door to the Fort Lewis College campus above Durango with views of the city and the La Plata Mountains. A privately owned course that is open to the public, Hillcrest is popular (65,000 rounds annually) because of its superb condition, affordable fees, family environment, and outstanding greens.

The Navajo Trail Open is staged here each year and in 2002 the PGA Tour's Notah Begay III finished in the top five. Hillcrest members take pride in their facility, with more than $2.5 million invested since 1981 and more than $500,000 recently, including a 2,000-square foot addition to the clubhouse.

THE DETAILS 970-247-1499. 2300 Rim Drive, Durango, CO 81301.
- Frank Hummel, 1969. 18 holes. Par 71. Black - 6,838 (71.2/125). Blue - 6,399 (69.1/118). Gold - 5,996 (67.2/114). White - 5,252 (67.9/121). Price - $$.

GETTING THERE Hillcrest is just across from Fort Lewis College. From Hwy. 550 go south to 6th, then east for 2 miles. At the top of the hill turn left and follow the road to the clubhouse.

DURANGO NOTES

After skiing or golf, grab a beer and some nachos at the **Cactus Cantina at the Glacier Club**, where you'll find Mexican dishes made to order and a picnic deck overlooking the golf course. It's best to get a reservation if you want to dine at Durango's Victorian-styled **Cyprus Café** (970-385-6884), where Mediterranean dishes appeal to the more experienced taste buds. Also consider the **Aspen Café** (970-259-8025) or **Carver's Bakery Café** (970-259-2545). **Lady Falconburgh's Barley Exchange** (970-382-9664) is a favorite local watering hole with every beer imaginable. The **Strater Hotel** (800-247-4431) was first built in 1887 and offers 93 Victorian-styled rooms. When Louis L'Amour, the western novelist visited, he always asked for the room directly above the **Diamond Belle Saloon**, Room 222, because the honky-tonk music helped set the mood for his novels of the Old West. Some say a good part of his Sackett's novels were written at the Strater, and the Belle still packs them in today. Another historic pick is the 1888 **Jarvis Suite Hotel** (970-259-6190), with 22 suites and on the National Register of Historic places. The **Apple Orchard Inn** (800-426-

Before the Snowmass re-make it was a nicely soft layout, but the new one will borderline on dramatic. It will be a radical change.—Jim Engh on his redesign at Snowmass

0751) is another popular choice. Ride the **Durango-Silverton Narrow Gauge Railroad** (888-872-4607) and revisit the Old West days when coal and steam powered the railroads. The trip takes you past sheer cliffs, criss-crossing the Animas River on its 45-mile trip to Silverton. Whitewater raft or fish in the Animas River, and consider a mountain-bike tour of the countryside. Check out **Mountain Bike Specialists** (970-247-4066), **Mountain Waters Rafting Inc.** (970-259-4191), **San Juan Outfitting** (970-259-6259), or **Duranglers** (970-385-4081) for outfitting services. **Vallecito Lake**, located 23 miles northwest of Durango in the San Juan National Forest, is a fisherman's paradise, and campers love the views. The **Vallecito** and **Pine River Trails** are gateways to the enormous **Weminuche Wilderness**.

GUNNISON

ELEV. 7,703 POP. 5,409

Named after a topographer who was mapping a railroad route to the Pacific in 1853 (Captain John W. Gunnison), Gunnison has become an ideal outdoors getaway. The Gunnison River area features more than 1.7 million acres of public land that offer nature in pristine abundance: sheer canyon walls, green lakes, stately peaks, and meadows full of wildflowers. Early inhabitants included the Ute Indians, ranchers, and miners, with the railroad bringing in many more pioneers.

Blue Mesa Reservoir, with 96 miles of shoreline, is a short drive from Gunnison within the Curecanti National Recreation Area. The Gunnison National Forest has more than 750 miles of trout streams and reservoirs. Also close by is the Aberdeen Quarry, which operated from 1889 to 1892 and supplied the stone for Denver's capitol. Thirty miles east is the Alpine Tunnel, which is now abandoned, accessible only via off-road vehicle. This tunnel bore through the Continental Divide at 11,523 feet, making it the highest railroad station in the country. Another great drive is the West Elk Scenic Byway through Almont and 30 miles north to Crested Butte. Needless to say, the charm and history of the town, along with the plentitude of outdoor activities, ensures that there's something for everyone in Gunnison.

DOS RIOS GOLF CLUB

THE GOLF Just south of Gunnison, Dos Rios Country Club features a beautiful-but-tight course that incorporates the natural landscape and intertwines with the tree-lined Gunnison River. The front nine was designed by John Cochran and the newer back nine by Dick Phelps. Dos Rios, or "Two Rivers," is a fitting

---

At this altitude, the ball goes farther, and off line shots also go farther, so we wanted to have wide fairways to help keep players on the course and not in the junk. —Tom Lehman on The Raven Golf Club at Three Peaks

name since this par-72, 6,566-yard course has water on 17 holes.

The scenic No. 13 is the most interesting hole, rolling 527 yards with water 290 yards off the tee. The second shot is a layup to a small area with the river crossing in front of the green and a cliff backdrop. Watch for marmots who might be searching for your golf ball.

THE DETAILS 970-641-1482. 501 Camino Del Rio, Gunnison, CO 81230.
- John Cochran, front nine, 1964. Brad Benz, Dick Phelps, back nine. 1980. 18 holes. Par 72. Blue - 6,566 (69.4/127). White - 6,044 (67.2/119). Red - 5,455 (69.4/125). Price - $$$.

GETTING THERE Take Hwy. 50 west from Gunnison. Cross the river and look for signs to the golf course on the left.

GUNNISON NOTES

The 1885 **Mary Lawrence Inn** (970-641-3343) has been renovated and is a great overnight option, and the **Inn at Rockhouse Ranch** (www.innatrockhouse.com, 888-641-0601)) is a restored 1904 stone home set on 1,000 private acres in the scenic Ohio Creek Valley. Fish the private section of Ohio Creek or try the hiking, biking, and horseback riding. Scenic drives abound around Gunnison, including US 50 west towards the 207-mile **West Elk Loop Scenic and Historic Byway**, as well as the road trip to the **Inn at Arrowhead** (970-862-8206, www.arrowheadinn.net), a remote, rustic lodge that requires a trip through **Blue Creek Canyon** to get there. The long-time Gunnison tradition is **The Trough Restaurant** (970-641-3724), where trout and wild game are on the menu along with live music on the weekends. Other dining options are **Backyard BBQ** (970-642-0200), **Cafe Silvestre** (970-641-4001), or **Katie's Cookery** (970-641-1958) is down-home, serving meals in a Mediterranean villa-style house built in 1938.

IGNACIO

ELEV. 6,420 POP. 669

The back roads southeast of Durango lead to the remote golf outpost of Ignacio, a town that was established in the 1870s at the southern end of the Pine River Valley. Home to the Mouache and Capote bands of the Southern Ute Indian tribe, the town was named after a Ute tribal chief. It's also home to a little nine-hole golf course that know one knows about.

There is nothing that I have ever played like this golf course. It is unique fun golf. I pushed the envelope a bit, but all of my courses do that. I would have liked to have done more like this at Red Hawk Ridge.—Jim Engh on Sanctuary

HUNTER'S RUN GOLF COURSE

THE GOLF Hunter's Run is charming, noted for its difficult 3,200-yard route as well as for being the only course in Colorado with redwood trees. Course owner and manager Robert Hardaway, who also designed the course, is a Colorado State University graduate (turf management degree) and is well qualified to serve as the course superintendent. His background includes working as a construction boss and superintendent for Wadsworth Brothers, who, Hardaway says, built two-thirds of all the Nicklaus courses. He's done the same work for designer Tom Weiskopf, and his experience shows.

The track's difficulty comes from lots of water, pesky trees, and small greens. Piñon and juniper are natural on the course, but Hardaway has also planted ponderosa pines, Austrian pines, and some aspen that combine to add some nice aesthetics to the course.

THE DETAILS 970-884-9785. 8400 Highway 172, Ignacio, CO 81337.
- Robert Hardaway, 1997. 9 holes. Par 36. 3,200 yards. Not rated. Price - $.

GETTING THERE From Durango take Hwy. 172 south 12 miles to Ignacio.

IGNACIO NOTES

Ignacio hosts the annual **Iron Horse Motorcycle Rally**, but most visitors come here for the **Sky Ute Lodge & Casino** (www.skyutecasino.com, 888-842-4180) or fishing at **Navajo Lake**. The casino has a hotel, outdoor swimming pool, the **Rolling Thunder Cafe**, and **Pino Nuche Restaurant**, making Ignacio the "Little Las Vegas" of southwest Colorado. Those who are unenthralled by the Indian casino scene can always find fun in Durango just 12 miles up the road.

MANCOS

ELEV. 7,040 POP. 1,119

Surrounded by mountains and rangeland, Mancos sits at 7,000 feet and offers a variety of outdoor recreational activities. The town was founded in 1894 near the site where early Spanish explorers first crossed the Mancos River.

The Mancos Valley is surrounded by the La Plata Mountains on one side and

---

This might sound a little crazy, but we want it to look as natural as possible even though the focus is on synthetic turf. Where the turf ends, we will have waste bunkers in low areas, wild grasses along the fairway borders and pine straw spread through the ponderosas. —Designer Matt Rauh V on Echo Basin Golf Club in Mancos, the world's first 18-hole synthetic turf golf course

the ancient cliffs of Mesa Verde on the other. Just south of Mancos through Weber Canyon is the eastern boundary of Mesa Verde National Park, where you can enjoy an old-fashioned, horse-drawn stage line run by the Bartels family. Hovenweep National Monument, 40 miles west, features unique Anasazi ruins, and you can venture to Jackson Gulch Reservoir for fishing, Mancos State Park for mountain biking, and the Echo Basin Golf Club to work in your hacks.

ECHO BASIN GOLF CLUB

THE GOLF When Dan Bjorkman bought Echo Basin Ranch in 1997, everyone told him the dude ranch didn't have enough water for an 18-hole golf course. But his vision was clear—combine a place where you can ride horses, fish, hike, enjoy summer concerts, explore the history of the area, and play the great game of golf.

When Bjorkman's nephew, Matt Rauh V, became the Western Slope dealer for TourTurf by FieldTurf, a light bulb went off. Why not build the world's first 18-hole synthetic turf golf course?

The first nine holes were scheduled for completion in the summer of 2003 but ironically, too much rain and a dock strike in New York gave the owners enough negative vibes to put off laying carpet until 2004. Two semis loaded with the carpet were scheduled to head west in the fall, but everyone thought cold weather was imminent and the glue might not bond well enough.

Rauh has designed what he calls a target-style layout through ponderosa pines and gambel oaks. The par-72, 7,250-yard layout starts at an elevation of 7,200 feet and climbs to 8,100 feet. The views include Star Mountain, Hesperus Peak, Shark's Tooth, Mesa Verde, and the San Juan Mountains.

Teeing areas will be small, but players should able to stick a tee into the turf just like real grass. And even though golfers won't take a divot, hitting down on the ball produces backspin, enabling shots to hit the greens and stop. The artificial blades of grass are filled with a rubber-like material called "Nike grind" that's made from ground-up tennis shoes.

The logistics of building the course are incredible. All told, it will take 1.4 million square feet of TourTurf, 12 million pounds of silica sand, 800,000 pounds of Nike grind, 12,000 tons of base material, and 25,000 tons of choke stone to finish the final 18 holes.

THE DETAILS 800-426-1890 or 970-533-7000. Not yet open.

Echo Basin Golf Club in Mancos, the world's first 18-hole synthetic turf golf course, will have 1.4 million square feet of TourTurf, 12 million pounds of silica sand, 800,000 pounds of Nike Grind, 12,000 tons of base material, and 25,000 tons of choke stone. Truck loads will come in stages. TourTurf will be rolled out just like carpet hole-by-hole. Silica sand will be stored in silos.

GETTING THERE From Cortez, head 15 miles east on Hwy. 160. After passing through Mancos, drive another 2.5 miles east until you see the large blue and white Echo Basin Ranch sign. Turn left on Echo Basin Road. Drive 3.5 miles to the ranch entrance.

MANCOS NOTES

The **Echo Basin Guest Ranch** (www.echobasin.com, 800-426-1890) offers much more than the world's first 18-hole synthetic turf golf course. Horseback riding and fishing are available. The staff can even schedule families for 1880s-style stagecoach rides with **Mancos Valley Stage Coach Tours**. **Cortez** and **Durango** (also golf towns) are nearby with more cititied amenities, and the fine pleasures of tribal gaming can be had south of Cortez at the **Ute Mountain Casino** (970-565-8800). To the east lies the town of Hesperus, (Pop. 75), home to the **Kennebec Café** (970-247-5674), which resides in the former 1940s Canyon Motel and offers Mediterranean-Mexican fares. Craft shops like the **Bounty Hunter** (970-533-7215) offer leather goods, cowboy gear, and other interesting items.

MONTROSE

ELEV. 5,806 POP. 12,344

Montrose serves as headquarters for the San Juan Skyway and the Ridgway State Recreation Area, a spot that offers great fishing on the Gunnison, San Miguel, and Dolores Rivers. Looks skyward are rewarded with views of golden eagles, prairie falcons, red-tailed hawks, and great horned owls that live here. Every road out of Montrose leads to an entertaining day-trip. Visit the Ute Indian Museum, the Black Canyon of the Gunnison National Park, or take a raft trip through the steep canyons. The Curecanti National Recreation Area created a series of dams that altered the Gunnison River's course. And the beauty of golf in Montrose is that the mild climate often allows for golf 10 months of the year.

BLACK CANYON GOLF CLUB AT MONTROSE

THE GOLF Now known as the Black Canyon Golf Club at Montrose, the former Montrose Golf Club features two differing nines and an affordable day of entertaining golf. The parkland front nine serves up hills and mature trees along with

---

At Jim Engh's new Snowmass Club the bunker complexes will be penal even if you aren't in them. "You probably will have a tough sidehill lie if you aren't in the bunker," Engh said. "They are linear with lots of shape, gnarly noses and small bottoms."

water and out-of-bounds. The back nine has more of a links feel with smaller greens guarded by deep bunkers.

Frequent players enjoy No. 9, a 310-yard par 4 that requires an accurate drive into a fairway that bends left. The second stroke plays to an open green protected by a bunker right and water left.

THE DETAILS 970-249-4653. 1350 Birch Street, Montrose, CO 81401.
- www.blackcanyongolf.com
- Joe Francese, 1959. 18 holes. Par 70. Blue - 6,246 (68.1/123). White - 6,042 (67.2/121). Women's White - 6,028 (72.5/127). Men's Senior - 5,617 (65.5/113). Red - 5,510 (68.1/118). Price - $.

GETTING THERE From Hwy. 50, head south on Hillcrest 6 miles to Birch. From Hwy. 550, head southeast on 12th to Hillcrest, and east to Birch.

THE BRIDGES AT BLACK CANYON

THE GOLF Slated to open in 2004, The Bridges at Black Canyon is a Steve Nicklaus design with Jon Garner as design associate. According to Garner: "The course design is centered around lakes and natural marshes and streams. Strong bunkering punctuates the natural features and leads The golfer on a memorable journey. Landscaping involves indigenous species of pine, spruce, ash, cottonwoods, as well as an array of natural shrubs and grasses. All of the lots that border the course will have excellent views of the course and the maintained turf limits will border the backyards. This will create a lush and expansive feeling for the homeowner. The Bridges at Black Canyon will have numerous wooden bridges with a unique rope rail treatment. The course will have a one-of-a-kind look that will identify and separate itself from other courses set in mountain communities."

Black Canyon's superintendent is Joe Distefano, who served at the Telluride Golf Course the past 13 years and also worked at Castle Pines. He will oversee the course's state-of-the-art irrigation system that takes water from the Loutsenhizer Canal, fed by Blue Mesa Reservoir. A 7,089-yard, par-71 route, The Bridges will include 11 lakes, a waterfall, 17 holes with water features, and plenty of bridges.

THE DETAILS 877-546-4653. 2500 Ogden Drive, Montrose, CO 81402.
- www.montrosebridges.com
- Steve Nicklaus, 2004. 18 holes. Par 71. Not yet rated. Price - $$$.

The Denver Open was first played in 1947 at Cherry Hills County Club and was won by Lew Worsham, who also won the US Open that same year.

GETTING THERE From Montrose take 550 or South Townsend to Ogden Drive. Head east 1 mile and follow the signs. From Ogden turn left and there is a short jog in the road.

THE LINKS AT COBBLE CREEK

THE GOLF The Links at Cobble Creek offers fun golf without the crowds in a pastoral setting where red barns, haystacks, and cornfields are framed against the mountain views.

The majestic San Juan Mountains provide the backdrop for a pleasing golf experience, with seven lakes and various creeks giving the track some character and bite. The water is needed to spice up the route, since the greens are large and there aren't many trees.

No. 6 is a short 262-yard par 4, with water in front of the green and out-of-bounds looming near, yet it's a birdie hole unless your mind really wanders. Another nice hole measures 608 yards, tempting macho big hitters to go for it in two.

Originally just a quaint 9-holer, the course opened its long-awaited back nine in September 2003 with the unusual layout of three par 3s, three par 4s, and three par 5s. It was worth the wait, according to the original homeowners, who patiently waited 14 years for the unveiling of the new back nine.

THE DETAILS 970-240-9542. 699 Cobble Drive, Montrose, CO 81401.
- www.cobblecreek.com
- Craig Cherry Inc./Pinnacle Golf, 1999. 18 holes. Par 72. Gold - 6,682 (71.2/126). Blue - 6,214 (68.8/121). White - 5,600 (65.6/112). Red - 5,100 (67.8/113). Price - $.

GETTING THERE Take Hwy. 550 south from Montrose. At Ute Indian Museum turn west and drive a half-mile to the Cobble Creek entrance. Turn left and find the pro shop a half-mile on the left.

MONTROSE NOTES

Restless types have plenty to do in and around Montrose. Just 20 minutes away is **Black Canyon National Park** (970-641-2337), the nation's newest national park where 2,000-foot-high black walls drop into canyons filled with gold-medal trout waters. Drive for 15 minutes and there's **Telluride's** historic western town and ski area. **Ridgway Reservoir** is packed with fishermen and campers. Another historic western

SOUTHWEST

Ben Hogan won The Denver Open in 1948 when the tournament was held at the Wellshire Golf Course.

town, **Ouray**, is 45 minutes away with opportunities for Jeep trips on the back roads. Fishermen love to test the **Gunnison River** and **Blue Mesa Reservoir**, the largest lake in the state. The **Black Canyon Motel** is a fun escape with **golf packages** to Fairway Pines in Ridgway as well as the Black Canyon Golf Course in Montrose. Also try the 100-year-old **Alexander Lake Lodge** (www.alexanderlakelodge.com, 970-856-2539) or **The Inn at Arrowhead** (888-862-8912), located in Cimarron next to Black Canyon National Park. The **Backwoods Inn** (970-249-1961) is good for steaks, the **Glenn Eyrie Restaurant** (970-249-9263) serves wild game and trout, and **Amelia's** (970-249-1881) is the place for greasy Mexican food. Wine connoisseurs can enjoy the **Rocky Hill Winery** (970-249-3765) by tasting their distinctive offerings in a shady picnic area next to a stream, with breathtaking views of the mountains.

PAGOSA SPRINGS
ELEV. 7,105 POP. 1,591

The Utes came to Pagosa Springs and called it "Pagosah" for the healing waters of the hot springs, considered by some to be the hottest in the world. At 145 degrees the Great Pagosa Hot Springs are too toasty for safe human use, but folks still want to see them. This scenic little town, not far from famous Wolf Creek Pass, is surrounded on three sides by the San Juan National Forest. Chimney Rock Ruins is another home of the Anasazi, and you can see where these ancient farmers lived some 1,000 years ago. The famous Old Spanish Trail, which went from Santa Fe to Los Angeles, came through the Pagosa Springs area, and the nearby Wolf Creek Ski Area is famous for receiving the most annual snowfall of any Colorado ski resort.

PAGOSA SPRINGS GOLF CLUB

THE GOLF Located in a spectacular rural setting, Pagosa Springs Golf Club challenges the best of golfers, yet is fair to the high handicapper. Ponderosa pines line some of the 27 fairways, which offer panoramic views of the San Juan Mountains.

Hole 3 on the Piñon/Ponderosa is the most memorable: a narrow, 354-yard par 4 with a sharp slope on the right and marsh on the left. The long and narrow green has some slope to it, so pick the correct landing area and avoid the nasty bunker.

Small-town friendliness is the highlight of vacations to Pagosa Springs. The course is open May 14 through October 16.

The Denver Open was canceled in 1949 because top pros were in Europe competing for the Ryder Cup.

THE DETAILS 970-731-4755. #1 Pines Club Place, Pagosa Springs, CO 81147.

- www.golfpagosa.com
- Johnny Bulla, 1972. 27 holes. Par 71. Price - $$.
- Piñon/Meadows: Blue - 7,132 (72.2/126). White - 6,385 (68.7/117). Red - 5,358 (68.8/126). Par 72.
- Piñon/Ponderosa: Blue - 6,515 (68.9/118). White - 6,072 (67/113). Red - 5,242 (67.4/117). Par 71.
- Ponderosa/Meadows: Blue - 6,849 (70.9/124). White - 5,991 (66.9/115). Red - 5,038 (66.2/118). Par 71.

GETTING THERE Take I-25 south to Hwy. 160. Take Hwy. 160 west to Pagosa Springs. The course is 3 miles west of Pagosa Springs on the right side.

PAGOSA SPRINGS NOTES

The charming little storefront café known as **The Irish Rose** (970-264-2955) is the ideal place for breakfast, and **JJ's Upstream** (970-264-9100), located right on the San Juan River, is the place to set up shop for after-golf philosophizing, seafood, and a whole lot more. **Ramon's** (970-731-3012) serves Mexican food and is lively because of its upstairs cantina. In the old days Indians skirmished here over the hot springs, but today there are two main spas that sometimes offer **golf packages**—the Springs' **Hot Springs Resort**, (www.pagosahotsprings.com, 800-225-0934) with more than 12 naturally heated, family-sized outdoor pools of different temperatures. And across the street is the **Spa Motel** (970-264-4168), which has a year-round outdoor swimming pool as well as men's and women's indoor hot baths. If you're looking for B&B accommodations, try **Oso Grande Ranch** (970-731-9548) otherwise take advantage of the **Pagosa Lodge** (800-523-7704) at the golf course. Lastly, consider pursuing lunker trout in nearby **Echo Lake Park** and **Williams Lake**, or get your legs in shape by hiking to **Treasure Falls**.

RIDGWAY

ELEV. 7,000 POP. 713

Historic Ridgway lies in the Uncompahgre Valley, surrounded by the snow-capped peaks of the Cimarron and San Juan Mountains. The town was named for a railroad superintendent by the name of Robert M. Ridgway, who founded the town in 1891. Back then railroad supply was a big business for the nearby mining towns in addition to ranching (some of the ranches extended all the way to the Utah border). Just a short drive from Ouray and Silverton, and the gateway to the Dallas Divide toward Telluride and 14,000-foot Mount Sneffels,

In the late 1950s the Denver Open resumed play at the Wellshire Golf Course and Tommy Jacobs won in 1959.

Ridgway is far enough away to avoid the tourist crowds and a great golf destination.

FAIRWAY PINES GOLF & COUNTRY CLUB

THE GOLF   Another of Colorado's true hidden gems, Fairway Pines is situated northwest of Ridgway on Loghill Mesa at an elevation of 8,000 feet, featuring panoramic views of the Cimarron Mountains. The course, recognized by the Audubon Society for environmental successes, was designed by local Byron Coker and has been awarded a 4-star ranking by *Golf Digest* six times.

Since the course is so vast, traversing 700 acres with fairways lined by ponderosa and juniper, it's rare to see other golfers throughout your round. Much of the day will be spent firing at targets, trying to keep the tee shot in play and out of the trees. Greens are small to medium in size, and the layout features a decent amount of water and some elevation changes. In a recent PGA West chapter event the winning score was one-under, a sign that the golf course is one you'll need to play more than once to learn the scoring nuances.

A testy driving hole, No. 4 is a par-5, 540-yarder with a 90-degree dogleg; it's difficult because of the towering trees and a well-placed fairway bunker. Take advantage of the 346-yard sixth hole, which requires a drive just short of the water that fronts the green.

THE DETAILS   970-626-5284. 117 Ponderosa Drive, Ridgway, CO 81432.
- Byron Coker, 1993. 18 holes. Par 72. Gold - 6,812 (71.8/128). Blue - 6,372 (70.8/118). White - 5,889 (68.7/115). Women's Blue - 6,372 (75/140). Women's White - 5,889 (72.4/136). Red - 5,317 (70.5/120). Price - $$$.

GETTING THERE   Exit State Road 62 between Ridgway and Telluride onto County Road 24A. Drive uphill to Log Hill Mesa. Or exit SR 550 south of Ridgway State Park (County Rd. 24) and follow the signs up to Log Hill Mesa.

RIDGWAY NOTES

Breakfast is best served an the **San Juan Mountain Bakery & Deli** (970-626-5803), but **Sandy's Sunshine Kitchen** is another nice spot with outdoor seating. Go for a burger and beer at the **True Grit Cafe** (970-626-5739), which is loaded with John Wayne garb. The **Adobe Inn** (970-626-5939) is one of the best Mexican food restau-

---

The 1970s Denver Open winners included Chi Chi Rodriquez at the Denver Country Club and Dave Hill at Meadow Hills.

rants in Colorado, then burn the calories off at **The Big Barn** (970-626-3600), which has a dance floor and live music. The **Chipeta Sun Lodge and Spa** (970-626-3737, www.chipeta.com) is the premium lodging option in Ridgway—a cozy full-service fitness center and spa, with hot tubs in many rooms. **Golf packages** are available in nearby Ouray at the **Box Canyon Lodge and Hot Springs** (800-327-5090), **Victorian Inn** (970-325-7222), and the **China Clipper B&B** (970-325-0565). Montrose is also nearby, and the **Black Canyon Motel** (800-315-0565) has **golf packages** for Fairway Pines and Black Canyon Golf Club. U.S. Highway 550 between Ridgway and Durango is called the **Million Dollar Highway**—a roller coaster of a drive surrounded by the San Juan Mountains. Just north of town is **Ridgway State Park**, rated one of the choice parks in Colorado. The 1,000-acre reservoir offers fishing, boating, swimming, hiking, and a full-service marina.

TELLURIDE

ELEV. 8,725 POP. 2,200

Utes, Spanish explorers, and fur trappers roamed this stunning box canyon area before the trains arrived, known to the Indians as "valley of hanging waterfalls." After the railroad boom of the late 1800s brought Finns, Irish, Swedes, Cornish, French, Italians, Germans, and Chinese to Telluride to work the mines, the population exploded to 5,000. Butch Cassidy robbed his first bank here in the canyons where Telluride sits along the San Miguel River in the midst of the San Juan Mountains. The entire town of Telluride is a National Historic District and people all over the world see views from its streets when the Telluride Film Festival brings countless Hollywood celebrities to town in September. Telluride is the most famous ski town of the San Juan Mountains, but its rich heritage and incredible charms make it a worthy destination any time of the year.

TELLURIDE SKI & GOLF CLUB

THE GOLF Sunshine Mesa, Wilson Peak, the San Sophia Mountains, and Utah's La Sal Mountains form the awesome scenic backdrop at Telluride Ski & Golf Club, a private club that is open to resort visitors of The Peaks Resort & Spa. The course is only open from mid-May to early October, but you'll experience a big boost in shot distance since the track's 9,564-foot elevation rests nicely at the foot of the 13,000-foot San Juan Mountains.

Some of the many distinguished participants of past Denver Opens are: Arnold Palmer, Bob Rosburg, Doug Sanders, Gay Brewer, Jerry Barber, Lionel Herbert, Jay Herbert, Ernie Vossler, Jack Burke Jr., Mike Souchak, and Davis Love Jr.

Designed by a group associated with the club, the construction of the course must have been an unbelievable effort given the difficult terrain. Some consider the course more of a links-style route; however, the elevation changes are mind-boggling as it follows the natural contours of the land. You'll run into six par-3 holes as you pass through woods, wetlands, ponds, and streams that are loaded with elk, deer, and the occasional red fox.

This one is first-class and in superb condition, with features like a Halfway House that serves lunch (at the junction of the 5th, 9th and 11th fairways) to make the day more enjoyable.

THE DETAILS 970-887-2606. 565 Mountain Village Blvd. Telluride, CO 81435.
- www.thepeaksresort.com
- 1992. 18 holes. Par 71. Gold - 6,691 (71.4/130). Blue - 6,211 (69.1/126). White - 5,446 (65.4/117). Women's White - 5,554 (70.4/130). Red - 4,936 (66.6/121). Price - $$$$.

GETTING THERE From U.S. Hwy. 550 south of Montrose or north of Durango, take Hwy. 62 west from Ridgway. Turn south on Hwy. 145, proceed to Mountain Village Blvd., and turn left on Vischer Drive.

TELLURIDE NOTES

Some say Telluride was once a hippie town, and you can still find the free spirits at **Baked** (970-728-4775), a hangout offering good food and malts, floats, and thick shakes. In order to experience Telluride's scene, don't miss the impressive **Sheridan Bar**, which is located in the historic **New Sheridan Hotel** (970-728-4351). Many boisterous bars with live music line Colorado Avenue. **Eagle's Bar & Grille** (970-728-0886) is another frequented watering hole, and **Harmon's** (970-728-3773) is located in the historic train depot. This cozy restaurant has a wide-ranging menu, mahogany bar, and the charms of an evening pianist. Aside from the New Sheridan, the pampering and golf are both first-class at **The Peaks Resort at Telluride** (800-789-2220), where you can relax in one of the three swimming pools, hike, or take a gondola ride. In Telluride's historic downtown you can find **Bear Creek B&B** (800-338-7064), a European-style inn with a rooftop hot tub. A mini-scenic drive takes you up **Alta Lakes Road** south of Telluride by Highway 145. Follow Forest Road 632 four miles to find the old mining camp of Alta and the lake. During summer and fall, the village is filled with festivals for jazz (www.telluridejazz.com), bluegrass (www.planetbluegrass.com, 800-624-2422) and chamber music. Anglers can cast into the **San Miguel** and **Dolores Rivers**, **Trout Lake** (12 miles south of town), or **Woods Lake** (10 miles north). Hikers should look for **Bridal Veil Falls**, Colorado's highest waterfall at 385 feet, and **Ingram Falls** for stunning photo opportunities.

Bob Newhart, Dow Finsterwald, and Johnny Dee posed for this photo at The Broadmoor in 1965.

I have the feeling when I'm taking my stance that someone has just pulled a chair from behind me and I'm waiting for him to put it back.—Arnold Palmer

Jack Nicklaus blasts from a Broadmoor East bunker on his way to the 1959 U.S. Amateur Championship. Runner-up to The Bear was a Colorado favorite—Charlie Coe.

The press surrounds Babe Didrickson Zaharias after she won the Broadmoor Ladies Invitational.

We all hit it into trouble at times. The key is to minimize the error and play smart. As they say, a bogey is a lot better than a double bogey—David Leadbetter

NORTHWEST

NORTHWEST

Northwest Mileage

	Aspen	Avon	Basalt	Battlement Mesa	Breckenridge	Carbondale	Copper Mtn	Craig	Eagle	Edwards	Fruita	Glenwood Springs	Granby	Grand Junction	Grand Lake	Gypsum	Keystone	Meeker	New Castle	Rangely	Rifle	Silverthorne	Snowmass	Steamboat	Vail	Winter Park	Wolcott
Aspen		91	18	92	101	29	81	158	71	87	140	41	166	128	181	64	94	157	160	67	92	16	150	96	145		82
Avon	91		73	101	49	62	20	149	23	11	166	57	129	140	115	27	65	89	79	209	61	25	115	78	35	85	10
Basalt	18	73		74	122	11	102	140	53	69	122	23	147	110	164	46	76	139	142	162	76	142	2	132	127	96	92
Battlement Mesa	92	101	74		150	62	130	113	81	97	48	51	198	36	213	39	143	91	16	118	25	141	78	194	124		
Breckenridge	101	49	122	150		111	20	174	53	69	208	91	79	174	89	72	15	159	124	242	77	10	108	92	37	67	60
Carbondale	29	62	11	62	111		91	129	42	58	111	12	147	99	167	35	95	128	8	159	27	104	24	124	88		52
Copper Mountain	81	20	102	130	20	91		154	34	48	178	72	99	152	99	53	7	124	105	189	74	9	89	71	30	46	40
Craig	158	149	140	113	174	129	154		87	102	85	118	121	103	131	134	167	61	101	90	97	142	145	41	108	104	114
Eagle	71	23	53	81	53	42	34	87		20	145	36	112	119	119	7	46	75	73	189	49	44	56	64	30	84	13
Edwards	87	11	69	97	69	58	48	102	20		164	54	120	135	131	23	61	83	83	174	61	30	71	30	25	113	6
Fruita	140	166	122	48	208	111	178	85	145	164		99	233	13	247	131	191	75	48	55	72	189	124	242		140	41
Glenwood Springs	41	57	23	51	91	12	72	118	36	54	99		135	86	174	27	83	118	14	150	27	96	44	112	79	107	14
Granby	166	129	147	198	79	147	99	121	112	120	233	135		219	13	131	92	177	173	230	124	91	164	124	144	25	107
Grand Junction	128	140	110	36	174	99	152	103	119	135	13	86	219		235	110	179	61	36	72	61	172	107	230		174	128
Grand Lake	181	115	164	213	89	167	99	131	119	131	247	174	13	235		143	83	197	172	242	143	96	186	120	113	21	
Gypsum	64	27	46	39	72	35	53	134	7	23	131	27	131	110	143		46	89	52	191	49	62	68	57	14	107	
Keystone	94	65	76	143	15	95	7	167	46	61	191	83	92	179	83	46		157	108	211	86	8	91	62	37	41	
Meeker	157	89	139	91	159	128	124	61	75	83	75	118	177	61	197	89	157		50	54	41	120	125	71	112	135	57
New Castle	160	79	142	16	124	8	105	101	73	83	48	14	173	36	172	52	108	50		93	8	105	97	121	82	107	
Parachute	67	209	162	118	242	159	189	90	189	174	55	150	230	72	242	191	211	54	93		116	196	120	159	174	283	160
Rangely	92	61	76	25	77	27	74	97	49	61	72	27	124	61	143	49	86	41	8	116		51	116	93			
Rifle Creek	16	25	142	141	10	104	9	142	44	30	189	96	91	172	96	62	8	120	105	196	51		135	36	76	88	
Silverthorne	150	115	2	78	108	24	89	145	56	71	124	44	164	107	186	68	91	125	97	120	116	135		88	66	15	
Snowmass	96	78	132	194	92	124	71	41	64	30	242	112	124	230	120	57	62	71	121	159	93	36	88		168	85	88
Vail	145	35	127	124	37	88	30	108	30	25		79	144		113	14	37	112	82	174		76	66	168		69	103
Winter Park		85	96		67		46	104	84	113	140	107	25	174	21	107	41	135	107	283		88	15	85	69		
Wolcott	82	10	92		60	52	40	114	13	6	41	14	107	128				57		160			88	103			

Globetrotters, presidents, legendary golfers, and celebrities flock to this spectacular section of Colorado—home to ski bums and zillionaires, log mansions and hostels. Rich man or poor man, there's plenty of world-class golf to be found here.

Colorado's most expensive golf game is here at The Lodge and Spa at Cordillera—a place the world has been exposed to because of Los Angeles Lakers star Kobe Bryant's recent visit. But you can also find spectacular more affordable golf options.

Count on gas prices jumping 20 cents a gallon in the Vail Valley, where the town was invented for skiing in the 1960s and the wealthy claimed it. Golf came second because the founding fathers knew summer would be important, too.

Just in the past few years, grand openings have drawn names like Jack Nicklaus to Cordillera's Summit Course and Arnold Palmer to Eagle Ranch. Then came Tom Fazio and Greg Norman to Red Sky Ranch. But the best new golf course in Colorado's Northwest Region was designed by Jim Engh of Castle Rock—that, of course, is The Golf Club at Redlands Mesa in Grand Junction.

Two old friends joined Palmer at the grand opening of Eagle Ranch—former PGA tour star Bob Toski and Dick Hauserman, a true Vail Valley golf pioneer. Hauserman was Vail's first resident, designed the logo Vail still uses today, and served on the board that launched the Vail Golf Club in the mid-60s.

In 1968 Palmer came to Vail to establish the Arnold Palmer Golf Academy. It was just the day after he tied Bob Charles for second place in the PGA Championship at Pecan Valley in San Antonio. "The Vail Valley area was sparsely populated and Vail was just a small town," Palmer remembered. Everyone agreed a golf academy was five years too early—it didn't last.

Today, driving from Denver to Grand Junction on an I-70 golf road trip, you get a rubbernecker's view of seemingly endless golf courses. Watch for Vail Golf Club, Sonnenalp in Edwards, Cordillera's Valley Course, and Wolcott's Eagle Springs as you zip down the interstate. Pass through spectacular Glenwood Canyon and enter an area called Glenwood Springs, where another new course, Bair Chase, was proposed and is now in limbo. Once past historic Glenwood Springs, where Doc Holliday is buried, veer onto Highway 82 south towards Ironbridge, River Valley Ranch, Snowmass, and the Aspen Golf Club. If you have the bucks, the private courses in this area are worth investigating.

Engh's brand-new Lakota Canyon Ranch in New Castle is just minutes west of Glenwood Springs, and don't pass up Battlement Mesa or Rifle Creek—two more affordable options before you arrive in Grand Junction, the largest town in the Northwest region. Explore the glories of the Grand Valley and don't miss playing the golf Club at Redlands Mesa and the local municipals.

Golfers who carry ball retrievers are gatherers, not hunters....Their dreams are no longer of conquest, but only of salvage.—David Owen

Make plans to enjoy a completely different Grand—Grand County—home to Winter Park and the golf treats of Pole Creek, Grand Lake, and Grand Elk. You can even hop aboard Amtrak or the Ski Train from Denver to get here. Life is a little more down-to-earth in Granby, and more affordable than in Vail. Back toward I-70 don't skip The Raven at Three Peaks or the Keystone Ranch and River Courses, if you have the time and bucks. Also, Nicklaus' only municipal in the world graces Breckenridge

Then, of course, there's Aspen. John Denver once called it home and Martina Navratilova still does. It's ritzy and expensive, but has posh powder in winter and marvelous golf in summer. Affordability is best at Aspen Golf Club and Carbondale's River Valley Ranch is a Top Ten layout. The redesign at Snowmass Club should prove to be another fun Engh experience when it opens in the summer of 2004.

The list is endless. There's another golf-rich area in the northwest— Steamboat Springs, an old ranching town and ski haven. More Winter Olympians have come from here than any other city in North America. The golf isn't bad either—Haymaker is one of the best courses in Colorado, but the Sheraton Steamboat Resort is also excellent and the hidden gem of the area is Craig's Yampa Valley Golf Course.

And don't be surprised if your ski instructor is a golf pro in summer. Two examples are Cordillera's Pentti Tofferi and Sheraton Steamboat's Gary Crawford.

NORTHWEST

Golf, like the measles, should be caught young, for, if postponed to riper years, the results may be serious.—P.G. Wodehouse

ASPEN

ELEV 7,907 POP. 5,914

John Denver was on a Rocky Mountain high when he lived in Aspen and mingled with the world's celebrities. Unlike Vail, which was invented specifically for skiing, Aspen has a history. Founded as a small mining camp in 1879, it became one of the world's richest silver-producing areas until the silver market crash of 1893.

Unlike many rural areas of Colorado, Aspen is more famous for culture than for agriculture. Art galleries, fancy restaurants, high-toned hotels like The Ritz-Carlton and Hotel Jerome, and frequent celebrity sightings are all part of the experience.

Aspen's ski pioneers arrived in 1935, when the town had just 700 residents. André Roch, a famous Swiss avalanche expert, found the right spot and developed a ski area. While World War II delayed his plans Roch formed the Aspen Ski Club, carved a trail system on Aspen Mountain, and constructed a boat tow that pulled skiers up the hill in two large sleds powered by a gas motor and an old mine hoist.

Winter visits here require a substantial amount of cash, but this elite ski resort can be a more affordable and appealing place for summer visits. And even the ultra cash-strapped can commute from Glenwood Springs (less than 50 miles away) and get a temporary job bartending or caddying in order to afford some time in Aspen.

ASPEN GOLF CLUB

THE GOLF Old-timers say that Aspen Golf Club's first head pro, Evon Tasha, and an area plumber staked out this ground more than 30 years ago for a 9-hole course. Things have certainly changed since then. Frank Hummel finished the golf course and in 1978 renowned Colorado golf architect Dick Phelps fine-tuned the full 18 holes.

The course recently completed another overhaul, with millions spent on a new pro shop, restaurant, and separate junior facilities. Now golfers can sit and enjoy lunch with views of the 18th green and snow-capped Pyramid Peak.

The greens are slick and the scenery (Aspen Highlands, and Buttermilk Mountain ski runs) is distracting. Groves of aspen, blue spruce, willows, and other trees are included in the layout. And in addition to bunkers and tight driving holes, the design features water on just about every hole—ponds, creek crossings, and hard-to-see irrigation ditches surrounded by thick rough are true hazards.

You can't go into a shop and buy a good game of golf. —Sam Snead

No. 16 is the course's best hole: a 453-yard par 4 that doglegs left around water into a green guarded by a pond and a bunker.

Golfers and skiers across the US probably think Aspen is snowed in the majority of the year, but in past years the golf course has opened in March, allowing lucky visitors the chance to ski and play golf in the same day.

THE DETAILS 970-925-2145. 39551 Highway 82, Aspen, CO 81611.
- Frank Hummel, 1970. Phelps Golf Design, 1978 remodel. 18 holes. Par 71. Gold - 7,137 (73.7/133). Blue - 6,458 (70.5/126). White - 5,545 (65.5/118). Men's Red - 5,150 (63.4/113). Women's Blue - 6,458 (75.6/137). Women's White - 5,590 (71/124). Women's Red - 5,238 (69.1/119). Price - $$$.

GETTING THERE From downtown Aspen head west 1 mile on Hwy. 82 to the course.

MAROON CREEK CLUB

THE GOLF Maroon Creek is everything you'd expect from an upscale Aspen golf club. Tom Fazio designed this sensational course, and *Golf Digest* tabbed Maroon Creek on its list of "Best New Private Courses" back in 1995 for good reasons: perfect conditioning, dramatic elevation changes at the base of the Buttermilk Mountain ski runs, difficult green sites, and caddies.

On the front, No. 9 stands out for its view of the Aspen Highlands ski area that rises 5,000 feet above the putting surface. On the back, No. 13 is an incredible downhill par 3 with aspens and Maroon Creek lining the left side.

THE DETAILS 970-920-1533. 10 Club Circle Road, Aspen, CO 81611.
- Tom Fazio, 1995. 18 holes. Par 70. Black - 7,129 (73.2/140). Gold - 6,792 (71.6/138). Blue - 6,323 (69.6/133). Green - 5,802 (67.1/125). Women's Blue - 6,323 (74.4/139). Women's Green - 5,802 (71.5/133). Women's Red - 5,109 (67.7/124). No reciprocal play accepted. Members and guests only. Price - $$$$.

GETTING THERE Take Hwy. 82 south from Glenwood Springs to Aspen. The course is just north of Aspen.

Think like the underdog. The underdog always has the advantage...The favorite, meanwhile, is prone to negativism, worrying about how embarrassing it would be to lose.—Dr. Bob Rotella

ASPEN NOTES

A book could be written about how to spend quality time in Aspen, famous for its world-class culture despite the preserved undercurrents of its mining history. The summer weather is phenomenal and there are countless festivals. There are very few bad places to eat. The shopping is tremendous. The Roaring Fork River snakes through town (**Aspen Outfitting Co.**, 970-925-3406). And the watering holes are unparalleled. Reserve a room with a golf package at the historic **Hotel Jerome** (800-331-7213), and plan for plenty of non-golf time in the **Jerome's famous J-Bar**. When in need of a change of scenery, mosey to the **Red Onion** (970-925-9043), Aspen's oldest bar, then **Bentley's** (970-920-2240) in the **Wheeler Opera House** (970-920-5770) for more quality drinking time. By then you'll have the nerve to appreciate the **Aspen Art Museum** (970-925-8050), and empty the ATM machine to prepare to shop and experience one of the countless fine dining establishments, where the classy cafés and restaurants generally charge over $25 for a main course. As for side excursions, the ghost towns of Ashcroft and Independence offer interesting day-trips into the silver mining past of the Aspen area. Summer wanderings east of Aspen through Independence Pass (12,095 feet) offer some of Colorado's most spectacular views. Seven miles north of town in tiny Woody Creek lies the **Woody Creek Tavern** (970-923-4585), and unpretentious locale where ranch hands shoot pool and dig into Tex-Mex.Colorado's most photographed mountain scene is minutes away—the Maroon Bells

AVON–BEAVER CREEK ELEV. 7,430 POP. 5,561

Styled after old European ski villages, the town of Avon sprang up around the Beaver Creek Resort and ski area and is one of the world's premier winter destinations. All kinds of ski terrain, expensive shops, and hotels dominate the landscape. Along with enjoying beautiful Gore Creek, which provides opportunities for fishing, kayaking, rafting, and relaxation, summertime visitors can get their golf fix in on two impressive 18-hole courses, as well as a charming little par-3 track.

BEAVER CREEK GOLF CLUB

THE GOLF Mountain scenery, babbling brooks lined with aspens, and a unique Robert Trent Jones, Jr. layout greet members and resort guests at the Beaver Creek Golf Club.

After the first four holes of this scenic layout, you'll wonder how Trent Jones

You will hit the ball farther more frequently when you don't try to hit it far—Sam Snead

Jr. did it. There isn't a whole lot of land to work with here, and the first shots of the day play downhill into target patches of green fairways. The challenge is vigorous, and might surprise those not familiar with this type of golf.

Holes 5 through 13 open up and the final five start climbing back toward the ski mountain, where old ranch buildings add character. No. 18 is demanding—the green is encircled by water and trouble and only a perfect shot will survive.

Members get the best early-morning tee times and resort guests are often bombarded by rain and lightning in the afternoon (bring rain gear).

For years Gerald Ford hosted an invitational tournament here to benefit charities.

THE DETAILS 970-845-5775. 103 Offerson Road, Beaver Creek, CO 81620.
- www.beavercreekclub.com
- Robert Trent Jones, Jr., 1980. 18 holes. Par 70. Gold - 6,752 (71.0/140). Blue - 6,464 (69.6/138). White - 6,026 (67.7/134). Women's Blue - 6,461 (75.8/146). Women's White - 5,973 (73/139). Women's Red - 5,088 (69.3/131). Price - $$$$.

GETTING THERE Take I-70 to Avon (exit 167) and proceed up the hill through several traffic circles to the gated entrance at Beaver Creek. Ask for directions to the golf course.

EAGLE-VAIL GOLF CLUB

THE GOLF Eagle-Vail's first hole, a 150-foot drop down to the fairway, is a good preview of what awaits throughout the round. The journey takes golfers up and down all day long on a route that is carved into the mountainside along the Eagle River. Six holes roll along the river, six through a housing development, and the remainder are mountainous. No. 16, a spectacular 346-yard hole highlighted by loads of aspens, has a sharp dogleg right and an approach to an elevated green.

Only 10 minutes from Vail Village, this layout has been spruced up with an influx of cash in recent years.

THE DETAILS 970-949-5267. 0431 Eagle Drive, Avon, CO 81620.
- www.eagle-vailgolf.com
- Bruce Devlin, Robert Von Hagge 1974. 18 holes. Par 72. Blue - 6,546 (70.6/127). White - 6,061 (68.6/118). Women's White - 6,061 (74.1/139). Women's Red - 4,790 (67.2/122). Price - $$$$.

Nonchalant putts count the same as the chalant putts. —Henry Beard

GETTING THERE Heading from Vail, take I-70 west to exit 171 (Minturn). Turn left at the stop sign and go 2 miles. Turn left at the traffic light to the main entrance.

WILLOW CREEK PAR 3 AT EAGLE-VAIL

THE GOLF The perfect spot for a quick round while the family is on vacation, and a low-key place for beginners to hack it around, Willow Creek is a testy little par 3 beautified by the typical Vail Valley scenery.

THE DETAILS 800-341-8051. 0646 Eagle Drive, Avon, CO 81620.
  • 9 holes. Par-3 course. Par 27. Not rated. Price - $.

GETTING THERE From Vail take I-70 west to Exit 171 (Minturn) and turn left at the stop sign 2 miles down. Turn left at the traffic light to the main entrance.

AVON — BEAVER CREEK NOTES

World-class lodging can be found at **The Pines Lodge** (970-845-7900), which is nestled on the western slope of the Beaver Creek Resort and short distance from the Beaver Creek Plaza area. A complimentary resort shuttle service takes guests to local destinations, and underground valet parking garages are convenient when it's cold. Try the **Grouse Mountain Grill** in The Pines Lodges, an American grill that features fresh, fine meats and the day's catch, live music, and an award-winning wine list. The rustic **Ritz-Carlton Bachelor Gulch** (800-576-5582) on Beaver Creek Mountain is your pass to golf in the area and Red Sky Golf Club. The 237-room resort offers panoramic mountain views and unlimited year-round activities such as skiing, golf, hiking, mountain biking, and cultural events. After a day in this Rocky Mountain lodge-styled playground, relax and rejuvenate in the 21,000-square-foot **Bachelor Gulch Spa**. In general the dining is more expensive in Beaver Creek than Vail, but places like **Beano's Cabin** (970-949-9090) are well worth it—a world-famous restaurant where you ride horseback up the ski slopes for a gourmet experience. In fact the dining in Beaver Creek is so ritzy, worn-out golfers might welcome the down-home **Dusty Boot Steakhouse & Saloon** (970-748-1146), where you can build your own burger and kick back over cold ones. **Cassidy's Hole in the Wall** (970-949-9449) is a country-western bar with a wooden dance floor that draws the rowdy crowd. And if you want a scenic drive, head for the mining towns of Minturn and Redcliff, and track down the town of Eagle and its authentically **Western Brush Creek Saloon** (970-328-5279) on the main drag.

Every golfer is on his honor.—Donald Ross

BASALT

Elev. 6,620 Pop. 2,681

Originally known as Frying Pan Junction, Basalt served as a simple railroad camp along the Colorado Midland Railroad in the late 1800s—a spot where coal and silver ore passed on its way to Aspen and Leadville over Hagerman Pass. Swiss and Italian immigrants came here and worked in the mines and for the railroad. In 1901 the name changed to Basalt because of the dense, black volcanic rock found throughout the region.

ROARING FORK CLUB

THE GOLF Fishing and golf meet luxury at the Roaring Fork Club, where the pro shop proudly displays upscale fishing tackle along with the best golf equipment. Don't be surprised to see a PGA Tour star casting into the Roaring Fork River—Billy Andrade, Tom Lehman, Mark Brooks, and Brandel Chamblee have all reeled in trout on these grounds.

Members like to think of this special golf experience in three parts—it has panoramic ranchlands spreading out in front of the Members' Lodge, wooded corridors that follow the Roaring Fork River and Spring Creek, and scenic upper plateaus.

Ranchland is on display on No. 5, where the tee overlooks ponds, wildflowers and bunkers sculpted by Mr. Nicklaus, and the valley and river views. The riverside portion of the layout has a pine and cottonwood landscape, and No. 6 is a short gem that plays over the Roaring Fork River to a tight fairway. The approach then must clear Spring Creek, which runs in front of the small, tree-lined green.

Take in the view of Basalt Mountain at the par-3 12th, which sits high above the valley floor and the Frying Pan River valley. Golfers must navigate one of the nine trout-filled ponds that come into play both in front of and behind the narrow green.

Even though it is a private club, Basalt residents and their guests can play by purchasing a Roaring Fork pass for $25 at Town Hall, showing proof of residency. Next you must go to the Basalt Recreation office and get a photo ID card and purchase a 10-play punch card at $35 a round. Roaring Fork may restrict these times, so call ahead and arrange tee times.

THE DETAILS 970-927-9100. 100 Arbaney Ranch Road, Basalt, CO 81621.
- www.roaringforkclub.com

Properly fitted clubs are the only part of improved golf that anyone can buy.—Tommy Armour

NORTHWEST

- Jack Nicklaus, 1999. 18 holes. Par 72. Black - 7,016 (72.8/138). White - 6,582 (70.6/133). Sage - 6,020 (67.9/123). Women's Sage - 6,020 (73.6/142). Women's Rose - 5,255 (69.4/129). Private, invitation only. No reciprocal play. Price - $$$$.

GETTING THERE Head out 1 mile east of Basalt on Hwy. 82.

BASALT NOTES

The Roaring Fork Club developers strive to be stewards of the land and in 1997 initiated the River Restoration Project to improve the fishery habitat, as well as enhance the beauty and channel stability of a one-mile stretch of the Roaring Fork River where it bisects club property. Roaring Fork members have several places to stay when visiting—with its chinked timbers and two-story cabins, the Member's Lodge is reminiscent of old fishing lodges. Luxury suites and cabins are also available. Aside from the club, the **Frying Pan River** is one of the most heralded great trout streams, and places like the **Taylor Creek Fly Shop** (970-927-4374) and **Frying Pan Anglers** (970-927-3441) are available to get you geared up and pointed in the right direction. Evenings are best spent at **Primavera** (970-927-3342) for Italian food and wine, and **Taqueria El Nopal** (970-927-1280) serves Mexican food. The best bet for lodging in Basalt is the **Shenandoah Inn** (970-927-4991), highly recommended because of its riverfront deck hot tub.

BATTLEMENT MESA   ELEV. 5,447 POP. 3,497

It's hard to find a stoplight in this small golf resort town, which is perched on a high plateau overlooking the Colorado River. The 3,200-acre residential community of Battlement Mesa is the home of one of only a handful of Joe Finger and Ken Dye designs in Colorado. A winner since its opening in 1987 and honored as a *GolfDigest* "Best New Course," the resort is popular because of its friendly reputation and affordability.

BATTLEMENT MESA GOLF CLUB

THE GOLF The Houston-based firm of Finger, Dye, and Spann is known for New Mexico's best layouts, including Black Mesa, Piñon Hills, and Paa-Ko Ridge. Here at Battlement Mesa, the architects make excellent use of the scenic views, sagebrush, and rolling terrain to route this 7,254-yard pleasure.

There is no surer nor more painful way to learn a rule than to be penalized for breaking it.—Tom Watson

The design involves lots of angles as it plays into the mountainside and along a raised plateau. Deep rough causes problems for golfers who stray from the fairway, and the large greens can be testy. However, there are few trees to get in the way and water comes into play only twice.

The ender is one of the better holes: a 445-yarder into the wind with a narrow landing area for the tee shot. Water looms right and the green has two tiers. There's nothing wrong with a bogey on the 18th.

THE DETAILS 970-285-7272. 888-285-7274. 3930 West Battlement Pkwy., Battlement Mesa, CO 81635.
- www.battlementmesa.com
- Joe Finger, Ken Dye, 1987. 18 holes. Par 72. Gold - 7,254 (73.7/135). Blue - 6,799 (72.2/125). White - 6,006 (68.7/116). Red - 5,386 (69.8/128). Price - $$.

GETTING THERE Find Battlement Mesa halfway between Grand Junction and Glenwood Springs on I-70. Take exit 75 and go 1 mile south to the course, which you can see from the interstate.

BATTLEMENT MESA NOTES

The resort offers newly renovated condominiums, a swimming pool, weight room, racquetball courts, and an outdoor playground. Fishing is nearby along with hunting, skiing, horseback riding, hiking, backpacking, mountain biking, snowmobiles, and more. Downtown Battlement Mesa is small and friendly with restaurants and gift shops, with the **White Buffalo** (970-285-1680) the best option for a meal. Those longing for the city can hop on I-70 and head for Grand Junction or Glenwood Springs, and the little town of Parachute has a joint called the **Hideout** with live music and spirits.

BRECKENRIDGE   ELEV. 9,603 POP. 2,803

First settled in 1859 when gold was discovered in the Blue River that runs through the middle of town, Breckenridge is where the largest gold nugget in North America was found in 1887—151-ounce chunk of gold—about the size of a human head. Today, no one knows where the nugget is.

It was a wild town in those days and the Gold Pan Saloon was the first drinking place. It's still open today, making it the oldest continuously operating saloon west of the Mississippi River.

The common error is taking the club back too far and decelerating through impact, which is like a boxer pulling his punches. It causes all sorts of mis-hit and misdirected pitch shots.—Tom Watson

NORTHWEST

The gold rush has given way to a powder rush—Breckenridge, Keystone, Copper Mountain, and Vail ski areas are all nearby. Breckenridge still maintains some of its charms, even though Vail Resorts bought the ski operation. The many shops and restaurants and a bustling main street provide relaxing leisure time. But golfers know this quaint little town as home to the world's only Jack Nicklaus-designed municipal golf course, now with 27 holes.

BRECKENRIDGE GOLF CLUB

THE GOLF Most golfers won't like the cart-path only rule here, but there's no doubt it has created some of the best-conditioned 27 holes in the mountains. After checking in at the clubhouse, which is perched at a lofty 9,324-foot elevation, golfers enjoy some of the most perfect fairway lies imaginable.

The newer Elk Nine, which opened in 2001, is a major challenge with long forced carries across rocky creeks and ditches. A beaver pond even comes into play in sight of the Ten Mile Range.

The Beaver and Bear Nines opened in 1987. The meadow holes move upward toward aspen groves and fairways lined with lodgepole pines. Penalizing native grasses and sagebrush add to the difficulty, and the Nicklaus Tees on the Beaver–Bear 18 plays to a tough 7,279 yards with a course rating of 73.3 and a slope of 150—one of the roughest in Colorado.

One memorable hole is No. 12 on the Beaver-Bear combo. Tee off from a chute of lodgepole pines to a fairway split by a stream. The native grass grows tall here as you near the elevated putting surface, bordered on the right by a beaver pond.

Breckenridge is difficult golf—you must pay attention all day while enjoying the cool summer temperatures. Thankfully, you will find holes that bend left and right—some of Nicklaus' earlier designs were fade-happy excursions. *GolfDigest* lists Breckenridge on its Places to Play list and rates it as a 4-Star Award Winner.

THE DETAILS 970-453-9104. 200 Clubhouse Drive, Breckenridge, CO 80424.
- Jack Nicklaus, 1987. 27 holes. Price - $$$$.
- Bear-Elk: Gold - 7,260 (73.5/143). Blue - 6,678 (70.8/136). Silver - 5,957 (67.2/121). Women's Silver - 5,971 (72.9/144). Women's Red - 5,149 (69.3/132).
- Beaver-Bear: Gold - 7,279 (73.3/149). Blue - 6,576 (70.1/139). Silver - 5,980 (67.1/128). Women's Silver - 6,031 (73.4/140). Women's Red - 5,063 (69.2/124).

Around the green, play the club that keeps the ball nearest to the ground.
It's easier to roll the ball up to the hole that fly the ball up and stop it by the hole. Putt rather than chip, and chip rather than pitch.—Billy Casper

NORTHWEST

- Elk-Beaver: Gold - 7,145 (73/148). Blue - 6,562 (70.2/140). Silver - 5,827 (66.9/124). Women's Silver 5,864 (72.7/145). Women's Red - 5,012 (68.9/131).

GETTING THERE Travel 7 miles south of I-70 (exit 203) and take Hwy. 9 to Tiger Road.

BRECKENRIDGE NOTES

The **Beaver Run Resort** (800-288-1282) offers golf packages for Breckenridge Golf Club. Located on the ski slopes, each room has stunning views and a kitchen. The **Fireside Inn** (www.fireside inn.com, 970-453-6456) is a 19th-century Victorian that's on the National Register of Historic Places. Breckenridge might have the best nightlife in Summit County. Don't forget the historic **Gold Pan Saloon** (970-453-8499) for post-round cold beers, the **Breckenridge Brewery** (970-453-1550) is a popular hangout, and **O'Toole's Roadhouse** (970-453-2004) is rough looking but attracts a unique clientele and is worthy of at least one cold beer. Other good options include **Mi Casa Mexican Restaurant** (970-453-2071), a favorite after-golf destination because of its views of the Blue River and ski slopes, as well as the **Hearthstone** (970-453-1148), a favorite locally for its solid food. Just north of Breckenridge is quiet Frisco, a quaint little village with a few good restaurants along its Main Street. The Creekside Inn (970-668-5607) is restful and provides a sense of solitude away from bustling Breckenridge.

CARBONDALE

ELEV. 6,170 POP. 5,196

Down the road 40 miles from Aspen in the Crystal River Valley is towering Mount Sopris, whose peaks reach 12,953 feet and tower over the small town of Carbondale. The White River National Forest surrounds this beautiful area, which is 12 miles from Glenwood Springs.

Carbondale began as the only stagecoach stop on the 40-mile run to Aspen, but today the little town has specialty shops, local arts and crafts, restaurants, and three great golf facilities. Explorers head for the Redstone-Marble area with its ghost towns and mining history, perhaps one of Colorado's best-kept secrets.

ASPEN GLEN GOLF CLUB

THE GOLF Aspen Glen has a lot to brag about. Designed by Jack Nicklaus and

Golf should be learned starting at the cup and progressing back toward the tee....If a beginner tries to learn the game at the tee and move on toward the green, postponing the short game until last, this is one beginner who will be lucky to ever beat anybody.—Harvey Penick

son Jack II, members claim the 18th green as Colorado's only natural island green—totally surrounded by the Roaring Fork River. *Golfweek* ranks it No. 2 in Colorado and in 2003 it co-hosted the Colorado PGA Section Championship with River Valley Ranch.

Exclusively private and locked behind a security gate, Aspen Glen has plenty of holes that lead to lively conversation. The 18th is a par 5 at 565 yards downhill. During grand opening festivities, Nicklaus used a driver and 3-iron to reach the green in two. Another scenic par 5 is No. 6, named "Sopris Springs" for towering Mount Sopris that looms over this neck of the Colorado woods.

There's also a par 3 called "Saddleback Hollow," a 219-yarder from the Bear tees that requires one of those Nicklaus long irons that fades and lands softly on the left center of the green. If you miss right, the return gives you a steep shot out of a saddleback hollow.

The view isn't bad from the elevated No. 7 tee box, either. The panorama includes a horseshoe-shaped piece of land along the Roaring Fork River, where members of Aspen Glen enjoy four miles of Gold Medal fishing. Also look for the bald eagle's nest in a ponderosa pine just off hole No. 10. The fairways are also a winter home for elk.

Lucky members get to dine in the Eagle's Nest Grille, with its rustic beams and vaulted ceiling, or golfers can dine outside on a terrace next to a huge stone fireplace.

Aspen Glen Club has reciprocal golf agreements with both Bookcliff Country Club in Grand Junction and The Country Club of the Rockies in Edwards. Both clubs require two Aspen Glen members per foursome.

The Details 970-704-1988. 0545 Bald Eagle Way, Carbondale, CO 81623.
- www.aspen-glen.com
- Jack Nicklaus, Jack Nicklaus II, 1997. 18 holes. Par 72. Gold - 7,455 (74.6/130). Blue - 6,830 (71.7/123). White - 6,191 (68.8/122). Green - 5,254 (64.8/104). Women's White - 6,181 (74.6/131). Women's Green - 5,345 (69.9/120). Limited reciprocal play, club pro must call. Price - $$$$.

Getting there From Glenwood Springs, take Hwy. 82 for 12 miles toward Aspen. The club is on the right side behind locked security gates.

RIVER VALLEY RANCH GOLF CLUB

The golf This Jay Morrish must-play is situated beneath Mt. Sopris in the

Every beginner ought to play with golfers better than himself. He will unconsciously by that means aim higher. It should be his ambition to beat somebody, and, having done so, to attack a still stronger adversary.—Sir Walter Simpson

Roaring Fork Valley, along the rippling Crystal River. No doubt, this is God's Country as well as golf country.

Stretching out to par 72 at 7,348 yards from the Ranch tees, RVR is a shot-maker's course with multi-fingered bunkers and risk/reward options. Seven holes either traverse or border the Crystal River, which is loaded with rainbows and browns—lunker enthusiasts will long for a fly rod for the nearby Gold Medal waters of the Roaring Fork and Frying Pan Rivers.

RVR finishes with a crescendo. The final four holes are a 237-yard par 3, a 485-yard par 4, a 623-yard par 5, and a 452-yard par 4. RVR and Aspen Glen co-hosted the PGA Section Championship in 2003, and the Colorado Golf Association Amateur Stroke Play Championship was held here. This is an idyllic golf experience, and should not be missed.

Other notes: Lew Ron Thompson, River Valley Ranch's maintenance chief, was born in a rustic cabin on the property and raised as a ranch hand.

After your round enjoy lunch at the Rock Creek Grill.

THE DETAILS 970-963-3625. 303 River Valley Ranch Dr., Carbondale, CO 81623.
- Jay Morrish, 1997. 18 holes. Par 72. Black - 7,241 (73.2/125). Blue - 6,597 (70.1/121). White - 5,975 (67.5/110). Women's White - 5,964 (73.4/132). Women's Red - 5,168 (69.8/120). Price - $$$.

GETTING THERE From Glenwood Springs drive south 12 miles on Hwy. 82 toward Aspen. Turn right on Hwy. 133. After 2 miles, turn right on River Valley Ranch Dr. and drive 1 mile to the clubhouse on the right.

THE RANCH AT ROARING FORK CLUB

THE GOLF This private residential community includes a public par-3 course, a 9-holer that is a tough short-game challenge. Situated on a flat piece of land, it has water on five holes and bunkers on six. No. 6, a 160-yard par 3, features a forced carry over water with sand traps surrounding the green.

THE DETAILS 970-963-4410. 14913 Hwy. 82, Carbondale, CO 81623.
- Unknown, 1987. 9 holes. Par-3 course. Par 27. Price - $.

GETTING THERE Take I-70 to Hwy. 82. Go toward Aspen and take Hwy. 133 south 2 miles to the course on the right.

Watch your opponent's (or partner's) ball and mark the spot carefully if it should land in trouble…It is a great comfort to know that those with you will extend the same courtesy to you.—Peter Dobereiner.

CARBONDALE NOTES

The **Comfort Inn & Suites** (800-228-5150) in Carbondale has golf packages just minutes from River Valley Ranch, and the **Ambiance Inn B&B** (970-963-3597) provides comfortable rooms and meals. The best breakfast in the valley is served at the **Village Smithy Restaurant** (970-963-9990), which began as an old blacksmith shop.

COPPER MOUNTAIN   ELEV. 9,720 POP. 1,500

Once known as Wheeler Junction, this town didn't get the name of Copper Mountain until 1972, when the ski area was born.

The area's mining past is no longer evident at the Copper Mountain Resort, where visitors enjoy a fabled ski experience in a self-contained pedestrian village. For convenience, all lodging is in a compact area complete with shops and restaurants. The resort offers expensive as well as affordable lodging options, along with a $3 million full-service athletic club. Keystone, Breckenridge, Arapahoe Basin, and Vail are all nearby, creating a unique summertime opportunity known as the "Summit County Golf Experience": mountain golf in and around some of Colorado's most amazing towns.

COPPER CREEK GOLF CLUB

THE GOLF Most wandering golf vacationers will love playing golf at the base of a world-class ski mountain. However, some purists consider this course too quirky with its abundance of bulkheads and narrow fairways.

At 9,700 feet, Copper Creek is a surreal experience: surrounded by 13,000-foot peaks and the highest championship golf course in North America. Part of what makes the experience special is that the climate limits the golf time, with frost-free days occurring for only a month in midsummer.

Railroad ties are abundant on this Pete and Perry Dye creation, which opened in 1976. The Dyes didn't have a large piece of property to work with, leaving some very tight holes that are difficult because of water. Unique for a track at this elevation, the course tips out at only 6,053 yards.

The front nine is strategic, taking golfers on a winding adventure through lakes, mounds, and alpine terrain with greens that are frequently bumpy (remember the frost-free days?). But picture-postcard beauty awaits when you make the turn and head up the mountain at hole No. 13, located at the base of

Remember that the object of most greenside bunker shots is not to "blast" the ball out, but to float it fairly gently from the trap on a cushion of sand, by skimming the club easily just beneath the ball.—John Jacobs

the "A" lift. Here the 508-yard par 5 slides through the upper parts of the course among the huge trees and remnants of an old mining town.

THE DETAILS 970-968-2882. 104 Wheeler Place, Copper Mountain, CO 80443.
* Pete & Perry Dye, 1976. 18 holes. Par 70. Gold - 6,053 (68.3/115). Blue - 5,674 (66.5/111). White - 5,135 (64.1/105). Women's Gold - 6,053 (72.3/135). Women's Blue - 5,674 (70.1/130). Women's White - 5,135 (67/122). Women's Red - 4,445 (63.2/111). Price - $$$.

GETTING THERE From Denver take I-70 west to exit 195 (Copper Mountain Resort). Proceed 1/4 mile on Copper Rd. and turn left on Golf Course Drive.

COPPER MOUNTAIN NOTES

For dining, don't miss the **Molly B's Saloon** (970-968-2318) for cold beers and hickory-smoked pork chops, and the **Double Diamond** (970-968-2880) has been the village's favorite eatery forever. The **Copper Mountain Resort** (800-458-8386) has everything, but another option is to stay in Silverthorne or Frisco, where you can hike the miles of trails in the **Arapahoe National Forest** nearby. Frisco in particular has some worthwhile stopping points, including the popular **Moose Jaw** (970-668-3931), and the inexpensive **El Rio Cantina & Grill** (970-668-5043).

CRAIG

ELEV. 6,186 POP. 9,189

Situated at the junction of U.S. Highway 40 and Colorado Highway 13, halfway between Denver and Salt Lake City, the old frontier town of Craig has a fascinating history. Locals recall stories of the days when this small town, set in the rolling hills and high plains of the Western slope, had its share of bandits, saloons, and cattle rustlers. Surveyors such as John Wesley Powell explored the area, and the remote canyons served as hideouts for bad guys like Butch Cassidy and the Sundance Kid. Ranching and farming have become the area's economic mainstays, but tourism is important since Craig serves as headquarters for numerous outdoors adventures and is home to the oldest and most affordable 18-hole layout in northwestern Colorado.

The great anxiety of the moderate player when making his stroke is to get the ball properly lofted, and in some obstinate cases it seems to take several seasons of experience to convince him completely that the club has been specially made for the purpose, and, if fairly used, is quite adequate. —Harry Vardon

YAMPA VALLEY GOLF COURSE

THE GOLF First opened as a 9-holer in 1967, Yampa Valley plays through 240 acres of cottonwoods, wetlands, native grasses, and sage.

Most city slickers envision cow-pasture pool here in the boondocks where deer and antelope sometimes roam the course. Locals call the front nine the "East Forty" because it's short. However, it offers some challenging and scenic golf as it rolls along with the Yampa River. The course then dives through a 75-year-old cottonwood forest and turns west onto the prairie, where stray shots find sagebrush, native grasses, and prickly-pear cactus.

The North Forty opened for play in 1986, and indeed started out as a cow pasture that was transformed into green grass, lakes, wetlands, and trees. It plays longer than the East Forty and has larger greens, more narrow-leaf cottonwoods, three lakes, bogs, and the Yampa River.

The 10th tee offers a beautiful view of Craig, Sand Rocks, Cedar Mountain, and the par-5 15th is home to a pair of nesting bald eagles that have inhabited the river bottom near the golf course since the 1980s.

The finale, the 591-yard, par-5 18th, affords a panoramic view of Breeze Basin and Buck Mountain, and is the longest hole, playing 591 yards from the back tees.

THE DETAILS 970-824-3673. 2179 Hwy. 394, Craig, CO 81625.
- www.yampavalleygolf.com
- John Cochran, Jeff Potts, front nine, 1967. William Neff, back nine, 1986. 18 holes. Par 72. Blue - 6,548 (70.6/123). White - 6,006 (68.2/116). Gold - 5,476 (65.6/110). Red - 5,124 (63.9/108). Women's Blue - 6,553 (76.2/139). Women's White - 6,022 (73.3/133). Women's Gold - 5,436 (69.8/125). Women's Red - 5,131 (68.1/120). Price - $$.

GETTING THERE Take Hwy. 40 west to Craig, and turn south onto Ranney Street. After crossing the river, turn east onto Hwy. 394 and drive a half-mile to the club on the left.

CRAIG NOTES

Steak dinners are a specialty at the **Eagle Watch Inn**—a full-service restaurant and bar at the Yampa Valley Golf Course; however, Craig has a good amount of family restau-

---

It is demonstrably more difficult to control a shot with a club of extreme loft than with one of moderate pitch. Therefore, the clubs of extreme loft should be left in the bag until the need for them becomes well defined.—Bobby Jones

rants, including the modest **Golden Cavvy Restaurant and Lounge** (970-824-6038), as well as the **Plaza Restaurant** (970-824-7345) if you're in the mood for Mexican. After golf head for **Brown's Park National Wildlife Refuge**, which lies on the Green River and covers more than 13,000 acres. Managed by the U.S. Fish and Wildlife Service as a refuge for migratory waterfowl, it serves as a home for elk, deer, and bald eagles in the winter, as well as golden eagles and peregrine falcons in the spring and summer. The **Taylor Street Bed and Breakfast** (970-824-5866) is an option for overnighters and offers home-style breakfast.

EAGLE

ELEV. 6,600 POP. 3,032

Eagle is not a high-toned resort, but instead a laid-back community about 30 miles west of Vail. Legend has it that William Edwards was the first to arrive in the Eagle area to ranch he built his home close to the railroad water tank. That first dwelling was a dug-out hut with rafters that were rubbed down with sagebrush and mud. The town originally was called McDonald, after Alex McDonald, but Eagle became the name in 1896 when it was sold for taxes totaling $210.42.

Eagle's calling card, in addition to Arnold Palmer's new golf course, is the short drive residents have to other famous Colorado resort towns. Beaver Creek, Vail, Copper Mountain, and Keystone are all nearby, and the incredible Glenwood Canyon lies in the opposite direction.

EAGLE RANCH GOLF COURSE

THE GOLF Arnold Palmer and staff were busy the day of Eagle Ranch Golf Course's grand opening, but they whisked him out to No. 12 when he arrived because this par-5, 614-yarder was befuddling a majority of the golfers, and it was becoming a ritual to pick up the ball and head to the next tee.

The hole requires a long straight first tee shot and some decision-making on the second. A natural wash borders the fairway on the right, then crosses diagonally in the line of fire on the second shot. The safe shot is to the right side of the fairway, just in front of a series of bunkers, opening up the view of the green for the third shot. Risk-takers, however, will go straight for the pin—a path only for the best players because you can't see the target, and trouble is everywhere.

Carved out of the Brush Creek Valley, Eagle Ranch is a walkable layout with only 1,000 feet in variation from the lowest to highest points. Playing to 7,468 yards with five sets of tees, the course forces golfers to negotiate big bentgrass

---

If I catch one of my amateur friends playing with a one-iron, he had better be putting with it.—Tommy Bolt

greens, lakes, and streams. Scenic mountain views abound here: the Sawatch Range, the Flat Tops, and Castle Peak are all nearby, and Eagle Ranch is a Certified Audubon Cooperative Sanctuary.

THE DETAILS 970-328-2882. 0050 Lime Park Drive, Eagle, CO 81631.

- www.eagleranchgolf.com
- Arnold Palmer, Ed Seay, 2001. 18 holes. Par 72. Black - 7,468 (74.8/141). Gold - 7,098 (73/131). Blue - 6,634 (70.8/126). White - 6,091 (68.3/119). Red - 5,401 (65.1/108). Women's White - 6,091 (73.2/137). Women's Red - 5,474 (69.8/126). Price - $$$.

GETTING THERE Motor I-70 west to exit 147 (Eagle), and drive south on Eby Creek Mesa Dr. to Hwy. 6. Go west to Sylvan Lake Road, turn left, and follow the signs to the course.

EAGLE NOTES

Enjoy the Eagle River and **Sylvan Lake State Park**, which is just 15 miles from town and loaded with **off-road Jeep trails**. The town's western heritage is on display at the annual Eagle County Fair and Rodeo, held since 1939. In June, Flight Days brings the locals together for concerts in the town park, food stands, crafts booths, and a parade in historic downtown. **Mi Pueblo Restaurant** (970-328-5156) is the preferred place for an evening on the town, and lodging is nearby along I-70 in the form of the **Best Western Eagle Lodge** (970-328-6316), **Comfort Inn Eagle** (970-328-7878), or **Suburban Lodge Eagle** (970-328-3000).

EDWARDS

ELEV. 7,430 POP. 8,257

Edwards is another one of those bumps in I-70 that continues to expand rapidly, and is a good spot to load up on gas and road-trip supplies when cruising for golf in Colorado. More affordable than high-toned ski resort towns like Vail and Beaver Creek, and loaded with golf courses, Edwards offers a nice shopping area, restaurants, a brewery, and plenty of worthy non-golf activities. Aside from the golf and world-class skiing, the town is a good base for outdoor adventures such as a float down the Eagle River, hiking in the wilderness area, or tapping into the unbelievable fly-fishing in the region.

Remember that you do not so often win holes as the result of your own brilliant play as by the mistakes that the other man makes.—James Braid

THE CLUB AT CORDILLERA—MOUNTAIN COURSE

THE GOLF Traditionalists sometimes complain about routes like the Cordillera Mountain Course; however, a trip around this layout for photo opportunities is a worthwhile adventure in itself. You'll have to decide for yourself, since the price tag is steep ($225 and up). You might also need to hire a forecaddie. Course critics claim that there's just not enough land, it's too severe slope-wise, and diabolical on the greens. Yet the incredible clubhouse, located at 8,250 feet, along with the interesting golf holes, make the Mountain Course worthwhile if money isn't an issue. The views of New York Mountain, the Gore Range, and beautiful aspen-covered hillsides are stunning.

No. 18 is amazing, playing more than 500 yards downhill and only a par 4. But most golfers walk away thinking the par-3 holes are the most enjoyable.

The Fenno family first came here in 1883 to raise sheep, cattle, and farm the slopes that now entertain golfers. Watch for signs of the old homestead all over the layout: the old Fenno cabin and barn just off No. 10 and a 1946 Case threshing machine that harvested grain and was operated by leather belts. The back nine is loaded with relics like a 1920s single-row planter, which was horse-drawn, and a potato digger.

THE DETAILS 970-926-5100. 650 Clubhouse Drive, Edwards, CO 81632.
- www.cordillera-vail.com
- Hale Irwin, Phelps Design, 1994. 18 holes. Par 72. Silver - 6,789 (71.5/137). Green - 6,653 (71.1/134). Blue - 6,165 (70/124). Women's Blue - 6,205 (74.3/143). Women's White - 5,675 (71.3/135). Women's Red - 5,226 (68.9/130). Private club and resort play only. Price - $$$$.

GETTING THERE Take I-70 west past Avon. Take the Edwards exit and go left down the hill to Hwy. 6 and turn right (west). Squaw Creek is 3 miles down, then turn left and drive 2 miles up past the first big gate. At the hairpin turn, the road turns into Fenno Ranch Rd., which takes you to the guard gate.

THE CLUB AT CORDILLERA—SHORT COURSE

THE GOLF The Mountain Course's diminutive sibling, designed by legendary short-game guru Dave Pelz, is a 10-hole practice facility unlike anything else in the world. Just a short walk from The Lodge and perched atop a scenic plateau, this short course and instructional facility is sophisticated enough for serious players who want to develop a stronger short game, yet laid-back enough for a

NORTHWEST

Bunkers are not placed on a course haphazardly, but they are made at particular places to catch particular kinds of defective shots.—James Braid

beginner.

Don't miss lunch at Grouse-on-the-Green, an authentic Irish pub that also serves as the Short Course clubhouse.

THE DETAILS 970-926-5550. 100 Kensington Drive, Edwards, CO 81632.
- www.cordillera-vail.com
- Dave Pelz, 1997. 9-hole par-3. 1,257 yards Par 27. Resort guests. Price - $.

GETTING THERE Motor down I-70 west past Beaver Creek to Edwards. Get off at the Edwards exit, go right, and follow the frontage road west about 1 mile to the guard gate.

THE CLUB AT CORDILLERA—SUMMIT COURSE

THE GOLF The first time Jack Nicklaus saw the spectacular piece of land that was to become the Summit Course, he wasn't so sure. "I thought it was too exposed to wind and weather. I asked Cordillera if they were sure they wanted to put a golf course up here, " Nicklaus said. "Then the longer we looked and the longer we thought, the more we knew that it would work."

The first visions of this layout perched at 9,200 feet was of an 8,000-yard golf course, playing with a boost of 20 percent more carry in the rarefied air; however, they eventually shortened it to 7,530 yards from the tips.

The layout's namesake summit is actually at the 18th tee box, a 473-yard, downhill par 4 that starts from the highest point on the golf course and offers a clear view of the New York Mountains, Bellyache Ridge, and the Gore Range. Thousands of acres of the White River National Forest loom over this slight dogleg left, which also features two bunkers in front and a stand of aspens in back to protect the small green.

The Summit Course used just 190 acres of Cordillera's massive area holdings, with only 80 acres of turf, and the Nicklaus team disturbed very little land. One of the most engaging features is the punchbowl green at the 592-yard, par-5 No. 8. But No. 12 might be the most visually stunning. This 504-yard par 4 has the only water on the course, a lake running down the left side of the green. A native rock outcropping cuts diagonally across the fairway and provides a cross-hazard that is easily carried from the upper tees, but not as easily from the back. The approach is tricky with a long, narrow green and hazard left.

NORTHWEST

If you really want to get better at golf, go back and take it up at a much earlier age. —Henry Beard

THE DETAILS 970-926-5300. 190 Gore Trail, Edwards, CO 81632.
- www.cordillera-vail.com
- Jack Nicklaus, 2001. 18 holes. Par 72. Gold - 7,530 (74/136). Silver - 6,861 (71.4/129). Green - 6,532 (69.7/127). Blue - 6,364 (68.9/125). Women's Blue - 6,428 (75/145). Women's Red - 5,430 (69.5/130). Private club and limited resort play only. Price - $$$$.

GETTING THERE Take I-70 west past Avon. Take the Edwards exit, go left down a hill to Hwy. 6, and turn right (west). Go almost 3 miles to Squaw Creek, turn left, and drive 2 miles up past the first big gate. At the hairpin turn, the road turns into Fenno Ranch Rd. Follow this to the guard gate. Drive past the Mountain course to the Summit.

THE CLUB AT CORDILLERA—VALLEY COURSE

THE GOLF For years this Tom Fazio desert-like links course, set amongst sage-brush and arid land, was ranked in *Golf Magazine's* "Top 100 You Can Play" list. It's no longer ranked, but with its near-desert terrain and Arizona-like look, the course is an enjoyable contrast to other Colorado layouts. Brown tints mingle with the rocks and sagebrush against blue skies and the bright green of the blue-grass fairways. The creek areas are abundant with cottonwoods and ancient junipers hug the rocky cliffside.

The Valley Course is a stern exam. "Every day I tell people to use the driver, but they think they can carry it with a 2-iron. Most days they are wrong," said one caddy of the 253-yard par-3 No. 14. At the 464-yard, par-4 No. 5, stare down the creek carry and take an angled approach to the green, which is sliced by a hump.

THE DETAILS 970-926-5950. 0101 Legends Drive, Edwards, CO 81632.
- www.cordillera-vail.com
- Tom Fazio, 1997. 18 holes. Par 71. Gold/Silver - 6,817 (71.5/129). Silver - 6,483 (70.1/128). Blue - 5,906 (67.2/121). Women's Blue - 6,033 (74.8/143). Women's White - 5,692 (72.6/137). Women's Red - 5,162 (69.4/128). Price - $$$$.

GETTING THERE Take I-70 west past Beaver Creek to Edwards. Get off at the Edwards exit, go right, and follow the frontage road west about 1 mile to the guard gate.

The first thing you should do when you see that your ball has settled in a divot is to tell yourself that it's a bad break, that it happens to everyone, and that you really want to concentrate on this shot...Oh, and you might also resolve never to leave a divot unrepaired yourself. —Ken Venturi

COUNTRY CLUB OF THE ROCKIES

THE GOLF Someone described the Country Club of the Rockies as "Jack Nicklaus on steroids." Some call it over-the-top with its artificial mounding, contours, and fairly flat land. The four holes that run along the Eagle River are aesthetically pleasing.

No. 12, a 477-yard straightaway par 4, is considered the signature hole because of the approach over the Eagle River.

No reciprocal play is accepted, making this a tough place to get on unless you are a member. In past years even sponsored guests were not allowed on the weekends.

THE DETAILS 970-926-3021. 676 Sawatch Drive, Edwards, CO 81632.
- Jack Nicklaus, 1984. 18 holes. Par 72. Green - 7,367 (73.7/136). Blue - 6,839 (71.2/131). White - 6,505 (69.6/126). Black - 6,099 (67.2/117). Women's Black - 6,099 (74.1/142). Women's Red - 5,373 (70.1/131). No reciprocal play accepted. Members and guests only. Price - $$$$.

GETTING THERE Take I-70 west of Avon to the Edwards exit. Take Avon Road to Hwy. 6 and turn right for 2.5 miles. You can see the course from the road.

SONNENALP GOLF CLUB

THE GOLF Sonnenalp hosted the Colorado Open until a surprising lack of sponsorship forced an abrupt cancellation in 2003.

Situated on the sunny side of the Vail Valley facing south, Sonnenalp runs along an elevation of 7,800 feet and covers 7,059 yards at a par 71. Locals declare it is in the "banana belt" of the Vail Valley, which means an April opening because of beautiful early-spring weather. The Jay Morrish-Robert Cupp layout takes in lots of morning sun and has a lower nine that is relatively level with strategically placed bunkers. The elevation is more severe on the back nine with terrain changes and stunning downhill shots.

The round opens with a blind par-5, 611-yarder, followed by a scenic 158-yard par-3 2nd hole. The gulch must be carried to reach the heavily bunkered, three-tiered green. Hooks are deadly on No. 2.

No. 12 dives straight downhill 423 yards, and the approach must negotiate a large stand of cottonwood trees on the right and a creek carry. Take in the scenery of the ski area in the distance on the tee at No. 15, then blast one down the steep hill. This par-4, 385-yarder doglegs left, with three ponds on the left

---

If the average American player would only realize how much easier it is to play well when he is swinging along at a good rate, he would surely gird up his loins and walk a little faster. —H.J. Whigham

to a strawberry-shaped green with back and right bunkers.

A youthful Tiger Woods competed here in an amateur event when he was 11, back when the club was known as Singletree Golf Club.

The Details 970-477-5370. 1265 Berry Creek Road, Edwards, CO 81632.
- www.sonnenalp.com
- Jay Morrish, Bob Cupp, 1980. 18 holes. Par 71. Black - 7,059 (73.1/139). Blue - 6,423 (70.3/129). White - 5,907 (67.8/117). Women's Blue - 6,423 (75.6/143). Women's White - 5,907 (72.7/137). Women's Green - 5,293 (69.4/125). Price - $$$$.

Getting There From Vail take I-70 west to Edwards (exit 163). Turn right at the bottom of the ramp, and immediately right onto Berry Creek Road. Drive straight 1.5 miles to the club on the right.

EDWARDS NOTES

The most exclusive place to stay in Edwards is **The Lodge and Spa at Cordillera** (800-877-3529), ranked 18th of the Top 75 Golf Resorts in America by *Golf Digest* in 2002. This is one of the most luxurious retreats in the world. The 56-room Lodge continually wins awards for its service, and the Spa is considered one of the Top 10 Spas in North America. Dine at **Restaurant Picasso** or **Chaparral** for certified prime-aged Angus steaks and chops, as well as seafood, pasta, and vegetarian entrees. The **Timber Hearth Grille** in the Mountain Course Clubhouse has western fare, but the laid-back favorite is **Grouse-on-the-Green**, which gives patrons an authentic Irish pub-style experience. The **Sonnenalp Resort of Vail** (www.sonnenalp.com, 800-284-4411) includes two other properties in Vail: the **Swiss Hotel and Spa** and the **Austria Haus Club and Hotel**. Owned by fourth-generation hoteliers from Bavaria, Germany, the resort opened in 1979 but was completely renovated in the 1990s. A more affordable option is the **Inn at Riverwalk** (970-926-0606), which is conveniently located near the **Cranberry Island Seafood Co.** (970-926-0639). Another popular local eatery is **Fiesta's Cafe & Cantina** (970-926-3540).

FRUITA

ELEV. 4,503 POP. 6,478

The unusual name of Fruita evolved from the early homesteaders who built their economy around acres of apricots, cherries, grapes, and peaches that they sold around the country. Fruita is the last golf town on the way into Utah and a

Some golfers seem to have no genius for figures. They cannot count correctly and, unfortunately, their general tendency is to be one stroke shy rather than one too many.—Jerome Travers

draw for mountain bikers and tourists coming to four festivals—the Fat Tire Festival, Mike and the Headless Chicken Days, Dinosaur Days, and the Fruita Fall Festival.

Home to the Colorado National Monument Visitor Center, tourists can get into the distinctive geology of the area, and explore dinosaur digs at Riggs Hill and Dinosaur Hill.

ADOBE CREEK NATIONAL GOLF CLUB

THE GOLF With views of the Colorado National Monument and Colorado River, this Ned Wilson design has three contrasting nines—a newer desert-styled layout, a long and windy par 37 on top of a mesa, and a scenic Monument nine. The land is rolling and treeless, but the views are noteworthy. Adobe Creek runs through a number of holes and the greens are fast and unpredictable. Watch out for out-of-bounds on every hole, even though the fairways are wide and forgiving.

THE DETAILS 970-858-0521. 876 18 1/2 Road, Fruita, CO 81521.
- Ned Wilson, 1991. 27 holes. Price - $.
- Mesa-Desert: Gold - 6,742 (70.2/121). Blue - 6,262 (68.1/114). White - 5,570 (64.8/101). Women's White - 5,934 (72/119). Women's Red - 5,433 (69.6/111).
- Monument-Desert: Gold - 6,946 (71.2/119). Blue - 6,293 (68.8/112). White - 5,787 (66.1/102). Women's White - 5,570 (69.8/115). Women's Red - 4,996 (66.6/109).
- Monument-Mesa: Gold - 6,998 (71.4/119). Blue - 6,453 (68.9/111). White - 5,731 (65.5/103). Women's White - 5,878 (71.6/115). Women's Red - 5,253 (67.6/109).

GETTING THERE Take I-70 to the Fruita exit (exit 19, about 10 miles west of Grand Junction). Go left to the first road, which is Frontage Road. Turn left and go about 1 mile.

FRUITA NOTES

After a morning of golf, have lunch at **Aspen Street** (970-858-8888), then dinosaur hunt in the afternoon before checking in at the relaxing **Stonehaven Inn** (800-303-0898). The **Dinosaur Diamond Scenic and Historic Byway** and the **Dinosaur Journey Museum** also offer opportunities to explore the age of the dinosaur. For moun-

Harvey Penick always wanted us to be good bunker players so we wouldn't be afraid to fire at a flag tucked next to one.—Tom Kite

tain bikers, the famous Kokopelli's Trail offers a 136-mile trek to Moab, Utah. And off-road types should look 8 miles north of town to the **Little Book Cliffs Wild Horse Range** for 4-wheeling adventures. The **Unaweep/Tabeguache Scenic and Historic Byway**, a 138-mile route, begins just outside of Grand Junction and follows the course of Unaweep Canyon through the vivid red desert of the Dolores River Canyon, opening up on the high plains. Finally, nearby Palisade, CO is home to five **vineyards** with tasting rooms and winery tours, as well as famous peaches.

GLENWOOD SPRINGS ELEV. 5,763 POP. 7,736

Glenwood Springs, established in 1888 by Walter Devereaux, is one of Colorado's top five tourist stops and is famous for several reasons. First is the world-famous Glenwood Hot Springs Pool, more than 100 years old and the world's largest. It's also the final resting place for Doc Holliday, who scrambled all around the state back in the 1880s as a part-time dentist and full-time hooligan and gambler. With 22 saloons in a two-block area, Glenwood Springs was probably his idea of heaven. Doc settled here in hopes that the hot springs would cure his ills, but tuberculosis claimed him and many still annually visit his grave. And in the early 1900s President Theodore Roosevelt spent time hunting bear in the area forests, and was supposedly presented with a handmade stuffed bear when he returned to the Hotel Colorado—thus the birth of the Teddy Bear.

Located in one of Colorado's most beautiful canyons, golfers sliding into Glenwood Springs become giddy from amazing driving experience—an impressively scenic route along a marvel of road engineering. Long known for its 9-hole municipal, Glenwood Springs has been graced with the impressive Ironbridge Golf Club, making the town a more viable golf weekend destination.

GLENWOOD SPRINGS GOLF CLUB

THE GOLF Glenwood Springs Golf Club is a 9-hole municipal course located in the west part of town. Running along the side of rising terrain, this one presents uneven lies while playing through narrow, tree-lined fairways. It's classic old-time golf with interesting features, such as a par 3 that has a huge dip in front of the green.

Locals say putts break toward the Colorado River, and the views of Red Mountain, with its iron-rich red streaks, might beguile you. No. 5 at 425 yards

Some players are never satisfied unless they are buying new clubs....This is not good for the player, but it is quite good for the clubmaker.—James Braid

NORTHWEST

is one of those side hill holes that requires accurate placement to the high side of the fairway.

THE DETAILS 970-945-7086. 0193 131 Road, Glenwood Springs, CO 81601.
- Henry Hughes, 1952. 9 holes. Par 35. Blue - 5,902 (67.6/112). White/Blue - 5,853 (67.3/112). White - 5,804 (67/111). Women's Blue - 5,904 (72.8/123). Women's White/Blue - 5,738 (71.8/122). Women's White - 5,572 (70.8/122). Women's Red/White - 5,352 (69.4/120). Women's Red - 5,132 (68/119). Price - $$.

GETTING THERE Take Glenwood Springs exit 116. Turn left at the first light (6th St.) and drive west until it forks (1 mile). Veer right to Donegan Rd. Turn right at Sunny Acres Road.

IRONBRIDGE GOLF CLUB

THE GOLF This 2003 Arthur Hills design is named for the historic old iron bridge crossing the Roaring Fork River nearby, and includes four holes on a rugged back nine that will leave you drooling for more.

Ironbridge includes two streams, five lakes, three tunnels, 19 bridges, and more than eight miles of continuous cart path. Don't even dream of walking the back nine, which includes tee boxes that dive downward and red-hued mountain vistas.

To build Ironbridge, Hills wiped out seven holes of a 9-holer known as the Westbank Ranch Golf Club, then routed the new course, a hefty 7,103 yards at par 72, over sections of the old track. A meadow-like front nine skirts the trout-laden Roaring Fork River, and a mountainous back nine climbs into ravines lined with piñons and junipers 300 feet above the river valley. Hills named this section The Lost Horizon.

A forced carry over a gorge is required on No. 10, a 457-yarder from the tips, where a draw is the play. The green is raised and heavily bunkered, so a par here is worth bragging about. The four holes located in the upper tiers are stunning and fun to play, and perfect conditions are impressive for a new course.

This is a private club, but the public can play through a golf package from the St. Regis Hotel in Aspen.

THE DETAILS 970-384-0630. 430 Ironbridge Drive, Glenwood Springs, CO 81601.
- www.ironbridgeclub.com

Would you like to know the fastest way to take several strokes off your game? Spend two hours in a bunker.—Greg Norman

- Arthur Hills, 2003. 18 holes. Par 72. Black - 7,103 (73.3/140). Blue - 6,667 (71.4/133). White - 6,158 (69.4/130). Women's White - 6,208 (75.9/148). Women's Red - 5,457 (71.7/141). Women's Gold - 4,916 (67.6/127). Private club. Price - $$$$.

GETTING THERE Take I-70 west to Glenwood Springs. Go 5 miles south on Hwy. 82 towards Aspen. Turn right at Westbank Rd. Cross the bridge through the housing area and follow Westbank Road to the course.

GLENWOOD SPRINGS NOTES

Just getting here from Denver is a visual delight. Driving through Glenwood Canyon is an adventure on I-70's new stretch of pavement through the tight canyon. The design has won environmental and architecture awards. For hundreds of years the Ute Indians revered the Yampah Hot Springs, which today feed the gigantic outdoor pool with 3.5 million gallons of hot, mineral-rich water a day. White men discovered the springs in 1860 when a party of geographic explorers led by Captain Richard Sopris stumbled by. Twenty years later, a group of British investors bought the Yampah Hot Springs and 10 acres of surrounding land. The summer calendar is loaded with festivals, making the town a lively place to visit for golf trips. Plan ahead and make reservations for places like the historic **Hotel Colorado** (800-544-3998), a 107-room lodge a block away from the hot springs. The historic **Hotel Denver** (800-826-8820) is located right off of the main street. Both are cozy options after quality time at the **Rivers Restaurant** (970-928-8813) and the **Glenwood Canyon Brewpub** (970-945-1276). Golf bums looking for non-stop golf should consider combining their visit to Glenwood Springs with time in **Carbondale**, where the **Comfort Inn & Suites** (800-228-5150) offers packages to River Valley Ranch, just minutes away.

GRANBY

ELEV. 7,939 POP. 1,525

Granby is a quiet, small town just a short drive from the ski slopes at Winter Park and on the way to the Arapaho National Forest with all its opportunities for outdoor activities. The mountain towns in Grand County are on the western entrance to Rocky Mountain National Park, and all have productive fishing lakes with beautiful, unspoiled views. Shadow Mountain Reservoir is right here along with Willow Creek Reservoir. Grand Lake, Colorado's largest natural lake, is only a few miles away.

Laid-back cowboy culture and lower gasoline prices await the roving golfer in

Poor chipping is the primary reason the handicap of the average golfer has remained frozen.—Corey Pavin

Granbury, which is void of valet parking and high-priced restaurants, and only minutes from outstanding golf at Grand Lake, Grand Elk, Solvista, and Pole Creek.

GRAND ELK GOLF CLUB

THE GOLF Envisioned by Jerry Jones, the man who invented the highly successful "Ski The Summit" pass in the 1970s, Grand Elk Golf Club was built as a getaway for golfers, fishermen, skiers, hikers, and lovers of the outdoors.

The Craig Stadler signature design was routed by Tripp Davis, and he calls Grand Elk a heathland-styled golf course because it reminded him of historic Gleneagles in Scotland, with a gentle roll of the mountain foothills located in a valley with rivers and streams. But gentle surroundings don't equal an easy golf course. Grand Elk traverses 7,208 yards at par 71 with several opportunities to fire at greens just over a stream, and wetlands that are difficult to see because of tall willowy shrubs or native grasses.

During grand-opening festivities Stadler said there were enough easy golf courses in the world. The design team wanted a fair golf course, but one that would play extremely difficult from the tips with the afternoon wind blowing hard.

At an elevation of 7,935 feet, Grand Elk has wide, charitable tee-shot fairways, but the approach demands attention. Yardage-wise, the back nine is shorter but plays longer because of the shot selections.

THE DETAILS 866-866-3557. 970-887-2540. 1321 Ten Mile Drive, Granby, CO 80446.
- www.grandelk.com.
- Craig Stadler, Tripp Davis, 2002. 18 holes. Par 71. Black - 7,208 (72.4/131). Blue - 6,410 (70.1/122). Green - 5,771 (67.2/114). Women's Blue - 6,411 (74.4/139). Women's Green - 5,771 (71/131). Women's Gold - 5,095 (69.1/115). Price - $$$$.

GETTING THERE Enjoy the I-70 trip from Denver west to Hwy. 40. Take Hwy. 40 north through historic Empire to Granby. The course is southwest of Granby on the left side.

SOLVISTA GOLF & SKI RANCH

THE GOLF Amtrak passes by on your journey through the front nine at SolVista, reminiscent of the old courses in Scotland. Located just across Highway 40 from Grand Elk, the course has panoramic views of red hillsides and the rush of the Fraser River.

Nothing is hidden at SolVista as the course routes through the valley-floor with native grasses and ponds coming into play. The greens have subtle breaks, which make them tricky to read, but overall this is a friendly layout susceptible to good scores.

Quarry Hill is in sight as the round begins with a reachable par 5, 567-yard hole that descends with a slight dogleg right to a large and undulating green. Even if you reach it in two, birdie is no gimme. The hole is lined on the right by the draw, a natural intermittent stream, and wetlands.

No. 4 is a 413-yard par 4 that tests accuracy. It's a slight dogleg right, guarded by a huge ponderosa pine on the right, but also in view is a large irrigation lake that guards the left side. SolVista is a fun golf course and a must-play when you come to the Grand County.

Michael Asmundson's front nine opened in the summer of 2001, but the back nine was delayed a few years due to the drought. Unlike the front, the back traverses up the hill toward SolVista's ski lifts and ski community (formerly Silver Creek) with an elevation change as it climbs into the sage arroyos and DeBerard Draw.

THE DETAILS 866-765-8478. 970-887-2709. 2579 County Road 894, Granby, CO 80446.
- www.solvista.com
- Michael Asmundson, 2001. 18 holes. Par 72. Gold - 7,210 (72.9/127). White - 6,602 (70/121). Green - 6,024 (67.2/113). Women's Green - 6,024 (72.2/127). Women's Rose - 5,310 (68.1/121). Price - $$$.

GETTING THERE Motor down I-70 west to Hwy. 40 about 42 miles to the SolVista Golf & Ski Ranch entrance. Follow the signs east 1.5 miles to the course.

GRANBY NOTES

Known as "the dude ranch of Colorado," six famous guest ranches are within a half-hour drive of Granby. Places like the **C Lazy U Guest Ranch** supply horses, family-style meals, cozy cabins and hot tubs. Visitors can ride the rails (www.amtrak.com) to

Not paying a golf debt is like ordering dinner, eating the damn thing, and then not expecting to pay for it.—Doug Sanders

NORTHWEST

Fraser or Granby on Amtrak's Chicago-Oakland route that passes through Denver's Union Station. The **Denver Rio Grande Ski Train** has day trips through the Moffat Tunnel to the slopes of Winter Park and SolVista Golf & Ski Ranch every Saturday and Sunday during the summer. *Colorado AvidGolfer Magazine* (www.coloradoavid-golfer.com, 720-493-1729) also offers a ski train golf trip in the summer. The **Inn at Silver Creek** has **Paul's Creekside Grill** (970-887-2484). Another favorite is the **Kicking Horse Lodges at SolVista** (www.solvista.com), which offers luxury condos with full kitchen and hot tubs overlooking the back nine of SolVista. Lunches to-go are available at **Mad Munchies**, which is across from **Remington's**, and **Carmelina's** is a local staple.

GRAND JUNCTION   ELEV. 4,597 POP. 41,986

The progression of ski-area terrain around Summit County and through Vail gradually changes as you head on I-70 toward Grand Junction. Here the landscape almost becomes a moonscape mixed with a verdant valley floor that is ideal for orchards and vineyards.

Grand Junction is the gateway city to the Colorado National Monument, and is bordered by the Little Bookcliffs—areas of steep reddish walls that plummet from mesas down to the valley floor where the Colorado River has carved a waterway through the Colorado Plateau.

Grand Junction's five-block North Seventh Avenue Historic Residential District is tree-lined and a nice walk for those interested in 100-year-old architecture. In late summer the peaches grown in this area are phenomenal. And while some consider Grand Junction merely a rest stop on the way to excursions west, or only as a mountain-bike destination, the golf is unparalleled—highlighted by the spectacular Golf Club at Redlands Mesa and several quality municipal tracks with lots of character.

BOOKCLIFF COUNTRY CLUB

THE GOLF Grand Junction's only private club, Bookcliff features mature trees, water, and views of the Bookcliffs and Grand Mesa.

It's a traditional-styled ego-booster with well-maintained greens and flat fairways. Water hazards in the form of lakes come into play on eight holes.

Walkers will enjoy Bookcliff. However, the best amenity at Bookcliff is the reciprocal golf agreements with Aspen Glen and The Country Club of the Rockies in the Vail Valley.

The overwhelming majority of unsuccessful putts are missed not because they were misjudged but because they were mis-hit.—Jackie Burke, Jr.

THE DETAILS 970-242-9053. 2730 G Road, Grand Junction, CO 81506.

- Press Maxwell, 1958. Dick Phelps, subsequent remodels. 18 holes. Par 71. Blue - 6,617 (70.3/120). White - 6,243 (68.5/115). Women's Blue - 6,632 (77/136). Women's White - 6,215 (74.7/132). Women's Red - 5,714 (71.9/126). Women's Gold - 5,370 (69.8/122). Private club, reciprocal play allowed Monday-Friday. Price - $$.

GETTING THERE Take I-70 to Grand Junction. At Horizon Dr. (airport exit), go south a half mile and turn right after the Pizza Hut. The course is immediately to the right.

CHIPETA GOLF COURSE

THE GOLF Chipeta is a scenic executive course with wide, tree-lined fairways and water hazards in play on only one hole (No. 7). Irrigation ditches run throughout the layout, which is flat with large, undulating, elevated greens of medium speed.

The backdrop includes scenes of the Grand Mesa. The 287-yard, par-4 14th is the signature hole. It's tree-lined from an elevated tee, making it a target for long drivers to nail in one stroke.

THE DETAILS 970-245-7177. 222 29 Road, Grand Junction, CO 81503.

- Wilson Golf Group, 1997. 18-hole executive course. Par 59. Black - 3,825 (58.6/88). Yellow - 3,395 (57.6/86). Women's Black - 3,749 (59.6/90). Women's Yellow - 3,395 (57.8/83). Price - $.

GETTING THERE Take I-70 to the Clifton exit (exit 37). Turn left on 32 Road. Follow 32 Road to B 1/2 Rd. Go west about 3 miles to 29 Rd. and turn left. Drive a half-mile to the entrance on the left.

THE GOLF CLUB AT REDLANDS MESA

THE GOLF When Redlands Mesa opened in 2001, the up-and-coming Jim Engh gained even more recognition, creating another outstanding Colorado course that wasn't designed by one of the more recognized architects.

Engh thought his Sanctuary design was a once-in-a-lifetime opportunity, but the Castle Rock-based designer changed his mind when he saw the future site of Redlands Mesa. He said it was spectacular, with boulders the size of houses and a moonscape on rolling terrain with large mesas and valleys, reminiscent of Utah's Canyonlands National Park.

The fact is that the ball is round and it's going to roll in the direction in which you hit it. High-speed video of golfers' putting strokes confirms this.—Dr. Bob Rotella

NORTHWEST

Redlands Mesa won *GolfDigest*'s Best New Affordable Course in 2001 and continues to be a favorite for travel golf enthusiasts. The par-72 layout plays at 7,007 feet from the Monument (back) tees, which display Engh's true genius. He saw a canvas of multiple earth tones and painted it with shades of green bordered by jagged sandstone boulders, ochre dirt, and numerous formations of balanced rock.

Eleven holes play downhill, inspiring outstanding views of the rolling mounds and deep bunkers.

In the distance look south for the pinks, reds, and browns of the 800-foot cliffs of the Colorado National Monument, north to the gray-purple Bookcliffs, and east to Mount Garfield and the Grand Mesa, the world's highest flat-topped mountain.

The 373-yard, par-4 No. 4 is exciting, especially from the back tee box where those with vertigo might have issues. You could almost hang glide from up here. Don't back up without looking, because it drops 100 feet.

No. 17 is another memorable climb to a tee-box perch. Again, the eagle's-nest tee box has a 150-foot drop and vista to a green 218 yards away, nestled in another natural bowl framed by rock. Those prone to take a mulligan may want to keep reloading.

Redlands Mesa, which hosted 28,000 rounds last year, has also won these accolades: Top Ten You Can Play by *Golf Magazine*, No. 3 Best New Golf Course in the World by *Sports Illustrated*, Colorado's No. 1 Public Access Course by *Golfweek*, and 23rd of the nation's top 100 Public Golf Courses by *GolfDigest*.

After your round, have lunch or dine in the Red Canyon Grille in the handsome new clubhouse.

THE DETAILS 970-263-9270. 2325 W. Ridges Blvd., Grand Junction, CO 81503.
- www.redlandsgolf.com
- Jim Engh, 2001. 18 holes. Par 72. Black - 7,007 (71.7/135). Blue - 6,486 (69.4/130). White - 5,838 (67.2/115). Women's Blue - 6,486 (75.8/141). Women's White - 5,838 (72.8/131). Women's Red - 4,916 (69//115). Price - $$$.

GETTING THERE Drive on I-70 west to Redlands Parkway-24 Road, and head south for 3 miles to Broadway. Turn east (left) on Broadway and go 2 miles to Ridges Blvd. Turn south (right) and travel through the Ridges subdivision. Take the right fork up the hill to the golf course.

Percentage golf is not so much the science of playing the game with the shots of which you are capable as it is of playing without the shot of which you are incapable. —Jackie Burke, Jr

LINCOLN PARK GOLF COURSE

THE GOLF Lincoln Park Golf Course's claim to fame is that it hosts the Rocky Mountain Open, the oldest open golf tournament in Colorado. This one is an easy-to-walk, old-school 9-holer with fairways that route back and forth, flat greens, water on three holes, and out-of-bounds on seven. Built back in 1926, it is conveniently located in the central part of town.

No. 1 is typical of Lincoln's holes: 402 yards straightaway with out-of-bounds right and the Grand Mesa within view.

THE DETAILS 970-242-6394. 800 Mantlo Circle, Grand Junction, CO 81501.
- Unknown architect, 1926. Dick Phelps, remodeling work. 9 holes. Par 36. Women's Yellow/Red - 6,071 (72.8/125) Red/Blue - 6,542 (68.6/119). Price - $.

GETTING THERE Take I-70 to the Horizon Drive exit and turn south on 12th St. Take 12th St. to Gunnison and turn left.

TIARA RADO GOLF COURSE

THE GOLF Designed in 1972 by Tom Kolacny as a 9-holer, Tiara Rado became an instant municipal favorite. It's a short, traditional design with a backdrop of towering rock walls, and has four lakes that come into play. Dick Phelps arrived in 1986 to add a back nine and re-work the front nine. And while Tiara Rado is a great ego-booster with impressive scenery, regulars benefit from knowing that the greens break away from the Colorado National Monument.

Post-round on a hot summer day, Rado's Piñon Grill is a popular spot to rehash the good and bad shots and enjoy a Colorado micro-brew on the flagstone patio.

A Dick Phelps master plan for remodeling has been in effect for about 10 years and the city is implementing the plan in phases.

THE DETAILS 970-254-3830. 2063 S. Broadway, Grand Junction, CO 81503.
- Tom Kolacny, 1972, front nine. Dick Phelps, 1986, back nine, subsequent updates. 18 holes. Par 71. Blue - 6,289 (69/120). White - 5,967 (67.4/117). Women's Blue - 6,152 (73.7/129). Women's White - 5, 907 (72.4/127). Women's Yellow - 4,919 (68/111). Price - $$.

NORTHWEST

The best advice I can offer for playing a ball out of water is – don't.—Tony Lema

GETTING THERE Take I-70 to exit 28 (the 24 Road exit) and turn south. Go about 7 miles to the course.

GRAND JUNCTION NOTES

Well-rounded weekends involve not only golf, but excursions into the Grand Valley's rich wine country as well as mountain biking and hiking in places like Rattlesnake Canyon, Mee Canyon, Knowles Canyon, or Jones Canyon. **Golf packages** to Redlands Mesa and other area courses are available at the **La Quinta** (970-241-2929), **Country Inns** (800-990-1143), and **The Adams' Mark** (800-444-2326). And right next to Redlands Mesa is **Los Altos Bed & Breakfast** (970-256-0964). Try the **Blue Moon Bar & Grille** (970-242-4506), or **The Winery** (970-242-4100) when looking for meals in town, and the **Rockslide Brew Pub** (970-245-2111) on Main Street is the perfect 19th hole.

GRAND LAKE

ELEV. 8,437 POP. 447

Grand Lake, the western entrance to Rocky Mountain National Park, is another one of those famous Colorado vacation spots popular for fishing and relaxation. Visitors love to stroll the boardwalk on a bright, cool summer day, or rent a boat and take a tour around the lake. The lofty altitude and scenic terrain create ideal conditions for enjoying golf at the Grand Lake GC, while significant others shop and wait in this charming village nestled against Colorado's largest natural lake.

GRAND LAKE GOLF COURSE

THE GOLF Referred to as "The Crown Jewel of Mountain Courses," the Grand Lake GC is a 6,650-yard, must-play beauty, carved through huge stands of lodgepole pines, located just minutes from spectacular Grand Lake. Henry Hughes designed the front nine in 1964 and Dick Phelps sculpted in 1978 to complete the 18 holes.

Tight and demanding at 8,420 feet, the elevated 17th tee is a challenge—many golfers gaze at Mount Baldy and lose focus. The hole is short and downhill at 363 yards, but the lodgepole pines eat up errant drives, and the smallish, subtle green is challenging.

THE DETAILS 970-627-8008. 1415 County Rd. 48, Grand Lake, CO 80447.

Every golfer should establish his own par on a hole and play for that par.—H.H. Ramsay

NORTHWEST

- www.grandlakegolf.com
- Henry Hughes, front nine, 1964. Dick Phelps, back nine, 1978. 18 holes. Par 72. Blue - 6,650 (70.5/119). White - 6,316 (69.5/117). Women's White - 6,310 (74.3/139). Women's Red - 5,678 (71/129). Price - $$.

GETTING THERE From Hwy. 40, take Hwy. 34 north 17 miles to Golf Course Road. Go left (west) on Golf Course Road 1.5 miles to the course.

GRAND LAKE NOTES

Peaks of the Never Summer Wilderness surround the tiny alpine village of Grand Lake, which has log-front stores, board sidewalks, and plenty of modern conveniences. Golf weekends should be combined with horseback rides, fishing, and rafting trips down the river followed by feasts at **E.G.'s Garden Grill** (970-627-8404). **The Mountain Inn** (970-627-3385) is rustic, serves juicy scrumptious steaks, and has an enjoyable ambience because it's crowded. The historic **Grand Lake Lodge** (www.grand-lakelodge.com, 970-627-3967) overlooks Grand and Shadow Mountain Lakes and offers its **Lodge Restaurant**; and the **Gateway Inn** (www.gatewayinn.com, 877-627-1352) is another alternative. For nightlife look to the **Lariat Saloon** or the **Stagecoach Inn** for live music.

GYPSUM

ELEV. 6,600 POP. 3,654

Gypsum, named after the mineral deposits found in the sagebrush-dotted hills, occupies a stop on the I-70 corridor that was surveyed in 1862 by C.W. Daggett. He was one of the area pioneers looking over nearby Dotsero for ranch land. By 1880 the area became a reservation for the Ute Indians just before the railroad rolled through in 1884. The terrain here is rugged ranch land, but close enough to the ski areas of Vail and Beaver Creek for residents to enjoy a day on the slopes. Thankfully for golfers, Pete Dye came along in 1997 to build Cotton Ranch Golf Club in the spot the Ute Indians used to call "hole in the sky."

COTTON RANCH GOLF CLUB

THE GOLF Located 35 minutes west of Vail, this 7,052-yard, par 72 course begins in Cottonwood Valley before climbing 200 feet to the top of a rocky mesa. Dye's design features a few tricky target holes.

The valley holes have plenty of streams, ponds, and native wetlands along

The muttered hint, "Remember, you have a stroke here," freezes my joints like a blast from Siberia.—John Updike

with testy bunkers. Greens are medium-sized with contours and quick rolls. The par-3 No. 8 is exciting, playing straight downhill 164 yards, with a panoramic view of the surrounding mountains and hills. Picking the right club is a challenge.

Locals prefer the signature No. 6, which rests atop a mesa. When this Pete Dye course opened in 1997, there was even a vertical lift to assist walkers to the higher plateau, but safety concerns closed it. No. 6 is a demanding hole of 568 yards surrounded by native sage, juniper, and piñon. Big hitters must carry it 300 yards for a chance to get home in two. The safe play is to lay up, which is no bargain since deep grass and bunkers on the right side must be carried.

Another scenic hole on the mesa, and a great photo opportunity, is the 411-yard No. 5. From the tee box the landing area appears tiny, but there's plenty of room. Then the approach must carry a draw to an island-like green.

THE DETAILS 970-524-6200. 530 Cotton Ranch Drive, Gypsum, CO 81637.
- www.cottonranch.com
- Pete Dye, 1997. 18 holes. Par 72. Black - 7,052 (72.9/130). Brown - 6,474 (71.5/123). Gold - 6,048 (70/118). Women's Brown - 6,474 (75.9/140). Women's Gold - 6,048 (73.7/134). Women's Green - 5,197 (70.1/117). Semi-private club gives 20 percent of tee times to non-members. Price - $$$$.

GETTING THERE Head out on I-70 west to the Gypsum exit (#140), turn left at the exit stop sign, and drive about a mile to Valley Rd. Turn right on Valley Rd., head 1 mile south, and the course is on the right.

GYPSUM NOTES

Vail and Beaver Creek offer luxury for a price nearby, but Gypsum has some enjoyable cafes and restaurants. The **Cotton Ranch Club** at the course is known for its signature Ahi tuna steak and Dirty Martini. **AJ Brink's** (970-524-7344) is on the lake and offers western fares, as well as lodging and summer fun via their **Sweetwater Resort**. **Sylvan Lake State Park** is about 40 miles away for fishing, boating, hiking, or picnicking.

From the roaring oceans to the majestic lakes, the rushing streams and quiet ponds and burns, water adds a test to golf that entrances.—Robert Trent Jones

KEYSTONE

ELEV. 9,166 POP. 825

In the old days Keystone was just a little stagecoach stop on the way to Denver. The bumpy ride back then included a towering climb up Loveland Pass with the optional excursion to a rustic little inn at 9,300 feet that has evolved into the Ski Tip Lodge. The lodge is still a popular place to stay—a Keystone landmark bed and breakfast and home to a gourmet restaurant that should not be missed. Back in the day, Hollywood stars like Henry Fonda lounged here on back-porch rocking chairs overlooking the Snake River, relaxing after a day of hiking in the cool Colorado summer.

Today's modern Keystone boasts River Run, a European-styled village with shops and restaurants on the first floors and condos on the upper floors—a great place to hole up for a weekend of golf at the village's two great golf courses.

KEYSTONE RANCH GOLF COURSE

THE GOLF The Ranch Course spreads across the grounds where the Ute and Arapaho Indians once hunted buffalo. Designed by Robert Trent Jones, Jr., this par-72, 7,109-yard route begins deep in the lodgepole pines before emerging into the open range after the early holes.

The sage meadows evoke a Scottish links feel and include 68 bunkers, a nine-acre lake, and a total of six water hazards. The greens are a combination bent and poa, with bluegrass and rye in the fairways.

Great photo opportunities abound, since the course is loaded with scenic golf holes routed around historic old ranch buildings. The par-3, 190-yard No. 5 is a good example. No. 9 is just as handsome. Playing 368 yards from the tips, it involves a huge carry of the lake and is mean because of the strong headwind.

The clubhouse, which also doubles as a gourmet restaurant, is a 60-year-old former ranch house once inhabited by the cattle ranchers who settled this area.

For the ladies, both The Ranch Course and The River Course have been rated high as friends of female golfers, and LPGA Hall of Famer Nancy Lopez lives in a house next to the first green.

THE DETAILS 970-496-4250. 1239 Keystone Ranch Road, Keystone, CO 80435.
- www.keystoneresort.com
- Robert Trent Jones, Jr., 1980. 18 holes. Par 72. Blue - 7,109 (72.5/137). White - 6,521 (69.4/133). Gold - 5,842 (66.9/117). Women's White - 6,521 (75/139). Women's Gold - 5,842 (71.2/132). Women's Red - 5,582 (69.9/128). Price - $$$$.

When your shot has to carry over a water hazard, you can either hit one more club or two more balls. —Henry Beard

GETTING THERE From I-70 take Hwy. 6 (exit 205) south 6 miles to the stoplight in Keystone. Turn right and follow the signs to the golf course (about 2 miles).

THE RIVER COURSE AT KEYSTONE

THE GOLF "Inspiring" might be a good word to describe the opening tee shot at Keystone's River Course. The fairway looms 100 feet below, snow-capped peaks surround the hole, and the Snake River is nearby.

Environmental award-winners Dana Fry and Dr. Michael Hurdzan presented generous landing areas on their design for The River Course. The muscular mounds make the fairways seem narrower than they are, while open green fronts allow bump-and-run shots. The first crossing of the Snake River is a par-3, 222-yard test. A trap looms on the right side of the green and anything right of that is in the river.

While the front nine plays close to the Snake, the back nine is threaded through a lodgepole-pine forest with lofty elevation changes, capricious bunkers, water hazards, and beaver ponds. In all, this $12 million layout includes 74 bunkers and five water hazards.

THE DETAILS 970-496-4444. 155 River Course Drive, Keystone, CO 80435.
- www.keystoneresort.com.
- Michael Hurdzan, Dana Fry, 2000. 18 holes. Par 71. Black - 6,816 (70.8/132). Blue - 6,393 (69.3/126). White - 5,874 (66.5/116). Gold - 5,265 (63.5/109). Women's Blue - 6,393 (74.3/140). Women's White - 5,874 (71.3/134). Women's Gold - 5,265 (68.5/128). Women's Red - 4,686 (65.1/123). Price - $$$$.

GETTING THERE Take the Dillon-Silverthorne exit (#205) from I-70. Go south on Hwy. 6 about 6 miles to course entrance.

KEYSTONE NOTES

Vail Resorts, Inc. purchased Keystone Resort in 1997, and golf trips to the area should be planned by visiting **www.keystoneresort.com**, where you can find special deals and advance tee times, and even make reservations to any of the restaurants by calling 800-354-4385. The **Keystone Ranch Restaurant**, heralded as "quite possibly the finest ski resort restaurant on earth" by *US News and World Report*, is THE place for post-golf revelry. It's in the same building as The **Ranch Golf Clubhouse**, a former 1930s ranch log homestead, the ideal spot for a six-course meal of wild game, elk, venison,

The man who can putt is a match for anyone.—Willie Park, Jr.

NORTHWEST

or fowl by the fireplace overlooking the Rockies and the golf course. Reveler types enjoy the **Snake River Saloon** (970-468-2788) for live music and beer drinking, and the **Kickapoo Tavern** is another worthy spot to hole up for a beer. Other Summit County options include the **Alpenglow Stube**, North America's highest gourmet restaurant, the **Ski Tip Lodge**, or **Fritz Alpine Bistro** (970-468-1420). Another macho hang out is **Gassy Thompson's** at the base of the mountain, sort of a hunting lodge grill named after an 1880s miner.

MEEKER

ELEV. 6.239 POP. 2,242

Meeker is a true ranch town located near the Flat Tops Wilderness Area, which is home to the world's largest herd of indigenous elk. Named for Nathan C. Meeker, who arrived in 1878 to head the White River Indian Agency, the little hamlet was called "land of shining mountains" by the Utes. Meeker's past is still visible in its old brick buildings on the square.

A Forest Service landscape architect named Arthur Carhart made some history here in 1919. He wanted to create wilderness preserves east of town. And his vision inspired the 1964 Wilderness Act, which was opposed by most Colorado politicians. Today Meeker is still sparsely populated, in the heart of a vast horse, sheep, and cattle country.

MEEKER GOLF COURSE

THE GOLF MGC offers the unusual opportunity to attack the signature hole with the first shot of the day. Course architect Henry Hughes, adamant about this aspect, worked it into this 9-holer when he laid it out in 1969. The hole plays only 295 yards, but requires strategic thinking. Macho men can play for the 220-yard carry of the stream that cuts the fairway, while those in the mood to warm up can lay it up and face a longer approach. Out-of-bounds lines the right side. All told, water hazards are the defining feature of this rolling course, with wet stuff on eight holes.

THE DETAILS 970-878-5642. 903 Country Road 13, Meeker, CO 81641.
- Henry Hughes, 1969. 9 holes. Par 34. White/Blue - 5,338 (64.1/111). Women's White/Blue - 5,344 (70.3/122). Women's Red/White - 4,740 (66.9/115). Price - $.

GETTING THERE From Meeker, take CR 13 south 1 mile to the course.

Play the game, strategically, from the green back to the tee. Design every shot for the easiest putt possible.—Jackie Burke, Jr

MEEKER NOTES

Elk Creek Lodge is the place outdoors enthusiasts stay while in the Meeker area for fishing, hunting, and golf. This gateway to the White River National Forest and the Flat Tops Wilderness (accessible only by foot or on horseback) offers 111 miles of fishable streams and 780 acres of lakes. The place to plan a drive on the 82-mile Flat Tops Trail Scenic Byway is either the **Market Street Bar & Grill** (970-878-3193) or the **Meeker Cafe**, next door to the historic **Meeker Hotel**. The best dining locale might be the **Sleepy Cat Lodge and Restaurant** (970-878-4413), which requires reservations and is twenty miles east of town, but serves unbelievable steaks. In Meeker, look to **The Bakery** (970-878-5500) for fresh bread and sandwiches.

NEW CASTLE

ELEV. 5,550 POP. 1,984

New Castle is a historic coal-mining town just 10 miles west of Glenwood Springs on Interstate 70. It was once home to 10 mines and nearly 500 miners. The population soared to 2,000 as the town expanded to include a local cannery, brickyard, brewery, 15 saloons, five restaurants, three livery stables, and several hotels. When coal mining subsided, New Castle turned to fruit growing and ranching. Golfers looking for links fun at the new Lakota Canyon Golf Club can explore three parks with fishing holes and boat ramps, and take in the historic museum, pizza place, cafe, bar, and grocery store.

LAKOTA CANYON GOLF CLUB

THE GOLF This new daily-fee, Jim Engh-designed course is projected to open in the summer of 2004. Lakota Canyon's layout traverses wild ridges, dives into huge canyons, and includes wetlands along the valley floor. Thanks to Engh's vision, golfers will find themselves bombing drives from high atop ridge lines into the valleys or striking par-3 shots from the ridge lines across canyons.

Holes 1 and No. 10, are parallel starting from atop holes, start from atop a hill, hitting down to the valley floor 160 feet below. Five other holes feature similar drives downhill. The par-5 18th requires hiking boots—it plays up into the valley, across a ravine, then back across the ravine again.

THE DETAILS 970-984-3909. 1000 Club House Drive, New Castle, CO 81647.
- www.lakotacanyonranch.com.
- Jim Engh, 2004. 18 holes. Par 72. About 7,000 yards from the back tees. Not yet rated. Price - $$$.

This is really the whole secret of good match play – simply to play your best and steadiest, and not to care about the opponent's game until it is absolutely necessary to do so.—James Braid

Getting There Take I-70 west past Glenwood to the New Castle exit (#105). Go north 1 mile on Castle Valley Blvd. to the golf course entrance.

NEW CASTLE NOTES

Consider a tip from course architect Jim Engh, who frequented the local bowling alley for dinner and sporting fun with his crew during construction of the course, and if you need to crash for the night, find the **Roadway Inn** (970-984-2363). However, the highlight of non-golf time in New Castle is the **Elk Creek Mining Company** (970-984-0828), which occupies a building that dates back to 1893. Steaks and ribs are the specialty, and the bar offers sports viewing, with an ambience accentuated by old photos of famous outlaws and lawmen. The **Colorado River** and **White River National Forest** offer 225 million acres for exploring, camping, hunting, and off-road four-wheel adventures. Sunlight, Aspen, Beaver Creek, and the Vail ski resorts are all a short drive from New Castle.

RANGELY

ELEV. 5,224 POP. 2,096

J.R. Ewing of the hit TV series *Dallas* would have been at home in Rangely. One of the nation's largest oil wells is here, just on the outskirts of town in the sagebrush and juniper, and an impressive 700 pump jacks dot the landscape in and around the town. Located near the Utah border, golfers can get their hacks in at the 9-hole Cedar Ridges Golf Course.

CEDAR RIDGES GOLF COURSE

The Golf Veteran Colorado designer Frank Hummel claims Cedar Ridges as one of his favorites. A 9-holer with some length, it is routed through rolling terrain and is generally in good condition. The dogleg-left No. 9 is the best challenge, featuring water and sand traps along its 436 yards.

The Details 970-675-8403. 502 County Road 108, Rangely, CO 81648.
- Frank Hummel, 1985. 9 holes. Par 36. Blue/Gold - 6,664 (70.6/126). White/Blue - 6,281 (68.8/122). Women's Red/Orange - 5,516 (69.9/118). Price - $.

Getting There Take I-70 to Rifle (exit 90) and head north towards Meeker on Hwy. 13. Turn left (west) on Hwy. 64, following the signs to Rangely. The golf

---

The neatest thing about playing was my ability to surprise myself. Under pressure sometimes I'd face a real hard shot I'd never played before and pull it off just the way I envisioned it. elements waiting to sabotage your game.—Tom Weiskopf

course is located in Columbine Park, 2 miles east of Rangely on the south side of the highway.

RANGELY NOTES

Take yourself on a self-guided, eight-site petroglyph tour; the ages-old rock art is here courtesy of the Ute and Fremont tribes. Maps and information are available at the **Rangely Museum**, just east of town. **Kenny Reservoir**, five miles east, is where the locals cool off in summer with boating, fishing, and swimming. At sunset take the awesome 20-minute drive to Rabbit Mountain, then cruise back into down for beers at **Magalino's**, **Cowboy Corral**, or **Giovanni's** (970-675-2670). Elk Park, a large, hillside town getaway, was paid for by the oil companies and includes cook-out grills, picnic areas, sports fields, and a recreation center. Motels are hard to find but look for the **4 Queens Motel** (970-675-5035), which offers access to the Rangely Recreation Center.

RIFLE

ELEV. 5,345 POP. 6,784

Rifle is located at the base of the White River Plateau, about an hour northeast of Grand Junction. Like so many small Rocky Mountain communities, Rifle is a hub for outdoorsmen, fishermen, and hunters who come to explore the White River National Forest or enjoy the scenic drives away from I-70. Golfers zipping down I-70 toward Grand Junction are in luck, since one of Colorado's surprising hidden gems is nestled here against the Hogback Mountain Range.

RIFLE CREEK GOLF COURSE

THE GOLF Rifle Creek Golf Course is a tale of two tracks. Owner Jimmy LeDonne of the Rifle Gap Land Company built the front nine in 1960, and Dick Phelps was hired in 1989 to add a rugged back nine and put a spectacular stamp on the layout. The front nine is open and friendly, but the back nine takes on a different personality—scenic, challenging, and dotted with elevated tees, rocky draws, and granite outcroppings. It's target golf and fun.

Some consider No. 1, which plays at 6,235 yards from the back tees, the most difficult. The opener plays 358 yards with a roller-coaster green that thrives on three-putts. Rifle Creek slices through the first six holes, forcing many carries.

The back nine begins after crossing over Highway 325, and on the 12th tee box golfers must strike it uphill to a green set in a hollow. No. 14 is the one that

Play the shot that makes the next shot easy. —Tommy Armour

sparks clubhouse conversation—railroad ties were used to build up the tee box looking out on a 100-foot drop to the end of the fairway. Right lies a bare hillside and left is a ravine lined with trees. Next, No. 15 is another scenic par 3 of 140 yards perched in the sky with a green that appears like an island. There's a steep drop-off and water guarding the front.

THE DETAILS 970-625-1093. 3004 State Hwy. 325, Rifle, CO 81650.
- Jimmy LeDonne, front nine, 1960. Dick Phelps, back nine, 1989. 18 holes. Par 72. Blue - 6,235 (70.2/123). White - 5,747 (67.9/115). Women's White - 5,830 (72.5/131). Women's Red - 5,140 (68.1/121). Price - $$.

GETTING THERE Head north from I-70 on Hwy. 13 for about 3 miles to the north side of Rifle Creek. Watch for a sign to the golf course and turn right (north) on State Hwy. 325, then drive 3 miles to the course.

RIFLE NOTES

The spectacular **Rifle Gap State Park** (970-625-1607) is 15 miles north of town and a favorite for those wanting to camp, fish, and spend time on the reservoir. And beyond that, the scenic drive into remote Buford is worthwhile for those exploring the backroads. Cave explorers can adventure into nearby **Rifle Mountain Park's** (970-625-2121) limestone caves, formed by a 50-foot waterfall. The **Coulter Lake Guest Ranch** is a great spot to spend the for weekend fun, and golf packages are available at the **Rusty Cannon Motel** (970-625-4004). While there's not many dining options in Rifle, Rusty Cannon's **Fireside Inn** (970-625-2233) and **Audrey's Cafe** are local mainstays.

SILVERTHORNE

ELEV. 8,790 POP. 3,196

Silverthorne is summed up easily: Ski in the winter, shop year-round, and enjoy the scenic fairways of The Raven Golf Club at Three Peaks during summers. This Summit County gateway to Keystone, Breckenridge, Copper Mountain, and Arapahoe Basin is right on I-70 and offers more reasonable lodging options than the slopes. Neighboring Dillon is on the other side of I-70, and the Ptarmigan and Eagles Nest Wilderness areas nearby are excellent for outdoor recreation of all kinds. The Silverthorne Factory Stores, featuring more than 70 name-brand stores and discount shops, probably draw as many tourists as skiers and golfers.

If there's one thing certain about putting, it is that it's an individual business. The great putters have used every conceivable type of grip, stance, and stroke.—Ben Crenshaw

THE RAVEN GOLF CLUB AT THREE PEAKS

THE GOLF Striking images set the scene at The Raven Golf Club at Three Peaks, an Alister MacKenzie-inspired route. The course offers multi-fingered bunkers, ragged grassy edges, a huge osprey nest on a man-made scaffold at the end of the third hole, yellow aspens quaking in the fall, and towering mountain scenes in all directions.

On the same spot where the old Eagle's Nest Golf Course used to be, Tom Lehman consulted with Michael Hurdzan and Dana Fry on this beauty, one of the most popular in the Rocky Mountains. The magnificent views include the Three Peaks in the Gore Range, Buffalo Mountain, William's Fork Range, the Ptarmigan Wilderness, Highline Creek, and the Blue River—just a short drive from the ski areas of Summit County. And the service is second to none, a trademark of Raven Golf.

The Raven measures 7,413 yards, par 72, from the tips. It's big and wide, and the front nine is fairly flat until you reach the ski-slope hill that is No. 9. The final four holes are daring, forcing tough decisions on how to carry streams and stay away from the dangers lurking in the groves of aspens.

No. 16 sweeps downhill, a par 5 with an awesome view of the Eagle River Valley. Playing over the stream is the keynote of the scary 431-yard, par-4 17th, which heads up toward an aspen grove. No. 18 runs uphill and has loads of trouble if you are long on the approach. The greens break off the mountain slope and are tricky.

THE DETAILS 970-262-3636. 2929 Golden Eagle Road, Silverthorne, CO 80498.
- www.ravengolf.com
- Michael Hurdzan, Dana Fry, Tom Lehman, 2000. 18 holes. Par 72. Black - 7,413 (73.4/142). Silver - 6,806 (71.2/135). White - 6,386 (69.3/126). Gold - 5,235 (64.6/108). Women's White - 6,386 (75.2/150). Women's Gold - 5,235 (69.9/129). Price - $$$$.

GETTING THERE Exit I-70 at the Dillon/Silverthorne marker (exit 205) and head right (north) on Hwy. 6. Go about 3 miles and the entrance is on the left.

SILVERTHORNE NOTES

The **Blue River** runs right through the factory outlet complex, offering die-hards the chance to throw flies at dumb, citified trout while waiting on shopping spouses. The **Historic Mint** is Silverthorne's most popular restaurant. Located in an 1862 building

A good golf course is like good music or good anything else. It is not necessarily a course which appeals the first time one plays it, but one which grows on the player the more frequently they visit it.—Dr. Alister Mackenzie

that was moved from nearby Dillon, they specialize in steaks prepared on a lava rock grill. Italian fare is best at **Matteo's** (970-262-6508), famous for its meatball sandwiches and, the **Dillon Dam Brewery** (970-262-7777) offers a brewpub menu and a summer beer garden. Affordable motel chains line the I-70 corridor in Silverthorne, and the centralized booking system for all budgets is **Summit County Central Reservations** (800-365-6365). **Wildernest** (800-554-2212) and the **Alpen Hutte Lodge** (970-468-6336) are the two options in Silverthorne.

SNOWMASS

ELEV. 8, 575 POP. 1, 822

Surrounded by the White River National Forest and the peaks of the Red Mountains, Snowmass Village is located at the southwestern end of the Roaring Fork Valley, a stretch that runs from the northeast end of Glenwood Springs to the Southwest end of Aspen. Long considered Aspen's little sister, the village is just 12 miles down the valley and offers more affordable dining and lodging, while sharing many of Aspen's cultural events and festivals. As for golf, the newly designed Snowmass Club Golf Course could redefine the area when it opens in the summer of 2004.

SNOWMASS GOLF CLUB

THE GOLF When The Snowmass Club asked Jim Engh to present a plan for updating its 1980 Arnold Palmer-Ed Seay layout, minutes from trendy Aspen, he presented a proposal the very next day that blew the Snowmass executives away. They'd envisioned updating the layout with today's technology and adding a few bells and whistles. But when Engh proposed a complete makeover at nearly the same price tag as what the executives had dreamed of for an update, they jumped at the opportunity to have a completely new golf course, designed by one of the best in today's design industry.

Snowmass is still trying to figure out if they want a new name, but that decision hasn't been made. There will be a new clubhouse, too, built by Cottle Graybeal Yaw Architects, which will honor the rich agricultural and ranching heritage of the area with metal roofing, timber trusses, old fencing, and lattice-work. The interior, by Slifer Designs, will offer authentic, hard-working furnishings in the tradition of early Snowmass settlers.

Engh's version of Snowmass, set to open in the summer of 2004, will offer all the ingredients that have made him the most decorated golf-course architect in the world. There will be pedestal tee boxes with dramatic downhill holes and

---

The proper putting stroke cannot be contrived or manipulated with the hands – it must be natural. —Ben Crenshaw

360-degree panoramas; awesome bunkers with fingers, small bottoms, and gnarly noses; as well as healthy doses of fun. Count on some daunting shots, including steep returns if you go over the contoured greens.

The Palmer-Seay Snowmass course was 6,662 yards long and had only three sets of tees. The new layout will have five sets of tees and stretches out to almost 7,000 yards (par 72). The drama will end at No. 18, a downhill, 585-yard par 5. Deck watchers drinking cold beers should enjoy the action.

"No. 18's pedestal tee box has a panorama of the Snowmass ski runs and the Elk Range, set up on a ridge," superintendent Al Ogren said. "The fairway looks narrow from up there, but it really has plenty of landing room. If you nail your drive you have a chance to reach the green in two, but there is a pond and wetlands right, and pot bunkers guarding the front and back."

THE DETAILS 800-525-0710. 970-923-5600. 0239 Snowmass Club, Circle Snowmass Village, CO 81615
- www.snowmassclub.com
- Jim Engh, 2004. Complete redesign of Arnold Palmer, Ed Seay course, 1980. Not yet rated. Opening summer 2004. Price - $$$$.

GETTING THERE Take I-70 in to Glenwood Springs, then Hwy. 82 south to Brush Creek Road. Turn right, go 2 miles to Highline Road, and turn left.

SNOWMASS NOTES

The unusual **Krabloonik** (970-923-3953) serves wild game and fine wines. Another traditional Snowmass eatery is the **Stewpot** (970-923-2263), affordable and known for its homemade breads. The grungy **Wood Creeky Tavern** (970-923-4585) is another good lunch spot serving bar grub and cold beers. Luxury chain hotels are the norm, but the family-owned **Pokolodi Lodge** (970-923-4310) is a solid alternative and a good place to headquarter for summertime adventures. The **Stonebridge Inn** (970-923-5889) is also preferred because it's located away from the village mall – check on renting one of their Tamarack Townhouses. Fishermen enjoy casting on the **Frying Pan River** here, and hiking, climbing, kayaking, and horseback riding are all available in the area.

NORTHWEST

STEAMBOAT SPRINGS ELEV. 6,695 POP. 10,115

Tourists have been coming for over 100 years to this town, which is named for the rhythmic chugging of the area's 157 hot springs. Steamboat Springs is such a famous ski town that it put a trademark on Champagne Powder® snow and is known as "Ski Town USA." Picture an Olympic-medal-winning downhill skier in a cowboy hat toasted by a community that is still immensely proud of its ranching history. The July 4th Cowboy Roundup Days involves a cattle drive down Lincoln Avenue.

Early settlers and ranchers learned to live in snow country and used snowshoes and skis to get around in winter. Then in 1912 Carl Howelsen arrived from Norway and introduced the cowboys to skis for recreation. He built a wooden ski jumping platform in 1914 on land that is now Strawberry Park. And he organized a winter carnival and jumping competition that even included the first high school band on skis—a tradition that is ongoing.

But for all its winter glories, Steamboat Springs is a truly awesome summer getaway, loaded with outstanding golf, excellent accommodations, many fine restaurants, and leads for every traditional Colorado summer activity.

CATAMOUNT RANCH & CLUB

THE GOLF Designed by Tom Weiskopf, Catamount Ranch is a golf course, cattle ranch, and environmentally sensitive habitat all rolled into one. This par-72, 7,088-yard route winds through working hayfields, a stone dairy barn, Walton Creek, and a sanctuary for migratory birds, elk, and other wildlife.

Catamount was Weiskopf's 40th design project and his fourth Colorado course (after Grandote Peak in La Veta, The Ridge at Castle Pines North, and Eagle Springs at Vail). At the grand-opening festivities in 2000 former Vice President Dan Quayle (a single-digit handicap), former Olympic ski jumper Moose Barrows, and Boulder native and former All-Pro defensive back Dick Anderson of the Miami Dolphins joined Weiskopf in the ceremonial first round.

Elevation changes make things more interesting, and golfers climb into groves of aspen, old-growth Douglas fir, scrub-oak brush, and rock formations. At 6,800 feet the ball zooms, as evidenced on the reachable 310-yard No. 5. No. 6 is also reachable at 315 yards, but there's a tricky 60-foot drop to a target spot.

Some golfers play an 8-iron on the 211-yard, par-3 No. 8! The Yampa Valley, Rabbit Ears Pass, and Flat Top Wilderness are in view, and Walton Creek rests 80 feet below.

Comparatively few golfers ever show that they are aware that the golf architect tries to design a course that rewards an intelligent golfer and penalizes a stupid one.—Tommy Armour

NORTHWEST

Catamount Ranch & Club was open to the public for a couple of years, but as promised, is now private. Memberships are available through the purchase of property at Catamount Ranch or Lake Catamount subdivision.

THE DETAILS 970-871-9200. 33400-B Catamount Dr., Steamboat Springs, CO 80477.

- www.catamountclub.com
- Tom Weiskopf, 2000. 18 holes. Par 72. Black - 7,088 (73.1/142). Gold - 6,565 (71/134). Silver - 5,880 (67.1/121). Women's Silver - 5,880 (72.6/142). Women's White/Silver - 5,452 (70.3/134). Women's White - 4,804 (66.9/120). Private club, reciprocal play allowed. Price - $$$$.

GETTING THERE Take Hwy. 131 north to Steamboat Springs. Turn right on Hwy. 40 and the course is about 1 mile ahead on the left.

HAYMAKER GOLF COURSE

THE GOLF Haymaker is the favorite course of many a wise travel golfer. Situated on the outskirts of town, with rolled hay stacks adjacent to Scottish-links-ike fairways, this Keith Foster creation is first-class and one that should not be missed.

Measuring 7,249 yards at a par 72, Haymaker is a perfect complement to the community's agrarian background. The city owns this 233-acre tract, which actually used to be an old rock quarry as well as a hayfield. And while there are no trees on the course, Foster forces strategic thought from golfers as they negotiate rock walls, deep bunkers, and native-grass rough. No houses surround the course, making it even more enjoyable.

On the 636-yard, par-5 sixth hole, known as "Cattle Drive," a working hayfield is visible along with the Yampa Valley, Flat Tops Wilderness, and Rabbit Ears Pass.

No. 8 is only 347 yards, named "Ring The Bell"—a consummate risk/reward hole. The routing makes a curve right over a marshy area, and tempts macho men to go for the green.

Appropriately named "Waterloo," No. 10 is a 454-yard par 4 that doglegs right with water all down the right. "Watering Hole" is the 11th, a 343-yard par 4 that tempts a carry of the bunker that rests squarely in the middle of the fairway. The peninsula-like green requires an accurate shot if the pin is set towards the right side.

The 163-yard No. 12 is named "Greywall" because of the rock wall stationed

The stroke must be made with rhythm. The change of direction should be smooth and unforced, just as it is with the pendulum of a grandfather clock.—Tom Watson.

between the water and the green. If the pin is on the right side, it is particularly challenging. The green narrows here, and traps are situated right and behind.

Haymaker, which opened for play in 1997, has hosted a Colorado Golf Association tournament and was nominated for *GolfDigest's* Best New Public Courses for 1998. The Colorado Mid-Amateur competition has also been held here.

The Haybale Bar & Grill is a full-service restaurant and bar at the course, serving to-go items, appetizers, hot and cold sandwiches (Sandwedges as they are referred to on the menu), and salads.

THE DETAILS 970-870-1846. 34855 US Hwy. 40 East, Steamboat Springs, CO 80477.

- www.haymakergolf.com
- Keith Foster, 1997. 18 holes. Par 72. Silver - 7,249 (73.3/131). Gold - 6,622 (70.3/124). White - 6,066 (67.7/118). Women's White - 6,183 (73.3/133). Women's Blue - 5,059 (66.9/117). Price - $$$.

GETTING THERE Located south of Steamboat Springs at the intersection of Hwy. 40 and Hwy. 131.

SHERATON STEAMBOAT GOLF CLUB

THE GOLF The Sheraton Steamboat Golf Club is a Robert Trent Jones, Jr. layout that opened with Tom Watson as its tour representative in 1974. And surprisingly for a ski town, the course is located at an elevation of 7,000 feet, which means the course is open approximately 150 days per year.

The course lies in the foothills near the Mt. Werner ski slopes, and putts break away from the big hill—it won't take long to figure out that dealing with the greens is the most difficult challenge here. The surfaces aren't too slick, but the combination of bent and poa turf along with the mountain-style breaks can make it a confusing day on the greens.

The scenery is spectacular, especially in the fall when the aspens gleam golden against the ski slopes in the background and beautiful Fish Creek babbling in the background. Some fairways are tight with evergreens lining the edges, and there are 72 total bunkers as well as water on seven holes.

The layout covers 6,902 yards from the tips and is a par 72. No. 10, a 542-yard par 5, is the signature hole with Fish Creek crossing the fairway 100 yards from the green. The par-4, 378-yard No. 15 includes two crossings of the creek. The par-3 holes stand out as well, and they require valor and accuracy from the

The chief reaction among amateurs to poor putting, it seems to me, is exasperation, combined with a sort of vague hope that, by some kind of mini-miracle, it will have all gotten better by the next time they play.—Jack Nicklaus

tee. The 190-yard No. 8 has a peninsula-style green, and Nos. 11 (200 yards) and 17 (191 yards) have highly elevated tee boxes to well-bunkered greens.

Gary Crawford, head pro at the Sheraton Steamboat Golf Club, is a former member of the U.S. Olympic Nordic Combined Ski Team. Appropriate, since two of the more famous Steamboat skiers are downhiller Billy Kidd and ski jumper Moose Barrows—both avid golfers as well.

THE DETAILS 970-879-1391. 2000 Clubhouse Dr., Steamboat Springs, CO 80487.
- www.sheraton.com/steamboat
- Robert Trent Jones, Jr., 1974. 18 holes. Par 72. Blue - 6,902 (72/138). White - 6,293 (70.2/131). Women's Red - 5,462 (72.2/125). Price - $$$$.

GETTING THERE Coming from Denver, take I-70 to Silverthorne, then Hwy. 9 to Kremling. Next take Hwy. 40 to Steamboat Springs. Turn right on Mt. Werner Rd., left on Steamboat Blvd., and right on Clubhouse Dr. The club is on the left.

STEAMBOAT GOLF CLUB

THE GOLF By far the most affordable option in town, the Steamboat Golf Club was built from scratch by the Steamboat Men's Club—a group that loved the great game of golf. Cottonwoods taunt certain shots, water teases players on every hole, and ponds and a diverted outshoot from the Yampa River make this fairly flat course a challenge.

Golfers should leave the driver in the bag and focus on giving up distance to keep the ball in play and maximize the chance to hit the small greens that require accurate approaches. Because it's friendly and affordable, the place is busy; however, it's worthwhile to play with locals and get the real flavor of the town.

No. 5, a 336-yard par 4, is the ultimate target golf hole. Pinpoint the drive and the approach, since water makes it narrow and fronts the elevated green. Trees and out-of-bounds also make this a tough hole.

THE DETAILS 970-879-4295. 26815 West Highway 40, Steamboat Springs, CO 80477.
- Steamboat Men's Club, 1964. 9 holes. Par 35. Blue - 5,606 (66/120). Red - 5,152 (68.4/120). Price - $$.

GETTING THERE Located 6 miles west of downtown Steamboat Springs on Hwy. 40.

A man who gets into a rage, swears, and breaks his clubs, and petulantly drives
his ball off into the woods should either reform or give up the game…Let him go beat carpets!
No true lover of golf will mourn his loss!—Jerome Travers

STEAMBOAT SPRINGS NOTES

Outdoor activities abound in this northern Colorado playground. Hike up to **Fish Creek Falls** with a picnic basket or buy a ticket for the **Steamboat Springs Summer Pro Rodeo Series** that runs from late June until the end of August. The rodeo grounds are at Romick Arena, one block west of Lincoln at 5th. Cowpokes can still find ranching supplies at **Soda Creek Western Mercantile** or western clothes at **F.M. Light & Sons**. Bed down in luxury by staying at the **Sheraton Steamboat's Morningside Condos** (970-879-2220)—massive condos with full kitchens and living rooms that overlook the Silver Bullet Gondola and ski slopes. The **Alpiner Lodge** (970-879-1430) is affordable and centrally located, and the **Hotel Bristol** (970-879-3083) is another solid option for downtown Steamboat. In the evenings look to **Antares** (970-879-9939) for creative American entrees, **La Montana** (970-879-5800) has solid Southwestern dishes, and for steaks find the **Old West Steak House** (970-879-1441). Other options include the **Cottonwood Grill** (970-879-2229) and the **Old Town Pub** (970-879-2101). In general the nightlife isn't too wild, but the Steamboat Today is an excellent source for finding out about visiting bands and dining deals. The **Cellar Lounge** (970-871-8917) might be the best local drinking establishment. The **Strawberry Park Natural Hot Springs** (970-879-0342) soothes sore muscles acquired from playing golf or spending time on the river with the **Steamboat Rafting Company** (888-888-7238) or fly fishing with **Bucking Rainbow Outfitters** (970-879-8747).

VAIL

ELEV. 8,380 POP. 4,531

Vail is a very young town, founded in 1960 by a group headed by Pete Seibert. Dick Hauserman, the man who designed Vail's logo, was there when Pete Seibert gathered a group of nine initial investors for the first board of directors meeting. A ski dynasty was formed from that meeting and the vision ultimately became Vail Resorts Inc., America's largest ski company.

In addition to the world-class skiing, Vail has become a popular summer destination, with outdoor adventures available in the White River National Forest, kayaking in Gore Creek, rafting down Eagle River, fishing in the area's six mountain lakes, and golf at the Vail Golf Club. Festivals are always available on the summer schedule, and Vail's 100-plus bars and restaurants create ample opportunities to get in the mood for shopping Vail's charming streets.

You get rewarded at the bottom of the club by what you do at the top end.—Jerry Barber

VAIL GOLF CLUB

THE GOLF The Vail Golf Club was the first course in the Vail Valley when it opened in 1963 with a Ben Krueger design. Robert Trent Jones and his son were considered as designers, along with Press Maxwell, but Krueger got the job and relied on members of the original founders of Vail (Dick Hauserman and Rod Slifer) to contribute.

Situated at 8,200 feet, the course's nine holes roll down from the clubhouse before the route heads back up at the base of the ski runs. Holes 6 through 13 offer views of the Gore Range, where golfers are repeatedly asked to hit large, slick greens guarded by huge traps. The tees are elevated and water comes into play on about half the holes.

No. 14 is one of the better holes: a 416-yard par 4 with a creek that crosses in front of the elevated green with bunkers left and right.

"Few people today realize that in the summer of 1968 there was the Arnold Palmer Golf Academy located in what is now Eagle Vail. It drew more than 500 boys between the ages of 12 and 17," said Hauserman. Palmer said it was five years ahead of its time, and he was right—it didn't last. But Vail Golf Club has survived.

THE DETAILS 970-479-2260. 1778 Vail Valley Drive, Vail, CO 81657.
- www.vailrec.com
- Ben Krueger, 1966. 18 holes. Par 71. Black - 6,740 (70.8/126). Blue - 6,260 (68.4/123). Women's Black - 6,740 (77/149). Women's Blue - 6,260 (74.3/143). Women's Gold - 5,875 (72/137). Women's Green - 5,277 (69.6/129). Price - $$$$.

GETTING THERE Scoot down I-70 to exit 176 (the main Vail exit). Head down the south Frontage Road east 2 miles to Vail Valley Drive.

VAIL NOTES

Plan vacations to **Vail** with a visit to www.vailresorts.com where there's countless options for lodging. It doesn't get any better than the **Austria Haus Club & Hotel** (970-477-5800) or the **Sonnenalp** (800-654-8312), which also offers packages to their course down-valley. Spouses will inevitably shop while the testosterone-plagued look for golf, fishing, and mountain biking on many nearby trails, including the mountain ski slopes (use the two available gondolas to carry your bike, then ride back down the mountain). Look to **Shrine Mountain Adventure** (970-827-5363) for information on

---

Forget about adding up your score, and live in the present moment.—Dr. Bob Rotella

trails and bike rentals. Try and work in a lunch at **Talon's Deck** on top of the mountain, and **Los Amigos** (970-476-5847) has been serving Mexican food in Vail forever and has the added bonus of an outdoor deck facing the slopes. Evenings should include the **Red Lion Inn** (970-476-7676), a Vail institution with live music, and the **Hotel-Gasthof Gramshammer's** (970-476-5626) Austrian restaurant **Pepi's** (970-476-4671), famous for the wiener schnitzel. The **Hubcap Brewery** (970-476-5757) also has live music. Another summer option is a drive to the town of Minturn, where the unique **Minturn Country Club** (970-827-4114) lets you pick your steak and put it on the grill. Afterwards, the **Minturn Inn** (970-827-9647) is a charming B&B option.

WINTER PARK
ELEV. 9,110 POP. 662

Located in the Fraser Valley, the village of Winter Park is home to the Winter Park and Mary Jane ski slopes, and is the gateway to Grand County and the golf courses of Pole Creek, Grand Elk, SolVista, and Grand Lake. More of an everyman's resort that is more affordable and ideal for families, Winter Park is popular for golf and mountain biking (660 miles of fat-tire paths), as well as fishing, rafting, and horseback riding.

POLE CREEK GOLF CLUB

THE GOLF Actually closer to Fraser, but listed with a Winter Park address, this is a slice of sheer Rocky Mountain heaven—just don't bring your slice to the award-winning 27 holes. Staffers say that Pole Creek is a 10,709-yard, par 108 with three challenging nines: Ridge, Meadow, and Ranch. *GolfDigest* gave acclaim immediately when the course opened in 1985, proclaiming it as one of the Best New Courses in the USA.

Aside from the outstanding golf, Pole Creek's best amenity is the down-to-earth staff, helpful rangers, great facilities, and general friendliness. The scenery is awesome with evergreen-lined fairways, elevation changes, dramatic doglegs, and breathtaking views of the 13,000-foot Continental Divide and Indian Peaks Wilderness. Holes play down the valley and back up, and involve crossings of Pole Creek. Seven lakes and ponds also get in the way.

Gary Player and Ron Kirby created the original 18—Meadow and Ranch. In 1998 the third Ridge nine was added by Denis Griffiths, and the design included homesites.

The Ridge's No. 9 is a wild ride—this par-5, 561-yarder with a 110-foot drop in elevation feels like a downhill ski experience. Even average hacks can poke

Above all, tempo is the great equalizer. It compensates for mechanical flaws in your swing, and will reduce your slices, hooks, and inconsistent contact.—Bill Moretti

it 300 yards. The fairways of the Ridge nine climb straight uphill behind the clubhouse and continue in a links fashion. Only one location has fairways that parallel each other.

The Ranch nine commences with a double dogleg left, a 593-yard par 5 that pushes straight uphill. The Ranch measures 3,609 from the back and water comes into play on five holes. The Meadow nine is 3,498 yards and the Ridge is 3,603.

The most talked about hole at Pole Creek since it opened in 1985 is No. 7 of the Meadow nine. It's a 584-yard par 5 that persuades golfers to cut the dogleg-left off the tee—a 90-degree bend. Anything less than perfect ends up in the lodgepole pines or with a downhill lie over a lake to an elevated green.

THE DETAILS 970-887-9195. County Road 51, Winter Park, CO 80482.
- www.polecreekgolf.com
- Gary Player, Ron Kirby, Meadow and Ranch Nines, 1985. Denis Griffiths, Ridge Nine, 1998. 27 holes. Price - $$$.
- Meadow-Ranch: Blue - 7,107 (73.7/145). White - 6,413 (71/135). Gold - 5,571 (66.5/122). Women's White - 6,398 (76.6/153). Women's Gold - 5,497 (71.5/138). Women's Red - 4,928 (69/127).
- Meadow-Ridge: Blue - 7,062 (73/136). White - 6,563 (70.5/130). Gold - 5,837 (67.2/118). Women's White - 6,563 (77.3/153). Women's Gold - 5,793 (72.8/140). Women's Red - 4,954 (69/125).
- Ranch-Ridge: Blue - 7,173 (73.5/139). White - 6,604 (71.7/127). Gold - 5,924 (67.7/125). Women's White - 6,589 (77.9/155). Women's Red - 5,026 (69.2/128). Women's Gold - 5,864 (73.5/140).

GETTING THERE Shoot down I-70 to exit 232 (US Hwy. 40) north. The first town is historic Empire. The road to Winter Park is pure Colorado mountains, steep and winding. Head through the towns of Winter Park, Fraser, and Tabernash before reaching Pole Creek. Keep going and look for the signs. The course is on the left.

WINTER PARK NOTES

It's a short drive to all four of the Grand County golf courses, so do your homework and book a golf package at one of the traditional hotel rooms, lodges, or resorts (log onto www.winterparkresorts.com, 800-979-0332). The brand-new **Kicking Horse Lodge** condos are available for rent, and views include the ski area and back nine of the **SolVista Golf Club** (www.solvista.com, 800-757-7669). The **Vintage Hotel, Iron**

NORTHWEST

Horse Resort, and **Winter Park Mountain Lodge** are solid lodging options. The Vintage's restaurant serves steaks, seafood, and pasta and has a place to talk golf in their 19th-century English bar. The **Moffat Station Bar and Grill** (970-726-4211) is a popular place, and the **Ranch House Restaurant and Saloon** (970-726-5633) is set in the former homestead of the **Devil's Thumb Ranch**. Impressive wines, fresh seafood, and gorgeous scenery complete the experience at the Ranch House. Roadtrippers looking for local flavor can head down towards Fraser and find the **Crooked Creek Saloon** (970-726-9250), where the motto is "Eat till it hurts, drink till it feels better."

WOLCOTT
ELEV. 7,100 POP. 50

Wolcott is a bump along I-70 that has a ranching past and a golf future. A post office, general store, and a hotel called The Yacht Club make this tiny spot an interesting candidate for growth. The Jouflas family first came here in 1926 and started a sheep-ranching business. Some of that original land is now Red Sky Ranch, home to two brand-new, very upscale golf courses (Fazio and Norman), both flaunting recent *Golf Magazine* new course awards.

EAGLE SPRINGS GOLF CLUB

THE GOLF Golf bums breezing westbound down I-70 can look right at Wolcott and spot this private Jay Morrish/Tom Weiskopf-designed beauty. Unfortunately, no reciprocal play is allowed—only members and guests can play this foothills gem that runs into arroyos and canyons, climbing uphill and back down again through sagebrush and over the Eagle River.

The 17th is known as "The Alley," a 447-yard par 4. It's guarded by native brush and grass on the left and the Eagle River on the right. Cottonwoods guard the right approach to the green. Non-member locals refer to this club as "Ego Springs."

THE DETAILS 970-926-4404. 28521 U.S. Hwy. 6 & 24, Wolcott, CO 81655.
- Jay Morrish, Tom Weiskopf, 1995. 18 holes. Par 72. Gold - 6,957 (73.2/133). Blue/Gold - 6,755 (72/128). Blue - 6,328 (69.5/129). White - 5,733 (67/124). Women's White - 5,722 (72.2/131). Women's Red/White - 5,591 (71.6/128). Women's Red - 5,112 (69.6/125). Private club. Members and guests only. Price - $$$$.

NORTHWEST

All swings have one thing in common: whatever the tempo, the speeds of the backswing and downswing are the same.— Johnny Miller

President Eisenhower and his grandson David on a ranch near Fraser.

GETTING THERE Head west on I-70 to the Steamboat Springs-Wolcott exit, then right on Hwy. 6 for 1 mile.

RED SKY GOLF CLUB - FAZIO COURSE

THE GOLF Named one of the Top Ten New Courses You Can Play by *Golf Magazine* in 2002, Red Sky Golf Club's Tom Fazio Course was the first of two award-winning layouts to open on 700 acres of sheep-ranching terrain in the Wolcott area.

It's a striking par 72 that spreads out on diverse terrain—sagebrush meets alpine here with aspen groves, evergreens, sandstone-rock outcroppings, and purple sagebrush. A huge ridge that separates the Fazio Course and the Norman Course also serves as a corridor for migrating deer and elk.

Views extend to Bellyache Ridge, Castle Peak, and the Back Bowls of Vail as lucky members and resort guests walk the gently sloping fairways and rolling ridges that frame shots to difficult Fazio putting surfaces. Most agree this experience is manageable tee-to-green, but three-putts are common.

On opening day, George Jouflas, whose family once ranched this land, shared

You wouldn't be foolish enough to try a different swing on every shot; you have to chose one way to think on every shot.—Dr. Bob Rotella

the podium with PGA Tour commissioner Tim Finchem, a frequent Vail visitor for skiing. Finchem was so impressed by the Red Sky Ranch area that he called Tom Fazio to ask him about the golf. Finchem said it took him about "18 minutes" to decide he wanted a retirement home at Red Sky Ranch, close to the Vail-Beaver Creek ski areas, where his young children enjoy Colorado skiing. Part-time Vail resident and former president Gerald Ford also attended the festivities.

Resort play is allowed for $200 if guests are staying in a Vail Resorts, Inc. hotel. The guest clubhouse, located at the Fazio Course, features a log exterior and architectural detail designed to present a Rocky Mountain atmosphere; it includes a restaurant with both indoor and outdoor dining and men's and women's locker rooms. Members have a separate clubhouse at the Norman Course. Red Sky Golf Club is proud of its service; valet parking greets you, and attendants on the practice range keep your clubs clean.

Red Sky Golf Club is also the home of a Chuck Cook Golf Academy. Cook is the Austin, Texas-based teaching professional who once tutored Payne Stewart and currently guides senior Tom Kite.

THE DETAILS 970-477-8425. 0376 Red Sky Rd., Wolcott, CO 81655.
- www.redskyranch.com
- Tom Fazio, 2002. 18 holes. Par 72. Black - 6,970 (72/135). Blue - 6,719 (70.7/133). Gold - 6,270 (68.7/129). Sage - 5,835 (67.3/115). Women's Gold - 6,270 (74.9/141). Women's Sage - 5,835 (72.1/136). Women's Red - 5,196 (68.2/125). Private club, resort play allowed on alternate days for guests of Vail Resorts, Inc. and other hotels. Call for information. Price - $$$$.

GETTING THERE Red Sky Ranch is just off I-70 west from Denver. Take the Wolcott exit. Turn left and proceed 1 mile up Bellyache Ridge Rd. Follow the signs to the golf course.

RED SKY GOLF CLUB - NORMAN COURSE

THE GOLF Greg Norman's first Colorado design opened in 2003 and captured a spot on *Golf Magazine's* Top Ten You Can Play List.

"The Shark" had an entertaining inaugural foursome that included John Elway, Dan Marino, and Denver Broncos' head coach Mike Shanahan. The two former quarterbacks bested Norman and the coach.

Measuring a brawny 7,580 yards from the tips at par 72, this differs from the

When you look down at your grip and see wrinkles in your wrists, chances are you are reaching for the ball and not using the club the way it was designed.—Tommy Armour

Fazio layout with tightly-mown bentgrass areas encircling perplexing contoured greens, giving the golfer an option to chip, putt, or bump it around the putting surfaces.

Like the Fazio Course, the route traverses aspens and junipers, uphill and downhill, past rock formations, through deep ravines, negotiating boulder-strewn water features and the shaven green fronts.

Norman's 16th hole, a 283-yard, downhill par 3, is definitely unique. Sideboards left of the green propel the ball toward the hole; some play short-irons towards the target.

The front side offers back-to-back daunting uphill par 4s. No. 4 is a 565-yarder that demands a 260-yard carry off the back tee to reach a fairway jutting at an angle. And if the 452-yard opening hole doesn't grab your attention, the 559-yard No. 9. definitely will—a ridiculously entertaining par 4 with a boulder-strewn, stream-fed pond fronting the green.

THE DETAILS 970-477-8377. 1099 Red Sky Rd., Wolcott, CO 81655.
- www.redskyranch.com
- Greg Norman, 2003. 18 holes. Par 72. Black - 7,580 (74.2/144). Blue - 6,841 (71.4/139). Gold - 6,464 (69.8/132). Women's Gold - 6,437 (75.3/142). Women's Sage - 5,969 (72.7/137). Women's Red - 5,227 (68.5/124). Private club, resort play allowed on alternate days for guests of Vail Resorts, Inc. and other hotels. Call for information. Price - $$$$.

GETTING THERE Take I-70 west from Denver to the Wolcott exit. Turn left and proceed 1 mile up Bellyache Ridge Rd. Watch for signs to the golf course. The Norman Course is past the Fazio Course.

WOLCOTT NOTES

The same Jouflas family that settled the area welcomes visitors for a dude ranch experience at the **Lazy J Ranch & Vail Rod & Gun Club** (www.lazyranch.net, 970-926-3472), and the **Four Eagle** (www.foureagle.com, 970-926-3472) is similar dude ranch experience in the area. But visitors who want to play golf at Red Sky must stay in a Vail Resorts, Inc. facility. Look to www.vailresorts.com for a complete list of stay-and-play options. At the top of the list is the rustic **Ritz-Carlton Bachelor Gulch** (800-576-5582) at nearby Beaver Creek, recently named to the *Conde Nast Traveler* "Hot List" of new hotels. The 237-room resort offers panoramic mountain views and unlimited year-round activities such as skiing, golf, hiking, mountain biking, and cultural events. After a day in this Rocky Mountain lodge-styled playground, relax and rejuvenate in the

---

Swing like you were being paid by the hour, not the job.—Davis Love, Jr.

21,000-square foot **Bachelor Gulch Spa**. The service and food at Remington's are unparalleled. Another world-famous hotel that allows you to play at **Red Sky** is **The Pines Lodge at Beaver Creek**, a nice option because of their **Grouse Mountain Grill**. In town the best spot for a quick sit-down meal is the **Wolcott Market** (970-926-3402) for deli items and big, fresh, juicy burgers. The **Wolcott Yacht Club** (970-926-3444) is a fish house with a full bar outside.

Golf Magazine's Top Ten New Courses - 2004

1. Red Sky Golf Course (Greg Norman) - Wolcott, CO
2. Black Mesa Golf Course (Baxter Spann) - La Mesilla, NM
3. The Bull at Pinehurst Farms (J. Nicklaus) - Sheboygan Falls, WI
4. Carter Plantation (David Toms/Glenn Hickey) - Springfield, LA
5. Circling Raven Golf Course (Gene Bates) - Worley, ID
6. Fossil Trace Golf Course (Jim Engh) - Golden, CO
7. Kaluhyat Golf Course at Turning Stone
   (Robert Trent Jones Jr.) - Verona, NY
8. Moorpark Country Club (Peter Jacobsen/Jim Hardy) - Moorpark, CA
9. The Rawls Course (Tom Doak) - Lubbock, TX
10. Wintonbury Hills Golf Course (Pete Dye/Tim Liddy) - Bloomfield,CT

Clifford Roberts, President of Augusta National, L.B. Maytag, washing machine magnate, Dwight D. Eisenhower, and pro Ed Dudley pose for this unique shot. The young caddie is Paul Ransom, who went on to become the long-time pro at Patty Jewett.

It is not necessary to go back and through the same length. That's hogwash,
unless it happens to work for you.—Jim McLean

FRONT RANGE

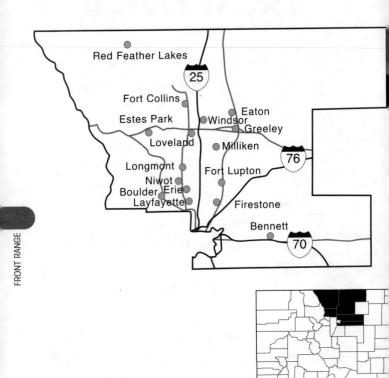

Front Range Mileage

	Bennett	Boulder	Eaton	Erie	Estes Park	Firestone	Fort Collins	Fort Lupton	Greeley	Layfayett	Longmont	Loveland	Milliken	Niwot	Red Feather	Windsor
Bennett		54	75	50	89	49	89	44	72	47	62	77	72	58	127	82
Boulder	54		59	19	36	22	46	28	19	12	15	34	45	8	85	48
Eaton	75	59		43	54	47	26	32	5	54	44	24	14	51	64	12
Erie	50	19	43		44	9	39	12	37	11	12	27	28	11	77	32
Estes Park	89	36	54	44		42	53	48	44	33	29	29	39	37	81	43
Firestone	49	22	47	9	42		41	12	41	14	16	22	30	14	80	35
Fort Collins	89	46	26	39	53	41		47	32	44	33	29	39	37	47	16
Fort Lupton	44	28	32	12	48	12	47		29	50	31	13	14	20	86	20
Greeley	72	19	5	37	44	41	32	29		21	20	22	39	46	70	9
Layfayett	47	12	54	11	33	14	44	50	21		12	35	11	11	70	46
Longmont	62	15	44	12	29	16	33	31	20	12		30	19	30	89	15
Loveland	77	34	24	27	29	22	29	13	22	35	30		37	11	70	14
Milliken	72	45	14	28	39	30	39	14	39	11	19	37		37	67	7
Niwot	58	8	51	11	37	14	37	20	46	11	30	11	37		77	41
Red Feather	127	85	64	77	81	80	47	86	70	70	89	70	67	77		54
Windsor	82	48	12	32	43	35	16	20	9	46	15	14	7	41	54	

The Front Range Region of Colorado is a diverse place—it's an agricultural hub, but also spreads out into the mountainous beauty of places like Estes Park and Rocky Mountain National Park, Boulder's foothills scenery, and the historic old mining and gaming communities of Black Hawk and Central City.

Road trips in these diverse terrains provide golfers a good sample of what Colorado is all about. It's not just the Rocky Mountains. It's also the agricultural plains and places like Greeley, where a lot of young men and their families headed west after an advertisement in the *New York Tribune* in 1869 asked adventurous folks to establish a colony in the West. "Go west, young man," the ad said. Today, a westward golf odyssey might begin in Greeley, a interesting college town known for its Greeley Stampede rodeo. Start with Boomerang Links and Highland Hills, then find a member to tee it up with at Greeley Country Club.

Fort Collins is next, the city with the largest population on the Front Range, and the opportunity to test the slick greens and narrow fairways of Collindale Golf Course and Southridge Golf Club. Those with connections will spend time at Ptarmigan Country Club.

Not far from Fort Collins are three newer offerings—Firestone's Saddleback Golf Course, Erie's Vista Ridge Golf Club, and the brand-new Highland Meadows in Windsor, set for a 2004 opening. Ute Creek in Longmont is one of only six Robert Trent Jones Jr. courses in the state. And how could you overlook the golf course with the strangest name in Colorado golf—The Mad Russian Golf Course in Milliken?

Moving toward the mountains, stop off in Loveland for The Olde Course at Loveland and Mariana Butte Golf Course before taking on the scenic drive to Estes Park for golf there and a stay at the world-famous Stanley Hotel, inspiration for Stephen King's *The Shining*. As the eastern gateway offers the chance to experience the 400-square-mile preserve of forests, meadows, tundra, and alpine ponds known as Rocky Mountain National Park. Slow down to view the bighorn sheep and glance upward for a circling eagle as you enjoy the world's highest paved through road, Trail Ridge Road, at 12,183 feet.

Wayward golf pilgrims will inevitably head for remote Red Feather Lakes, home of Fox Acres Country Club, a Troon Golf-managed private club with fishing and other outdoor activities. Highlights here include exploring the depths of Poudre Canyon, a granite-walled encampment, and discovering the exhilarating Peak-to-Peak Highway.

Heading south for Boulder, home of the University of Colorado, savor the foothills, the rock protrusions called the Flatirons, and the city's 33,000 acres of

When I hit a shot into trouble, I expect the worst…When I get there and find that I can actually hit the ball – which you usually can – it changes my mood for the better right away.—Corey Pavin

parks and trails. Golf highlights in Boulder include the Flatirons Golf Course, a favorite since 1933, and the private Boulder Country Club.

A road trip on the Front Range wouldn't be complete without wandering into Central City and Black Hawk, where mining history abounds and casino gambling is available. And while there's no golf there now, that could change when Rick Phelps implements a master plan for golf that would straddle the city lines. If the politicians can work it out, Colorado tourists will be able to gamble, play golf, and experience these two charming towns.

Summers in the Front Range in search of golf might also lead you to the captivating town of Georgetown, or towards the world's highest paved highway, Mount Evans Highway, at 14,264 feet. Or a night's stay at Colorado's oldest hotel—the Peck House, which opened in 1862 in Empire.

Golf, mountain scenery, mining history, and agricultural plains: the Front Range of Colorado has it all.

My first rule is, "Distance without direction is worse than no distance at all."—Nancy Lopez

BENNETT

ELEV. 5,483 POP. 2,021

Located 25 miles east of Denver, this small town was named for Hiram Pitt Bennett, Denver postmaster. Its claim to fame has been that the state's highest temperature was recorded here on July 11, 1888, at 118 degrees; however, now the town will surely become known for its new Rick Phelps-designed Antelope Hills Golf Course.

ANTELOPE HILLS GOLF COURSE

THE GOLF Antelope Hills is a new prairie-links style track that takes advantage of the special beauty of the eastern plains of Colorado—unobstructed views of the rolling hills and Rocky Mountains that Nebraskans envy.

The course is lengthy at 7,261 yards with wide landing areas. Rick Phelps provided short treks from tee to green, making it walker-friendly.

THE DETAILS 303-644-5992. 600 Antelope Drive West, Bennett CO 80102.
- Rick Phelps, 2002. 18 holes. Par 72. Black - 7,261 (73.6/12). Blue - 6,698 (70.8/124). White - 6,076 (68/114). Red - 5,352 (68.9/115). Price - $$.

GETTING THERE Take I-70 east to Exit 305, and drive south 2 miles to the course on the left.

BENNETT NOTES

Antelope Hills could be played either before or after flights at the Denver airport, since it's just a short drive. Post-round golf time generally points towards Denver, but the **Willow Tree Country Inn** (800-257-1241) invites you to relax in pampered luxury with a complimentary hydrotherapy foot bath and gentle herbal cream foot massage. This great B&B includes a stocked refrigerator and basket of snacks in each room.

BOULDER

ELEV. 5,344 POP. 94,673

The drive from Denver to Boulder can be a beautiful experience—especially when there's no traffic. At 5,430 feet above sea level, Boulder offers a postcard-perfect view of the rugged, jagged Flatirons as well as the Rocky Mountain

No power on earth will deter men from using a ball that will add to the length of their drive.—Golf Illustrated, 1902

foothills. On a crisp fall day when the fall foliage is ripe with yellows and reds, there's nothing quite like driving out to Boulder to play golf and see the Colorado Buffaloes play football in a scene that some describe as "the city nestled between the mountains and reality."

Boulder is located 35 miles northwest of downtown Denver, and has remained an environmentalist haven loaded with countless recreational opportunities. It's home to the University of Colorado, which has the most beautiful campus in America and was founded in 1874.

Boulder's first residents were Southern Arapahoes who maintained a village near Haystack Mountain. The Utes, Cheyennes, Comanches, and Sioux also visited the area. Seekers of gold established the first non-native settlement in Boulder County on October 17, 1858 at Red Rocks near the entrance to Boulder Canyon; less than a year later A. A. Brookfield organized the Boulder City Town Company.

Amazingly for such an active, sizable town (*Outside* Magazine named Boulder "America's number one sports town"), Boulder only claims two golf courses—the private Boulder Country Club and the historic Flatirons GC.

BOULDER COUNTRY CLUB

THE GOLF The greens are fast, undulating, and well maintained on this course, which is one of the homes of the Colorado Buffalo golf team. The layout has plenty of mature trees that can alter your shots; additionally, water hazards (two streams and four lakes) come into play on a number of holes. Spectacular mountain views make a scenic backdrop for this Press Maxwell-designed course.

THE DETAILS 303-530-2226. 7350 Clubhouse Road, Boulder, CO 80301.
- Press Maxwell, 1965. 18 holes. Par 72. Black - 7,031 (73.3/135). Blue - 6,625 (71.3/131). White - 6,309 (69.6/126). Gold - 5,834 (66.7/123). Men's Red - 5,408 (64.9/116). Women's White - 6,309 (76.4/148). Women's Gold - 5,834 (73.3/137). Women's Red - 5,408 (70.2/131). Private club, reciprocal play allowed. Price - $$$.

GETTING THERE Take the Denver-Boulder Turnpike toward Boulder. Take the Superior exit, and go north to S. Boulder Rd. Turn west to 76th St. Turn north on 76th, drive to Baseline Rd., and turn west again. Take 76th St. north to Clubhouse Rd., then turn left and find the course.

Amateur golf is a game of trouble shots and one-putt pars. It follows therefore that good scrambling is the amateur's fastest, most direct route to better golf.—George Peper

FRONT RANGE

Hale Irwin, Les Fowler, and Larry McAtee probably discussing Irwin's fancy plaid shorts.

*The golfer obsessed with his putter or his grip is focusing on the props,
and not on the core of his performance.*—Dr. Bob Rotella

FRONT RANGE

FLATIRONS GOLF COURSE

THE GOLF Flatirons Golf Course has been popular since 1933 when it opened as a private country club. In 1985 the facility opened to the public and continues to be an area favorite.

Water features, strategic bunkers, narrow, mature tree-lined fairways, and fast greens make the course a challenge. Water guards the left side on the par-4 16th hole, a 449-yard test that requires perfect tee-shot placement. The bail-out area is limited on this difficult hole. Drives left find cottonwoods that block your path, and a slice right finds more trees or even out-of-bounds to kill your chance for par. If you're fortunate enough to be in solid position after a nice drive, the approach is also difficult. The green is small and a steep slope defines the right side. A bogey isn't bad on No. 16, one of the best holes in Colorado for ruining a round quickly.

THE DETAILS 303-442-7851. 5706 E. Arapahoe Road, Boulder, CO 80303.
- Robert Bruce Harris, 1933. 18 holes. Par 70. Black - 6,782 (71.7/126). Blue - 6,445 (69.8/124). Yellow - 5,910 (67.4/118). Green - 5,226 (64/110). Women's Black - 6,782 (77.3/139.5). Women's Green - 5,226 (68.3/119). Women's Yellow - 5,910 (72.5/129). Women's Blue - 6,445 (75.6/135). Price - $$.

GETTING THERE Take either Hwy. 36 to Arapahoe Rd. or Foothills Parkway to Arapahoe Rd. in Boulder. Turn right (east) on Arapahoe Rd. and follow it for about a mile to the entrance of the course on the right.

BOULDER NOTES

Thanks to everything that comes with being a university town, Boulder has an outstanding evening scene, with a few small bars on University Hill and the lively downtown area centered around Pearl Street. In fact Boulder is a beer drinker's heaven, with several brewpubs and even a few wine bars in town. Look to the **Walnut Brewery** (303-447-1345), **Mountain Sun Brewery** (303-546-0886), or **BJ's Brewery** (303-402-9294) for spirits. The best post-golf cold beer-burger options are the **14th St. Bar & Grill** (303-444-5854) or **Tom's Tavern** (303-442-9363). The best sit-down options are the dressier **Flagstaff House** (303-442-4640), the **Boulder Chop House** for steak, **Chautauqua Dining Hall** (303-440-3776) for the true Boulder experience, or particularly for romantic summer evenings, **Bacaro** (303-444-4888), which offers upscale Italian fares on an outdoor deck. Reserve a room at the **Alps Boulder Canyon Inn** (www.alpsinn.com, 800-414-2577), a historic, luxury country inn in Boulder

With either a downhill lie or an uphill lie, always play the ball nearer the higher foot.—Jackie Burke, Jr.

Canyon, or the national historic landmark **Hotel Boulderado** (303-442-4344), once the most high-toned spot in Boulder when it opened in 1909. The **Inn on Mapleton Hill** (800-276-6528) is a charming, affordable B&B. The **Boulder City Parks trail system** is a must for outdoors lovers who come to visit this beautiful city. Don't miss the Chautauqua Park, and **Flagstaff Mountain**. The west end of the path winds out of the city and up through Boulder Canyon for four miles. Adventurers should explore the mountains west of Boulder, where the towns evoke a 1960s hippie-era charm. Nederland is the gateway to the **Indian Peaks Wilderness**, and places like Ward, Eldora, Rollinsville, and Jamestown are all intriguing stops; at Gold Hill appears as if it hasn't changed since the gold mining days.

EATON

ELEV. 4,839 POP. 2,690

The loneliness of the Front Range greets you as you drive into Eaton. A sign reads "Beef, Beets and Beans," and no doubt lots of folks wear overalls in this small farming community just seven miles north of Greeley on U.S. Highway 85. The town's namesake, former Colorado Governor Benjamin Eaton, helped found the town in 1892 and was instrumental in getting irrigation to the area. Surprisingly, Eaton's golf scene has been around since 1923, and the facility is definitely worth a visit if you can figure out a way to work your way on the grounds of the hallowed Eaton CC.

EATON COUNTRY CLUB

THE GOLF The ECC's calling card is its well-conditioned, subtle, hard-to-read greens, which some consider the best in Northern Colorado. The 18-hole route rolls through agricultural plains, but the rolling terrain offers some surprising elevation changes, and the design has been spiced up over the years with the persistent addition of trees. A lake that comes into play on the signature 18th hole has been deepened and widened. This par-4 hole measures 432 yards and is a tough ender due to the lake.

THE DETAILS 970-454-2587. 37661 Weld County Road 39, Eaton, CO 80615.
- Frank Baumgarner, 1967. 18 holes. Par 71. Black - 6,606 (70.8/118). Blue - 6,339 (69.4/117). White - 6,078 (68.4/115). Women's White - 6,119 (73.9/128). Women's Red - 5,758 (71.9/125). Women's Red - 5,691 (71.6/125). Private course, but reciprocal play allowed if pro calls. Price - $$.

If rough is growing in the direction of the shot, the ball will come out easier and faster; if it is against that direction, the grass will resist the club, so you must swing harder. —Raymond Floyd

GETTING THERE Take I-25 to I-76, and go north to Hwy. 85. Take 85 north to Eaton, and turn east on WCR 74. Proceed 1 mile to WCR 39 (stop sign) and go north 1.5 miles to the course.

EATON NOTES

The first option for post-round fun is at the golf course. If you must spend the night, the **Cottonwood Motel** (970-454-2380) will get you through the night. A quick lunch can be had at **Eaton Pizza** (970-454-1068), which also serves sub sandwiches.

ERIE

ELEV. 5,034 POP. 6,291

The former coal mining town of Erie was settled by a Methodist minister from Erie, PA, near a string of fur trading posts built along the South Platte River in the 1830s and 40s. At the time this was part of the Nebraska Territory, which included what are now 17 Colorado counties, and eventually also included the Pony Express and Union Pacific routes that crossed the northeastern corner of Weld County. Erie is an active, growing city due to its location just north of Denver, and its suburban role is evident in the new Jay Morrish-designed Vista Ridge Golf Club.

VISTA RIDGE GOLF CLUB

THE GOLF Built by The Redstone Group, Vista Ridge is a Troon Golf-managed facility that has a prairie links look and impressive bunkering. Routed over an expansive 232 acres, the roomy layout allows for broad fairways and generous landing areas for tee shots, as well as a nice buffer zone from the homes that border the course. Morrish says Vista Ridge is "wide-open prairie and features lots of native areas, creative bunkering, and prairie grasses."

THE DETAILS 303-665-9590. 2700 Vista Parkway, Erie, CO 80516.
- www.vistaridgegc.com
- Jay Morrish, 2003. 18 holes. Par 72. Black - 7,404 (74/138). Gold - 6,897 (71.7/129). Copper - 6,230 (68.6/115). Women's Gold - 6,763 (78.1/143). Women's Copper - 6,086 (74.4/135). Women's Silver - 5,400 (70.7/125). Women's Jade - 4,693 (67/114). Price - $$$.

FRONT RANGE

It's OK to have butterflies. Just get them flying in formation.—Francisco Lopez

GETTING THERE Take I-25 exit 229 (Hwy. 7) and drive west 2.5 miles to Vista Parkway. Turn right on Vista Parkway.

ERIE NOTES

With Boulder and Denver nearby, Erie isn't a prime overnight destination. Local food joints include the **Uptown Erie Cafe** (303-828-2501) and **Paraiso Azteca** (303-828-3477). Kids love the **Anderson Farm Corn Maze** (303-696-6659), no doubt a place that can keep them busy while dad is playing golf at Vista Ridge. Erie is also home to the **Colorado National Speedway** (www.coloradospeedway.com, 303-665-4173) in case you have a thing for fast cars and racing.

ESTES PARK

ELEV. 7,522 POP. 5,413

Beautiful Estes Park is the eastern gateway to the famous park and where Joel Estes and his family settled in 1859. At one time in the early history of Colorado tourism, a visit here, complete with a drive through Rocky Mountain National Park, a glance at the 14,259-foot summit of Longs Peak, and a stay in the Stanley Hotel, constituted America's ideal family vacation. Once journalists wrote about climbing Longs Peak, the rest of the world discovered this scenic town and adventurers from all over the world came to experience it for themselves. Bombarded by tourists in the summer, the town's reputation grew when Stephen King used the setting as the inspiration for his novel *The Shining*.

Aside from the summer crowds, Estes Park is definitely worth a golf visit, particularly if the trip is planned in conjunction with quality family time in the area. Estes Park has two gorgeous golf courses – 18-hole Estes Park and the 9-hole Lake Estes—where you'll experience the unusual hazard of roaming elk.

ESTES PARK GOLF COURSE

THE GOLF Loaded with elk and outstanding views, this unspoiled golf locale rates as one of the most beautiful layouts in the state. There's something about the 7,600-foot elevation, surrounding mountains, and laid-back atmosphere that makes Estes Park special.

Scratch golfers welcome the ego-boost this course can provide, but must putt well on the poa annua greens and find the Kentucky bluegrass fairways, which tend to be flat on the front nine and hilly on the back. On No. 17, a 541-yard

---

Golf is a game to be played with two hands. Your left hand guides the club and keeps the face in the desired position for the hit, and power pours through the right hand and the club. Whack the hell out of the ball with the right hand.—Tommy Armour

doglegger right, Fish Creek awaits any weak approaches into the green.

THE DETAILS 970-586-8146. 1080 South Saint Vrain Ave., Estes Park, CO 80517.
- www.estesvalleyrecreation.com
- Henry Hughes, 1957. Dick Phelps. 18 holes. Par 71. Blue - 6,326 (69/121). White - 5,869 (66.8/112). Women's White - 5,869 (71.9/131). Women's Red - 5,250 (68.3/125). Price - $$.

GETTING THERE Take I-25 to Hwy. 66 (west). Go to Estes Park to Hwy. 7 and turn left (south). The golf course is 1 mile down Hwy. 7 on the left side, just a few miles east of Rocky Mountain National Park.

LAKE ESTES EXECUTIVE 9 GOLF COURSE

THE GOLF The Big Thompson River snakes along five holes on this scenic executive course. And while the route is flat and void of bunkers, holes like the 100-yard, par-3 sixth hole keep golfers entertained. No. 6 features two streams connecting in front, then curving around the sides—a fun hole for single-digit hacks and a nervous hole for beginners.

THE DETAILS 970-586-8176. 690 Big Thompson, Estes Park, CO 80517.
- www.estesvalleyrecreation.com/9holegolf.html
- Henry Hughes, 1971. 9-hole executive course. Par 31. White - 4,418 (60.2/96). Women's White - 4,348 (62.6/106). Women's Red - 4,176 (61.6/105). Price - $.

GETTING THERE Go about a half mile east of downtown Estes Park on Hwy. 34. The course is just a few miles east of Rocky Mountain National Park.

FRONT RANGE

ESTES PARK NOTES

Estes Park is one of Colorado's best golf destinations simply because there is so much to do. The list of outdoor excursions is too long to detail here, the historic streets are loaded with shops, and the restaurants are nothing short of excellent. Plan your visit at www.estesparkresort.com. Weary golfers should look first to the **Estes Park Brewery** (970-586-5421), a popular microbrewery known for its Samson Stout, a brew named after a magnificent bull elk that was poached illegally in the park a few years back. The restaurant and outdoor deck are perfect for warm afternoons spent gazing at Longs

The primary reason players often make spectacular trouble shots, causing the ball to go under, around, and over obstacles, is that they work harder on visualizing these shots that on those from less demanding positions.—Gary Wiren

Peak. While there aren't too many lively nightspots, watering holes like the **Wheel Bar** (970-586-9381) and **J.R. Chapins Lounge** (970-586-2332, at the **Holiday Inn**) get the job done. Of the many **dining options** available, first consider the following:

• Cascades at the Stanley Hotel	Western fare
• Grumpy Gringo	Mexican
• Orlando's Steak House	Steak and seafood
• The Other Side	Traditional Western American
• Silverado at the Lake Shore Lodge	Western bistro
• Sweet Basilico Café	Italian
• Twin Owls Steakhouse at the Black Canyon Inn	Continental and Colorado
• The Woodlands Restaurant	Intercontinental
• Grubsteak Restaurant	Elk and buffalo burgers
• Big Horn Restaurant	Breakfast
• Ed's Canina and Grill	Mexican

As you might expect from such a premier tourist destination, the city offers a comprehensive selection of lodging for every type of visitor. The world-famous **Stanley Hotel** heads the pack (800-976-1377, www.stanleyhotel.com). It was built in 1909 by F. O. Stanley, inventor of the Stanley Steamer automobile, who came to Estes Park for health reasons (tuberculosis). Make reservations, though, as the summer tourist season is extremely busy. For breaks from the tourists, don't miss a drive up Trail Ridge Road, a majestic byway through **Rocky Mountain National Park** and the highest continuous motorway in the United States. More than eight miles are above 11,000 feet and it climbs to 12,183 feet.

FIRESTONE
ELEV. 4,961 POP. 1,908

Once a lonely outpost off of I-25, Firestone is another of Denver's growing north-side suburban areas and the sixth-fastest-growing municipality in the nation from April 1, 2000, to July 1, 2002. Outdoor recreational opportunities abound with 35 parks, 12 miles of scenic trail, as well as the relatively new Saddleback Golf Club.

FRONT RANGE

Let your love of winning drive your practice habits. Practice shouldn't be viewed as an exercise in self-denial or sacrifice. It should be viewed as an integral part of the process of improvement.—Dr. Bob Rotella

SADDLEBACK GOLF COURSE

THE GOLF Built on a former 250-acre alfalfa farm with views of the Rockies to the west and the plains to the east, Saddleback's green fairways stand out beautifully in the wheat-colored terrain of the prairie. The course features raised mounds, fairway bunkers, manmade ravines, and over 3,000 cottonwood, oak, maple, spruce, pine, and ash trees that will add character once they mature. Architect Andy Johnson inserted shelved areas in the fairways to create definition in the pathways to the greens. Saddleback qualifies as a hidden gem: a good layout placed on an extremely plain site.

THE DETAILS 303-833-5000. 8631 Frontier Street, Firestone, CO 80520.
- www.saddlebackgolf.com
- Andy Johnson, 2001. 18 holes. Par 72. Black - 6,928 (72.3/125). Gold - 6,423 (70/123). Blue - 6,009 (68/118). White - 5,455 (65.4/111). Women's Blue - 6,009 (73.1/130). Women's White - 5,455 (70.1/124). Women's Red - 4,834 (66.6/115). Price - $$.

GETTING THERE Take I-25 to exit 235 (Hwy. 52). Go east 2 miles on Hwy. 52 to WCR 13. Go north 3 miles (past Safeway) and turn east on WCR 20. Drive 1 mile and the course entrance is on the right.

FIRESTONE NOTES

Try **Tom & Ski's Tavern** (303-833-9917) for a meal over cold beers, and discuss tackling the Firestone Trail, which is over 12 miles long and provides a unified pedestrian connection to area parks, the regional St. Vrain Legacy Trail, and the **Colorado Front Range Trail** system.

FORT COLLINS
ELEV. 5,003 POP. 118,652

French fur trappers came here in the early 1800s and found bounties in Northern Colorado, and the U.S. Army eventually established Camp Collins to protect wagon trains rolling through the Overland Trail. In 1870 the Agricultural College of Colorado opened and established Fort Collins as a city. Since then the community has grown into one of the nation's most livable cities, centered around modern-day Colorado State University, the Cache La Poudre River (named for the French words "hide" and "powder"), and a thriv-

About the only positive contribution of uncontrolled pursuit of power is to make golf ball and equipment manufacturers rich.—Jim Flick

ing historic Old Town district surrounded by tree-lined streets and charming houses. And for its size, Fort Collins is jammed with golf courses (8 facilities), earning a *Golf Digest* ranking in 1999 as the Ninth Best Place for Affordable and Accessible Golf.

ADRIEL HILLS GOLF COURSE

THE GOLF The 6-hole, par-3 golf course at Adriel Hills is an amenity for the condo association—no outside play is allowed. The design features a 2-acre lake with islands and a few holes with water approaches, as well as a few bunkers on rolling terrain. The bentgrass greens are great, but rather slow because the maintenance staff doesn't have the ability to roll them. A sparse gathering of spruce, cottonwoods, and honey locusts defines the layout.

THE DETAILS 970-484-3098. 1900 Kedron, Fort Collins, CO 80524.
- Private. No reciprocal play allowed. Information for this course is unavailable.

GETTING THERE Find Adriel Hills by taking Exit 50 off of I-25 and heading west.

CITY PARK NINE GOLF COURSE

THE GOLF Designed by the Fort Collins Golf Association, City Park is an old-school 1940s 9-holer with tight fairways, old-ass trees, and tiny greens. Accuracy off the tee is imperative, since anything crooked takes you into the trees.

THE DETAILS 970-221-6650. 411 South Bryan, Fort Collins, CO 80521.
- Fort Collins Golf Association, 1940. 9 holes. Par 36. Women's Red/White - 5,726 (71.5/127). White/Blue - 6,297 (69.9/123). Price - $.

GETTING THERE Take I-25 north to exit 269-B. Follow Mulberry just past the lake in the park and turn right (north) on Bryan. Take a left immediately past the fire station into the course entrance.

COLLINDALE GOLF COURSE

THE GOLF The Collindale Golf Course is solid—good enough to host an annual U.S. Open qualifier because of its long par 5s and outstanding greens. The greens, considered some of the best and quickest in the state, sometimes run 10

Missing a short putt does not mean you have to hit your next drive out of bounds.—Henry Cotton to 12 on the Stimpmeter. Accuracy is a must because of the mature cottonwoods and pines that line the course, along with five lakes and a ditch that winds its way through the course.

THE DETAILS 970-221-6651. 1441 East Horsetooth Road, Fort Collins, CO 80525.

- Frank Hummel, 1971. 18 holes. Par 71. Blue - 6,935 (72.3/127). White - 6,403 (70/123). Gold - 5,857 (67.5/114). Women's White - 6,403 (76.2/140). Women's Gold - 5,728 (72.2/133). Women's Red - 5,423 (70.4/126). Price - $.

GETTING THERE Take I-25 to Harmony Rd. (Exit 265), turn west, and continue to Timberline Rd. Turn right (north) to Horsetooth Rd. and head left (west). The Golf course is on the left.

FORT COLLINS COUNTRY CLUB

THE GOLF Members proudly exclaim that Fort Collins Country Club is the only member-owned golf and country club in town. Velvet-smooth putting surfaces, warm hospitality, great food, and a family-oriented experience is the story at FCCC. Recently renovated by the folks at Dye Designs in Denver, the course measures 7,150 yards with five par-3 holes.

THE DETAILS 970-482-9988. 1920 Country Club Road, Fort Collins, CO 80524.
- www.fcgolf.org
- Henry Hughes, 1959. Dye Designs renovation. 18 holes. Par 71. Gold - 7,150 (73.6/133). Blue - 6,583 (71.3/128). White - 6,162 (69.4/125). Women's White - 6,162 (75.3/139). Women's Red - 5,329 (70.4/125). Private, but reciprocal play is allowed. Price - $$$$.

GETTING THERE Take I-25 to exit 271 near Fort Collins. Turn left (west) and find County Road 11. Turn right and go north to Country Club Rd. Turn left (west) on Country Club Rd. and follow it to the clubhouse.

LINK-N-GREENS GOLF COURSE

THE GOLF Watch out for the water on this 18-hole executive course located in the northern part of Fort Collins. The layout is fairly flat, making it a fun walk with few bunkers and mildly contoured greens. There is one hefty 3-shot par 5

Be prepared to get it up and down on the first hole. That way, you always expect the unexpected and you're ready for anything.—Jackie Burke, Jr.

on the course—the 605-yard No. 6, which doglegs left with water on both sides of the fairway.

THE DETAILS 970-221-4818. 777 East Lincoln Avenue, Fort Collins, CO 80521.
- C.A. Musgrave, 1982. 18 holes. Par 64, executive course. Blue - 4,809 (61.6/93). White - 4,601 (60.8/91). Women's Blue - 4,900 (66.3/103). Women's White - 4,548 (64.4/102). Women's Red - 3,727 (59.8/95). Price - $.

GETTING THERE Take I-25 and turn west at the Mullberry exit. Turn north on Lemay and go west on Lincoln.

MOUNTAIN VISTA GREENS GOLF COURSE

THE GOLF The newest course in Fort Collins, this 9-holer was created by Victor Tawara, who routed the course through his tree farm. It's an easy walking course, a favorite of area seniors, and has wide fairways and large bentgrass greens.

The decade-old trees are maturing each year and adding beauty and challenge to the course. The best hole is No. 8, a 179-yard par 3 that has mountain views, a shallow, long green surrounded by bunkers, and a lake in the rear.

THE DETAILS 970-482-4847. 2808 N.E. Frontage Road, Fort Collins, CO 80524.
- Harold Garrison/Victor Tawara, 1992. 9 holes. Par 36. White/Blue - 6,684 (70/117). Women's Red/White - 5,847 (72/123). Price - $.

GETTING THERE Take I-25 north to exit 271, turn right, then left on the frontage road. Go 1 mile north and the course is on the right.

PTARMIGAN GOLF & COUNTRY CLUB

THE GOLF Ptarmigan's layout traverses water and a myriad of elevation changes, boasting all the score-busting features of a Jack Nicklaus signature design. Modern features such as mounding, large undulating greens, and more than 80 bunkers challenge golfers repeatedly.

Avoid the large lake that runs down the entire left side of the 609-yard No. 16. Out-of-bounds is right and the green is elevated and narrow, protected by water on the left and bunkers on the right.

A Ladies NCAA Fall Classic is staged here with female college golfers coming from as far away as San Francisco. Denver University, Montana, Kansas,

FRONT RANGE

CSU, CU, and other colleges also take part.

THE DETAILS 970-226-6600. 5416 Vardon Way, Fort Collins, CO 80528.
- www.ptarmigancountryclub.com
- Jack Nicklaus, 1988. 18 holes. Par 72. Black - 7,201(73.8/132). Blue - 6,586 (71.1/124). White - 6,077 (68.2/119). Men's Red - 5,287 (64.1/108). Women's White - 6,062 (74.3/137). Women's Red - 5,287 (70/126). Private, but reciprocal play is allowed. Price - $$$$.

GETTING THERE From I-25 take the Windsor exit (exit 262) east to the course.

SOUTHRIDGE GOLF CLUB

THE GOLF Rolling hills and elevation changes are trademarks of Southridge, which features a brand-new clubhouse. One of the most difficult holes is No. 16, a 206-yard par 3 with a diagonal creek in front. The wind on this hole, which is considered one of the toughest in Northern Colorado, can knock your shot into trouble if you're short or left, and trees and sand will gobble up anything too far right.

THE DETAILS 970-226-2828. 5750 South Lemay Ave., Fort Collins, CO 80525.
- Frank Hummel, 1986. 18 holes. Par 71. Blue - 6,378 (70.2/124). White - 5,837 (67.4/114). Women's Blue - 6,250 (74.5/141). Women's White - 5,696 (71.5/133). Women's Red - 4,821 (66.6/121). Price - $.

GETTING THERE From I-25 take the Harmony Rd. exit west to Lemay Ave. At Lemay turn south for about 1 mile. The course is on the left.

FORT COLLINS NOTES

Most post-golf revelry should begin in **Old Town**, where it's a summertime tradition to linger in the square, sample a microbrew, and listen to a free concert. Fort Collins is becoming famous for beer, with brewers like **New Belgium Brewing Co.** (970-221-0524), **Anheuser-Busch** (970-490-4691), **Linden's Brewing Co.**, and **CooperSmith's** (970-498-0483) all offering delicious cold beverages – the latter two offering food as well. For meals **Austin's American Grill** (970-224-9691) is a favorite because of its patio, and the oyster bar at **Nate's Steak & Seafood Place** (970-223-9200) is phenomenal. Other popular Fort Collins eateries are **Rio Grande** (970-224-5428) for margaritas, **Charco Broiler** (970-482-1472) or **Cozzola's Pizzas** (970-

Don't let the bad shots get to you. Don't let yourself become angry. The true scramblers are thick-skinned. And they always beat the whiners. —Paul Runyan

482-3557) for a monster 16-inch Italian pie. Consider staying at the historic **Edwards House B&B** (800-281-9190), built in 1904 and featuring eight rooms with fireplaces, high ceilings, complimentary adult beverages each evening, and a full breakfast every morning. It's located one block from historic Old Town, a great place to drink, eat, shop, and start a tour of Fort Collins after golf. Another good choice is the cozy **Sheldon House B&B** (970-221-1917), originally built at the turn of the 20th century by banker Charles Sheldon. Hikers have **Horsetooth Mountain Park** and many other great locales for working their legs, and the Cache la Poudre River has picnic spots along the highway and rafting for hot summer afternoons after golf.

FORT LUPTON

ELEV. 4,906 POP. 6,787

The fertile Platte River Valley in the southern part of Weld County is home to 1890s-era Fort Lupton, a town that looms on the fringes of Denver and offers affordable golf without the crowds. Located only 30 minutes from Denver and 15 miles from Denver International Airport, Fort Lupton makes a fun golf stop for business travelers with time to kill between meetings and connecting flights, or road-trippers on the way to and from Greeley.

COYOTE CREEK GOLF COURSE

THE GOLF Snow-capped mountains and open stretches of prairie surround the Coyote Creek Golf Course, a modern prairie-links track that tests golfers with five lakes, more than 50 bunkers, undulating greens, and a pesky canal. Course designer Matt Eccles routed the layout through gently rolling terrain, with mounding and some clever risk/reward challenges along the way. It's worth going for the par-4 14th, a drivable 295-yarder, but bunkers and mounding near the green give the hole some bite.

Coyote Creek includes a learning center, driving range, practice greens, and generally great amenities.

THE DETAILS 303-857-6152. 222 Clubhouse Drive, Fort Lupton, CO 80621.
- www.golfexperience.com/coyotecreek
- Matt Eccles, 1999. 18 holes. Par 71. Blue - 6,412 (69.5/118). White - 6,097 (67.9/116). Red - 5,166 (67.7/116). Price - $.

If a putt looks straight, don't stare at the line for a long period of time trying to see if there's something you overlooked. Sooner or later, you'll invent a break that isn't there.—Corey Pavin

GETTING THERE Take I-25 to the Dacono-Ft. Lupton Exit 235. Go east on Hwy. 52 about 9 miles through the town of Fort Lupton, and the course is about half a mile east of town.

FORT LUPTON NOTES

With no rush to get into Denver, Coyote Creek's clubhouse is a nice place to enjoy the bar and grill and work up the buzz to spend some cash in the full-service golf shop. Restless turistas should visit the **Fort Lupton Museum** (303-857-1634) or go horseback riding at **Gloraloma Ranch** (303-833-4040). During the summer **Anders Farm** (303-857-2158) is a fun roadside stop for every kind of fresh produce imaginable.

GREELEY

ELEV. 4,664 POP. 76,930

Located at the junction of the South Platte River and Cache La Poudre, Greeley was the locale touted in 1860s *New York Tribune* ads that immortalized the term "Go west, young man." Pioneers came and developed the area, basing the economy on farming and beef. Today Greeley is home to the University of Northern Colorado, a frequent power in small-college football and the inspiration for the town's culture and vitality. Agriculture and ranching are staples, and Greeley is known for its annual Greeley Stampede, one of the nation's largest outdoor rodeos. Golfers can get their fix on the public Boomerang Golf Links and Highland Hills Golf Course, or use connections to get onto the 1930s-era, Tom Bendelow-designed Greeley Country Club.

BOOMERANG GOLF LINKS

THE GOLF On this links-style course that weaves around the numerous water hazards of the Boomerang Canal, the design features huge, fast greens, loads of wet stuff, and tall buffalo grass that lines fairways and can be deadly.

Boomerang, host of recent Colorado Golf Association Public Links Qualifying events, offers panoramic views of the Front Range as golfers navigate the "Down Under Nine" (front nine) in an effort to avoid the water.

The Northern Territory (second nine) feels more secluded; first-time golfers here should pay close attention to the diagram books that come with the carts. Shot selections are not intuitive and it's imperative to think through strategy.

After-golf time should be spent at the course's Outback Restaurant.

I have never seen a pocket billiards player lose his stroke. He's not thinking about his stroke. He's thinking about what's in front of him, as athletes in other sports do. His concern is moving the cue ball to a certain point with a certain amount of speed, not how he's holding the darn cue stick.—Roger Maltbie

THE DETAILS 970-351-8934. 970-351-8947. 7309 4th St., Greeley, CO 80634.
- William Neff, 1991. 18 holes. Par 72. Black - 7,214 (73.4/131). Men - 6,800 (71.4/128). White - 6,264 (68.8/125). Women's White - 6,264 (74.2/134). Women's Red - 5,285 (68.3/120). Price - $$.

GETTING THERE From I-25 take the Greeley/Loveland exit (Exit 257). Follow Hwy. 34 east and take the Business Loop as it turns north. Follow the Business Loop (becomes W. 10th St.) to 71st Ave. and turn left (north). Take 71st Ave. north to 4th St. At 4th St., turn left and follow it to the course.

GREELEY COUNTRY CLUB

THE GOLF Tom Bendelow, famous for some of America's favorite old golf courses (Medinah in Illinois and the East Lake Golf Club in Atlanta), routed the front nine way back in 1932. Then Press Maxwell came through 30 years later for a redesign of Bendelow's route, which included an additional nine. Old-school all the way, the design features small greens, plenty of out-of-bounds, water, bunkers, and some 2,000 mature trees that wreak havoc on wayward hacks. The course's signature is the challenging greens—tiny targets and subtle breakers that make this a Northern Colorado favorite.

THE DETAILS 970-353-2431. 4500 W. 10th Greeley, CO 80634.
- Tom Bendelow, front nine, 1932. Press Maxwell, back nine, 1962. 18 holes. Par 70. Blue - 6,469 (70.8/132). Women's Red - 5,656 (72.7/ 128). Women's White - 6,175 (75/138). White - 6,189 (69.9/127). Private, but reciprocal play is allowed. Price - $$$.

GETTING THERE From I-25 take exit 257 (Greeley exit). Follow Hwy. 34 east about 5 miles to the business loop exit. Take the business exit as it goes north. Stay on this road, and it will turn into 10th St. Take 10th all the way past 47th Ave. to the course on the right.

HIGHLAND HILLS GOLF COURSE

THE GOLF Stretching out on top of a hill, Highland Hills is a traditional tree-lined golf course, with lakes, sharp doglegs, undulating fairways, and tricky greens. Two of Colorado's most prolific architects designed the course nine holes at a time. Press Maxwell arrived first and laid out the East Nine in 1959. Frank Hummel, who designed the West Nine about 10 years later and decided to retire

When a putter tries very hard not to three-putt, he generally winds up three-putting more often, and, at the very best, two-putting a lot.—Dr. Bob Rotella

here, still lives on the course. Hummel says he prefers his West Nine—a challenging 6,741 yards—because of the larger greens: "What I like are the big greens that are not very severe. It also has a lot of variety in its holes and the par-3 holes are some of the best in Northern Colorado."

Erik Hogan, a course member and UNC golf team player, fired a course-record 60 here in 2003. This shattered the 1977 mark held by Allan Abrams, head pro at Indian Tree.

THE DETAILS 970-330-7327. 2200 Clubhouse Drive, Greeley, CO 80634.
- Press Maxwell, east nine. Frank Hummel, west nine, 1960. 18 holes. Par 71. Blue - 6,741 (73.1/129). White - 6,491 (72.1/126). Women's White - 6,491 (76.9/142). Women's Red - 6,002 (74.3/136). Price - $$.

GETTING THERE From I-25 take the Greeley exit (US 34) east to 47th Ave. (stay on the bypass, avoid the business loop). At 47th turn left and go to the next stoplight (20th St.). Turn left, follow 20th up to the water tower, and look for a sign to the parking lot.

GREELEY NOTES

A stroll through Greeley's **Old Town Square** reveals that it's more than a cow town, and the best option for weekenders in the historic district is the **Sod Buster Inn** (970-392-1221). Another option is the **Greeley Guest House** (970-353-9373). For meals locals prefer **Fat Albert's** (970-356-1999) for lunch, and they'll point you towards **Coyote's Southwestern Grill** (970-336-1725) for an evening Mexican feast. Don't miss the Cajun Boil at the **Union Colony Brewery** (970-356-4116). Explore the town's history at **Centennial Village Museum**, which displays the architecture and lifestyle of the early Union colonists, who traveled here from New York. Greeley is sort of a rodeo town, known for its **Greeley Independence Stampede** from the end of June to July 4 each year.

LAFAYETTE

ELEV. 5,236 POP. 23,197

In 1863, newlyweds Lafayette and Mary Miller joined an ox-team train of 50 wagons and headed for Colorado, landing in the Lafayette area in 1871. In addition to farming and raising six children, the industrious couple operated a stage coach stop and ran a meat market, before coal was discovered on the Miller Ranch in 1884. The Cannon mine turned out to be the richest vein of coal in

---

One very simple tip will infinitely improve the timing of most golfers. Merely pause briefly at the top of the backswing.—Tommy Armour

the area, giving Mary reason to lay out the town site in 1889 and name it after her late husband. The area has been home to farmers, ranchers, and miners ever since. Sandwiched between Denver and Boulder and convenient by shooting up US 287, Lafayette is a worthy side trip golf destination for warm fall weekends before CU football games.

INDIAN PEAKS GOLF COURSE

THE GOLF This Hale Irwin signature course is not too far from where Irwin competed in both football and golf for the University of Colorado. Situated a few miles east of the foothills, the open course layout at Indian Peaks offers unspoiled views of the snow-covered mountains.

The course is routed over rolling terrain and features six lakes and two creeks. Recently a construction crew planted 1,100 trees, which are still fairly small. The greens are large and contoured, but 83 bunkers get in the way during a round. No. 1 is a favorite hole: a big, dogleg-left par 5 that tempts a huge drive over a lake, cutting the corner of out-of-bounds. Consider playing a safer shot to get home in three. Take advantage of the downhill par-4 10th before the back nine levels out and finishes back uphill.

The course has hosted numerous events, including the 1994 Colorado State Amateur, 1996 Local U.S. Open Qualifying, 1996 Titleist Pro/Assistant Championship, 1998 Local U.S. Open Qualifying, 1999 State Public Links Championship, and 2002 State Public Links Championship.

THE DETAILS 303-666-4706. 2300 Indian Peaks Trail, Lafayette, CO 80026.
- Dick Phelps, Hale Irwin, 1993. 18 holes. Par 72. Black - 7,083 (73.4/133). Blue - 6,617 (70.9/125). White - 6,000 (67.9/117). Women's White - 6,000 (73.7/129). Women's Red - 5,468 (70.8/122). Price - $$.

GETTING THERE From I-25 in Lafayette take Hwy. 7, which becomes Baseline Road. Don't turn north at 287; instead continue west 1 mile after crossing 287 and take a right on Indian Peaks Drive.

LAFAYETTE NOTES

The **Ninety-Fifth Street Spa & Salon** (303-666-7036) makes a worthy excursion for significant others who are awaiting golfers. Locals recommend **Spice China** (720-890-0999) or **Ting's Place** (303-666-9559) for a meal, but nearby Boulder is preferred for lodging, good eats, and nightlife.

There is only one categorical imperative in golf. And that is to hit the ball. There are no minor absolutes. —Sir Walter Simpson

LONGMONT

ELEV. 4,942 POP. 71,093

Back in 1871 the St. Vrain Valley must have looked awfully good to a group of pioneers from Chicago who purchased 70,000 acres and headed west. They built the town of Longmont on the higher ground of the north bank of the St. Vrain River, where they could enjoy the Longs Peak view. Today Longmont is a big city with loads of golf, and an entertaining Main Street lined with shops and restaurants.

FOX HILL COUNTRY CLUB

THE GOLF Designed by Frank Hummel in 1972 with subsequent remodeling by Dick Phelps, Fox Hill offers a tight test of golf, with out-of-bounds on nine holes and lakes and streams to cause trouble on seven others. The greens and fairways are heavily contoured, and the bentgrass greens are quick. Course management is paramount here because of the mature trees lining the fairways. The 401-yard, par 4 No. 16 requires a great tee shot over water to a tight fairway lined with trees, followed by an approach that must carry a creek to a two-tiered, well-bunkered green.

THE DETAILS 303-772-1061. 1400 E. Hwy. 119, Longmont, CO 80502.
- www.foxhillcc.com
- Frank Hummel, 1972. Dick Phelps, remodel master plan. 18 holes. Par 70. Blue - 6,806 (72.4/136). White - 6,454 (70.9/128). Green - 6,180 (69.5/122). Gold - 5,758 (67.5/117). Men's Red - 5,471 (66.2/112). Women's Blue - 6,806 (78.9/146). Women's White - 6,454 (76.9/143). Women's Green - 6,180 (75.1/140). Women's Gold - 5,758 (72.3/135). Women's Red - 5,471 (71/128). Private, with limited reciprocal play allowed. Price - $$$.

GETTING THERE Take I-25 to exit 240 (Route 119)and drive west 5 miles. The course is on your right.

LAKE VALLEY GOLF CLUB

THE GOLF Built in 1965, Lake Valley is a Press Maxwell design that started out a public layout until it turned private in 2000. Rick Phelps designed a master plan for remodeling that is being implemented in phases.

The point is that it doesn't matter if you look like a beast before or after the hit, as long as you look like a beauty at the moment of impact.—Seve Ballesteros

The course is nestled in the foothills just north of Boulder, and measures 6,825 yards with a links-style look. The front nine is hilly and the back nine smoothes out as ponds come into play on three holes. Bunkers are scarce.

Members love the view of the Flatirons from the clubhouse, where they can enjoy good eats and cold beverages at the Persimmon Grill. A new short-game practice area opened in 2001 and Phelps' long-range improvements will include more bunkers and water hazards.

THE DETAILS 303-444-2114. 4400 Lake Valley Drive, Longmont, CO 80503.
- www.lakevalley.com
- Press Maxwell, 1964. Rick Phelps, master remodeling plan. 18 holes. Par 70. Black - 6,825 (72.1/128). Blue - 6,548 (70.7/126). White - 6,261 (69.3/122). Green - 6,002 (68.0/120). Men's Red - 5,516 (65.2/116). Women's White - 6,261 (75.5/136). Women's Green - 6,002 (74/134). Women's Red - 5,516 (71.2/127). Private club, but reciprocal play is allowed. Price - $$$.

GETTING THERE Take Route 36 (Denver-Boulder Turnpike) to the north side of Boulder. Five miles north of Boulder turn east on Neva Road, go 1.5 miles and turn right at the Lake Valley sign.

MISSING LINKS GOLF AT FREDERICK

THE GOLF We're not sure what you'll find at the confusing "Missing Links at Frederick," which lists a Longmont address. We've heard of an executive track with little character and a few synthetic turf tee boxes, but attempts to secure a tee time were unanswered or met with hostility. "We are under construction," they say before hanging up. Suffice to say that there's probably a better use of your golf time until the mystery of the Missing Links is solved.

THE DETAILS 303-682-2758. 5830 WCR 20, Longmont, CO 80504.
- Jack Finley and Rob Finley, 1995. 9 holes. Par 34. Men's - 4,138 (60/81). Women's Back - 4,138 (60.6/104). Women's Forward - 3,898 (60/103). Price - $.

GETTING THERE Take I-25 to Exit 235 and go 2 miles east on Hwy. 52 to County Rd. 13. Then go north 3 miles to the course.

We all have particular quirks and faults in our golf swing we wish were not there. We anguish over how to make them go away. But they never do and they never will. It's all part of our 'thumb print.' Don't forsake your thumb print. It is who you are. Work with it, not against it. —Roger Maltbie

SUNSET GOLF COURSE

THE GOLF Regulars claim that Sunset is one of the more scenic 9-holers in the state, with excellent conditioning. An old-school design that dates back to 1924, the course is conveniently located near historic Old Town and offers inspiring views of Longs Peak.

THE DETAILS 303-776-3122. 1900 Longs Peak Ave., Longmont, CO 80501.
- Bink Young, 1924. 9 holes. Par 34. White/Blue - 5,871 (66.6/113). Women's White/Blue - 5,872 (73.4/127). Women's Red/White - 5,607 (71.8/124). Price - $.

GETTING THERE Take I-25 to Hwy. 119 (Longmont exit). Go west on 11 to Main St. where it turns into 3rd Ave. Turn right on Sunset and left at Longs Peak Ave. Drive around the water tower and find the clubhouse on the right.

TWIN PEAKS GOLF COURSE

THE GOLF The Frank Hummel-designed Twin Peaks course is a traditional par-70 route with well-bunkered, tree-lined fairways, elevated and undulating greens, and water hazards on seven holes. No. 16 is the best hole, a long dog-legger right with water on each side and an approach into an elevated green.

THE DETAILS 303-772-1722. 1200 Cornell Drive, Longmont, CO 80503.
- Frank Hummel, 1978. 18 holes. Par 70. Blue - 6,830 (71.7/123). White - 6,349 (69.3/118). Women's White - 6,394 (75.6/131). Women's Red - 5,816 (71.3/124). Women's Gold - 5,408 (69/120). Price - $$.

GETTING THERE From I-25 take the Longmont exit (exit 119). Drive west to Hover Rd., north to Mountain View Ave., then west to Cornell Drive. Go south on Cornell to the course.

UTE CREEK GOLF COURSE

THE GOLF Ute Creek is one of only six Robert Trent Jones, Jr. courses in Colorado, and the only one in the northern Front Range. The hefty course length, along with five lakes, multi-tiered fairways, Ute Creek, and plenty of nasty native grass, all combine to make this a very formidable challenge.

Post-round at Ute Creek finds golfers in the clubhouse discussing the 470-

---

The most important single move in establishing your tempo and rhythm is your takeaway. It sets the beat for everything that comes later. Strive on every shot to move the club back as deliberately as possible, consistent with swinging it back rather than taking it back.—Jack Nicklaus

yard, par-5 finishing hole. If you can deal with the summer wind, avoid the bunkers on the left and the lake on the right; the green is fair and offers a good shot at a one-putt.

THE DETAILS 303-774-4342. 2000 Ute Creek Drive, Longmont, CO 80501.
- Robert Trent Jones, Jr., 1997. 18 holes. Par 72. Black - 7,167 (73.2/132). Gold - 6,750 (71.4/125). Blue - 6,196 (68.7/120). Women's Blue - 6,196 (74.6/137).Women's Red - 5,509 (70.4/128). Price - $$.

GETTING THERE From I-25 take the Hwy. 119 exit and go west 4 miles. Turn right on Weld County Rd. 1. Follow for 2 miles and turn left on E. 17th Ave. The course is a half-mile down on the right.

LONGMONT NOTES

Thirsty golfers can find a whole lot of good beer at the **Left Hand and Tabernash Brewing Co.** (303-772-0258), one of Colorado's largest handcrafted breweries. Tours are available on Saturdays or by appointment, and the tasting room is open Monday through Saturday, offering samples of Left Hand's Black Jack Porter or Sawtooth Ale, or the German-style Tabernash Weiss. Weekenders should take advantage of a couple of local B&Bs: **Dickens Bed & Breakfast** (303-774-0071) and **Ellen's Bed & Breakfast** (303-776-1676)

LOVELAND

ELEV. 4,982 POP. 50,608

When New Mexican pioneer Mariano Medina came here in 1858, he opened a trading post west of what is now Loveland. It didn't take long for the Overland Stage Line to put Namaqua, the name of Medina's store, on their route in 1862. Over the years the town shifted in other directions; eventually, the Loveland Hotel was built, and the town's opera house opened its doors in 1884. Thanks to William Austin Hamilton Loveland, the town's namesake, the Colorado Central Railroad routed its line from Cheyenne, Wyoming, through Loveland on its way to Denver. In the early 1900s, Loveland was a sugar beet capital with one of Colorado's first sugar mills. Despite the slow pace of life, Loveland continues to grow and prosper, leaving great links options for those wandering the Front Range in search of golf.

FRONT RANGE

If you are in the woods, don't act like a seamstress. Your job is not to thread needles but to get the ball back into the fairway.—Arnold Palmer

CATTAIL CREEK GOLF COURSE

THE GOLF Cattail is an entertaining par-3 track with plenty of challenges. Approaches that miss the green can find uneven lies on the rolling terrain, and there is water on five of nine holes. No. 6 might be the best hole: a 152-yarder with water and sand fronting the green.

THE DETAILS 970-669-5800. 2116 W. 29th Street, Loveland, CO 80538.
 • Dick Phelps, 1991. 9 holes. Par 27. Not rated. Price - $.

GETTING THERE Take I-25 to the Loveland/Greeley exit 257. Head west on Hwy. 34 and turn north at the first light past Lake Loveland (Taft Ave.). Follow Taft Ave. to 29th St. and go west to the golf course on the south side of 29th St.

MARIANA BUTTE GOLF COURSE

THE GOLF Dick Phelps designed Mariana Butte in 1992, and the beautiful course has received high praise ever since (*Golf Digest*—four stars). Views of Devil's Backbone and Mariana Butte frame the holes, and elk traverse the course in the fall. Phelps utilized the Big Thompson River and the severe elevation variations to his advantage. The view from the clubhouse, the highest point on the property, is impressive looking down at the Big Thompson wetlands and rock out-croppings. No. 7 is the hole everyone talks about: a difficult par 4 with a small-ish green fronted by water on three sides. Note: Mariana Butte plans to add GPS carts sometime in 2004.

THE DETAILS 970-669-5800. 701 Clubhouse Drive, Loveland, CO 80537.
 • Dick Phelps, 1992. 18 holes. Par 72. Blue - 6,612 (70.8/130). White - 5,956 (67.5/117). Women's White - 5,956 (72.7/135). Women's Red - 5,353 (70/121). Women's Yellow - 5,057 (68.4/117). Price - $$.

GETTING THERE From north I-25, go west at exit 255 (Hwy. 402). Head west for 6.5 miles and turn north on Wilson Ave., then drive a quarter mile west on 1st Street and turn north on Rossum Dr. to the clubhouse.

THE OLDE COURSE AT LOVELAND

THE GOLF As the name implies, this 1959 Henry Hughes design is all about tra-ditional golf. Don't look for the frills found at today's high-dollar, daily-fee

---

Let your attitude determine your golf game. Don't let your golf game determine your attitude.—Davis Love, Jr.

courses, but do look for the $2.5 million upgrade and facelift that improved the golf experience here just a few years back.

Some compare Olde to Cherry Hills in the old days, noting that the round becomes more challenging toward the end on both courses. By the time you reach their version of "Amen Corner" (holes 14-16) you'll realize that your "A" game is required in order to finish well; otherwise, the course can eat you alive.

Mature, tree-lined fairways are dominant—such as on No. 5, a 535-yarder. Here the tee shot must find a fairway with a plateau. The approach faces a green surrounded by water on three sides. The course routes around six ponds, including the chance to hit an island green on No. 14.

THE DETAILS 970-667-5256. 2115 W. 29th St., Loveland, CO 80538.

- Henry Hughes, 1959. Dick Phelps remodel. 18 holes. Par 72. Blue - 6,870 (71.6/128). White - 6,448 (69.5/125). Red - 5,829 (72.4/128). Women's Yellow - 5,411 (70.2/124). Price - $$.

GETTING THERE Take I-25 to Loveland-Greeley exit 257. Head west on Hwy. 34 and turn north at the first light past Lake Loveland (Taft Ave.). Follow Taft Ave. to 29th St. and go west to the golf course on the north side of 29th St.

LOVELAND NOTES

One of the favorite local getaways is **2 Eagles Resort** (866-834-4722), where year-round adventurers seek outdoor opportunities on the Big Thompson River between Loveland and Rocky Mountain National Park. And while in the Loveland area, don't miss the chance to drive the **Peak-to-Peak Scenic Highway** through the spectacular Big Thompson Canyon. **Benson Park** displays the work of leading area and national sculptors. **Carter Lake** is nearby and offers 100 acres of fishing and water sports. There's also a new 38-store **factory outlet mall** just west of the junction of U.S. 34 and I-25, and the **Trail Ridge Winery** (970-635-0949) is a nice way to wrap up a day of golf or souvenir shopping.

MILLIKEN

ELEV. 4,750 POP. 2,888

Milliken's claim to fame when it was founded in 1909 was that a cowpoke could belly up to the bar and have a drink. Early settlers said it was common to see these drinkers wobbling down the same streets through which cattle were

---

If you attend professional golf tournaments, it might help you to follow a good putter for a couple of rounds and notice how often he misses very remarkable putts. Then, watch his response and how, on his next putt, his routine stays the same.—Dr. Bob Rotella

herded to the train station. Today the outpost of Milliken offers golf at the interesting Mad Russian Golf Course, and there could be more in the future, with the Centennial Crossing master-planned community offering a new town hall, softball-baseball complex, trail system, outdoor amphitheater, athletic facilities, and an 18-hole golf course.

THE MAD RUSSIAN GOLF COURSE

THE GOLF Legend has it that a Russian by the name of Ted Blehm dreamed of making big money here back in 1979, and decided a golf course community was his ticket to riches. The endless stories about an angry man who would never back down from a fight resulted in the nickname "The Mad Russian."

First, Blehm hired Greeley Country Club superintendent Dave Tooley to design the layout and named it Jack Rabbit Trail Golf Course. Then he built his own $1.2 million house on top of a hill by the 18th tee—a 12-sided, revolving house on pillars. Eventually the name was changed to The Mad Russian Golf Course and he adopted a dancing Cossack, golf club in one hand and shotgun in the other, as his logo.

Today his golf course lives on, with gently rolling terrain as well as some dramatic hilly features and uneven lies. The Nicklaus design team recently renovated four holes and six greens, and there are future plans to add length, rebuild tee boxes, and improve the bunkering.

No. 11 is one of the better holes, requiring a 240-yard carry over a lake from the tips, followed by a short pitch to the green if the lake is carried.

THE DETAILS 970-587-5157. 2100 Country Club Parkway, Milliken, CO 80543.
- Dave Tooley, 1969. Nicklaus design team remodeling project. 18 holes. Par 70. Blue - 5,550 (65.5/114). White - 4,809 (64.3/103). Women's Blue - 5,182 (69.8/117). Women's White - 4,850 (67.7/113). Women's Red - 4,027 (63.3/95). Price - $$.

GETTING THERE Take I-25 to the Johnstown/Milliken Exit (252). Go east to Hwy. 257, then north 2 miles.

MILLIKEN NOTES

Play golf in Milliken on the way to weekends in Greeley, where food and lodging are abundant (also Longmont). The **Fort Vasquez Museum** in nearby Platteville is worth a drive by if you have some spare time.

I've never known anyone to get from an average handicap to scratch in much less than two years. It may take you four to six years if you sustain a regular commitment to practice and playing.—Dr. Bob Rotella

NIWOT

ELEV. 5,095 POP. 4,160

Chief Niwot, leader of the Arapahoe tribe, is the namesake of this town platted in 1875 along the railroad tracks between Golden and Boulder. Samuel Dobbins applied for a post office, and the city grew with a general store, blacksmith shop, post office, and the rail depot. A local dairy was also established and Niwot continued to grow, basing its economy on agriculture – the perfect place for a day of 9-hole, down-home, dirt-road golf and a tour of Niwot's historic downtown district.

HAYSTACK MOUNTAIN GOLF COURSE

THE GOLF Haystack isn't fancy, but it's fun. Farm buildings surround the golf course, and the views of Haystack Mountain, a geological feature shaped like a cone, add character to this rural track. Consider walking this 9-hole executive course, which features rolling terrain and medium-sized greens with some contours. The layout is generally open, despite the presence of some large trees. No. 5 is an entertaining par-4 hole, playing only 275 yards with a few trees getting in the way of a birdie or eagle.

THE DETAILS 303-530-1400. 5877 Niwot Road, Niwot, CO 80503.
- Clarence Ebel, Jr., 1966. 9 hole executive course. Par 32. Red/Blue - 3,961 (59/81). Women's Red/Blue - 3,961 (62.2/99). Price - $.

GETTING THERE From I-25 take exit 235 (Hwy. 52) west about 16 miles to Hwy. 119 and turn left. Next turn right (north) on 63rd St. and go approximately 2 miles to Niwot Rd. Turn left (west) and look for the sign on the right side down Niwot Rd.

NIWOT NOTES

Pretend that the statue of Chief Niwot (on the Boulder Creek Path near Settlers Park) is a tribute to the Golf Gods and pay your respects accordingly. And **Haystack Mountain Goat Dairy** (303-581-9948) is the largest goat dairy farm between Colorado and Wisconsin, with grounds open to the public and a fun spot for a family detour. **Old Town Niwot** is two blocks long and loaded with antique shops. Overnighters can reserve a room at the **Niwot Inn** (303-652-8452), which offers 14 "country-contemporary" rooms near downtown.

FRONT RANGE

Many amateurs hit a putt too hard and turn away in disgust as the ball passes the hole. I watch closely as a putt goes by the hole to see how the comeback putt will break.—Tom Watson

RED FEATHER LAKES

ELEV. 8,200 POP. 525

Somewhere in the mountains on the way to Wyoming northwest of Fort Collins, you'll run into tiny Red Feather Lakes—a serene spot surrounded by the year-round outdoor playground that is the 612,000-acre Roosevelt National Forest. Ranchers and loggers were the first to inhabit the area around 1900. Today it's a great place to enjoy a little golf, explore the town's art gallery and antique store, and look for adventures on Colorado's first designated Wild & Scenic River—the Cache La Poudre River.

FOX ACRES COUNTRY CLUB

THE GOLF Stunning views, spring-fed mountain lakes, and the pleasures of golf away from the big city are what you'll experience at Fox Acres Country Club. Imagine granite-rock outcroppings that bump up against pristine putting surfaces surrounded by quaking aspens. Here the mountain meadows have been turned into verdant fairways—the No. 9 signature hole, named Eagle's Nest, will take your breath away. It's a short 154 yards from an elevated tee, but the green is narrow, sloping from the right, and water awaits behind the green.

Members and guests also enjoy tennis, a fitness trail, hiking, horseback riding, whitewater rafting, mountain biking, cross-country skiing, sleigh rides, and fly fishing in the club's 15 private lakes.

THE DETAILS 970-881-2510. 3350 Fox Acres Dr. W. Red Feather Lakes, CO 80545.

- www.foxacrescc.com
- John Cochran, 1983. 18 holes. Par 71. Blue - 6,236 (69.3/131). White - 5,686 (67.1/119). Men's Green - 5,286 (65.2/113). Women's White - 5,716 (71.9/143). Women's Green - 5,217 (68.8/135). Women's Red - 4,817 (65.7/131). Private club, members and guests only. Price - $$$.

GETTING THERE Take I-25 to exit 269B. Take Hwy. 14 west to US 287 north toward Laramie. Go north to Livermore. Turn left (west) on Red Feather Lakes Rd., and drive west 25 miles to Red Feather Lakes. Turn right, and go north 1 mile.

RED FEATHER LAKES NOTES

The **Red Feather Ranch B&B & Horse Hotel** (877-881-5215, www.redfeather-

Head-lifting is caused by fear and anxiety. You are seeking the result before you have struck the ball. You did not trust your swing.—Ernest Jones

ranch.com) is the place to stay for the weekend and enjoy mountain outdoor activities. The local food options are down-home, and places like **Dal-Rae High Country** have a little bit of everything and tasty pies. The **Rawah Wilderness Area** is a premier place for a boondocks hike—it is within Roosevelt National Forest, which offers 25,580 acres of primitive outdoors opportunities. Side trips to the ghost towns of the North Park area, which includes Gould, Rand, and Walden situated at 8,000 feet, are always interesting, and Red Feather Lakes is also a popular spot to fish and relax. For information about fishing check in with **St. Peter's Fly Shop** (970-498-8968) in Fort Collins before your trip.

WINDSOR

ELEV. 4,798 POP. 9,896

Windsor is a growing community known as the hub of Northern Colorado. Its location between the three major communities of Greeley, Fort Collins, and Loveland, and its proximity to both Denver and Cheyenne, Wyoming make this town of almost 10,000 an easy stop-off for the traveling golfer in search of rounds at the Pelican Lakes or Highland Meadows golf courses.

HIGHLAND MEADOWS GOLF CLUB

THE GOLF One of Colorado's newest golf courses, Highland Meadows was designed by CU alum Art Schaupeter, who apprenticed under Keith Foster. Located in a master-planned community, this one is a daily-fee beauty that plays 7,050 yards to a par 71. Schaupeter created some drama by routing eight holes through arroyos. No. 11 is a good example, teeing from the top of a mesa with views of Longs Peak in the distance. The hole plays 180 yards into a wide green surrounded by bunkers.

Terraced and split fairways, bunkers, various uphill and downhill lies, water features, canyons, and arroyos all come into play here, but a GPS system is available to help the first-time player.

And while there aren't a lot of trees on the property, one cottonwood dominates the middle of the first fairway, a 560-yard par 5. Whether you can carry the tree or not, an island green awaits the approach, a rarity for an opening hole.

THE DETAILS 970-204-4653. 6300 Highland Meadows Parkway, Windsor, CO 80550.

- Art Schaupeter, 2004. 18 holes. Par 71. Not rated yet. Back tees - 7,050. Price - $$.

No matter how skillfully one may lay out the holes and diversify them, nevertheless one must get the thrill of nature....The puny strivings of the architect do not quench our thirst for the ultimate. —George Thomas, 1927

FRONT RANGE

GETTING THERE Coming from Denver on I-25, exit east on County Rd. 392 or the Windsor exit. Go about 2 miles and look for the Highland Meadows Parkway entrance on the right side and follow it to the clubhouse.

PELICAN LAKES GOLF & COUNTRY CLUB

THE GOLF This water-splashed golf course was designed by Ted Robinson, Sr., who's better known for his numerous layouts in the Southern California desert. Supposedly Pelican Lakes has more shoreline than any course in the world: more than 7.5 miles. The Poudre River corridor also comes into play here, forcing carries at least four times. The par-4 No. 18, all 449 yards of it, requires a strong shot to hit an elevated green guarded by bunkers and water on the approach.

Robinson, Sr. has designed more than 140 courses worldwide. Sahalee Country Club in Redmond, Washington, the site of a recent PGA championship, is his most widely-known accomplishment.

THE DETAILS 970-674-0930. 1600 Pelican Lakes Point, Windsor, CO 80550.
- Ted Robinson, Sr., 1999. 18 holes. Par 72. Black - 7,067 (72.9/132). Blue - 6,566 (70.6/128). White - 6,039 (68.4/121). Women's Blue - 6,566 (76.9/151). Women's White - 6,039 (73.9/143). Women's Red - 5,266 (69.9/125). Price - $$.

GETTING THERE Take I-25 to the Windsor exit 262. Go 4 miles east into town, and turn south on 7th St. Turn left at Eastman Park Dr. then right onto Water Valley Parkway. The golf course is on the right.

WINDSOR NOTES

Windsor doesn't offer a huge selection of eateries, but **The Border** or **Tortilla Marisa's** serve Mexican food and get the job done, and the **Egg and Eye** serves a great breakfast. Another new restaurant called the **Chimney Park Bistro** recently opened. Spend the night at the **Porter House Bed and Breakfast Inn** (888-686-5793), which is a short walk from the Country Store, **Walden's Ice Cream Parlor**, and **Kate Marie's Coffee Shop**. You might also wander Windsor's historic old town and its museum, which also boasts a **Farmer's Market** in summer months.

FRONT RANGE

The road to improvement is filled with moments of great joy and satisfaction, as well as with plateaus and setback.—Dr. Bob Rotella

FRONT RANGE

Jack Nicklaus and Arnold Palmer were reunited at Cherry Hills 1993 for the Senior's U.S. Open. Nicklaus won the tournament.

It is quite certain that, had the ground on which ordinary inland golf is played today been the only available ground for the purpose, the game would never have been invented at all.—Garden G. Smith, 1898

NORTHEAST

NORTHEAST

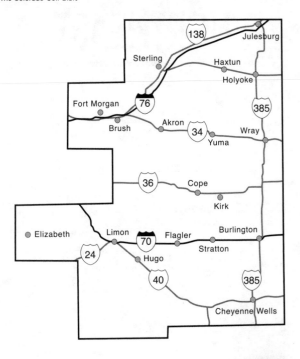

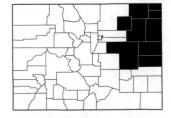

Northeast Mileage

	Akron	Burlington	Brush	Cheyenne Wells	Cope	Elizabeth	Flagler	Fort Morgan	Haxtun	Holyoke	Hugo	Julesburg	Kirk	Limon	Sterling	Stratton	Wray	Yuma
Akron		109	24	148	52	145	93	35	64	81	98	91	76	86	36	92	53	27
Burlington			151	38	59	131	48	160	110	93	84	124	37	142	179	18	56	83
Brush				161	81	120	84	10	170	130	73	87	105	76	37	133	78	52
Cheyenne Wells					95	141	48	170	148	130	162	92	105	179	88	54	94	120
Cope						125	84	90	80	96	128	124	75	86	41	133	60	40
Elizabeth							83	110	170	185	140	211	149	24	70	157	30	172
Flagler								114	110	122	68	172	66	88	142	41	104	81
Fort Morgan									74	92	97	172	66	138	88	128	88	61
Haxtun										17	150	101	149	157	142	54	41	63
Holyoke											167	40	89	176	101	149	157	142
Hugo												176	24	31	103	72	141	118
Julesburg													101	176	72	142	136	118
Kirk														89	115	66	54	63
Limon															128	112	136	81
Sterling																128	74	80
Stratton																	74	57
Wray																		26
Yuma																		

A s the sun sets on the Eastern Plains of Colorado, a lone windmill is framed against another day of farming and ranching. When droughts clamp down on this land, dust trails whip down dirt roads and roll forever. In winter, blinding blizzards squeeze the horizon, signaling that it's time to stay home in front of the fire, read a good book, and keep the woodpile stocked.

If you've ever driven the long, straight roads of the high plains—whether across the Texas Panhandle, the tiny notch of Oklahoma Panhandle, or even western Kansas—you've experienced the same flat, almost featureless panoramas where the geography gives way to endless stretches of sky. U.S. 385 from Springfield to Julesburg is a perfect example. The Pawnee Buttes, 300-foot tall knobs of earth, served as navigational guides for westbound wagon trains, and still tower today at the junction of Weld County Roads 111 and 112. But in the big scheme of things out here, they're still only blips on the screen.

The people who live in Northeastern Colorado have big dreams and love the wide-open spaces. The pioneer spirit lives on here; the stretch between Sterling and Julesburg, once called the Overland Trail, served as a byway for thousands of restless settlers in covered wagons looking for a place to call home back in the 1860s. Now that the railroads and the interstates have taken over from the covered wagons, this vast land is bounded on the south by Interstate 70, on the north by Interstate 80, and is linked by Interstate 76. Carriers like the Union Pacific and Burlington Northern-Santa Fe provide rail service with connections to the Gulf Coast, West Coast, and the Midwest markets.

What would the USA have without places like this? "A lot less beef, beets, and beans," as they say in places hereabouts where farmers can wear overalls to play golf on flat, minimalist courses with sand greens. This is normally a dry, open country, since storms from the Pacific hit the Rocky Mountains and dump their moisture on the western slopes. When it rains or snows on the high plains, the storms come up from the Gulf of Mexico.

The golf here isn't legendary, other than maybe at Yuma where a young Steve Jones honed his skills and later won the U.S. Open. However there is an aura to this remote golf outpost—guidebooks never cover places like this. Loaded with small towns where you can play a round in an hour for the price of lunch, then move down the road for the next golf stop, Northeast Colorado is prime for friendly, pass-through golf.

However, the golf fortunes are changing. A new Tom Doak project is slated for the sand dunes of Holyoke. On a patch of land where some of the dunes reach 50 feet high, a new private golf course is taking shape: it will be rugged and wild and named Ballyneal, taking its roots from Ireland's Ballybunion. Already golfers are itching to try another example of Doak's minimalism; the

NORTHEAST

project has been compared to Sand Dunes in Nebraska, with on-course lodging for golfers in summer and hunters in winter.

President Gerald Ford, a part-time Vail resident, chipping for birdie at The Broadmoor in 1978.

Continuing to trust your stroke as you practice is part of the discipline you must learn. —Dr. Bob Rotella

AKRON

ELEV. 4,661 POP. 1,711

Named for Akron, Ohio, this seat of Washington County has surged in recent years with a population growth of 167 percent since 1990. Yet Akron is still a little farming community centered around a historic old courthouse and known as one of the top wheat producers in the state. Places like Hardamon Drug, an old drug store with a fountain serving cold drinks, and C.N. Yeamans and Son Hardware, the oldest business in town, offer old-time opportunities to experience Akron after rounds at the 9-hole Washington County Golf Club.

WASHINGTON COUNTY GOLF CLUB

THE GOLF The WCGC is a flat course with a few hills that can cause the occasional uneven lie. It is a favorite for average hacks because of its ego-boosting length. The greens vary in undulation and can be a challenge to read. Trees and bunkers come into play, but the predominant hazard along the fairways is native buffalo grass. Two sets of tees provide for different looks on additional rounds.

The buffalo-grass fairways end at the 150-yard markers, with bluegrass from there to the greens. The straightaway 412-yard No. 9 is the toughest hole on the course because of its length.

THE DETAILS 970-345-2309. 59469 Hwy. 63, Akron, CO 80720.
- Unknown, 1972. 9 holes. Par 36. White/Blue - 5,861 (65.8/101). Women's Red. White - 5,772 (72.3/119). Price - $.

GETTING THERE Go half a mile south of Akron on Hwy. 63.

AKRON NOTES

The **Washington County Museum** displays relics and information about the old days, and the **Eastern Colorado Roundup** is Akron's big fair, celebrated each August. If you're absolutely determined to bed down in Akron, reserve a room at the **Gin Jer Snap Ranch** (970-345-2955) where hay rides and chuck wagon dinners are popular. **Crestwood Manor** (970-345-2231) is the preferred place for sit-down dining.

NORTHEAST

When it's breezy, hit it easy.—Davis Love, Jr.

BRUSH

ELEV. 4,231 POP. 5,117

A northern plains city named in honor of Jared L. Brush, a Colorado cattle pioneer, Brush is situated on the banks of Beaver Creek and served as a supply point in 1866 for cattle drivers along the Texas-Montana Cattle Trail. The trail began in the panhandle of Texas and continued to the grasslands of eastern Montana. Located on I-76 just nine miles from Fort Morgan and 80 from Denver, Brush was platted in 1882 when the railroad arrived. These days Brush offers a golf break during road trips to and from Lincoln, NE, which is especially appropriate when the Buffs visit Memorial Stadium.

BUNKER HILL COUNTRY CLUB

THE GOLF A Frank Hummel-designed 9-holer that stretches to 6,478 yards when played twice, Bunker Hill opened in the early 1970s. Head Pro Steve Samuels chuckles when he thinks back to golf in 1971 when Bunker Hill was built.

"I was talking to Hummel recently, and we looked at the scorecard that has two par 4s that are about 355 and 368 yards. When this course was designed, Jack Nicklaus was hitting them 280 yards so that would have given him just a sand wedge into these holes. But not everyone hits it that far, and the golf course does have challenging greens."

Bunker Hill also has buffalo-grass rough and sugar-sand traps. The greens are quick, sometimes running 10 or 11 on the Stimpmeter, but not overly undulating.

Steve Jones, the former U.S. Open champ and native of nearby Yuma, has graced the fairways over the years. So has course record holder (61) Ray Rodriguez, who grew up in Fort Morgan, played golf for the Colorado School of Mines, and has toiled on the mini tours.

THE DETAILS 970-842-5198. 2301 West Mill Rd., Brush, CO 80723.
- Frank Hummel, 1971. 9 holes. Par 36. Blue - 6,478 (70.4/115). White/Blue - 6,322 (69.6/114). White - 6,146 (68.8/113). Women's White/Blue - 6,322 (75.2/130). Women's White - 6,146 (73.4/127). Women's White/Red - 5,772 (71.9/126). Price - $.

GETTING THERE Take I-76 east to the Hospital Rd. exit. Drive 1 mile and turn right on Mill Rd. for another mile.

Rhythm is best expressed in any swing directed at a cigar stump or a dandelion head.—Grantland Rice

NORTHEAST

BRUSH NOTES

Brush wouldn't be Brush without **Drover's** (970-842-4218), where 25-cent coffee, $6.95 steaks, homemade pies, and cinnamon rolls tantalize locals and visiting golfers. Other dining options are the **Clayton Street Grill** or **Carillo's Mexican Food.** Cheap lodging can be had at the **Microtell Inn** (970-842-4241), but the working elk and buffalo ranch known as **Elk Echo Ranch Country B&B** has more character. Brush celebrates the Fourth of July each year with the **Brush Rodeo**, staged since 1925.

BURLINGTON
ELEV. 4,167 POP. 3,678

Just 13 miles from the Kansas border, Burlington is a refueling spot going to and from Denver on I-70, and one of the most remote Colorado golf outposts. Some might be interested in the 1905 Kit Carson County Carousel, a hand-carved wooden merry-go-round that is a tourist stop along with the Old Town Museum and town square; however, golfers craving links time while speeding along I-70 will be more interested in the 9-hole Prairie Pines Golf Club.

PRAIRIE PINES GOLF CLUB

THE GOLF No-frills Prairie Pines is buffalo-grass fairways, pine trees, rolling terrain, and known for a par 3 that plays 199 yards downhill with a sloped green and bunker. Trees frame the backside of this popular course, which tends to be loaded with a heavy schedule of league play from locals. The scattering of trees can alter some shots, and a pond comes into play on one hole. Lots of out-of-bounds stakes make accuracy important.

THE DETAILS 719-346-8207. 48680 Snead Dr., Burlington, CO 80807.
- 1979. 9 holes. Par 35. Women's Red/Blue - 5,573 (68.6/111). Men's Red/Blue - 5,625 (65.1/101). Price - $.

GETTING THERE Take I-70 east to Burlington near Colorado's eastern border

BURLINGTON NOTES

Grab a bite at the **Smoky Hill Trail** (719-346-8790), which specializes in tasty hickory-smoked meats. Burlington is a pass through town, but if you have car problems there is a **Comfort Inn** (719-346-5361).

NORTHEAST

CHEYENNE WELLS

ELEV. 4,290 POP. 1,010

Cheyenne Wells is the seat of Cheyenne County and a farming hub with a nice little 9-hole golf course affectionately known as the Smoky River Golf Club. The countryside offers glimpses of the sod dugouts that date back to the arriving settlers in the 1860s. After the gold rush died out, homesteaders started looking to the central high plains of Colorado, where the railroad was expanding. Today, wheat and cattle industries combine with oil and gas development to define this tiny town.

SMOKY RIVER GOLF CLUB

THE GOLF Natural hills and valleys roll through the Smoky River Golf Club, causing a few uneven lies but generally offering an easy day of golf. Highlighted only by a dry creek that runs through the course, a lack of sand bunkers and water hazards give confidence to golfers who whale away toward the large greens. The only other consideration is the strong winds of the open plains. Two sets of tees spice up the route the second time around.

Mark Stephenson, the high school golf coach, commented on the pace of play and that price rules here. "You can just drive up and get on anytime," he said, "and it is a relaxed pace of play. You can't beat $15 for 18 holes, either."

Watch out for No. 5, a 349-yard par-4 dogleg right with an approach to an elevated green and out-of-bounds in back—plan to fade it around a huge tree. "There's also a huge gully to carry it over," Stephenson said. "And it's a tough recovery from the gully because of some dense rough."

The other difficult hole is No. 7 (16 on the back), with out-of-bounds left and thick rough right and left. There's variety, too, with five blind tee shots. The green collars have bluegrass and the huge bentgrass greens have subtle contours. Place the ball in the wrong spot and you'll have a long, difficult two-putt.

THE DETAILS 719-767-5021. 161 South First East, Cheyenne Wells, CO 80810.
- Marty Johnson, 1991. 9 holes. Par 35. White/Blue - 6,087 (67.9/117). Women's White/Blue - 6,087 (72.5/129). Women's Red/White - 5,296 (68.3/118). Price - $.

GETTING THERE From Denver take I-70 east. At Burlington go south onto Hwy. 385. The course entrance is on the left side of the road just before you arrive in town. It's at the intersection of U.S. Hwy. 40 and U.S. Hwy. 385, 16 miles from the Kansas border.

When you stroke with timing and rhythm, the ball sails straight down the fairway, and for distance. It is effortless power, not powerful effort.—Ernest Jones

CHEYENNE WELLS NOTES

Spend the night at the **Trail Inn Motel** (719-767-5637) and eat your meals at **Country Charm** (719-767-8775) or **Aunt Deb's** (719-767-5200). Just for history's sake, The Smoky Hill Trail, also known as the Starvation Trail, routes along Highway 40 west of Cheyenne Wells and continues through Elizabeth. The Cheyenne County Courthouse is listed on the National Register of Historic Places and worthy of a split-second glimpse.

COPE
ELEV. 4,400 POP. 100

Founded in the late 1880s by Jonathan Cope, the town lies where U.S. Highway 36 crosses the Arickaree River.

Wheat and corn are the mainstays of this tiny community, which is the largest between Byers, 60 miles west, and St. Francis, Kansas, 60 miles east. Eldred Sidebottom, a former pastor at the Cope Community Church, says the dry-land corn hasn't amounted to anything over the past couple of drought years. However drought doesn't bother the sand greens at the 9-hole Prairie GC.

PRAIRIE GOLF COURSE

THE GOLF The Prairie GC is a 9-hole, par-34 sand-green track designed by local John Rudnik, who still lives across the street from the golf course. Talk about a bargain. A family membership is $30 a year and visitors can play all day for $4.

"Most of the visitors we get are golfers from Pueblo, Colorado Springs, or Denver who have never played a sand-green course," said Sidebottom. "It has rolling terrain, very few trees or bunkers, some blind shots, and is basically open prairie." Buffalo grass defines the fairways and small pine trees are planted at the 100-yard markers.

THE DETAILS 970-383-2211. 36460 County Rd. 8, Cope, CO 80812.
- John Rudnik, 1971. 9 holes. Par 34. Sand greens. Middle/Back - 4,900 (61.1/85). Price - $.

GETTING THERE Take I-70 to Hwy. 36 east to County Rd. NN south. Drive 1 mile south, then left on County Rd. 8 for about 8 miles.

NORTHEAST

Take responsibility for your own ball and your own score the only things you have control over.—Sam Snead

COPE NOTES

The **Prairie Motel** (970-383-2211) is the place to stay and the **Western Steakhouse** is the place to dine. After your round, head for the Idalia area for **Bonny Lake State Park**, which offers year-round recreational opportunities on the 1,900-acre lake. The surrounding prairie is ripe with bird-hunting, hiking, and camping, and fishermen will find walleye, northern pike, and bass in the river-fed reservoir. The **Cope Old Settlers Picnic**, scheduled every May, is the highlight of the year.

ELIZABETH

ELEV.6,448 POP. 1,434

The town of Elizabeth, located near Parker and only 20 minutes from Denver, has grown since the early 1990s as urban escapees look to leave the hustle and bustle. It was founded in 1859 as a logging center, with dense ponderosa forests that lead to the area known as Black Forest. The area's elevation ranges from 5,000 feet to 7,350 and the Palmer Divide is the area's east-west spine. Water flows north to the Platte River and south to the Arkansas River. Small and rural, but worthy as a golf road-trip destination, the town's Spring Valley Golf Club has been known as one of the best bargains in the state since it opened in 1997.

SPRING VALLEY GOLF CLUB

THE GOLF Surrounded by plowed fields, the Ross Graves-designed Spring Valley GC features a wide-open front side followed by a more rugged back side that is defined by Running Creek. Characteristics such as native grasses, bunkers, canyons, water, and small, flat greens make Spring Valley a challenging test of golf.

In the spring wildflowers and lilacs beautify the layout, which begins with a 426-yard par 4. The signature hole is the 212-yard No. 17, a par 3 that has a wooded creek almost surrounding the green with lots of marshy areas to hide golf balls. The course hosted the Colorado Junior Golf Association Championship in 2003.

THE DETAILS 303-646-4240. 42350 County Rd. 17-21, Elizabeth, CO 80107.
• Ross Graves, 1997. 18 holes. Par 72. Black - 6,930 (72.2/132). Blue - 6,498 (70.1/128). White - 6,204 (69.1/122). Women's White - 6,191 (74.1/135). Women's Red - 5,156 (68.3/118). Price - $$.

NORTHEAST

Nobody ever swung a club too slowly.—Bobby Jones

Getting there From Hwy. 83 in Parker, take Hilltop Rd. east. Go 5 miles left into Singing Hills, then 6 miles east to County Rd. 17-21. Turn north on 17-21 and drive about a mile to the clubhouse on the right.

ELIZABETH NOTES

Folks in Elizabeth drive to the Franktown area to enjoy **Castlewood Canyon State Park** (303-688-5242), where a day-use permit allows rock climbing, hiking in canyon trails, picnicking, and an Outdoors Colorado nature program. **Smokey Jack's** (303-646-4227) serves barbecue and **Botana Junction** (303-646-3163) offers Mexican fare. On the way back to Denver, stop in Parker and enjoy a meal at **Italian Family** (303-805-4744). The biggest event every year is the **Elizabeth Stampede Rodeo** held at Casey Jones Park the first week in June.

FLAGLER

ELEV. 4,188 POP. 612

Built along the Rock Island Railroad in 1888, Flagler was originally called Mallow, but later renamed for Henry M. Flagler, one of the founders of Standard Oil. Today Flagler is the center of a farming and ranching area comprising the western part of Kit Carson County. Located at Exit 395 on I-70, it is 60 miles from the Kansas border and 120 miles from Denver.

Agriculture here relies heavily on the huge Ogallala aquifer, which flows all the way to the South Plains of Texas. On the prairies that surround Flagler and stretch to the Kansas border, gigantic circular systems irrigate wheat, corn, and sunflowers from the pool of water hundreds of feet below the farmland. The water also benefits golfers who get their hacks in at the Mossland Memorial GC.

MOSSLAND MEMORIAL GOLF COURSE

The golf Mossland Memorial is a hilly, narrow, and tree-lined track that routes around a lake with small, undulating greens. Unlike many small-town 9-holers, this one is rugged and difficult to walk.

The signature hole is No. 2, a 403-yard, par 3 that is a sharp dogleg right. No. 7, a 281-yard par 4, is probably the most talked-about and handsome. It plays uphill to a green surrounded by pine trees. From the tees, a golfer can only see the top of the flag stick.

Learn to bear your ill fortune without appealing for sympathy.—Harold H. Hilton

THE DETAILS 719-765-4659. 100 3rd St., Flagler, CO 80815.
- Flagler Golf Club, 1986. 9 holes. Par 36. White/Black - 5,951 (67.7/108). Women's White/Black - 5,500 (69.6/112). Women's Orange/White - 5,185 (68.5/106). Price - $.

GETTING THERE Take I-70 east past Limon to exit 395, and drive south to the course.

FLAGLER NOTES

Head for the **Flagler State Wildlife Area**, only minutes away, for hunting, fishing, and boating. The places to eat are **J.C.'s Bar & Grill** on Main Street or **Crawford's Bar and Grill**, popular for steaks. The **Little England Motel** has lodging and an RV park.

FORT MORGAN
ELEV. 4,324 POP. 11,034

When Hollywood wanted to film James Michener's *Centennial*, the story of Colorado pioneers, they picked the wide-open prairies near Fort Morgan, the gateway to the Pawnee National Grassland. Glenn Miller and the Overland Trail are Fort Morgan's most heralded claims to fame. The big-band leader was born here and became famous before World War II; his plane disappeared over the English Channel in December 1944.

The Overland Trail passed right through town back in the day; its stage station and fort were welcome stopping points for ranchers and farmers travelling from the Missouri River to Denver. When you visit, look for the marker on Riverview Avenue that honors the site of the fort.

Named for Colonel Christopher Morgan, Fort Morgan has three museums and more than 40 historic downtown sites for history buffs. Fishermen flock to Jackson and Bijou Reservoirs and Jackson Lake State Park. Springtime is the best time to visit, since the wildflowers bloom then and the summer heat has yet to set in.

FORT MORGAN GOLF COURSE

THE GOLF The Fort Morgan Golf Course is one of the best and busiest golf courses in northeastern Colorado, offering views of the Platte River Valley and two distinctive nines.

On the course, what is feared is like a magnet. Water, bunkers, trees, ravines, high grass—whatever you fear turns magnetic. —Wiffi Smith

NORTHEAST

Colorado Golf Hall of Famer Dale Douglass played golf for the CU Buffs and went on to stardom on the PGA Tour and Champions Tour.

The Henry Hughes-designed front side originally opened in 1920 and features mature, tree-lined fairways, small greens, and water on two holes. The contrasting different back nine was added in the 1960s and offers larger greens, lofty elevation changes, native grasses, and yucca and cactus bordering the fairways. The signature hole is No. 18, playing 530 yards downhill with water right and out-of-bounds left. The green is large and golfers may have some out-of-bounds trouble if behind the green.

The facility is an Audubon Cooperative Sanctuary and promotes native wildlife and habitats.

Fort Morgan was also home to Colorado Golf Hall of Famer Dale Douglass, who played golf for the CU Buffs and went on to stardom on the PGA Tour and Champions Tour.

THE DETAILS 970-867-5990. 17586 County Rd. T 1/2, Fort Morgan, CO 80701.
- www.fortmorgangolfcourse.com
- Henry Hughes, 1920. 18 holes. Par 72. Black - 6,579 (71/128). Blue - 6,223 (69.3/124). White - 5,760 (67/115). Gold - 5,427 (65.1/113). Women's Blue - 6,224 (74.5/128). Women's White - 6,188 (71.9/122). Women's Gold - 5,474 (70.2/118). Price - $.

GETTING THERE Head down I-76 to Fort Morgan and take exit 80. Turn north and go approximately 1 mile to Golf Course Rd. Turn left and follow it to the Fort Morgan Golf Course.

FORT MORGAN NOTES

Most golfers take advantage of the **Tea House** at the golf course, where freshly made burritos and desserts are the specialty. **Queen's Lounge** is the place to have a 23-ounce pilsner draft beer (970-867-9945) and browse the curiosities hanging on the walls. Or head to **Cable's Italian Grille** (970-867-6144) for calzones or strombolis. The **In the Mood Coffeehouse** (970-867-7378) is a great spot for contemplation and the morning paper. Fort Morgan's **Rainbow Bridge**, just north of town on Highway 52, is a historical attraction and marks one of the entrances to the **Pawnee Pioneer Scenic and Historic Byway**. The bridge was built in 1922 to cross the South Platte River. In Fort Morgan proper, the **Central Motel** (970-867-2401) stands out among the chain motels and mom-and-pops, and the **West Pawnee Ranch** (970-895-2482) offers the chance to really get away with three guest rooms on their working cattle ranch.

The secret in the rough is to take a few dozen practice swings with a 2-iron (a scythe is good, too). —Tom Callahan

HAXTUN

ELEV. 3,700 POP. 982

For more than 100 years the small town of Haxtun, situated in Colorado's akward high plains agricultural region, has been home for farmers and ranchers. It is located at the crossroads of U.S. Highway 6 and Highway 59, about 30 miles from Interstate 76. The local motto is "Small City with a Big Heart." The golf is small-time too, with the clever 9-hole pasture course known as the F&H Golf Club—a course that continues to improve through the decades. As you drive into Haxtun you'll see a tall white water tower that marks the primary reason for a golf trip to this outpost—it is across the street from the landmark Haxtun Inn, a B&B and one of the few historic, fine dining establishments in Eastern Colorado.

F&H GOLF CLUB

THE GOLF Rustic and friendly F&H offers the chance to experience golf on the prairie. This down-home route will never be mistaken for an upscale daily-fee Denver course. Once a sand-green course, it is flat and easy to walk. The best hole is No. 2, a 191-yarder that plays uphill into a large, contoured green. Sloping sides to this green make it a tough up-and-down if the approach misses.

THE DETAILS 970-774-6362. 43355 County Rd. 30, Haxtun, CO 80731
- Marty Johnson, 1972. 9 holes. Par 36. White/Blue - 6,433 (68.9/107). Red - 5,676 (71.6/117). Price - $.

GETTING THERE The course is between Fleming and Haxtun, just off of Hwy. 6. The course is 6 miles west of Haxtun.

HAXTUN NOTES

Base your trip around a stay at the **Haxtun Inn** (970-774-4900), a historical B&B and restaurant that dates back to its butcher shop and ice house existence in 1919. Hunters recognize Phillips County as a superb habitat for chasing pheasant, and local wildlife includes pheasant, coyote, deer, duck, geese, and dove.

NORTHEAST

You should want to hit the ball as far as you can; don't be ashamed of that.—Davis Love, Jr.

HOLYOKE

ELEV. 3,736 POP. 2,261

Holyoke, the seat of Phillips County, was established in 1888 in the sand hills area of northeastern Colorado, not far from the Nebraska border. Located at the crossroads of U.S. Highways 6 and 385 and surrounded by excellent dry and irrigated cropland, it's a beautiful town with charming lawns, mature trees, and picnic parks.

Corn, wheat, sugar beets, and pinto beans are all grown by local farmers, who will no doubt be shocked by what is coming in the near future—an impressive private golf complex named Ballyneal that will flow through the sand hills and attract a national membership.

BALLYNEAL GOLF COURSE

THE GOLF The O'Neal brothers have hired award-winning architect Tom Doak (Pacific Dunes in Bandon, Oregon) to design their sand-dune minimalist layout. Course construction is scheduled to begin in spring 2004 and the course could open for play sometime in 2005.

"We will start the member interviewing process in early 2004. Ballyneal will be built on a singularly unique dunes property with a hard and fast fescue surface-giving our national members a great links golf experience," said Rupert O'Neal.

The northeastern Colorado plains landscape is dominated by a wild, grassy look and dotted with 40- to 50-foot-high sand dunes. Don Placek, a designer on Doak's staff, said the project compares to the highly-ranked Ben Crenshaw-Bill Coore Sand Hills in Nebraska, but says this course will have rough, wild lines compared to Sand Hills' smoother lines.

THE DETAILS 970-854-3540. Opening 2005.
- Tom Doak, 2005. Not yet rated. Not yet open. Private course with national members, on-site lodging for winter hunting and summer golf.

GETTING THERE To be determined.

HOLYOKE GOLF COURSE

THE GOLF A traditional course in the middle of nowhere, Holyoke is loaded with elm, cottonwood, hackberry, poplar trees, and few hazards (three bunkers total). Bluegrass fairways lead to tiny bentgrass greens. The 195-yard par-3 No. 2 includes a carry over a dry creek with out-of-bounds behind the green.

The good player swings through the ball while the awkward player hits at it.—Ken Venturi

THE DETAILS 970-854-3200. 415 E. Carnahan, Holyoke, CO 80734.
- Unknown, 1972. 9 holes. Par 36. Blue - 6,445 (68.8/136). Red - 5,938 (72.5/123). Price - $.

GETTING THERE Take I-76 to Sterling, then Hwy. 6 to Holyoke. The course is one block north of Hwy. 6.

HOLYOKE NOTES

Typical small-town charms are available in Holyoke, where you can visit the **Phillips County Historical Society Museum** (970-854-2129), attend the **Dandelion Daze festival**, held annually in June, and dine at **The Skillet** (970-854-2150) or **Kardale's Restaurant** (970-854-3455). Weekenders can spend the night at the **Golden Plains Motel** (970-854-3000) or the **Cedar Inn Motel** (970-854-2525), and Ballyneal is slated to have on-site lodging for winter hunting and summer golf.

HUGO

ELEV. 5,360 POP. 885

Hugo has a cowboy history, with old-timers who remember the day when local cooks served steak and biscuits from a chuck wagon to President Teddy Roosevelt. In the 1880s, folks traveled the Smoky Hill Trail and the Butterfield Overland Stage came through, as did the Leavenworth & Pikes Peak Stage. The region has fertile soil that's watered by the Big Sandy Alluvial and Ogallala Aquifer.

Anyone traveling through Colorado's Central Plains is likely to pass through this part of Lincoln County known as "The Hub City of the Plains." The golf here is nothing but old-school— a sand-green course that some believe opened in 1898.

HUGO GOLF CLUB

THE GOLF Hugo Golf Club is one of the few sand-green golf courses left in the state. To say it is isolated is an over-statement. They don't even have a tele-phone at the course.

Joe Clark, president of the Hugo Golf Club, says no one knows exactly when golf began in Hugo, but some believe 1898. "Actually, there was a golf course across the street from today's present course that was called Shepherd's Golf Course," said Clark. "The existing course was moved to its present spot in the

It would be an insult to your good taste and intelligence to tell you how to behave on the links, because it is only necessary to remember that for the time being the golf course is your garden and the clubhouse is your temporary home.—Henry Cotton

1940s and Jack Owens, who is now deceased, led the members in the building of the new one."

Clark admits that a lot of golfers from other parts of the state show up to play just because they have never seen sand greens. And he said one Denver family joined the club because they thought it would be an ideal place to learn the game. It's certainly affordable golf, with $5 green fees and a family membership for $50 a year.

Buffalo-grass fairways play mostly straightaway, although there are a couple of slight doglegs. No. 5 moves left and recent tree plantings of fir, cedar, and cottonwoods should give the hole some bite when they reach maturity in a decade. The course did have sand traps at one time, but they were removed.

The toughest hole might be No. 3, a 175-yard par 3 that goes uphill. Only the flag is visible from the tee. "You don't see many pars here," said Clark. "If you stand on the bench behind the green you can see the sand splash if someone hits the green, but not many do."

THE DETAILS No telephone. Hwy. 287, Hugo, CO 80821.
- Unknown, 1898. 9 holes. Not rated. Sand greens. Price - $.

GETTING THERE Take I-70 east to Limon, and drive south on Hwy. 287 to Hugo.

HUGO NOTES

Head for the **Hugo State Wildlife Area** and **Kinney Lake**, located just south of Hugo, to fish as well as to hunt game birds, antelope, and deer (like Teddy Roosevelt). Sleep at the **Trailblazer Motel** (719-743-2474) and discuss golf with the locals over breakfast or lunch at **Jean's Family Kitchen** (719-743-2716).

JULESBURG

ELEV. 3,477 POP. 1,467

Established in 1859 and named for Jules Beni, a French trader, the border town of Julesburg was an important stop even before the Overland Trail became established. For a short time in its history, the Pony Express stopped in Julesburg, which is just two miles from the Nebraska border in the Colorado's far northeast corner.

Julesburg was once home to wild saloons and dance halls on the Union Pacific Railroad route, and named "the wickedest little town of the West." It was even torched and burned to the ground as a reaction to the infamous skirmish

Make a longer swing for a longer bunker shot. Swing smoothly, not violently. A rehearsal swing outside the bunker will give you the feel.—Butch Harmon

called the Sand Creek Massacre. Modern Julesburg is tamer—an agricultural community set amid a landscape of buffalo grass and flat prairies. After golf at the Sedgwick County Golf Course, discover the lurid details of the town's Wild West history at the Fort Sedgwick Depot Museum and its sister site, the Fort Sedgwick Museum.

SEDGWICK COUNTY GOLF COURSE

THE GOLF The Sedgwick County GC offers buffalo-grass fairways, winter rules, rolling land, and tiny greens, which were made of sand until about 15 years ago. The par-3 No. 4 is one of the better holes at 203 yards. The green slopes from back to front, making the tricky hole more difficult because it's easy to be too long off the tee.

According to local Butch Stone, the course's Father's Day Tournament is one of the best in the state. "We are already booked up for next year's event and have a 20-team waiting list. The tournament format is a two-man team scramble."

"The par-3 holes on this course are tough," says Stone. "I think that's what most people like about it. Also, No. 1 is one of those frustrating holes at 530 yards where you can make eagle or double bogey. There's out-of-bounds trouble and thick rough if you go over the green."

U.S. Open champ Steve Jones of nearby Yuma won the Colorado State Sand Green Tournament at Julesburg back when he was attending CU.

THE DETAILS 970-520-2626. Hwy. 11, Julesburg, CO 80737
- Designed by locals, date unknown. 9 holes. Par 36. Blue - 2,936. White - 2,786. Red - 2,685. Not rated. Honor system pay box. Price - $.

GETTING THERE Go 2 miles north of Julesburg off Colorado Hwy. 11.

JULESBURG NOTES

In the fall and spring birdwatchers migrate to Julesburg to drive down the country roads and watch the fauna. Birds flock to the **South Platte River**, which branches off the **Missouri River**. The South Platte is also home to local fishing. Bed down at the **Platte Valley Inn** (970-474-3336) or the **Holiday Motel** (970-474-3371). Try the **D & J Cafe** (970-474-3556) or **Thad's Flying J** (970-474-3366) for eastern-plains-style good eats.

The part shot from 50 to 60 yards out is golf's "money shot." When warming up before playing, always devote time to 60-yard shots, even if that's all you do. —Jim Flick

KIRK

ELEV. 4,220 POP. 200

The thriving metropolis of Kirk is one of Colorado's smallest golf towns, a farming and ranching community that flourishes thanks to the irrigation of the Arickaree River. Golfers passing through to the Plainsman Golf Club, where the greens never turn brown, have the added amenities of a bank, gas station, store, and post office in case there's business to be attended to.

PLAINSMAN GOLF CLUB

THE GOLF About 10 years ago, says local banker Roger Maag, the PGC's sand greens were replaced by contoured, artificial-turf greens. It's a pasture golf course, he says, with 53 acres they molded with buffalo-grass fairways. Local Otis Collette designed the course in 1964.

"What we have is sufficient for our little community," Maag said. "We have men's and women's leagues and a few tournaments. From time to time Colonel Carl Comer, who owns the Runaway Inn, has events with steak dinners following the golf."

How do you play approach shots into 10-year old fake turf? "Very good players who can hit it high and spin the ball can fire at the greens," Maag said. "But for novices you have to learn to run the ball onto the greens. You can hit it about 50 yards short and bounce them on. It just takes some practice."

No. 8, a 130-yard par 3, stands out. The green is set into the side of a hill and there's out-of-bounds on the right. The course even includes a wildlife habitat area.

THE DETAILS No telephone. 9785 County Road 4, Kirk, CO 80824.
• Otis Collette, 1964. 9 holes. Par 34. Not rated. Price - $.

GETTING THERE From Kirk, go 1 mile north to County Rd. 4, then 1 mile west.

KIRK NOTES

The Runaway Inn (www.runawayinn.com, 970-358-4567) is a excellent place for pheasant hunters and golfers to congregate for rural getaways. Like a hunting lodge B&B, meals are served and it's ideal for corporate outings, weddings, or family reunions. Road-tripping pilots even have two runways where they can land their planes in for a golf visit.

How many people realize that every part of the swing is associated with irrelevant and putting-off thoughts? It is these irrelevant thoughts, always latent, which the gamesman must try to bring to the surface, however buried and fleeting they may be. —Stephen Potter

NORTHEAST

LIMON

ELEV. 5,365 POP. 2,071

They say you can see six states from the Genoa Tower Museum, close to Limon, an indication that this is the famous flatlands of the Colorado high plains. A tornado destroyed downtown Limon in 1990, but the town lives on after an extensive rebuilding project.

In 1888, Limon got its start as a railroad stop and work camp for the new Chicago and Rock Island rail line that connected Kansas to Colorado Springs. Named after one of the railroad's original construction foremen, five highways intersect here and the town is equidistant to Denver and Colorado Springs, making it a hub city of sorts.

TAMARACK GOLF COURSE

THE GOLF A course of many names, Tamarack opened as Tri-County Golf Course and was also known as Limon Municipal. An unhurried place to walk on slightly rolling land, the course sports wide fairways with large greens, both flat and contoured. There's water on two holes and a handful of bunkers. No. 3 is 500 yards and the dogleg around the lake is notorious for grabbing wayward shots.

THE DETAILS 719-775-9998. Highway 71, Limon, CO 80828.
- Henry Hughes, 1967. 9 holes. Par 35. Blue/White - 6,017 (67.5/112). Women's Blue/White - 6,002 (72.4/124). Women's Red/Blue - 5,620 (70.5/120). Price - $.

GETTING THERE Go east on I-70 to Limon and follow the business district signs. Head south on State Hwy. 71 (first right) and go 1.5 miles to the course.

LIMON NOTES

Head for the **Fireside Junction Restaurant** (970-775-2396) for chile rellenos, brisket, and homemade pies. The **Craig Ranch Bed & Breakfast** (www.craigranch-bandb.com, 719-775-2658) is for those who want to spend the night in B&B style, but lodging is also available at the **Best Western** (719-775-0277) or the **Comfort Inn** (719-775-2752). The **Limon Heritage Museum** (719-775-0430) explains High Plains agricultural and railroad history.

NORTHEAST

Too much thought about the mechanics is a bad thing for anyone's game…You must be mindful but not thoughtful as you swing. You must not think or reflect; you must feel what you have to do. —Percy Boomer

STERLING

ELEV. 3,939 POP. 11,360

Sterling's moniker is "The City of Living Trees," and throughout town dead trees have been transformed into sculptures that have brought the trees back from the Dutch Elm disease. Sterling is a trade center for farming and ranching operations in northeastern Colorado and southwestern Nebraska. It is also headquarters for much of the oil and gas activity in this part of the state. Fishing and other water sports are available at three area reservoirs, and the town offers two 18-hole golf courses.

RIVERVIEW GOLF COURSE

THE GOLF On this modern course with a wide variety of trees (silver maple, cottonwood, Russian olives, green ash, and ponderosa and Austrian pine), regulars are able to navigate the route because the trees are scattered sparsely and they know which ones to avoid.

Difficulty enters in the form of tricky, 5,000-square-foot contoured bentgrass greens that are slick and extremely challenging with certain pin locations. About 50 sand traps dot the gentle, rolling terrain, and the pace of play and the price are right.

No. 2 is a long, straight par 3 of 207 yards. The green is small and guarded by a large bunker on the left. The fifth hole is a 440-yard dogleg left with a tough approach over a pond.

THE DETAILS 970-522-3035. 13064 County Road 370, Sterling, CO 80751.
- Val Heim, 1980. 18 holes. Par 71. Blue - 6,418 (70.5/126). White - 5,784 (67.4/120). Women's Blue - 6,148 (73.6/125). Women's White - 5,815 (71.8/120). Women's Red - 5,016 (67.6/113). Price - $.

GETTING THERE Travel I-76 to Sterling and exit left at Hwy. 6. Turn right at the information center and go half a mile to the course on your right.

STERLING COUNTRY CLUB

THE GOLF Host of the longest, continuously run Labor Day Tournaments in Colorado (some 77 years), Sterling Country Club began as a sand-green cow-patty field of dreams, dating back possibly as far as 1902.

Long-time pro Milo Luckett is said to have designed one nine, but Henry Hughes also has his name attached to the first nine in what locals describe as "a

---

I used to play golf with a guy who cheated so badly that he once had a hole in one and wrote down a zero on the scorecard.—Bob Brue

little hidden gem that doesn't look like much on the scorecard, but just try and score low."

This traditional layout rolls through cottonwood and elm trees, and has very tricky, subtle breaking greens. The 2003 Colorado Golf Association Four Ball was staged here and birdies were surprisingly scarce. Other tournaments include the Northeast Amateur championship in June, and the Ladies Invitation is also an annual Sterling event.

An irrigation ditch runs through the course, affecting play on about nine holes. The signature hole is the 211-yard, par-3 No. 12. The green has two tiers and anything short rolls backwards. A couple of bunkers also guard the putting surface.

Even though this is a private club, county residents can play once a month and golfers statewide can also call up and get a tee time.

THE DETAILS 970-522-3776. 17408 Hwy. 14, Sterling, CO 80751.

- Henry Hughes, front nine, 1921. Milo Luckett, back nine, 1956. 18 holes. Par 72. Blue - 6,290 (69.1/118). White - 6,112 (67.6/114). Women's White - 6,112 (75.2/132). Women's Red - 5,522 (71.4/124). Semi-private, reciprocal and outside play allowed. Price - $$.

GETTING THERE Drive 2 miles west of Sterling on Hwy. 14.

STERLING NOTES

The **North Sterling Reservoir** is popular with locals for water sports, fishing, and camping. The **Ramada Inn** or **Days Inn** on the interstate are adequate stops for overnighters, and the **Elk Echo Ranch** is a fun B&B in Stoneham on Pawnee National Grassland. **Delgado's Dugout** (970-522-0175) doesn't have a sign, but is located by an old church at the corner of 2nd and Beech Streets, and serves tasty, greasy, cheap Mexican food. Other dining options include **Momma Conde's** (970-522-0802), **J 'n L Cafe** (970-522-3625), **T.J. Bummer's** (970-522-8397) for green chile, and the popular **River City Grill** (970-521-7648), the best place for sports watching.

NORTHEAST

One of these days in your travels, a guy is going to come up to you and show you a nice, brand-new deck of cards on which the seal is not yet broken, and this guy is going to offer to bet you that he can make the jack of spades jump out of the deck and squirt cider in your ear. But, son, do not bet this man, for as sure as you stand there, you are going to wind up with an earful of cider.—Damon Runyon

STRATTON

ELEV. 4,414 POP. 669

Travelers know Stratton as a convenient rest stop during the long, straight stretch of I-70 that runs from Colorado's eastern border to Denver. Located in the irrigated cornfields nudged against Kansas, Stratton is primarily a farming and ranching community. Corn, wheat, soybeans, and sunflowers form the cornerstone of the agricultural industry in the area. Post-golf drives down Main Street and Colorado Ave. reveal gift shops, convenience stores, family restaurants, and even an ice cream shop.

STRATTON GOLF COURSE

THE GOLF The 9-hole Stratton Golf Course is tree-lined, narrow, hilly, with buffalo grass in the fairways and speedy greens.

The course's lone pond is in play on No. 2, a 492-yard par 5 that also features out-of-bounds. No. 5, a 182-yard par 3, plays downhill to a receptive green that slopes from back to front.

The honor system is used for paying green fees.

THE DETAILS 719-348-5412. First and Wyoming, Stratton, CO 80836.
- Box Hemburger, 1976. 9 holes. Par 34. Men's Red/White - 5,022 (62.2/94). Women's Red/White - 5,022 (66.2/107). Price - $.

GETTING THERE Head for Stratton on U.S. Hwy. 50, 30 miles west of the Kansas border.

STRATTON NOTES

The expansive prairies and the sandhills to the north are superb hunting grounds, and Stratton is known for its deer, antelope, and pheasant hunting. **Bonny State Park** and **Flagler Lake and State Wildlife Area**, both west of Stratton, are excellent places to explore. In Stratton stay at the **Best Western Golden Prairie Inn** (719-348-5311) or the **Claremont Inn** (719-348-5125). Locals point towards the **Brand Inn Iron** (719-348-5209) for sit-down meals.

He who have fastest cart never have to play bad lie.—Mickey Mantle

WRAY

ELEV. 3,522 POP. 2,187

Wray, a flat-prairie town in Yuma County, is situated just 13 miles from the Nebraska border. The North Fork of the Republican River runs right through the community, which was established more than 100 years ago.

The Wray area includes buttes, canyons, and cliffs to the south of town and is one of the largest corn-producing counties in the USA thanks to water from the Ogallala Aquifer and the huge, central-pivot irrigation systems.

Locals enjoy 255 days of sunshine each year, important to the wayward golfer because it means that the Wray Country Club can be experienced year-round.

WRAY COUNTRY CLUB

THE GOLF Frank Hummel came along in 1962 to lay out this short, hilly course with mounding, wide-open fairways, few trees, and elevated greens. Wind is a factor on the plains, but there's only one sand trap and zero water hazards.

Only two holes bend and one is the 535-yard No. 7. With an extreme uphill par 3 of 131 yards, No. 2 requires accuracy. The green slopes back to front and presents a small target that is hard to hold. The inability to see the green makes it even more difficult.

THE DETAILS 970-332-5934. 36357 Hwy. 385, Wray, CO 80758.
- Frank Hummel, 1962. 9 holes. Par 35. White - 5,974 (67.4/114). Women's White - 5,974 (72.8/119). Red - 4,858 (65.8/101). Price - $.

GETTING THERE Head 1 mile north of Wray on Hwy. 385.

WRAY NOTES

Lodging options include the **Butte Motel** (970-332-4828) and **Travelers Inn** (970-332-4848), and the **Sandhiller Motel & Restaurant** (970-332-4134) offers the chance to stay and dine. In late July check out **Wray Daze**, a festival of silly fun and rubber duck races (970-332-3484). Even the diminutive prairie chicken is celebrated here. In March the quirky mating habits of the prairie chicken are on display, and tours are available to watch the strange love dance (970-332-5063). The **Wray Museum** (970-332-5063) houses an extensive paleo-Indian exhibit, as well as information and artifacts from the Battle of Beecher Island in 1868.

If you arrive at the course with just a few minutes to warm up before a round, use that time to hit chip shots. The chip shot, being a short version of the full swing, tells your muscles and your golfing brain to get ready to play.—Harvey Penick

YUMA

ELEV. 4,131 POP. 3,285

When the first white settlers arrived here in covered wagons in the 1870s, they kept on going. A drought gripped the area back then and it looked like a desert. Yuma was the middle of nowhere, but the Santa Fe Trail was south of Yuma and the Oregon Trail was north.

Yuma County actually became part of the land the United States bought from France in the 1803 Louisiana Purchase. Then it became Missouri Territory and in 1854 was split by the Kansas-Nebraska act. Even when Congress created the Colorado Territory in 1861, this part remained mostly unoccupied. It wasn't until Texas cattle herds were driven through here after the Civil War that the area finally gained an identity. When the Union Pacific railroad headed toward Yuma from Ogallala, Nebraska, the high plains grasslands here became a place for cattle to munch and become beefier before being loaded onto cattle cars.

Located about 150 miles east of Denver between I-70 and I-76, Yuma has a dry farming climate and comparatively mild winters for this area, with a growing season of about 138 days and even more for golf.

Yuma is on the Colorado golf history map thanks to hometown boy and CU grad Steve Jones. In 1988 Jones won the Colorado Open at Hiwan Golf Club with a four-stroke victory over Bruce Summerhays—a sign of future success since he went on to win the 1996 U.S. Open at Oakland Hills Country Club in Birmingham, Michigan.

INDIAN HILLS GOLF COURSE

THE GOLF The course that Steve Jones played as a youngster features large greens and is tree-lined, but wide fairways make it a good driving course. One large lake comes into play on two holes, and a teardrop-shaped portion of that water affects another approach shot.

Expect some uneven lies on the hilly terrain, but there's only one hole that doglegs—No. 6, a 413-yard par 4 that fires over a hill and requires a carry of 190 yards. It is a tough par if you don't carry the hill. No. 7 is a par-4, 372-yarder that has water protruding about 10 yards in front of the green. No. 6 requires a shot over trees cutting the corner of the dogleg and unforgiving rough.

Visitors always comment on the course's great conditioning, says Dean Metzler, who runs the Sweet Spot Cafe, the golf course's eatery. "We have our own wells so during the past couple of drought years we've been green and beautiful."

Don't get into the habit of playing "winter rules." If you do, you'll never learn to play the shots you need to be a decent golfer. Winter rules are generally an amusing delusion. They aid neither in the development of the turf nor of the player.—Tommy Armour

"No. 2 might be the toughest," said Metzler. "It's about 450 from the back tee and you have to strike two solid shots to even dream of a birdie. The large bent greens can be nasty with some of the pin placements, but overall long hitters love this course."

Recently the club added a mogul that affects play on No. 4 and a sand trap on No. 5; members hope to build a new clubhouse in the near future.

Metzler said Jones comes back from time to time because his parents and two brothers still live in Yuma.

THE DETAILS 970-848-2812. 5294 County Rd. 39, Yuma, CO 80759.
- Unknown, 1970. 9 holes. Par 36. White/Blue - 6,817 (70.7/118). Women's Red/White - 6,325 (74.5/128). Price - $.

GETTING THERE Take I-76 to Hwy. 34 and go east to Yuma. Take Hwy. 59 north 1 mile to CR 39, and go east to the course just down the road.

Steve Jones, the 1996 U.S. Open champion, is from Yuma, CO and attended Colorado University.

YUMA NOTES

The **Sweet Spot Cafe** is convenient because it's in the clubhouse, and **Woody's Drive-In** (970-848-5647) is another option for good eats. Accommodations include the **Harvest Motel** (970-848-5853) and the **Sunrise Inn** (970-848-5465).

SOUTHEAST

Eads	327
Fowler	328
La Junta	329
Lamar	331
Las Animas	332
La Veta	333
Pueblo	334
Rocky Ford	339
Springfield	340
Trinidad	341
Walsenburg	343

SOUTHEAST

Eads

385

Pueblo

Fowler

Las Animas

50

Lamar

Colorado City

Rocky Ford

La Junta

287

350

Walsenburg

25

160

La Veta

Springfield

160

Trinidad

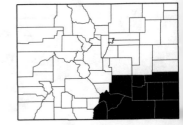

Southeast Mileage

	Colorado City	Eads	Fowler	La Junta	Lamar	Las Animas	La Veta	Pueblo	Rocky Ford	Springfield	Trinidad	Walsenburg
Colorado City		138	60	89	144	107	34	24	78	182	60	24
Eads	138		78	76	36	57	159	114	73	85	158	149
Fowler	60	78		28	84	47	94	36	18	133	100	84
La Junta	89	76	28		55	19	84	64	11	105	82	74
Lamar	144	36	84	55		36	139	120	66	49	137	129
Las Animas	107	57	47	19	36		103	83	30	86	101	92
La Veta	34	159	94	84	139	103		58	79	169	47	10
Pueblo	24	114	36	64	120	83	58		54	86	84	48
Rocky Ford	78	73	18	11	66	30	79	54		115	82	68
Springfield	182	85	133	105	49	86	169	86	115		122	159
Trinidad	60	158	100	82	137	101	47	84	82	122		37
Walsenburg	24	149	84	74	129	92	10	48	68	159	37	

Rounding the curve at Stonewall Gap, Colorado State Highway 12, known as the Scenic Highway of Legends, bends to the north. It has been a typically warm fall day, with the aspens gleaming gold and the ponderosa pines emanating that sweet smell that's heaven to a visitor from the sweaty realms of the southwest. As twilight aims a red-hued spotlight at the Sangre de Cristo Mountains to the west, the breeze of a traffic-free day grinds to a halt. The Trinchera elk herd, which outnumbers locals 100 to 1, is cutting a path across the highway. When the road opens up again, Monument Lake and the tiny defunct ski town of Cuchara await in the distance.

A golf road trip here follows this mountainous, scenic Highway of Legends, an 82-mile route that first began as a dirt trail carved out by the Ute Indians in the 1770s as a pathway through the valleys to neighboring Apache tribes and to bountiful hunting grounds and sacred sites.

The people here have a distinct lifestyle. It's a laid-back atmosphere with friendly folks who love nature. Any day visitors are greeted with amazing scenes—double rainbows following an afternoon thunderstorm, a flock of wild turkeys winging it over Purgatoire Campground Road, or wild strawberries growing along the high-altitude trail at Fishpaw Pass among gnarled, centuries-old bristlecone pines.

It's a land with cattle roaming on an open range, where highway traffic sometimes stops for a cattle drive right down the center line.

It's a land of an off-season hush—some days fishermen can cast a nymph upon Monument Lake with only silence as a companion. No motor boats, zero chatter of neighboring fishermen, just a diving osprey zeroing in on a rainbow trout.

It's a land of geological wonders—the world's largest concentration of volcanic granite dikes are here, protruding from the Spanish Peaks like spokes on a wheel. From an airplane the sight is even more impressive.

And golf legends abound here as well. Just 10 minutes past Cuchara in the middle of nowhere is La Veta's Grandote Peaks Golf Club, designed by Jay Morrish and Tom Weiskopf. Opened in 1986, Grandote Peaks is stunning and challenging—a hidden diamond located in the boondocks of Huerfano County, south of Pueblo. Within an hour of here the wayward golfer finds three more hidden gems that must be experienced—in addition to Grandote, the list includes Pueblo's Walking Stick Golf Course, Alamosa's Cattails Golf Course, and the Trinidad Golf Course, just over Raton Pass from New Mexico. Texas Panhandlers love to flock to Trinidad, which some consider the best 9-holer in Colorado.

The southeast region of Colorado is mainly eastern plains—places like La

You must always, during the match, try to give your partner in a foursome an impression that you are more than pleased with him. This impression is usually a very false one.—Horace Hutchinson

Junta, home of historic Bent's Fort on the Santa Fe Trail, and Rocky Ford, where the sweetest cantaloupes and watermelons in the world are grown. Both small towns have 9-hole courses—La Junta Golf Club and Rocky Ford Country Club. There's also the Spreading Antlers Golf Course in Lamar and the surprising golf town of Pueblo. Cross the forests and plains, gaze at the Sangre de Cristo range and the Spanish Peaks in the distance, and discover some great off-the-beaten-path golf in this rugged area.

Many consider Trinidad Golf Course the best nine-hole layout in Colorado.

If everybody could learn to hold his head still there wouldn't be any golfers around still trying to break 100.—Arnold Palmer

COLORADO CITY

ELEV. 5,858 POP. 2,018

Colorado City is located barely west of I-25, just 27 miles south of Pueblo in the Greenhorn Valley. Venture off I-25 here on the 103-mile national Frontier Pathways Scenic & Historic Byway and the countryside displays the remains of mills, cattle ranches, and the original homesteads of hard-rock miners. Places like Pueblo, Hardscrabble, Greenhorn, Buzzard's Roost, and Fowler's Lookout served as the original outposts for early 1870s explorers, trappers, and traders. These days wandering golfers can experience the Hollydot Golf Course in Colorado City, an interesting locale nestled against Greenhorn Mountain and the 1,237,920-acre San Isabel National Forest, and an easy stop-off while venturing along speedy I-25.

HOLLYDOT GOLF COURSE

THE GOLF Hollydot is the combination of two names: Holland Duell, one of the first residents of the area and owner of the property, and his wife Dorothy.

Duell, a local rancher, was actually a modern-day pioneer. He introduced Colorado's first master-planned development concept at Colorado City in 1963. As Duell planned roads and envisioned growth, he included golf as part of the scheme. Before going bankrupt in the 1980s, the course was known as Meadow Creek Country Club.

Hollydot's opening nine, the East Course, plays out in a meadow setting that is wide and forgiving. When Frank Hummel came along and redesigned the course, he added the back nine known as the Links Course. The Links features large, contoured greens, tighter fairways, and thick rough. One of the most attractive holes is No. 18 on the Links, a par-5 585-yarder that plays with Greenhorn Mountain as its backdrop. The green has two tiers and wind is predominately in your face.

The third nine, the West Course, was basically laid out by Duell and is hilly and tree-lined. Most golfers prefer the East and Middle nines.

Hollydot is known for its friendly, small-town staff, as well as possibly the best bentgrass greens in Colorado. Variety is another plus, since visitors enjoy the chance to play three distinctively different nines. The course hosts 80 to 90 tournaments a year, including the Colorado high school boys' and girls' state championships over the years.

The good players are almost always the ones who ask me to watch them on the putting green. The high-handicappers, who need it the most, would rather do anything than have a putting lesson. —Harvey Penick

THE DETAILS 719-676-3341. 55 N. Parkway, Colorado City, CO 81019.
- Frank Hummel, 1974. 18 holes. Par 71. East and Middle Nines combined and called Gold Links. Back - 7,009 (71.9/126). White - 6,163 (68.2/110). Women's White - 6,163 (73.6/125). Red - 5,224 (68.2/113). Price - $.
- West Nine designed by Holland Duell, 1963. Par 35. White - 6,420 (69.3/122). Price - $.

GETTING THERE Take I-25 south of Pueblo to exit 74A (Colorado City, Rye, San Isabel exit). Follow Hwy. 165 west 1 mile from exit 74A. The course is easily visible from Hwy. 165.

COLORADO CITY NOTES

Look for post-round meals in Colorado City at **Colella's** (719-676-2462) and **Espey's BBQ** (719-676-4022). For lodging, consider the **Greenhorn Inn** (719-676-2340). And one of the more unusual tourist attractions in Colorado is **Bishop Castle**, where Jim Bishop and family have been hard at work for more than 30 years building a gigantic castle stone by stone. Follow the signs along Highway 165.

EADS

ELEV. 4,260 POP. 850

The railroad town of Eads was founded in 1887, but lean times in the 1890s pretty much sealed its fate as a small town forever. It's the seat of Kiowa County, which boasts a whopping 850 folks and serves as the gateway to the Great Plains Reservoirs (www.kiowacountycolo.com). When traveling through this remote spot of southeast Colorado, consider a few hours at the uncrowded 9-hole Eads Golf Course in conjunction with excursions on the areas six fishing lakes.

EADS GOLF COURSE

THE GOLF Eads Golf Course is the place to take in the pasture pool experience of $5 green fees and sand greens. The birth of golf in Eads is an interesting story: on land south of town that local farmer Kelley Jackson originally rented for $1 an acre, local engineer R.H. Musselman designed a course around hills and a creek. Just as the project got rolling, Jackson decided he wanted more money for the land, explaining to Musselman that they could either move the course or he

The golfing area of the brain is a fragile thing that is terribly susceptible to suggestion.—Harvey Penick

would fence it off and let his cattle graze there. Jackson ended up selling another tract of 67 acres for $50 an acre, and Musselman had to do his design work once again. The land has a huge gravel pit in the middle of the course; members call it the "Big Divot." Locals planted the trees, created a watering system, and built the cart paths, greens, and tees.

THE DETAILS No telephone. Eads Fairgrounds, Eads, CO 81036.
- R.H. Musselman, golf members, 1960. 9 holes. Par 36. Regular - 6,290 (67.7/112). Price - $.

GETTING THERE Head for the fairgrounds located on the west side of Eads.

EADS NOTES

Grab a meal at either **Betty's** (719-438-2099) or **Our Place Restaurant** (719-438-5686) before you head to the next golf destination, and ponder the fact that the town is named after James Eads, the engineer who designed the bridge over the Mississippi River in St. Louis.

FOWLER

ELEV. 4,341 POP. 1,206

The little prairie town of Fowler is located on the south side of the Arkansas River on U. S. Highway 50 in Otero County, 34 miles east of Pueblo. Arapahoe, Comanche, Kiowa and Ute Indian tribes lived here before the arrival of O.S. Fowler, a professor who entertained visions of building an irrigation ditch that would attract settlers and make fruit growing possible. One mile of the ditch was complete before Fowler passed on, but the community has survived over the years thanks to the Arkansas River and its resources.

COTTONWOOD LINKS GOLF CLUB

THE GOLF Cottonwood does indeed have a links-style feel, with bluegrass fairways as wide as the eastern plains vistas and nothing but newly-planted trees on the first five holes. However the remaining holes involve a small pond and a creek (Nos. 8 and 9), and some mature cottonwoods get in the way. Thick rough lines some of the fairways, and the bentgrass greens vary—some are flat and some have slopes.

The par 4 No. 7 is only 272 yards but tricky, doglegging right with out-of-

You can't hit a good five-iron if you're thinking about a six-iron on your backswing.—Charles Coody

bounds and a huge cottonwood on the left side of the fairway. Large mounds and grass bunkers surround the green.

You won't need a tee time here. Just walk up, say hello, and play a round for less than the cost of a steak dinner.

THE DETAILS 719-263-4500. One Cottonwood Lane, Fowler, CO 81039.
- Lee Terry, 1994. 9 holes. Par 36. White/Blue - 5,838 (67.2/107). Red/White - 5,256 (68.7/112). Price - $.

GETTING THERE Take I-25 east on Hwy. 50 to Fowler. Next take a left on Main Street, and just past the railroad tracks take another left straight into the golf course about 1 mile down the road.

FOWLER NOTES

Pueblo's charms are just a short drive away, but Fowler is the place to come for a weekend of bird hunting and golf, an adventurous combination in the fall when quail, dove, duck, and geese frequent the southeastern Colorado plains. For lodging, try the **Blue Spruce Inn** (719-263-4271). Locals head for dinner at **C J's Restaurant** (719-263-4441), **Stockman Restaurant** (719-263-9994) or **Tamarack Grill** (719-263-4092). And **Injection** is a new restaurant in town that specializes in steak and seafood.

LA JUNTA

ELEV. 4,066 POP. 7,568

The Santa Fe Trail and the Santa Fe Railroad played significant roles in the growth of La Junta, named for the Spanish word for "junction." The city got its start as the crossroads of three divisions of the historic Santa Fe Trail: 182 miles southeast of Denver, 63 miles east of Pueblo, and 83 miles northeast of Trinidad. The Bents built a fort here during the fur-trade era and historic Bent's Old Fort saw it all—Indian Wars, massive buffalo herds, and the coming of the Santa Fe Railroad, which really put La Junta on the map. On May 15, 1881, La Junta became a town; legend says a herd of antelope ran down Main Street, leading to the presence of the animals on the city seal today. Today bustling La Junta is the center of the Arkansas Valley, county seat of Otero County, and home to a fun little 9-hole golf course.

SOUTHEAST

Everyone has his own choking level, a level at which he fails to play his normal golf. As you get more experienced, your choking level rises.—Johnny Miller

LA JUNTA GOLF CLUB

THE GOLF During World War II the Air Force, called the Army Air Corps back then, came to the flat prairie of La Junta to train pilots and scraped up the dirt that became La Junta Golf Club. A few years after the war the Corps of Engineers came in and continued the construction. The course has evolved over the years, but today the La Junta course has bentgrass greens, punishing buffalo grass rough, very few bunkers, and loads of trees lining the fairways.

Aside from the solid, affordable golf, La Junta's reputation for serving the best food in town is well deserved. Sandwiches, steaks, burgers, and Mexican dishes are all on the menu.

THE DETAILS 719-384-7133. 27696 Harris Road, La Junta, CO 81050.
- Army Corps of Engineers, 1950. 9 holes. Par 35. Black - 6,557 (69.5/114). White/Blue - 6,306 (67.9/112). Red - 5,217 (68.3/112). Price - $.

GETTING THERE Take I-25 to the Hwy. 50 exit at Pueblo, and go east to La Junta. In town continue to Hwy. 109 north about 4 miles to Industrial Park. Turn east into Industrial Park and proceed to the course.

LA JUNTA NOTES

Mountain bikers head to the **Picketwire Canyonlands**, an 18-mile loop through desert and canyon country. Late Summers in La Junta display **roadside stands** piled high with fresh produce, and you can load up on the world's best cantaloupes and watermelons. History buffs should consider a trip back in time by visiting **Bent's Old Fort National Historic Site** (719-384-2596), a reconstruction of the old trading post that was once a frontier hub of activity. Museums include one dedicated to Kit Carson as well as the **Koshare Indian Museum** (719-384-4411).**La Junta** is jammed with fun restaurants. **Café Grand'Mere** (719-384-2711) is the more upscale dining option, and offers the charming 1900 **Amanda House** (719-384-2744) for overnighters next door. But also consider **The Barista** (719-384-2133), **Felisa's Mexico Food** for lunch (719-384-4814), **El Azteca** (719-384-4215), and the **Hog's Breath Saloon** (719-384-7879) for cold beers. **Mexico City** (719-384-9818), located in the former 1950s **Country Club Restaurant**, serves spicy chile rellenos. The best option might be four miles west of town in Swink, where the roadhouse bar called **Dry Bean BBQ & Steakhouse** (719-384-2326) smokes it slow and is considered the best barbecue in the valley. For lodging look to the **Holiday Inn Express** (719-384-2900), the

Sometimes a particular hole will cause a choke—a choke hole…Like the 18th at Cypress. It's like walking into a certain room in a big dark house when you were a kid—you get this fear that hits you.—Dave Marr

Stagecoach Inn (719-384-5476), and the historic **Finney House Bed & Breakfast** (719-384-8758).

LAMAR

ELEV. 3,622 POP. 8,343

Lamar, like so many in towns of the west, was born from the railroad and has an interesting story behind its founding. A.R. Black, who owned everything in sight at railroad milepost 499 (the distance from Atchison, Kansas), was perfectly happy running cattle on the rich grasslands, which were fertile from the Arkansas River's irrigation and loaded with cottonwood and plum trees. But old man Black became annoyed with all the farmers moving into the area, and when they organized in 1866 and asked him to donate some land for a town, he refused. The folks said they would just move three miles away to post 502 and take the railroad depot, too. Black thought they were bluffing. He was wrong and Lamar was born on May 24, 1886.

SPREADING ANTLERS GOLF COURSE

THE GOLF Like many courses on the southeastern plains of Colorado, the scenery is bleak here, and the course takes pride in their fun, challenging layouts that is in excellent condition. Willow Creek is present on six of nine holes and there are some trees and some moderately hilly sections. Spreading Antlers is another track where a tee time is generally not required.

THE DETAILS 719-336-5274. South Hwy. 287, Lamar, CO 81052.
- Labron Harris, 1965. 9 holes. Par 35. White/Blue - 6,069 (68.8/117). Gold/White - 5,716 (67/114). Red/Gold - 5,228 (69.2/116). Price - $.

GETTING THERE Located 2 miles south of Lamar at Hwy. 287 and 385. The course is on the east side and the pro shop is in the Elks Lodge building.

LAMAR NOTES

The best place to bed down is the **Cow Palace Inn** (719-336-7753), where you can spend the night and have steak and lobster, and homemade pie for dessert. Other options include the **Blue Spruce** (719-336-7454) and **Day's Inn** (719-336-5340). Other dining options include the **Hay Stack Steak House** or the **Hickory House**. Folks in Lamar celebrate the coming of the white snow geese in spring with the **High**

Golfers who claim they never cheat also lie.—Henry Beard

Plains Snow Goose Festival and Arts and Crafts Fair. The birds roost on the lakes and prairie in the area, a favorite stop on their annual migration. Other doings includes a celebration of Lamar's Birthday with a parade in May and the **Little Britches Rodeo** at the Prowers County Fair Grounds. **Oktoberfest** is a big hit in the fall.

LAS ANIMAS

ELEV. 3,893 POP. 2,758

The old ranch town of Las Animas is famous as the final home of legendary mountain man Kit Carson. Road-trippers passing through can partake of his legend by visiting the old buildings and historic relics of that time, working in a round of golf at the entertaining local 9-hole golf course, and taking a side-trip excursion to Boggsville (Carson's actual home around 1860), just three miles south of town on State Road 101.

LAS ANIMAS GOLF COURSE

THE GOLF The beauty of the Las Animas route is that it's mild-mannered and easy on your game. Expect wide fairways, flat terrain, short par 3s with no trouble, and a laid-back atmosphere. In fact, when we called for our tee time, the nice lady who answered the phone asked if we could call back because she was "holding onto a wild dog right now." The course has a little spice, with water in play on five holes, including a fun 382-yard par 4 that plays straight but involves a water carry on the approach.

THE DETAILS 719-456-2511. 220 Country Club Drive, Las Animas, CO 81054.
   • Ray Hardy, 1984. 9 holes. Par 34. Blue - 5,425 (65.1/108). White - 4,968 (66.9/111). Price - $.

GETTING THERE From Pueblo on I-25 take Hwy. 50 to Las Animas. Drive through town and turn right before the Arkansas River bridge and continue to the golf course.

LAS ANIMAS NOTES

The **John Martin Reservoir** is just east with its state park, and you'll also find fish in **Blue Lake** 18 miles away. The **Best Western Bent's Fort Inn** is a 38-room motel near the historic Santa Fe Trail, and 13 miles west is **Bent's Old Fort** National Historic Site.

I work to the rule that if the green appears to be fast, I will aim my putt at
an imaginary hole six to twelve inches short of the hole. —Bobby Locke

LA VETA

ELEV. 7,000 POP. 924

Located on the eastern side of La Veta Pass, tiny La Veta is known for its gigantic views, with the massive Spanish Peaks shadowing the town. The Sangre de Cristo Mountains loom to the west and the Cuchara River Valley is south. The beautiful location serves as the idyllic inspiration for a community of writers and artists, yet the cattle ranches and the cowboy culture still predominate.

Golfers passing through for rounds at the Grandote Peaks Golf Club can visit old Fort Francisco, the birthplace of the town in 1862. In 1877 a rail depot was built and for many years, the stretch of rail line between La Veta and Wagon Creek was the highest in the world. The old rail grade can still be seen west of town on the Old La Veta Pass route. The old depot building at the summit is listed on the National Register of Historic Places.

In 1836 Texas won its independence and claimed a narrow panhandle-like strip of mountain territory extending northward through Colorado to the 42nd parallel. Grandote Peaks was part of the territory declared as part of The Republic of Texas.

GRANDOTE PEAKS GOLF CLUB

THE GOLF If there was an award for Comeback Golf Course of the Year, surely Grandote Peaks would win it. By May 2002 Grandote Peaks had run out of water. The fairways turned brown, water had to be trucked in to keep greens and tees alive, and by the end of the summer every national golf magazine in the U.S. had written about Grandote Peaks' water woes.

But 2003 was a banner year for conditioning at this remote hidden gem. Green was the theme and visitors found the course in almost perfect condition to match its flawless views of the Spanish Peaks and Sangre de Cristo Mountains. What a difference a year makes!

The route, designed in 1984 by Tom Weiskopf and Jay Morrish, has been rated four stars by *Golf Digest*, and you'll see one of the reasons why from the No. 1 tee—a 570-yard, dogleg-left par 5.

The swift and cold Cucharas River roars past you on several holes and is definitely an intimidating presence, preparing you for the arduous finishing holes. No. 15 is the third-toughest hole, No. 16 is ranked fourth-hardest, and No. 17 is the most difficult: a 458-yard par 4 that plays into the prevailing south wind. No. 18 is a 522-yard par 5 with water crossing the fairway and a lake guarding the right side of the green.

SOUTHEAST

Practice is the only golf advice that is good for everybody.—Arnold Palmer

During the week this place is a dream, with very few golfers on the course, and the twilight rate might be the best bargain in Colorado.

THE DETAILS 719-742-3391. 5540 U.S. Hwy. 12, La Veta, CO 81055.
- www.grandotepeaks.com
- Tom Weiskopf, Jay Morrish, 1984. 18 holes. Par 72. Black - 7,085 (72.9/133). Blue - 6,630 (70.9/128). White - 6,315 (69.4/124). Red - 5,608 (70.6/130). Price - $$$.

GETTING THERE Take I-25 south to Walsenburg. Turn right (west) on US 160 to State Hwy. 12 and follow Hwy. 12 in to La Veta. The golf course is on the south side of La Veta on Hwy. 12.

LA VETA NOTES

Oktoberfest fills up Main Street in La Veta and many summer weekends are full of street vendors. Lodging options include four B&Bs: **Francisco Plaza Inn** (800-530-3040), Southwestern-styled Inn at the **Spanish Peaks B&B** (719-742-5313), 1899 **Bed & Breakfast Inn** (719-742-3576), and the **Hunter House B&B** (719-742-5577). Also consider the **La Veta Inn** (719-742-3700), where you're guaranteed a home-cooked meal along with affordable rooms. **La Veta Sports Pub & Grub** (719-742-3093) is also someplace to consider. Pre-golf breakfast is best served at the **Ryus Avenue Bakery** (719-742-3830). Don't miss **Charlie's**, an old-fashioned grocery store that offers supplies, a soda fountain, and ice cream. And Cuchara is a tiny resort town with fun food options just 12 miles south. **The Boardwalk** (719-742-3450), also known as the "Dog Bar", is famous for pizza, and **The Silver Spoon** (719-742-6133) is a mountain-rustic place to splurge for an evening.

PUEBLO

ELEV. 4,662 POP. 102,121

With one of the lowest elevations on the I-25 corridor, Pueblo is extremely warm in the summer. But the quality affordable golf, the abundance of places to find a cold beer and a meal in the historic Union Avenue District, and the charming Arkansas River Walk all make this a pleasant place to visit even though it's not too obvious with just a cursory look from I-25.

Travelers must stray from the interstate to discover that the town is loaded with shops and makes the ideal spot for a family weekend getaway, since there are plenty of non-golf activities to entertain restless spouses.

"Never had a lesson in my life" is a phrase uttered with smug satisfaction by a good many people. The correct reply is, of course, "That's why you are no better than you are." —Henry Longhurst

DESERT HAWK AT PUEBLO WEST

THE GOLF Desert Hawk at Pueblo West is in the city's newest growth corridor and features sweeping vistas of the Sangre de Cristos and Spanish Peaks to the south and Pikes Peak to the north. The brawny 7,341-yard route features lengthy par 3-tests of 200 yards or more and receptive greens that have recently been rebuilt. Other recent renovations include facelifts of bunkers and the rerouting of hole 5 around a new lake.

THE DETAILS 719-547-2280. 251 McCulloch Boulevard, Pueblo, CO 81007.
  • Johnny Bulla, 1972. 18 holes. Par 72. Gold - 7,341 (73.6/123). Blue - 6,805 (71/118). White - 6,328 (68.9/115). Red --5,588 (70.4/122). Price - $.

GETTING THERE Take I-25 to Hwy. 50, then head west to McCulloch Blvd. and turn left.

A 1923 shot of Pueblo Country Club's original clubhouse.

Golf and wagering go together as smoothly as "double" and "bogey."—James Y. Bartlett

ELMWOOD GOLF COURSE

THE GOLF The former City Park Golf Course, Elmwood assumed its old name (from the 1950s) in 2002, perhaps searching for some of the nostalgia for which the course is known.

In 1963 during the Southern Colorado Open, Tommy Bolt was paired with Bob Blanton when Blanton nailed one into some deep rough and took relief. When he showed up on the next tee and started to hit, Bolt said: "Hey, fella, who gave you the honors?" As the story unfolded, Blanton asked for relief and got it from a guy selling root beer in the gallery.

Babe Didrikson Zaharias was from Port Arthur, TX, but married George Zaharias, a professional wrestler from Pueblo. After winning the British Women's Open in 1947, she was presented with Denver's "Key to the City".

While Bolt and Blanton bickered about it over the next few holes, Mo Springer, the City Park pro, arrived and negated the ruling. Then another area pro, Pat Rea, passed both of them on the way to the tournament title.

Then there's the story of the tipsy widow who asked to spread her husband's ashes over the course, but decided just to dump the whole vase into the 15th cup. When the superintendent heard the news he had to shovel the gray stuff out. Gary Gettman, who has worked in the pro shop since 1975, says every time he reaches No. 15 green he thinks of the deceased golfer.

Elmwood is an easy walk, a traditional course built in the 1930s and then upgraded in 1965 with a new clubhouse and another executive nine. The fairways and greens are immaculately groomed among mature trees that add beauty and challenge.

An irrigation ditch marches through the shorter course, providing some trouble for worm-burners. The greens are mostly flat with bentgrass of moderate speed.

By whatever name, this course has seen some interesting history, and thanks to Pueblo's moderate climate it stays busy, hosting as many as 100,000 rounds in one year.

Certainly when you're playing for a lot of dough, you should hole everything. From four feet to two feet to one inch—putt it into the hole. It only takes a moment and it avoids all arguments.—Sam Snead

THE DETAILS 719-561-4946. 3900 Thatcher Avenue, Pueblo, CO 81005.
- John Cochran, 1932, WPA Project. Course update - George Boyd, 1965. 18 holes. Par 70. Blue - 6,483 (68.9/111). White - 6,263 (67.9/109). Red - 5,984 (72.3/120). Black - 4,322 (60/96). White - 4,046 (31.4/92). Red - 3,808 (30.6/90). Price - $$.
- Executive Nine. Price - $.

GETTING THERE Take I-25 to Hwy. 50, then head west to Pueblo Blvd. Turn south on Pueblo Blvd. and go over the river, turn left on Thatcher. The course is on the right.

PUEBLO COUNTRY CLUB

THE GOLF The PCC's initial president, O.G. Pope, first pushed for a golf club back in 1893 at the Fountain Lake Hotel, but panic over the price of silver and the economic depression that followed delayed progress. Finally momentum built, and the group shaped the rugged sagebrush and cacti-infested property into a 9-hole course that opened for play in June 1903. Members paid dues of 50 cents per month. Paul Reitemeier, the first golf pro, showed up from Scotland in 1919. With his hickory-shafted clubs he amazed the locals with 300-yard drives in the light, humidity-less air of the semi-arid Colorado plains.

More that a century later, more than 700 members call Pueblo Country Club home. They get their rounds in on a short front nine that offers tree-lined fairways and round, flat greens, and a newer back nine with wide-open fairways and larger, more contoured greens. No. 9, a 404-yard par 4, plays into an uphill dogleg left and is a favorite hole despite out-of-bounds trouble.

THE DETAILS 719-542-2941. 3200 8th Avenue, Pueblo, CO 81008.
- Henry Hughes, 1903. 18 holes. Par 71. Blue - 6,428 (69.3/122). White - 6,094 (67.8/117). Red - 5,597 (70.7/127). Private, reciprocal play accepted when pro makes tee time. Price - $$$.

GETTING THERE Take I-25 to 29th St. (exit 100B), then turn west on 29th St. to 8th Avenue. Drive north on 8th Ave. to the course.

WALKING STICK GOLF COURSE

THE GOLF One of the must-play hidden gems of Colorado golf, Walking Stick is city-owned and Keith Foster-designed. Since it opened in 1991, the links-style track has consistently been heaped with praise, winning awards and becoming

---

Don't give anything and don't expect to be given anything. I've seen the best players in the world miss putts inside two feet, so no putt is a sure thing. If there's any kind of a sidehill or downhill contour, you'd be surprised how many "gimmes" can be missed. —Sam Snead

the favorite Pueblo municipal. The layout traverses barren arroyos with beautiful mountain views, quick greens, and fairways that were once forested by the native cholla (cacti). The cholla, when dead and dried, looks like a walking stick or cane, hence the course name.

This 7,142-yard, par-72 layout has a reputation for "funky" greens that are challenging because of their roller-coaster nature. Locals know to take advantage of the par 5s because the par 4s are tough.

The par-5 fourth hole is a 544-yard dogleg left with an arroyo down the entire left side. This one is reachable in two, but the green has two climactic tiers. If the pin is on top and you're on the lower tier, this is one tough putt to get close. No. 6 is a 197-yard par 3 that has a long bunker below the putting surface on the left.

One real treat is the post-round festivities in Nachos Fireside, the Stick's restaurant. Non-golfers come here just for the foot-long Monster Burrito smothered in green chile.

THE DETAILS 719-584-3400. 4301 Walking Stick Blvd., Pueblo, CO 81001.
- Keith Foster of Arthur Hills, 1991. 18 holes. Par 72. Black - 7,142 (73/134). Blue - 6,600 (70.8/126). White - 6,000 (68.1/119). Red - 5,191 (68.6/121). Price - $$.

GETTING THERE From I-25 go east on Hwy. 50 and look for the exit at the University of Southern Colorado. Go left over the highway and follow the zigzagging road. Look for Walking Stick signs. The clubhouse is on your left.

PUEBLO NOTES

The elegant **Abriendo Inn** (719-544-2703, www.abriendoinn.com) is the preferred locale for weekend getaways, a turn-of-the-century house near the downtown district. For breakfast try the Italian Egg & Vegetable Oven Frittata, South of the Border Potatoes, and Apple Oven Omelet. Other options include the **Pueblo Marriott** (719-542-3200) and **Jeanie's Hotel** (719-542-0796). Downtown look to the storefront café known as **Steel City Diner & Bakeshop** (719-295-1100) for microbrews, wines, and tasty meals. And Mexican food lovers head to **Jorge's Sombrero** (719-564-6486) for authentic fare, as well as the easy-going **Mexi-Deli** (719-583-1275). For Italian find **Joe Tomato Italian Delicacies** (719-584-3007), an impressive shop with a full deli that is ideal for lunch. The best watering hole is the **Irish Brewpub** (719-542-9974), an old family-owned brewery that serves outstanding, unique fare (lamb, ostrich, and buffalo burgers), and began serving its own trademark beers in 1996.

SOUTHEAST

There is no other sphere in which a belief in oneself has such immediate effects as it has in golf.—P.G. Wodehouse

The Pueblo area offers some of the best whitewater rafting in the state on the Arkansas River, where you'll find plenty of guide services:

- American Adventure Expeditions (800-288-0675)
- Echo Canyon River Expeditions (800-748-2953)
- River Runners LTD (800-525-2081)
- Whitewater Adventure Outfitters (800-530-8212)
- Bill Dvoraks Kayak & Rafting Expeditions (800-824-3795)
- Raft Masters (800-568-7238)
- Adventure Quest Expeditions (888-448-7238).

Gamblers can get their fix on greyhound races or thoroughbred simulcasts at the Pueblo **Greyhound Park** (719-566-0370), where live racing runs from October through April. The **El Pueblo Museum** (719-583-0453), **Rosemount House Museum** (719-545-5290), **Sangre de Cristo Arts Center** (719-295-7200), and the **Pueblo City Zoo and Park** are all worthy venues for killing time.

ROCKY FORD

ELEV. 4, 178 POP. 4,286

Rocky Ford, named by Kit Carson because of the rocky, graveled crossing on the Arkansas River, is famous for the sweetest cantaloupes in the world, which are in season from late summer to early fall. And since 1878 they've celebrated Watermelon Day, where you can dig in and devour watermelons for free. The wayfaring golfer is welcome here, since the sport is popular in Rocky Ford; over 200 members partake of the great game at the immaculate Rocky Ford Country Club.

ROCKY FORD COUNTRY CLUB

THE GOLF Rocky Ford residents take pride in their challenging little 9-hole lay-out, which is open to the public and in great condition even during times of drought. Hills, canals, doglegs, and quick bentgrass greens give this course some bite.

Course manager Jim Hamm, who is improving the course by enlarging and extending the tee boxes, says folks from Pueblo drive here, get out of their car, and tee off. "You can't do that in the big city," Hamm says. "They can drive here and play quicker than they can stand in line at a golf course in Pueblo."

SOUTHEAST

If the green appears to be slow, and particularly if during the last two or three feet to the hole the ground is uphill, I hit it firmly for the back of the hole.—Bobby Locke

THE DETAILS 719-254-7528. 91 Play Park Hill, Rocky Ford, CO 81067.
- Architect unknown, 1927. 9 holes. Par 35. White/Blue - 5,677 (66.7/119). Red/White - 5,521 (70/117). Price - $.

GETTING THERE Head through town on Hwy. 50 and drive south on Main Street for about a mile.

ROCKY FORD NOTES

Set aside some post-golf time in the **RFCC Clubhouse Grill**. "We are practically the only place in town to get real American food," Hamm said. "You can get hamburgers to T-bone steaks." The **Country Morning Coffee Shop** (719-254-6596) and the **El Capitan Dining Room** (719-254-7471) are other choices. Spend the night at the **High Chaparral**, which has been remodeled and includes an indoor swimming pool. Look for the melons at **Smith's Corner** (719-254-6960), located on Highway 50 and open from July to October.

SPRINGFIELD

ELEV. 4,365 POP. 1,562

Springfield is the county seat and largest town of Baca County in the southeastern corner of Colorado. Agriculture dominates this part of the plains where the road though Springfield was once a main stagecoach route between the Texas line and the Canadian border. Road trips here are worthy of consideration since the municipal golf course is one of only three left in Colorado with sand greens, and Springfield serves as headquarters for excursions into the southern unit of Comanche National Grassland—a remote area characterized by rolling plains dotted with farms and ranches, tree-lined creeks, and scenic stops like Picture Canyon and Carrizo Creek.

SPRINGFIELD MUNICIPAL GOLF COURSE

THE GOLF The Springfield course, built by a committee of World War II vets after returning home from battle, includes a dry creek that runs through the course, buffalo-grass fairways that generally need a good amount of water (there is no irrigation system), and thick, wild rough loaded with rattlesnakes, cactus, and soapweed.

Springfield, Hugo, and Eads are reportedly the only three sand greens left in Colorado, and some locals will argue that it's time for Springfield's to go. A fund

Consider, if you will, that on a par-72 course you can bogey 17 of the 18 holes and still break 90. –Cliff McAdams

SOUTHEAST

drive is underway to replace them with artificial greens because dealing with the sand is old hat for the regulars. Once on the green you use a "drag" to smooth out a path to the hole, which is just a cup full of sand. To putt remove the cup, then replace it when you're finished and rake in a circular motion around the hole.

It's worth the $5 honor system green fee (see the pay box) just to experience such a wild way to play the game of golf.

THE DETAILS 719-523-4609 for the Club Secretary. No course phone. Hwy. 160 East, Springfield, CO 81073.

- Member-designed, 1945. 9 holes. Par 35. Sand greens. Men - 5,608 (64.2/96). Women - 5,588 (70.7/124). Price - $.

GETTING THERE Go one mile south of Springfield on Hwy. 287, then west on Hwy. 160. The course is on the right.

SPRINGFIELD NOTES

Pre-golf all-you-can-eat pancakes can be had on Saturdays at the **Longhorn Steakhouse** (719-523-6554), which also serves steaks, burgers, and everything else for lunch and dinner. Also dig in at the **Cobblestone Grill** (719-523-6831), **Trails End** (719-523-6788), or the **Bar 4 Corral** (719-523-4065), then bed down at the historic **Stage Stop Hotel** (719-523-4737, www.stagestophotel.com). In March and September the city celebrates the **Equinox Festival** (www.springfieldcoloinfo.com) at Picture Canyon, where a prehistoric calendar rock marks the first day of spring and fall. Springfield is the **"Goose Hunting Capital of the USA"** and serves as the winter home to thousands of ducks and Canada geese. Hunters can find them at **Two Buttes Reservoir**.

TRINIDAD

ELEV. 6,019 POP. 9,078

In this old mining town situated on the Mountain Branch of the Santa Fe Trail, it's not hard to walk the historic streets and imagine a rambunctious Old West scene of saloons and a red-light district with the likes of Marshal Bat Masterson and Doc Holliday attending to business.

After coal was discovered in 1876, folks from all over the world came here to give Trinidad its culturally diverse population that includes Northern Europeans, Hispanic, Italian, Greek, Polish, Irish, Lebanese, and Slavic families. Trinidad is the first stop in Colorado, just 13 miles across the border from

Much dripping wears away a stone, and continual fussing and fretting…wears away the golfer.—Bernard Darwin on too much waggle

New Mexico and lofty Raton Pass. Road-trippers who actually slow down to stop and play golf here will come back year after year. And there may be more golf in the future, since a development named Stone Ridge has been approved with an 18-hole Baxter Spann-designed course as part of the master plan.

TRINIDAD GOLF COURSE

THE GOLF Located off of I-25, the TGC is basic, traditional golf at its finest, with superb conditioning when the area is void of drought. Some say this is the best 9-hole route in Colorado—"a Cadillac course at Chevrolet prices."

Although the course's architect is unknown, some speculate that its opening dates back as far as 1915, designed by either Donald Ross or one of his crewmen while working on Broadmoor East. In May of 1940 the layout re-opened as a "grass course" following a WPA project that was sponsored by the city and interested local golfers. The WPA planted the Chinese elm trees that line most fairways to accentuate the native piñons. Wildlife is abundant, and the occasional bear has been known to mosey across the links.

The greens here are excellent, but demonic. You will see Ross traits in the putting surfaces—some have false fronts and some are bowled, making this short course a challenge. Most slope from back to front (except No. 1), and there aren't too many flat, straight putts. The par 5s are definite birdie holes, but the par 3s are tough. Rather than taking dead aim at the flag on the par 3s, play the contours and let them carry the ball toward the hole.

The slightly uphill 181-yard No. 7, with a ravine in front, could test the most accomplished hack. Missing the green calls for a miracle recovery, but hitting the green is no bargain, either. Many a forlorn golfer has nailed a beautiful tee shot three feet above the hole and three-putted. Two putts on this green are cause for celebration.

The other par 3, the 135-yard No. 5, has a sloped green from back to front and takes proper placement to remain on the green or get near the pin. Follow the contour by hitting to the right side of the green to keep it on; if you miss just a hair right of the green, the ball will just bounce straight down the slope. On No. 5 it's imperative to keep it within the green's collar so the ball will take the slope to the left.

No. 3 is spectacular: the highest spot on the layout and the best view of the Sangre de Cristos and the Spanish Peaks. However, the trademark is a "bell hole" with a blind tee shot. No. 2, a 326-yard par 4, has a sign telling you to wait for the bell signal. Stroke the tee shot down the left fairway boundary. When the tee shot lands it kicks hard right following the wicked slope. Those in the neigh-

---

As I stood addressing the ball I would watch for my right hand to jump. At the end of two seconds I would not be looking at the ball at all. My gaze would have become riveted on my right hand. I simply could not resist the desire to see what it was going to do.—Harry Vardon on the yips

borhood of the bell have 125 yards to an elevated green. It's all carry with a false front and two tiers—impossible to run it on in lush conditions.

This is a busy course and its Labor Day Tournament is the second longest running in Colorado, dating back 64 years. Only Sterling Country Club eclipses that run with 77 years. Trinidad's Memorial Day Tournament has been hosted for 38 consecutive years.

THE DETAILS 719-846-4015. 1417 Nolan Drive, Trinidad, CO 81082.
- Architect unknown, 1915. 9 holes. Par 36. Blue - 6,158 (68.8/119). Red - 5,348 (68.9/121). Price - $.

GETTING THERE Exit I-25 at mile marker 13A, and head east toward Santa Fe Trail Drive. Drive uphill for a quarter mile, and look for the course on the right.

TRINIDAD NOTES

The carne asada at **Estivins Mexican Family Restaurant** (719-846-7491) is note worthy, and you can also find good meals at **El Capitan**, the **White Spot Cafe**, and **Nana & Nano's Pasta House**. Also consider The **Rock House Cafe** down I-25 in Aguilar. Weekenders should look to set up shop at the western **Black Jack's Saloon Steakhouse & Inn** (719-846-9501), a former brothel complete with reminders of hooligan Black Jack Ketchum and Bat Masterson, along with solid B&B accommodations. **Chef Liu's** (719-868-3333) is packed at lunch and only a block from the golf course. Overnighters should look to the **Chicosa Canyon B&B** (719-846-6199) or the **Inn at the Santa Fe Trail B&B** (719-846-7869). The historic Victorian architecture offers plenty of sights worth visiting, including an adobe named **The Baca House** built in 1908. The old West Theater, which now houses the **Fox Movie Theater**, is Colorado's last remaining theater with a double-tiered balcony. Trinidad's locale places gasoline in high demand, so beware of the high prices and fill up before you arrive.

WALSENBURG

ELEV. 6,182 POP. 4,182

Originally settled as Plaza de los Leones in 1862, Walsenburg was named after Fred Walsen, a businessman who settled here about 1870 and opened the first coal mine in the county just west of town in 1876. Located just off I-25, Walsenburg is a natural stopping place for the restless golfer, and the gateway to La Veta Pass and the San Luis Valley Lathrop State Park is home to two lakes and the golf course. The charming towns of La Veta and Cuchara are nearby,

---

Directly, as I felt that it was about to jump (right hand), I would snatch at the ball in a desperate effort to play the shot before the involuntary movement could take effect. Up would go my head and body with a start and off would go the ball, anywhere but on the proper line.—Harry Vardon on the yips.

and the town is the starting point for the Highway of Legends Scenic and Historic Byway.

WALSENBURG GOLF COURSE

THE GOLF The WGC can be testy, for fairways that roll up and down relentlessly and raised, contoured greens that never seem to leave you with a straight putt. The design also features a few piñon trees that can get in the way. Your best bet for eagle is the 285-yard, par-4 No. 5, but beware of the severe back-to-front slope of the green.

At one point, plans were in place to expand the course with an additional nine; however, water issues and political struggles have slowed the process.

THE DETAILS 719-738-2730. Lathrop State Park, Highway 160, Walsenburg, CO 81089.

- Clyde Young, Gerald Aliano, 1966. 9 holes. Par 36. Blue - 5,768 (66/102). White - 5,498 (68.1/110). Price - $.

GETTING THERE Go west in Walsenburg on Hwy. 160 to Lathrop State Park, located just outside and west of town.

WALSENBURG NOTES

Lathrop State Park, packed on weekends with productive fishing, is nestled among the piñons and junipers on the prairie west of Walsenburg. The majestic Spanish Peaks serve as a stunning background for campers and fishermen. **Martin Lake** has a nice beach for swimming. **Horseshoe Lake** is crystal clear and smooth, and loaded with muskies, catfish, largemouth bass, and rainbow trout. The locals recommend **George's Drive Inn** for breakfast and lunch—one of those "nobody goes there because it's always crowded" kind of places. Other options include the **Aly's Fireside Café** (719-738-3993), maybe the best restaurant in town, or the eclectic **Tes' Drive Inn** (719-738-1710), where the sopapilla burger is preferred. For lodging the isolation and views are best at the **Rio Cucharas Inn** (719-738-1282), just outside of town heading toward La Veta. In town try the **La Plaza de Leones B & B** (719-738-5700), conveniently located downtown and kid-friendly.

SOUTHEAST

The art or practice of winning a sports contest by expedients of doubtful propriety (as by distracting an opponent) without actual violation of the rules of the game.."—Webster's definition of Gamesmanship

BORDER CROSSINGS

Some argue that there's no justification for leaving the beautiful state of Colorado for golf excursions across the border in neighboring states. However the restless golfer is always in search of variety, and Utah, Wyoming, New Mexico, Nebraska, and Kansas all offer unique golf experiences different from what Colorado offers. Who would have thought in the 1960s that playing golf through sand dunes would be a modern trend in the USA? But after all, the Irish, Scottish, and English have been doing it for centuries.

Utah has its red-rock country. New Mexico has more starkly beautiful desert courses. Wyoming has its own mountain beauty. Nebraska has its sand hills. And Kansas may be as flat as a cornfield in many areas, but plains golf is golf. You can have fun anywhere.

When you're ready to extend the golf road trip, here are a few nearby border crossings.

FARMINGTON, NM
51 miles from Durango, CO

Piñon Hills Golf Course (505-326-6066), is the best, most affordable golf course in the US. This 7,249-yard, 18-hole gem (74.3/140) is open year-round and traverses canyons and arroyos among sandstone rock outcroppings. Designed by Ken Dye, it is a must-play for any travel golfer in the world.

Built in the high desert, with bentgrass greens and water hazards, the course's signature hole, No. 15, is a 228-yard par 3 that plays through a canyon. Water hazards come into play on a few holes. Since opening in 1989, Piñon Hills has been honored by every major golf magazine in the country. Locals can buy an annual pass for a mere $425 and non-residents can still walk it for under $30.

The par-3 "pitch and putt" known as **Civitan Golf Course** (505-599-1194) is a Jack Snyder design built in 1950 and is a favorite place to hone your short-game skills. A water hazard comes into play on one hole of this par-27, 1,300-yard shorty.

KIRTLAND, NM
60 miles from Durango, CO

Legend has it that **Riverview Golf Course** (505)-598-0140 came to be when some El Paso Gas Company folks were having a chat in a coffee shop. The course was built for their employees. That was 1954 and nine more holes were added in 1998 by Finger, Dye and Spann. Trees line the fairways on flat terrain, but No. 9, a 405-yard par 4, has a sharp incline up to the green. Riverview spreads out at 6,853 yards (70.5/121). The La Plata Mountains and Shiprock Monument are included in the vista on this wide-open course.

AZTEC, NM
36 miles from Durango, CO

Hidden Valley Golf Club (505-334-3248) is a new 18-hole, par-70 course that opened in 2001. Testy greens make this one a toughie, but you can manage it tee-to-green. Putting surfaces at Nos. 6, 7, and 8 are severely sloped. There's just one sand trap, but hidden sand washes might catch an errant shot. It measures 6,104 yards (6.76/110).

MONTICELLO, UT
167 miles from Grand Junction, CO

The Hideout (435-587-2468) is a lengthy drive from anywhere, but this 1961 gem, situated at 7,000 feet, is a traditional wonder that's worth the drive. First known as Blue Mountain Meadows, it is a difficult course because of the countless trees lining the fairways. Located in the heart of Canyon Country, it measures 6,700 yards, is surrounded by national and state parks, and has a canal running through the course. It was expanded to 18 holes in 2002. Legends claim that many outlaws and cattle rustlers came to hide out on this spot.

MOAB, UTAH
112 miles from Grand Junction, CO

Moab Golf Club (435-259-6488) is located in the awesome rock formations of this scenic town. This 6,819-yard, par 72 (72.2/125) borders along an impressive natural setting, and trees can play havoc with your shot selection. Three holes have water hazards and the signature hole is No. 6, a 475-yard, par 4 with a vista from a cliff that overlooks the entire city. The course was built in 1986.

VERNAL, UT
51 miles from Rangely, CO

Dinaland Golf Course (435-781-1428) is a 1993 design that covers 6,773 yards (71.5/129) with trees, open fairways, ponds, and streams. Bunkers dot each hole and the signature hole is No. 12, a 452-yard par 4 requiring a huge tee shot up a fairway that is protected by lakes on both sides. The approach is long and tough.

ROCK SPRINGS, WY
161 miles from Rangely, CO

White Mountain Golf Course (307-352-1415) is a long way from Dinosaur, but closer to the border of Colorado. Its award-winning 7,072 yard layout (72.4/122) is demanding and presents narrow fairways. It's scenic, with trees and lakes; *Golf Digest* named it No. 8 in the state back in 1996.

CHEYENNE, WY
46 miles from Fort Collins, CO

Airport Golf Course (307-637-6418) is a 1927 municipal gem of 6,121 yards (67.1/99) that still presents a challenge because of all the mature trees. Water hazards (lakes) come into play on several different occasions. The Wyoming Open is held here every July.

Prairie View Golf Course (307-637-6420) is a 9-hole course that features some flat and some rolling terrain with wide fairways, great for the beginner. The wind can get blustery, giving this one some bite, but it is an easy walk. The course lays out at par 36, 3,080 yards (34.4/109).

KIMBALL, NE
76 miles from Sterling, CO

Four Winds Golf Course (308-235-4241) is flat and wide open, but the greens are sloped on this 6,551-yard course (70.4/116), which was built in 1970. Golfers must negotiate a ditch and lake with a river coming into play on four holes.

CHAPPELL, NE
16 miles from Julesburg, CO

Chappell Golf Course (308-874-2729) is a 9-hole course located on I-80, with wide fairways and many trees that line fairways. Sloped greens and water hazards can make it a challenge. The signature hole is No. 9, which requires a shot over a pond to the green. This par 36 course is 3,315 yards (35/111).

ENDERS, NE
78 miles from Julesburg, CO

Enders Lake Golf Course (308-394-5491) is a 9-holer with large, contoured greens and fairways lined by trees. Built in 1969, it traverses 6,592 yards (70.9/115) and has four holes that dogleg. The layout consists of wide, straight bluegrass fairways and bentgrass greens that are small.

GRANT, NE
50 miles from Julesburg, CO

Grant Golf Club (308-352-9978) is demanding, locals say, with plush fairways, large greens, and 9 holes. It rolls out at a short 5,724 yards (64.8/106).

BIRD CITY, KS
70 miles from Burlington, CO

Bird City Golf Course (785-734-2708) is your chance to play sand greens in a small town of 500 folks. There's an honor system for paying green fees, so just drive up and tee off. Members say that rabbits and ground squirrels might be in your line of fire at any time on this course, which is located in a cow pasture. There are water hazards that come into play after it rains. It's a par 36 at 2,700 yards.

SAINT FRANCIS, KS
65 miles from Burlington, CO

Riverside Recreation Association Golf Course (785-332-3401) is a 9-hole, bentgrass greens course that opened in 1969. Residents say it's the best in northwestern Kansas. A river runs through it and comes into play on several holes. Ladies tee off from the same set of tees as the men, but their par is 39 instead of 36.

SHARON SPRINGS, KS
60 miles from Burlington, CO

Sharon Springs Golf Course (785-852-4220) is a 9-hole, 1961 golf course with bentgrass greens, buffalo-grass fairways, rolling terrain, uneven lies, and tall rough. There are eight natural greens and one that's artificial. The greens here are also surrounded by gnarly, wicked taller grass. The course plays to par 34 at 2,711 yards.

GOODLAND, KS
32 miles from Burlington, CO

Routed by Kenny Yoke in 1969, **Sugar Hills Golf Club** (785-899-2785) is an 18-holer with large greens and many trees on its 6,210 yards (69.6/112). The club hosted the State Women's Amateur Tournament in 1993. Locals say it's a natural beauty. The back nine was added in 1993.

SYRACUSE, KS
49 miles from Lamar, CO

Tamarisk Golf Course (316-384-7832) is a 9-hole course designed in 1996 by Denver's Ric Buckton. Undulating bentgrass greens, mature trees, bunkers, and tamarisk bushes highlight this layout, which has water on two holes. A few Canada geese live here year-round. This is a par 36 measuring 3,251 yards (34.9/111).

RATON, NM
21 miles from Trinidad, CO

Small Raton is a scenic and historic, just minutes from the Colorado border on I-25 with views of the Spanish Peaks and Sangre de Cristos. Situated at 6,500 feet, **Raton Country Club** (505-445-8113) is actually a municipal located in the foothills with piñon and juniper trees lining the fairways. The nine holes were built in 1922 by a coal-mining baron and have bentgrass greens, lots of trees, water, and natural hazards from the rugged terrain.

RED RIVER, NM
92 miles from Alamosa, CO

Red Eagle Golf Course (505-377-3396) is located minutes from the summer haven and winter ski resort of Red River. This 18-hole, 7,002-yarder was actually closed in 2002 because of the drought, so be sure to call before you head this way. Views of the Sangre de Cristos make it scenic; there are several dogleg fairways, and some holes have water in play. Bentgrass greens are medium in speed and size. The signature hole is No. 9, a 572-yard par 5. It heads downhill and is protected by water on the front and right of the green. The 1997 layout was designed by Brett Glenn and Bill Gill.

TAOS, NM
90 miles from Alamosa, CO

Taos Country Club (888-TAOS-GOLF, 505-758-7300) is a Top Ten New Mexico course—target golf in deep sagebrush. The course is in mint condition and has hosted the State Amateur and Northern New Mexico Senior Championships. This par 72 measures 7,302 yards (72.8/124). Views include the Taos Box Canyon and surrounding peaks. At one time before the New Mexico daily-fee boom, it was ranked as high as No. 3 in the state by *Golf Digest*.

LONGER TRIPS, BUT WORTH THE EFFORT

NEBRASKA

Think you can finagle a round at private **Sand Hills Golf Club** (308-546-2437) near Mullen? It is No. 1 on *Golfweek*'s list of modern golf courses. Even though it's a five-hour drive from Denver, this is a must-play for any world traveler. Befriend a member and make the drive to this Ben Crenshaw- and Bill Coore-designed prize routed among the rolling terrain and sandhills of north-central Nebraska. This is exclusive, par-71 7,089-yarder is one of the best courses in the U.S.

A Colorado note—four Denver investors have purchased 3,000 acres next door to Sand Hills and plan on a national membership golf club with attached lodging for its members. This foursome includes restaurant owner Tony Pasquini, technology executive Timber Notestine, and two lawyers, Tim Kratz and Bill Martin, who assembled together the team. Jack Nicklaus has already visited the property and an invitation might also go to Tom Doak.

Gothenburg is 297 miles from Denver, but **Wild Horse Golf Course** (play-wildhorse.com, 308-537-7700) is a minimalist wonder. Grassy prairies define this Scottish-links public course, a 1998 design by Dave Axland and Dan Proctor. Wild Horse is ranked No. 6 in the state by *Golf Digest*. Opened in 1999, this wild looking layout has thick native grasses on the borders and measures 6,805 at par 72 (73/125). Bring plenty of golf balls.

Another tough test near Ogallala is **Bayside Golf Course** (www.bayside golf.com, 308-287-4653) that is known for forced carries on just about every hole. It's located on a rugged land of many dry washes and arroyos with numerous blind or semi-blind shots. This one was designed by Wild Horse's Axland and Proctor.

KANSAS

Private **Prairie Dunes Country Club** (www.prairiedunes.com, 620-662-0581) in Hutchinson hosted the 57th U.S. Women's Championship. It will also host the 2006 U.S. Senior Open. But the top daily-fee course in the state is Colbert Hills in Manhattan, Kansas State's home course.

Colbert Hills (www.colberthills.com, 877-916-4653 or 785-776-6475) was designed by Jim Colbert and Jeff Brauer and locals call it the "Big Course." They also call the back tees the "bruiser tees," measuring a 7,525 yards. Both courses are highly ranked by national golf magazines.

UTAH

Home to red-rock wonders, Utah is serious golf. St. George is only 120 miles north of Las Vegas and gateway to Zion National Park, Bryce Canyon National Park, Lake Powell, and the Grand Canyon. Don't miss **Entrada at Snow Mountain** (www.golfentrada.com, 435-674-7500) and Coral Canyon (www.coralcanyongolf.com, 435-688-1700). Entrada is No. 3 in the state and **Coral Canyon** No. 4 in the *Golf Digest* state rankings. **Sunbrook Golf Club**, Sun River, South Gate, Oasis Golf Club, Green Spring and Dixie Hills are other options (www.cityofstgeorge.com/golf).

In Park City, the talk is about five planned championship 18-hole golf cours-es—part of the **Pete Dye Canyon Golf Trail**, which includes Promontory. It trav-erses sagebrush meadows and rolling hills with panoramic views of the Wasatch Mountains—home to Deer Valley, Park City Mountain Resort, The Canyons, and Utah Olympic Park. (www.parkcitygolf.com).

NEW MEXICO

Check out Golf on the Santa Fe Trail (www.golfonthesantafetrail.com) for Black Mesa Golf Club, Paa-Ko Ridge, Twin Warriors, Isleta Eagle, The Championship Course at the University of New Mexico, Santa Ana, Pueblo de Cochiti, and Marty Sanchez Links de Santa Fe. Also discover Towa Golf Resort near Santa Fe (www.towagolf.com).

WYOMING

Play golf in the shadows of the Tetons and minutes from Yellowstone National Park at either **Jackson Hole Golf Resort** (www.jhgtc.com, 307-734-3855) or **Teton Pines** (www.tetonpines.com, 307-733-1005, 800-238-2223).

Jackson Hole was opened in 1963, and Robert Trent Jones Jr. arrived in 1973 to redesign it and showcase some of Wyoming's most famous Grand Teton views. Multiple USGA National Championships have been staged here, and the course is consistently ranked No. 1 in Wyoming by *Golf Digest*.

Designed by Arnold Palmer, Teton Pines in Jackson Hole is No. 2 in the state. This resort course is a must-play course for any avid golfer.

Sheridan's **The Powder Horn** (www.thepowderhorn), designed by Dick Bailey in 1997, has 27 holes named, Mountain, Stag, and Eagle overlooking the Big Horn Mountains. It was originally built as a private club, but the public can still play here. It features a replica of the famous Swilcan Burn Bridge at St. Andrews.

Kendrick Golf Course is Sheridan's municipal (307-674-8148, www.sheridan-wyoming.org).

COLORADO GOLF PROJECTS

Despite the drought and a multitude of new golf courses that have opened in the past 10 years, Colorado's golf boom continues at full steam. All of the projects listed below are in the planning stages and could become reality or get put on hold for lack of water, financing issues, or a number of reasons.

FOUR MILE RANCH IN CAÑON CITY

Jim Engh's most recent Colorado project comes on the heels of another award—*Golf Digest* named him Architect of the Year for 2003.

Four Mile Ranch in Cañon City is situated on land east of town with terrain that includes piñon and juniper trees and views of the Sangre de Cristos. It begins on flatter land, but climbs into the hills with elevation changes of 130 feet or more. Mini-buttes 20 feet high are also in sight.

One par 5, No. 15, will have a drop of 130 feet to the fairway. Engh says he will mix styles to make extreme variety. Some holes will include modern features, and some will have pure Irish characteristics.

"On probably four or five holes I won't touch a thing," Engh said. "No. 6 is a par 5 that is cut through a dune but the rest of the terrain remains as it is today—it will be a wild little Irish golf hole."

Four Mile Ranch will be a master-planned community, but semi-private, making it a daily-fee course for the public. Ground-breaking is scheduled for spring 2004.

BLACK HAWK, CENTRAL CITY

The old mining towns of Black Hawk on Highway 199 and Central City, a mile uphill, certainly have their share of tourists with gaming, but thus far have been void of golf.

Rick Phelps says it could happen in the near future. He's done about 10 routing plans that would include a course that straddles the two cities around Miners

Mesa and climbing up to Signal Hill. Both cities have political issues, but they are discussing the possibility of a golf project.

The Teller House Bar in Central City is an authentic old-west tourist stop that includes the famous "face on the barroom floor" from the old song. It's a painting of Baby Doe Tabor, a famous character in the area's history.

BAIR CHASE NEAR GLENWOOD SPRINGS

Bair Chase seems to be in limbo since the Texas developers have filed for bankruptcy. It was supposed to be a golf-course development with limited memberships, 150 rental units, 33 home lots, and 56 cabins on the 285-acre Sanders Ranch. Named the Bair Chase Golf & Rod Club, it would have views of Mount Sopris, overlooking the Roaring Fork River, and would have been Rees Jones' first design in Colorado.

STILLWATER RANCH IN SILT

This projected Scott Miller design, located between Glenwood Springs and Rifle just off I-70, will be called Stillwater Ranch (par 72, 7,400 yards). It is situated just south of the Colorado River, which separates the project from the small town of Silt.

Owners are securing financing, and it is tentatively set to begin construction in May 2004 with a late 2005 opening. Troy Grondahl of Scott Miller Design says it will have a lot of topographical variety with views of the Colorado River and strategic holes along Dry Hollow Creek.

"Since the elevation is about 5,600 feet, weather should be good for 10 months of play a year," said Grondahl. "It's a natural beauty in sagebrush terrain, and was a former cattle ranch that was grazed heavily. It does have cottonwoods, but we will also be adding piñon and juniper trees," he said. Wide-open fairways, native grasses, and large, blowout-type bunkers will be part of the design.

Miller, who designed the highly acclaimed We-Ko-Pa Golf Club in Fountain Hills, Ariz., is a protégé of Jack Nicklaus. He designed Deer Creek Golf Club at Meadow Ranch in Littleton as well as the 27 holes of Kierland Golf Club in Scottsdale and The Coeur d'Alene Resort Golf Course in Coeur d'Alene, Idaho.

HEADWATERS IN DOUGLAS COUNTY

This project just southwest of Castle Rock in Douglas County received opposition as soon as it was announced. Headwaters will include two Tom Fazio 18-

hole private golf courses near Jackson Creek Road. Home prices would range from $1.8 to $4.5 million.

Insufficient water during drought is the cry of the opponents, and the county denied a plan submitted in 1997 that called for three golf courses and a hotel on the same property. However, the plan passed some hurdles in 2003 and developers say they own sufficient water rights for the project.

FLYING HORSE RANCH IN COLORADO SPRINGS

Flying Horse Ranch, a 1,600-acre, mixed-use development by Classic Homes, is in the planning stages just north of Colorado Springs. They hope to begin construction this summer on the Tom Weiskopf design. Flying Horse Ranch will be managed by Troon Golf and will be a high-end private course with a possible 250-350 room resort spa next door.

STONE RIDGE GOLF CLUB IN TRINIDAD

The developer has been super-secretive about this project. Baxter Spann of Houston's Finger, Dye and Spann designed Stone Ridge Golf Club, to be located in a Trinidad subdivision that could attract more than 4,000 new residents to the historic mining town. The layout will be located on 235 acres in the shadows of Fisher's Peak, with distant views to the Spanish Peaks and the Sangre de Cristos. Developer Pete Schrepfer, needs to line up the financing, but he wants the project to include a 100-room lodge-styled hotel built by the Bison Hotel Group.

VALAGUA IN GYPSUM

Valagua is an Arthur Hills-signature design, with Chris Wilczynski as lead designer. The same team that brought you Ironbridge Golf Club in Glenwood Springs in 2003 has designed a 7,800-yard layout that maximizes the beauty of the Gypsum Creek area surrounded by overhanging cliffs. Valagua, which means "valley of water," could include 27 holes when completed with facilities for tennis, swimming, and fitness as well as hiking trails and fishing areas.

This will be a private golf and residential community with 963 acres of landscaping and abundant water. Vistas include rocky cliffs above Gypsum Creek and strategic use of water hazards.

"The par-3 4th hole on the lake nine is one of the most visually exciting holes at Valagua," said Wilczynski. "At 145 yards the hole is short enough, but with bunkers and the 30-foot deep Gypsum Creek ravine guarding the green, perfect shot placement will be imperative."

Construction schedules and an opening date have not been set.

RENDEZVOUS IN GRAND COUNTY

Rendezvous, a 1,150-acre, master-planned community located adjacent to Winter Park at the entrance to Fraser, is on the drawing board. Long-term plans include a championship golf course, resort, hotels, residential opportunities, and an extensive trails network.

STAGECOACH IN STEAMBOAT SPRINGS

Brian Stahl wants to develop the old Stagecoach area, which is 20 minutes south of Steamboat Springs and east of Highway 131. This area features Colorado's largest defunct ski area, which had a brief run in the early 1970s. Stahl's preliminary plans call for an upscale 18-hole golf course. Steamboat Springs has a bright future in tourism, which includes world-class skiing, golf, and outdoor adventures—the city was selected by *Money Magazine* as one of the 12 best places for a summer vacation in the U.S.

ASCENTPOINTE IN PARKER

This planned 27-hole master-planned community in Parker is lead by the team of John Prestwich, Alan Cunningham and Paul Shoukas—all former employees of Denver-based Redstone Group, the same company that built award-winning Rio Grande Club in South Fork. Cunningham says the project is still in its early stages and still on the drawing board. It proposes 6,300 residential units and a commercial development.

HIGHPOINTE AT DENVER INTERNATIONAL AIRPORT

In the last few years, several new prospective projects have aimed for the Denver International Airport area. Dye Designs announced it was going to build one called The British 18 at DIA; however there is no news on this project.

HighPointe at DIA is expected to include an 18-hole golf course, a 350-room hotel, a complex of office buildings, and a shopping district. This one is proposed to be shared by Denver and Aurora and will include an 1,800-acre real estate development near DIA.

Landmark Properties Group and Catellus Development Corp. are projected to partner in the construction, worth $1.5 billion over the next 20 to 25 years.

This proposed project could start by spring 2005. Hopefully, the golf course, conference center-hotel, and first residential phase will be built first; some of them could open in 2006. But principals say the entire project could take 20 years or more.

THE CANYONS IN CASTLE ROCK

Tom Doak's Renaissance Golf Design has been hired to design The Canyons, a semi-private golf club in Castle Rock. Look for more of Doak's minimalist philosophy, with very little movement of dirt. The location includes sandy washes and should be a rugged design, much like those built back in the 1920s. Smaller greens than today's norm are also set for the layout.

The Canyons is part of a 3,500-acre development north of Crowfoot Valley Road in Castle Rock. It will include 1,500 homes on the north section of the site, to be platted after the golf course is designed. Construction could begin in the summer of 2004 with an opening date tentatively set for 2005.

RAVENNA NEAR ROXBOROUGH PARK

Jay Morrish says Ravenna, a private golf course in Waterton Canyon that is scheduled to break ground in 2004. The spectacular site sits at the doorstep of spectacular Roxborough Park. It will include a 27,000-square foot clubhouse, swimming pools, tennis courts, and fishing facilities.

COLORADO'S PROFESSIONAL TOURNAMENTS

THE INTERNATIONAL

Davis Love III won the 2003 tournament wire-to-wire, but nothing could outdo the finish in 2002 when Rich Beem held off Steve Lowery in one of the most exciting PGA Tour event conclusions ever at Castle Pines Golf Club.

When Beem registered an eagle on the par-5, 492-yard 17th hole, he had a nine-point lead on 1994 champion Steve Lowery in The International's modified Stableford scoring system. Little did Beem know, Lowery was coming down the stretch with an eagle at 15 and a double eagle at 17, when he holed out a 6-iron shot from 217 yards. Lowery narrowly missed a birdie putt at 18 to give Beem the win. Two weeks later, Beem won the PGA Championship at Hazeltine Golf Club in Chaska, Minnesota.

But probably the story at The International and Castle Pines is more about the man who brought the tournament to Colorado. Jack Vickers is the reason the PGA Tour pros love coming to Castle Pines. Vickers, who grew up in Oklahoma, was good friends with amateur great Charlie Coe and has formed a close friendship with Jack Nicklaus. Last year he received the prestigious Ambassador of Golf award from the PGA Tour and Northern Ohio Golf Association charities.

THE INTERNATIONAL SCORECARD
Castle Pines Golf Club
www.golfintl.com
7,559 yards, Par 72
Designed by Jack Nicklaus

MODIFIED STABLEFORD SCORING SYSTEM
Double Eagle +8 points
Eagle +5 points
Birdie +2 points
Par 0 points
Bogey -1 point
Double Bogey or more -3 points

THE INTERNATIONAL PAST CHAMPIONS (SCORE IN PARENTHESIS)

2003 Davis Love III (46)	1997 Phil Mickelson (48)	1991 Jose Maria Olazabal (10)
2002 Rich Beem (44)	1996 Clarence Rose (31)	1990 Davis Love III (14)
2001 Tom Pernice, Jr. (34)	1995 Lee Janzen (34)	1989 Greg Norman (13)
2000 Ernie Els (48)	1994 Steve Lowery (35)	1988 Joey Sindelar (17)
1999 David Toms (47)	1993 Phil Mickelson (45)	1987 John Cook (11)
1998 Vijay Singh (47)	1992 Brad Faxon (14)	1986 Ken Green (12)

COLORADO OPEN

Talk about a shock out of nowhere. On the eve of the 2003 Colorado Open, set for Sonnenalp Golf Club in the Vail Valley town of Edwards, the tournament was canceled for lack of sponsorship. It was the first time in 39 years that the tournament had not been staged. In 2004 the tournament will be played at Green Valley Ranch.

This historical golf championship began in 1964 and has included winners like Al Geiberger, Brandt Jobe, Dave Hill, Willie Wood, Mark Wiebe, Steve Jones, and Jonathan Kaye. Some low amateurs have included future pros Phil Mickelson, Steve Elkington, Bob Tway, Corey Pavin, Mark Hayes, Peter Jacobsen, Jones, Wood, and Jobe. In 2002, Kevin Stadler, with his father, 1982 Masters champion Craig Stadler serving as his caddy, won his first event in his first professional start.

The Colorado Open, which was set to mark its 40th anniversary with the 2003 tournament, was first played at the Hiwan Golf Club in Evergreen in 1964.

Inverness Golf Club hosted it from 1992-97 and then Saddle Rock Golf Club from 1998-2000. It was staged at Sonnenalp in 2001 and 2002.

COLORADO OPEN PAST CHAMPIONS

1964 Bill Bisdorf, Denver
1965 Bill Bisdorf, Denver
1966 Bob Pratt, Las Vegas, NV
1967 Bill Bisdorf, Denver
1968 Vic Kline, Arvada
1969 Ted Hart, Scottsbluff, NE
1970 Wright Garrett, Albuquerque, NM
1971 Dave Hill, Denver
1972 Gene Torres, Las Vegas, NM
1973 Bill Johnston, Scottsdale, AZ
1974 Gary Longfellow, Denver
1975 Pat Rea, Pueblo
1976 Dave Hill, Denver
1977 Dave Hill, Denver

1978 Paul Purtzer, Scottsdale, AZ
1979 Larry Mowry, Maitland, FL
1980 Larry Webb, Chandler, AZ
1981 Dave Hill, Denver
1982 Dan Halldorson, Manitoba
1983 James Blair, Jeremy Ranch, UT
1984 Willie Wood, Stillwater, OK
1985 Al Geiberger, Beaver Creek
1986 Mark Wiebe, Littleton
1987 James Blair, Stansbury Park, UT
1988 Steve Jones, Phoenix, AZ
1989 Chris Endres, Glendale, AZ
1990 Bob Betley, Ogden, UT
1991 Bill Loeffler, Littleton

1992 Brandt Jobe, Englewood
1993 Bill Loeffler, Littleton
1994 Brian Goetz, Littleton
1995 Mike Zaremba, Pueblo
1996 Jonathan Kaye, Boulder
1997 Doug Dunakey, Fort Charlotte, FL
1998 Shane Bertsch, Parker
1999 Bill Riddle, Phoenix, AZ
2000 Scott Peterson, Denver
2001 Brett Wayment, Logan, UT
2002 Kevin Stadler, Englewood
2003 Cancelled—lack of sponsorship

DENVER OPEN

You have to call it historic when past winners include Ben Hogan and Chi Chi Rodriquez. That's the Denver Open, which has announced a change to Buffalo Run Golf Club in 2004. Green Valley Ranch was the host course in 2003. This was once a tournament on the PGA Tour.

Lew Worsham won the first Denver Open in 1947 at Cherry Hills Country Club and he went on and won the U.S. Open that year. Ben Hogan made headlines by winning in 1948 at Wellshire Golf Course. Thinking he had no chance of winning, Hogan's round ended early in the day and he took off for the bus station without knowing he had won the championship.

There wasn't a Denver Open in 1949 because many of the top pros were in Europe competing in the Ryder Cup, but the tournament resumed in the late 1950s at Wellshire. Denver-born Tommy Jacobs won in 1959; the popular Rodriquez won in the Denver Country Club and Dave Hill won at Meadow Hills. Through the years top pros have played in the Denver Open including Doug Sanders, Arnold Palmer, Bob Rosburg, Gay Brewer, Jerry Barber, Lionel Herbert, Jay Herbert, Ernie Vossler, Jack Burke Jr., Mike Souchak, and Davis Love Jr.

George Fazio, President Eisenhower, John Rodgers, and PGA Tour pro Dick Metz. Rodgers was head pro at Fort Morgan, Park Hill, and Denver Country Club.

MILE HIGH OPEN

It has been more than 30 years since a Mile High Open was played, but a new version has been scheduled for July 16-18, 2004 at Deer Creek Golf Club. This 54-hole tournament will have championship and senior flights. Amateurs with a 2.4 or better index can enter. No cuts will be made.

COLORADO WOMEN'S OPEN

The Colorado Women's Open is an annual event that Valley Country Club hosted in 2003. In 2004 the tournament is set for June 14-17 at Green Valley Ranch. This tournament began as a flight of the Colorado Open known as the Heather Farr Division. H.G. Godbey was the organizer.

By 1995 it was so popular that First Data Corporation sponsored the event and charity was the winner. The CU Cancer Center benefitted from a tournament that started with 15 local entries to more than 100 today from as far away as Australia. In 2003 the charity contributions helped out St. Anthony's Flight for Life, the CU Cancer Center, and Samaritan House.

In 2003 Lisa DePaulo of Austin, Texas won the event at Valley Country Club. Canadian Isabelle Beisiegel captured the trophy in 2002.

COLORADO WOMEN'S OPEN PAST CHAMPIONS

1995 Shelley Rule, Tequesta, FL

1996 Stephani Martin-Cobb, Colorado Springs, CO

1997 Lanny Whiteside, Woodland Park, CO

1998 Dawn Kortgaard, La Veta, CO

1999 Shannon Hanley, Lakewood, CO

2000 Janice Littlefield, Round Rock, TX

2001 Tamara Johns, Queensland, Australia

2002 Isabelle Beisiegel, Norman, OK

2003 Lisa DePaulo, Austin, TX

GOLF & COLORADO WEATHER

A cowboy poet once said, "Heaven is playing golf in Colorado on July 4 without sweating." In normal times that statement rules, but lately Colorado has been in the grip of one of the worst droughts it has ever experienced. The records say that 2002 was the driest year in 100 years. Golf courses were affected greatly, and for a short time the Denver municipals had to close in winter because of turf loss.

Since then, game plans have been formed. The drought is still here, but golf courses have been planning for more wells on their property, securing water rights, or using effluent sewage water.

In the summer of 2002, Grandote Peaks Golf Club in La Veta ran out of water. Fairways turned brown and greens and tees were kept alive by trucks hauling water in daily. By the end of the summer ever major national golf publication had followed with a story about Grandote Peaks.

The next summer things changed drastically – there was enough snow and rain early to bring the course back to life, green and lush. Cucharas Creek was full and alive.

Some projects got axed because of the drought. Melby Ranch, a 35-acre ranchette development in the San Luis Valley, cancelled its golf-course project.

Probably one misconception about Colorado golf is that we are snowed in during the winter. Wrong! The mountain golf courses are closed, but on the front range it is not uncommon to have plenty of days in the 60s and a few in the 70s during the winter. Denver golfers frequently play when it is in the 50s if the sun is out.

A Chamber of Commerce fact: Denver has 310 days of sunshine per year – more than Florida. And in December 2001 there were 2,400 rounds played at Overland Park in the Mile High City.

Tom Woodard, Director of Golf for the city municipals, said golfers can normally play 30 of the 60 days in February and March. But in 2001 there was only one play date in February. So you never know.

Colorado weather is constantly changing. Just when a storm passes through and chills the state to the bone, the Chinook winds take over and warm things up. Chinook is an Indian word for "snow eater."

The most interesting thing coming to Colorado golf in 2004 is Echo Basin in Mancos. This year they will be building the world's first 18-hole synthetic turf golf course, and one appealing fact emerged from this revelation.

Joe Niebur, whose Niebur Golf Construction of Colorado Springs was selected as the general contractor of the project, thought of another plus for having synthetic turf. He said most Coloradoans are always telling friends outside the state how we can experience a foot of snow one day and have it be 60 degrees the next.

"All you have to do with this turf is remove the snow and you can be back playing almost immediately. And just think about those golf courses situated high in the mountains. Keystone sometimes has only 30 frost-free days a year – if they can make a turf that holds up to the elements, it will add days to play golf in similar climates," Niebur said.

Never a dull moment – Colorado weather.

WHEN IT'S COLD

First thing, buy Footjoy's Winter Sof gloves.

Yep, the key is proper attire. Use a layered clothing strategy so you can easily add or remove items as needed. Watch out for the dreaded "Nanook of the North" syndrome that can leave you looking like a Pillsbury Doughboy, totally unable to swing a golf club. The best single investment is a shell—either a vest or windbreaker—made with tough but light GoreTex fabric to block the cold, wind, and wet. Some of these clothing items can be expensive, but think of it as good equipment rather than fancy apparel. When wearing layers, do as Tom Watson says and "Swing more slowly, so the sequence of the motion in the swing stays intact." That's good advice even on a warm day. Rain suits are another good layer.

On cold days, 75 percent of your body heat can be lost through your head, so wear a winter hat, preferably fleece that covers your ears. Special winter gloves are also available at retail stores around the state. Gloves take bit of an adjustment but are well worth it if you're determined to brave the elements, especially since your hands are how you connect with the club.

The next piece is knowing how to play winter golf. First, have the right attitude. Remove your expectations of low rounds, since it's just not the same. Take a macho approach and be ready to toughen up to the elements rather than complain about the conditions. And carefully select your playing partners, since it's easier to handle tough weather conditions when you're out there having fun with your non-whining golf companions.

Be sure to warm up more than you normally would for a summer round. Extra stretching can loosen the muscles up and make cold temps bearable. Once you've teed off, don't forget to hit "more club." The ball isn't going to carry as much when it's cold. Also, practice "knock-down" shots to keep the ball out of the swirling winds. The advantage is twofold here: You're never going to man-handle the wind, and less spin means less margin for wayward shots. Secondly, fairways that are not overseeded will be firm with dead grass, and you can take advantage of the extra roll with a lower trajectory shot.

With a little preparation, dealing with the Colorado weather can be a breeze. Tote the right gear so you can avoid miserable rounds and keep the weather from ruining your day.

WHEN IT'S HOT

If you play golf in Pueblo or Grand Junction, you know that it can still get to 100 degrees in Colorado. Last year I played at Cordillera's Summit Course and Breckenridge at 9,000-feet plus and it got almost uncomfortable. I couldn't believe I would ever see 80+ degrees at those altitudes.

Four simple rules: first, remain hydrated with water. That's right, water, not beer. Only water really gives your body what it needs to stay loose and cool during a sweltering day. Beer, while very enjoyable, is an extra beverage, not a water substitute. Second, wear light-colored, lightweight fabrics; dark colors absorb sunlight, while light colors reflect it. However, if you have already experienced sun cancer, dark colors are recommended. Third, use plenty, and I mean plenty of SPF 30 or higher sunscreen all over before facing the sun. Fourth, seek shade wherever you can find it. Even a moment or two under a tree or canopy will help cool you down.

LIGHTNING

Typically in Colorado, three people are killed by lightning each year, while 13 are injured. Casualties were down during 2002 and that was attributed to the drought, which meant less thunderstorms than normal. What is normal in Colorado? Beautiful mornings and chaotic afternoons loaded with rain and lightning.

Thunderstorms always carry lightning. There are more than 40 million lightning strikes every year in the United States, resulting in more than 100 fatalities.

In Colorado, lightning is the No. 1 life-threatening weather hazard. More than 100 people have been killed by lightning in the state in the last 50 years. Lightning heats the surrounding gases in the air to around 50,000 degrees and unfortunately causes forest and grass fires, an awful thought during a drought.

Despite what Lee Trevino said, God actually can hit a 1-iron. And he proved it to Trevino in June 1975 when a lightning bolt struck the Merry Mex and permanently damaged the vertebrae in his lower back. Luckily for Trevino, he was able to recover somewhat after a series of operations, but his days of total dominance on the PGA Tour were lost forever.

Thankfully golf is the only sport that has a regulation related to lightning. The USGA has accounted for dealing with lightning in their Rules of Golf (Rule 6-8), which allows players to discontinue play if they believe there is a danger from lightning. Most golf courses provide some kind of help in the form of restrooms or shelters. Golfers caught off guard by a quick moving storm should quickly determine the nearest safe place. Avoid trees, since they attract lightning, and look for a large permanent building.

GOLF GEAR – COLORADO WEATHER SURVIVAL CHECKLIST

- ❏ Rain suit
- ❏ Footjoy's Winter Sof golf gloves
- ❏ Extra towels
- ❏ Lip balm
- ❏ Fleece hat
- ❏ Umbrella
- ❏ Extra socks
- ❏ Extra shoes
- ❏ Sun screen SPF 30 or higher
- ❏ The right attitude
- ❏ Beverages – drink plenty of water in summer and winter. You can get just as dehydrated in cold weather as hot.
- ❏ Avoid alcohol.

ROMANCE & GOLF IN COLORADO

O K, first of all I'm probably not the right person to write this little chapter. Guys, especially travel golf writer guys, don't write about romance. Would the Tool Man, Tim Taylor, ever be caught dead with a romance chapter assignment?

Well, here's goes. I do have a story to tell. Back in the '80s as a journalist for *The Dallas Morning News* I invited my female friend Cheryl on a vacation to Colorado and a stay at The Broadmoor. I told her I was planning to play golf and she said, "Fine, while you are on the golf course I'll just go visit my brother at Fort Carson."

So we checked in to this world-famous hotel and I watched as her eyes grew as big as the Rocky Mountain sky. "Wow," she said, several times. "I've never seen anything this beautiful?" she repeated over and over. Once we got situated, I suggested a walk around the grounds, which is worth a stay just for the opulent landscaping, Cheyenne Mountain scenery, a stroll around Cheyenne Lake, feeding the ducks, and people-watching. The circular pathway that does a loop passes by the first tee of The Broadmoor's West Course. Guess whose eyes got big?

Yep, my eyes got bigger than Dallas. "I gotta play, right now," I told her. She was not a happy camper. Long story short, we had a little tension until that evening when we had dinner at The Tavern, which opened in 1934 celebrating the end of Prohibition. The prime rib and a couple of glasses of wine made her a much happier camper.

The bottom line—finding a romantic getaway in Colorado is an easy assignment. But if your significant other is not a golfer, romance and golf in Colorado needs to be handled with the deft touch of an experienced family psychologist. You must be diplomatic, you must share time—time for things that make her happy and a smidgen of time for your golf.

The Broadmoor is a perfect spot for couples—golfers and non-golfers alike—because guests rarely spend much time in the rooms. There's just too many activities. The resort surrounds Cheyenne Lake, and the new swimming pool offers a water slide and old-style cabanas. She can also go to The Spa at The Broadmoor for a paraffin body wrap. Guests can enjoy horseback riding, fishing, trips to the Cheyenne Zoo and Seven Falls, or end a day with a movie in The Broadmoor's own theater.

So where to go for romance and golf in Colorado? Here are my suggestions. But, you can't go wrong with hundreds of getaways in one of the most beautiful spots on earth. This list just scratches the surface.

- The Broadmoor, Colorado Springs, www.broadmoor.com
- The Lodge and Spa at Cordillera, Edwards, www.cordillera-vail.com
- The Sonnenalp Resort of Vail, www.sonnenalp.com
- The Ritz-Carlton Bachelor Gulch in Beaver Creek, www.ritzcarlton.com
- The Peaks Resort, Telluride, www.thepeaksresort.com
- Inverness Hotel & Golf Club, Englewood, www.invernesshotel.com
- Sheraton Steamboat Resort & Conference Center, Morningside Luxury Condos, www.steamboat-sheraton.com
- Grand Lake Lodge, Grand Lake, www.grandlakelodge.com.

CAMPING, FISHING, RAFTING, & GOLF

L ong before I hit my first drive from the tee box of a Colorado golf course, I cast a fly into the Rio Grande River at Thirty Mile Campground, 30 miles down a dusty Rio Grande National Forest road from Creede. My Boy Scout troop came here annually, but perhaps the most intriguing experience was our 50-mile hikes into the Weminuche Wilderness in southwestern Colorado.

Climbing to elevations that make you gasp for that next breath, trudging along the Rincon la Vaca Trail, past the peak that is called The Rio Grande Pyramid and stopping for a photo of La Ventana, a notch of rock missing from a stretch of a sandstone ridge line—this was something few city slickers ever experience.

I will never forget the afternoon we found a series of lonesome ponds, far up on the Continental Divide, where cast after cast landed tasty, small brookies. Our arms grew weary as our Scoutmaster started frying the fish, but we kept on to our limits. And just for fun's sake, someone got the brilliant idea to just toss a bare hook in. Bingo, that even worked.

Our camping experiences were unforgettable. Inside rows of musty, olive-green tents, we slept on army cots on blow-up air mattresses inside zero-degree-tested sleeping bags. When the sun set, we were either in bed or telling ghost stories by the campfire. It was downright cold at night, even in August.

But on the 50-mile hikes it was even more primitive. We hauled rolled-up "mummy" sleeping bags and backpacks filled with dry changes of clothes and socks and non-perishable food. A poncho was ever-present and we shared the drudgery of lugging a Dutch oven and trail kit, complete with cooking pot, frying pan, plates, and cups. At times, on the abandoned trails, it wasn't as much fun as it is today, thinking back on that time in our lives.

Later in life I found myself working on a two-year, temporary writing-editing project for that same Rio Grande National Forest, headquartered in Monte Vista. My boss, Tom Lonberger, eagerly would take me to a spot just west of Del Norte, where we donned waders and fly fished the Rio Grande's Gold Medal waters. I'll never forget the late afternoon when we stopped on the trail for an adjustment to my waders and a skunk stopped right at my feet, looked up at me, and then just lumbered on down the path.

Little did I know that some 10 years later a championship golf club, The Rio Grande Club, would open minutes away in South Fork, and that one of its amenities would be a scenic stretch of the Rio Grande bordering the golf course so members could fish. In 2003, *Golf Digest* named this Ric Buckton design No. 6 on its list of Best New Upscale Courses in the USA.

This scenic South Fork area on Highway 160 is a favorite of tourists wanting to experience rural Colorado. It's a long, long way to any town of size and the fishing and camping experiences are unparalleled. Now the golf is as spectacular.

THE ROARING FORK CLUB IN BASALT

Transition from the down-to-earth San Luis Valley's Alamosa, Monte Vista, Del Norte, and South Fork, and travel north to Basalt, near Aspen. Here, The Roaring Fork Club offers luxury in a rustic, rural setting. This exclusive and pricey private club has a Jack Nicklaus-designed gem of a course, and also has a Fly Fishing Guide Staff. PGA Tour players Brandel Chamblee, Mark Brooks, and Billy Andrade have all fished here, as does Mr. Nicklaus when he wants a break from his busy schedule.

In fact, The Roaring Fork Club, which includes the Roaring Fork River, has recently acquired U.S. Forest Service Permit Days for its members and guests, extending access to other local waters in the area. Management says the premier locations secured include the Upper Frying Pan River from the dam down to the lower-river public water, said to be the most prized fly fishing water in the state and the West.

In addition, members can cast into Maroon Creek and Castle Creek in Aspen and Maroon Lake, at the base of one of Colorado's most photographed scenes: the Maroon Bells. Roaring Fork management says that only four fly shops and guide services have the ability to fish these waters.

Back at the club, members and guests fish in eight stocked ponds, a .75-mile-long section of Spring Creek, and a 1.5-mile stretch along the famous Roaring Fork River for rainbow, brown, brook, and cutthroat trout.

Another Gold Medal fishing experience can be found in the Blue River, just minutes from The Raven Golf Club at Three Peaks in Silverthorne and Breckenridge Golf Club. Down in Crested Butte angler/golfers can enjoy The Club at Crested Butte while dreaming of casting into the Gunnison River. And throughout the Vail Valley, with its ritzy list of high-end courses, the Eagle River is a favorite of anglers.

THE ARKANSAS RIVER

The Arkansas River cuts a path through a geological rift, running from Leadville in the north along Highway 24 through Salida in the south. It then turns east on Highway 50 through The Royal Gorge and on to Cañon City and Pueblo. Along this historic river the trout population is said to be 90 percent browns and 10 percent Colorado River rainbows

Some say the rafting and kayaking along this river is some of the best in the world, and you can hook up with experienced guides in Buena Vista, Breckenridge, Royal Gorge, or Salida.

The Arkansas Headwaters Recreation Area is a river park created more than 10 years ago for whitewater enthusiasts. The AHRA consists of about 24 recreational sites located at intermittent stops off major highways between Buena Vista and Salida. AHRA headquarters are in downtown Salida. Call 719-539-7289 or visit online at www.parks.state.co.us/arkansas. The area also has an informative website at www.nowthisiscolorado.com.

And fishing usually means ample opportunities for camping. Log on to www.campcolorado.com or www.gocampingamerica.com for more information.

Not far from Leadville are the Summit County golf courses—Copper Creek, Keystone, Breckenridge, and The Raven Golf Club at Three Peaks. You can also play at Salida Golf Club or in Buena Vista at Collegiate Peaks Golf Course. And as the river turns east there's a brand-new Gary Player-signature golf course in Florence called Sumo Golf Village.

These fishing, rafting, camping, and golf opportunities are just a sampling of what Colorado offers. Here are some helpful references for your next experiences:

FISHING

- Royal Gorge Anglers, Cañon City, 719-269-3474
- Colorado Fishing Guides, Buena Vista, Out of state: 800-356-4992. In state: 719-395-2302, www.coloradoflyfishingguides.com
- Alpine Angling, Carbondale, 970-963-9245 or www.worldwidefishing.com
- Breckenridge Outfitters, 970-453-4135 or 877-898-6104
- Bucking Rainbow Outfitters, Steamboat Springs, 888-810-8747, www.buckingrainbow.com
- Duranglers, Durango, 970-347-4346, 888-FISH-DGO, www.duranglers.com

- The Fly Fisher, Denver, 303-322-5014, www.theflyfisher.com
- Fly Fishing Outfitters, Avon, 800-476-FISH, www.flyfishingoutfitters.net
- Kirks Mountain Adventurers, Estes Park, 970-577-0790, 877-669-1859, www.kirksflyshop.com
- Matt Owens Fly Company, Cedaredge, 970-856-7894, www.mattowensflycompany.com
- Telluride Angler Fly Shop, Telluride, 970-728-3895, 800-831-6230, www.tellurideoutside.com

RAFTING

American Adventure Expeditions	800-288-0675	Arkansas River
Echo Canyon River Expeditions	800-748-2953	Arkansas River
River Runners LTD.	800-525-2081	Arkansas River
Whitewater Adventure Outfitters	800-530-8212	Arkansas River
Bill Dvoraks Kayak & Rafting Expd.	800-824-3795	Arkansas River
Raft Masters	800-568-7238	Arkansas River
Adventure Quest Expeditions	888-448-7238	Arkansas River
Clear Creek Company	303-567-1000	Clear Creek
Clear Creek Company	800-353-9901	Arkansas River
Raven Rafting	800-332-3381	AR & CO Rivers

CAMPING IN COLORADO

STATE PARKS
www.parks.state.co.us/default.asp?parkID=89&action=park

NATIONAL PARKS
www.nps.gov, reservations: www.reservations.nps.gov

NATIONAL FORESTS
www.reserveusa.com, www.fs.fed.us

COLORADO CAMPGROUND AND LODGING OWNERS ASSOCATION
www.campcolorado.com

THE COLORADO DIRECTORY
www.colorado-directory.com

COLORADO TOURISM
www.colorado.com

BUSINESS & GOLF

(Courtesy of Fandango Publishing's *Golf Bible* series)

Civilization may be falling apart, the ozone is disappearing, and culture is in the crapper. But for the businessperson who loves golf, there's never been a better time to be alive. More than ever, even the bean counters in Accounting are willing to admit that a round of golf is a small but very powerful tool of goodwill in the battle to gain new clients. In the old days, taking a client out for 18 holes involved faking a major illness; today, no Watergate-style cover-up is necessary. The smart executive who secures "face time" with the client over a round of golf is lauded as an example of "hustle"...even if he's really a hustler!

Golf and business go hand in hand, sure, but not everyone understands the art of blending the two. This brand of golf is more about fellowship than score. Call it "golf with a purpose"—a game to help achieve other social and financial ends. If your playing partner is sizing up a 20-foot putt while you're trying to negotiate a tricky lie in the bunker, you quickly become comrades in pursuit of a common goal: a respectable score. Later, when it's time to close the deal, you'll have a deeper understanding of each other.

Where else but a golf course can executives spend a leisurely four hours in such a private, sociable setting? What better way to cement a relationship with a client than lifting a glass together after a round? Believe it or not, there is solid behavioral science to back up the fact that men open up and share more freely when they engage in an activity, such as golf, as opposed to a formal conversational environment, like a meeting.

There is a distinct difference between playing golf with your buddies versus playing golf in a business setting, and you'll need some savvy when dealing with employees, partners, or customers on the golf course. How well you comport yourself over those 18 holes—balancing business and friendship, dealing with competition and success—suggests to others how you might behave in the boardroom or around the bargaining table. Since your actions will speak volumes, here are some suggestions on how to send the right message and make it through the round.

LEARN THE ETIQUETTE

Follow the basic protocols: stay quiet when your partners are hitting and always treat the course with the utmost respect. Don't allow your partners to lose face because you've stepped in their putting line or failed to rake a bunker. The bumbling hack who finds himself (dis)gracing the fairways of an upscale private club will embarrass himself and lose the deal.

GRACEFULLY ENGAGE YOUR PARTNERS

Don't worry about closing the deal during a round. Instead, focus on getting to know your partners. Be sure to find out personal things like the names of their spouse and children, and what they like to do away from the office. Also, know when it's appropriate to talk business. Avoid diving into your core business conversations right away and at all times be aware of their demeanor while looking for the signals of opportunistic timing.

RELAX AND BE LOW-KEY

Don't be intimidated by the situation. Show clients you can handle the pressure with good humor; otherwise, you'll tense up and doom your chances of pulling off an effective golf swing. Golf is difficult enough as it is! If you start hacking it around, prove your mettle by keeping your composure and taking it like a man. Announce your high score with a smile. Besides, your partners might not even notice since they'll be so focused on their own games.

You want people to remember how enjoyable it was playing with you, so watch how you react to bad bounces and swing crises. If you lose your temper, you're done. If you get used to dealing calmly with struggles on the course, it will help your overall game even in casual golf situations.

DON'T OFFER ADVICE

It's okay to talk shop and discuss the latest swing fads, but if your partner is hacking away, refrain from opening your mouth with inappropriate swing tips. You don't know what the hell you're talking about, anyway. Just play and have fun.

READING PEOPLE

The best approach to the dicey details of business and golf is to learn how read people on the golf course. Are they serious about the game, and how do they approach their decisions during the round? Knowing the answers to those questions helps you feel easier in the setting, and can even clue you in to the appropriate timing to initiate that important business discussion you've been waiting for.

Golf nuts avoid business discussions on the course. They love the game and want to soak it all in, and would probably prefer playing golf on vacation rather than in a business setting. Power executives, on the other hand, strongly associate golf with business. They love the camaraderie of the game and the competition. Be ready to gamble a dollar or two since they believe it makes the game more enjoyable. Gamblers might identify with an executive golfer more than another archetype, yet are a little too sloppy for the uppity businessman. To them risk is everything and they'll do anything to get an edge, sometimes pushing it too much to form a true bond with a more emotionally balanced golfer. Finally there's the non-serious golfer; the one who doesn't compete or track his handicap. The one who plays the game for fun and relaxation, and is into it more for the relationship possibilities than anything else.

THE ESSENCE OF GOLF MACHISMO

(Courtesy of Fandango Publishing's *Golf Bible* series)

MACHISMO: 1. A strong or exaggerated sense of masculinity stressing attributes such as physical courage, virility, domination of women, and aggressiveness; 2. An exaggerated sense of strength or toughness

Follow me on this one if you will. For the purposes of this chapter, machismo, used in a light-hearted yet somewhat serious sense, is a term used to describe someone who has the savvy and experience to handle themselves confidently and effectively in every situation. Clint Eastwood's characters always smoothly deals with outlaws, James Bond always handles things better than we would, and Harrison Ford's Indiana Jones always efficiently takes care of business.

The bottom line: Knowing the intricacies of the often misunderstood aspects of the game such as rules and etiquette, or gamesmanship and wagering, sets you apart from the layman. It breeds confidence. It is machismo.

EXAMPLES OF GOLF MACHISMO

(Courtesy of Fandango Publishing's *Golf Bible* series)

A few years back when the Ryder Cup came to Brookline, Phil Mickelson and Jarmo Sandelin found themselves dueling at the par 3 No. 2 hole. After sticking his shot close to the pin, the diminutive Sandelin looked at Mickelson in anticipation of him conceding the putt. In what might be considered a rare macho gesture for the happy-go-lucky non-major champion, Mickelson reached into his pocket and pulled out a ball marker for Sandelin, who subsequently missed the putt.

Slammin' Sam Snead never won the PGA Tournament, but he definitely had the chance in 1947. In those days the championship was decided by match play, and Snead and Lew Worsham went toe to toe for 36 holes, with Worsham routinely giving the Slammer the short gimmes. Yet on the final hole, Worsham waxed machismo and stared in silence after Snead lagged his putt within the leather. Flustered, Snead butchered the putt and lost the match. Another story says that Snead left the putt way short, then as he set up to putt again, Worsham interrupted by asking Snead "Are you sure you're away?"—upsetting the Slammer enough to blow the putt. Either way, history shows that golf machismo was the order of the day, resulting in the edge Worsham needed to overcome the favored golfer.

The 2002 U.S. Open at Bethpage, NY was marred by nasty weather, and conditions became virtually unplayable despite the USGA's insistence on continuance of play. Tiger Woods persevered and kept his mouth shut. Sergio Garcia whined like a baby about the unfair conditions. Tiger followed the creed of the golf macho and won the tournament. Sergio, a fiery Spaniard, uncharacteristically avoided the machismo option and proved that he was the lesser man.

HANDICAPPING

I have a few degenerate buddies who will immediately flip to this chapter expecting tips on how to handle horse (or even dog) wagering at one of the eclectic Colorado tracks. Sorry, guys, but this isn't about picking a winner. This section is here because for every avid golfer who uses the handicap system effectively, there are a dozen weekend hacks who have no idea of how the system works.

While the USGA has done an admirable job of designing and promoting the handicap system, many of us don't take the time to use it, so keeping an accurate handicap falls by the wayside. Some of us use the system sporadically and make a guess at our handicap level when asked. Others never use it and don't care. It doesn't have to be that way. Knowledge is power, my friends, and knowing your actual handicap will help you in a variety of ways.

Without getting into the details of how course ratings and slope are computed, understand that the United States Golf Association uses those figures to determine how many strokes a given hack should get in an attempt to level the playing field for everyone. Because of this system, any two players can theoretically go out and compete against one another. Think about it. You can't do that in any other sport.

In another classic scene from Caddyshack, the Judge asks: "You don't keep score? Then how do you measure yourself against other golfers?" Ty (Chevy Chase): "By height." That's funny, but it's a shame because a golfer without a handicap really can't compete at any meaningful level. Establishing a handicap is easy: Simply play ten or more rounds, keep your score, and turn in the scorecards with two signatures: yours and one of your partner's.

Many public facilities have their own handicap computers, so choose a convenient area course where you play frequently to turn in your scores. You don't have to be a member of a club, which is nice for the roving golfer. At any given time, your handicap is the average of the 10 best scores of your previous 20 rounds. As a general rule, your handicap is the number of strokes over par it should take you each time out. Thus, a 10 handicapper should shoot an 82 on a par 72 course.

The most important point to this entire discussion is that handicapping is imperative when you're playing for cash. Most of your golf will typically be matches with other players. If the computer posts you as a 12 and your buddy as a 17, you'll give him 5 strokes a round. Circle the five most difficult holes on the card, and don't forget that you're spotting him a stroke on those holes.

In order to reach the next level and give yourself a huge advantage over 98% of all other golfers, there are certain rules you need to follow every time you play:

- Know the rules of golf and play by them. If you don't know them, start learning.
- Eliminate the psychological crutch of needing to improve your lie. Always play the ball as it lies. That's the way the game is meant to be played.
- Get into the habit of knocking down the short putts to finish a hole. If you start relying on your buddies to give you the "gimmes," you're in trouble when it counts the most.
- Start counting every shot. None of what I've mentioned above applies until you follow this basic tenet. Swallow your pride and write your real score down every time—even the quadruples that so often ruin a decent round.

KEEPING SCORE

While keeping score helps you measure your progress against the game, the courses, and even other golfers, it's easy to get too caught up in how many shots it takes you to make it through the day. Have some perspective and remember that scoring isn't everything. Many times you'll be playing matches against other players or teams, and the only thing that matters is how you come out compared to your opponents. Remember both sides of it and balance your approach to achieve the most enjoyment from the game. If you're having a bad hole, concede it and move on.

RULES

The rules of golf, while important, can sometimes be totally overwhelming, and are often too much to grasp for the average golfman. Understand that your knowledge of the rules of golf will develop over time. The best approach is to start becoming aware of certain scenarios while you play, then over time you'll patiently absorb the intricacies of the game. Watch more accomplished golfers on the tee and on the green to see how they behave. When they lose a golf ball, how do they handle it? Eventually you'll get the hang of the basics, and if you start playing frequently the rest will fall into place. Below we've included a few important rules from the United States Golf Association's The Rules of Golf.

- Dropping the ball: Lift and clean the ball, find the nearest spot where you have complete relief and mark it with a tee, measure one club length from that mark (use your driver), then naturally drop the ball.
- Off the tee: Tee it up between the markers, not in front, and no more than two club lengths behind them.
- The lost ball: You have five minutes to find it, then you must return to the tee or to the point from which you last hit the ball and play another. It'll cost you stroke and distance. If you slice it wildly off the tee but you think it might still be in, hit a provisional to avoid the long walk back. When it's lost in a water hazard, drop behind the hazard keeping the point where the ball last crossed the hazard between you and the hole. And don't forget to add a one-stroke penalty.
- Unplayable lie: You can play from where you hit your last shot, drop within two club lengths of where the ball is (no closer to the hole), or you can go back as much as you like, provided that you keep the same line to the hole. Whatever you decide, give yourself a one-stroke penalty.
- Play it as it lies: It's a hard thing to get in the hang of, but once you do you'll never play another way.
- Ball in a hazard: Remember that when you're in a hazard (bunker, water, etc.), you cannot touch the ground or water with your club before impact.

ETIQUETTE

Similar to grasping the rules, learning the ins and outs of proper golf etiquette takes time, and is something you should patiently pursue as you succumb to the lures of the game. Entire books have been written about golf etiquette, and we've included a few pointers below, but just remember that the golf machismo knows how to handle himself on the course.

- As a general rule, smile and keep your mouth shut. Don't go crazy in complimenting every shot your partner hits. Don't immediately dive into questioning your partners about what they do for a living, where they live, etc. The quiet golfman is a more confident golfman. It will help you in match play and make you more likable to other players. Rare men like Lee Trevino can pull it off, but most of us are better off in zipping it shut. Another point that goes along with keeping quite is to avoid giving advice to other golfers.
- Respect the course and the Golf Gods, and repair divots and ball marks.
- For general hacks, "ready golf," which means forgetting about whose honor it is, is the best way to play. Even if you don't play that way, be ready to hit at all times.
- If you hack it into another group, always, always, always yell "FORE!"
- Don't lollygag at the turn. Get your stuff and go.
- When you're done on a hole, get the hell off the green. Write your scores down elsewhere and make room for the duffers behind you.
- Avoid the drunk-college-guy trick of tearing ass all over the course with your cart. Keep it away from the greens and on the cart path at all times. Watch for the group in front of you and refrain from slamming on the brakes while they're on the tee.

STATISTICS

The number of stats kept for PGA Tour players is amazing: average driving distance, sand saves, trips to the bathroom. While tracking all of your golf statistics is burdensome, the dedicated hack will enjoy the game much more by keeping a few basic statistics in addition to score. Things like how many greens you hit in regulation (G.I.R.), how many fairways hit off the tee, how many putts averaged, and how many strokes it takes to get down from a greenside bunker help you detect strengths and weaknesses in your game. And if you wisely elect to invest in golf instruction, these stats are extremely beneficial to your pro.

GAMESMANSHIP AND WAGERING

How ingrained is wagering in golf? The USGA has a "Policy on Gambling" section within its voluminous Rules of Golf that states in part: "The USGA does not object to informal wagering among individual golfers or teams of golfers when the players in general know each other. Participation in the wagering is optional...and the amount of money involved is such that the primary purpose is playing the game for enjoyment." Translation: bet away, boys!

In fact, nowhere is betting more popular than on the PGA Tour. During Tuesday practice rounds, pros bet thousands with each other. And when you see two pros lining up putts on the practice green before a round, you can count on the fact that there's money on the line. Indeed, the PGA Tour itself is really a gamble: every week, 156 players pay to tee it up on Thursday knowing that almost half of them will miss the cut and go home without making a penny. The other half will stay and compete for purses of up to $6 million. "Golf is just a gambling sport," says Dallas' Harrison Frazar, a UT grad and tour player since 1996. "We spend $3,000 to $5,000 a week just to come out and see if we can make more money. In a sense, we're betting on ourselves."

For the rest of us, golf is recreation, a way to have fun. We get plenty of stress at the office, so that added pressure of a hefty bet can ruin the whole enterprise. What we're talking about is betting for fun—a small, reasonable amount—to enhance the experience and build camaraderie. Some old codgers even play for dimes. In other words, it's not the amount, it's the bragging rights, and the chance to slap a friend on the back and say, "Hey, I just got into your wallet!"

There are a million games and types of wagers invented just for golf. We've chosen just a handful that are popular at courses around Texas. Try them out the next time you and the gang get together. By the way, in most of these games, you need to take handicaps into consideration and figure out who gets strokes from whom on each hole. An extra stroke can make a huge difference to the outcome.

GOLF BETTING GAMES

BINGO, BANGO, BONGO: A simple game that can be played with two, three, or four players. Each hole has three available points, with each point equaling, say, a dollar. The first ball hit on the green—"Bingo"—wins a dollar. The person closest to the pin after every player's ball is on the green— "Bango"—is the second point. "Bongo," the first ball in the hole, earns the last buck.

HAMMER: A popular country club game that also is a favorite of tour players during practice rounds. The "hammer" is open at the start of each hole. If at any point of playing the hole a player believes he has the other player beat, he can "hammer" his opponent. That player has a choice of conceding the hole or accepting the hammer, which doubles the bet. If that player believes he gains the upper hand on the next shot, he can hammer back. So a bet can be doubled multiple times. Beware overusing the hammer late in the round: this can get expensive.

HONEST JOHN: On the first tee, each player predicts what score he will shoot that day. The player who finishes closest to his prediction without going over wins the pot.

LAS VEGAS: Play this game with four players divided into two teams. On each hole, each team combines its score to come up with the lowest possible two-digit number. In other words, if one teammate gets a 3 and the other gets a 4, their score is 34. If the other team posts two 4s, its score is 44 and it loses the hole by 10 points.

NASSAU: The classic golf betting game involves three match-play wagers: front nine, back nine and entire round. Perfect for two guys just having a leisurely round.

NINES: The perfect three-man game, probably invented by guys who could never scare up a foursome. Each hole has a total value of nine points. The player with the lowest score earns five points, the second lowest earns three points, and the highest earns one point. When there is a two-way tie for lowest score, those players get four points. When two players tie for the high score, they get two points each. A three-way tie is worth three points.

QUARTERS: A game designed to pass the time while you're standing on the tee box waiting to hit. Using only their drivers, players "tee off" from the tee marker of the men's tees and must hit to the tee marker of the ladies tees, striking it, then hitting back up to the men's tee marker. Each shot is worth a quarter, with the loser paying the winner 25 cents (or whatever amount) for every stroke above the winning total.

SKINS: You've probably seen the big-money version of this on TV. Players place a dollar value per hole. If one player gets the lowest score on a hole, he wins one skin. If two or more players tie for low score, the skin is carried over to the next hole, and so on, until a hole is won outright.

THOUSAND-DOLLAR-NO-BOGEY: A popular game among pros during British Open and Masters practice rounds. A foursome decides before the round that if anyone in the group plays bogey-free, he gets $1,000 from each of his playing partners.

TREES: A game made popular by Dallasite Lee Trevino and his buddies. Each time a player hit a tree, he had to pay the others in the foursome $10. If a ball bounced off one tree and hit another, each playing partner got $20.

WOLF: Players take turns on each tee being the designated "wolf." The wolf hits first and then watches the tee shots of the other players. The wolf then chooses one as his partner to play against the others. Or, the wolf may choose to play the others on his own. Some call that "pigging it."

GOLF BETTING LINGO

FORT WORTH RULES: This rather crude rule states that "Any male golfer whose tee shot does not go further than the ladies tees must play the rest of the hole with his manhood exposed from his trousers."

PRESS: A bet made by a player who is behind in a match. Many match bets have automatic presses. For example, if a player is one or two holes down, an additional bet will begin from that hole onward. Often, on the 9th or 18th hole there is a get-even bet that enables the player who is behind to recoup his losses.

SANDBAGGER: A golfer who exaggerates his handicap or purposely plays poorly the first hole in an attempt to lure an unsuspecting opponent into a higher bet.

TRASH: Sometimes referred to as "garbage" or "junk," these are smaller side bets. Players earn money for getting up and down from a greenside bunker ("sandies"), hitting the green off the tee on a par 3 ("greenies"), making par despite hitting a tree ("woodies"), or sinking a putt longer than two flag sticks ("polies"). Reverse-trash means loss of money for three-putts, hitting a ball into a bunker or water, or making worse than a bogey.

STYLE

These days a few professional golfers have made it a point to dress uniquely in an attempt to create their own special brand, thus capitalizing on the advertising and sponsorship dollars that often follow being a celebrity along the lines of Dennis Rodman or Deion Sanders. Jesper Parnivek wears his hat pointed to the sky and tight, colorful clothes, and is perhaps the only one who call pull off his different look. Charles Howell goes too far with his tight pants and ridiculous colors, and Aaron Baddeley isn't much different, combining outrageous threads with a white belt. However how can one argue with the suave, casual look of Freddy Couples, or the classic Polo-draped Davis Love III? Yet no matter what you wear, the important thing is how you wear it. so we've included a few suggestions on how you can ensure a decent look on the course.

- Wear your pants on your waist for a balanced look. The belt buckle should always be visible.
- Be sure that your pants aren't too short, and that the cuffs have a slight break that rests on your shoes. A nice-fitting pair of pants will not allow your fans to see your socks.
- The proper shirt-sleeve length is right at the elbow, and should not hang down any further on your arms.
- The shoulder seam should rest just off the shoulder blade.
- Avoid Dork Syndrome and refrain from buttoning your shirt all the way to the top. A little bit of a gap is best.
- Avoid the Duval look and refrain from wearing shades on the course. It just doesn't work.

GOLF RESOURCE GUIDE

From apparel manufacturers to web sites, *Colorado AvidGolfer* annually compiles a list of golf-related companies that call the Centennial State home. The following roster appeared in the magazine's Spring 2004 issue.

Apparel Manufacturers

IMPERIAL HEADWEAR
5200 E. Evans Ave., Denver
303-757-1166
imperialheadwear.com

SPORT-HALEY INC.
4600 E. 48th Ave., Denver
303-320-8800
sporthaley.com

TEHAMA APPAREL
550 S. Wadsworth Blvd., Suite 200,
Lakewood
800-955-9400
tehamainc.com

Club Makers, Repair Shops

ACE OF CLUBS
2843 Keystone Circle,
Colorado Springs
719-278-2261

BASS CUSTOM GOLF CLUBS
7251 Lowell Blvd., Westminster
303-427-7078

D'LANCE GOLF
151 W. Mineral Ave., Littleton
303-730-2717
dlancegolf.com

DIMENSION Z
14700 W. 66th Place, Suite #9,
Arvada
303-403-8344
dimensionz.com

GOLFSMITH
Englewood: 9667 E. County Line
Road, 303-708-1858
Westminster: 9440 Sheridan Road,
303-426-7775
golfsmith.com

PHOTON GOLF
1130 W. 127th Court, Westminster
303-522-7198
photongolf.com

YES! GOLF
7808 Cherry Creek South Dr., Unit 103, Denver
800-845-4327
yesgolf.com

CLUBHOUSE ARCHITECTS
William Zmistowski Associates LLC
1877 Broadway, Suite 100, Boulder
303-449-4831
zdesigngroup.net

COURSE ARCHITECTS
Andy Johnson Golf Course Design
P.O. Box 2018, Edwards
970-926-3436
andyjohnsondesign.com

DYE DESIGNS
5500 E. Yale Ave., Denver
303-759-5353
dyedesigns.com

JAMES J. ENGH GOLF DESIGN GROUP INC.
900 W. Castleton Road, Castle Rock
303-663-1000
enghgolf.com

PHELPS GOLF COURSE DESIGN
P.O. Box 3295, Evergreen
303-670-0478
phelpsgolfdesign.com

RATHERT GOLF DESIGN
1301 E. Green Meadow Lane, Greenwood Village
303-794-2400
rathertgolfdesign.com

Driving Ranges (all feature plastic mats unless indicated)

AQUA-GOLF
501 W. Florida Ave., Denver
303-778-9975

CENTRE HILLS LIGHTED PRACTICE RANGE
16300 E. Centre Tech Parkway, Aurora
303-343-4935
Chipping & putting greens
Denver Family Golf Center
6901 S. Peoria, Englewood
303-649-1115

Double-decker hitting area, grass and plastic mats, chipping and putting greens

GATEWAY PARK FUN CENTER
4800 N. 28th St., Boulder
303-442-4386

GRAND GOLF & RECREATION
9655 S. Quebec, Highlands Ranch
303-470-9300

NORTHRIDGE GOLF RANGE
14079 W. 96th Ave., Arvada
303-431-9268
Chipping green

NORTHWEST GOLF PRACTICE & LEARNING CENTER
4301 W. 120th Ave., Broomfield
303-438-6512

WORLD GOLF
6865 Galley Road, Colorado Springs
719-597-5489
Grass and plastic mats, chipping
greens

Golf Carts

Colorado Golf & Turf Inc.
11757 S. Wadsworth, Littleton
303-761-3332
cologolfandturf.com

E-Z-GO COLORADO
5867 N. Broadway, Denver
303-292-6609
ezgo.com

MASTER QUALITY CARTS INC.
2255 Busch Ave., Colorado Springs
719-448-0742
masterqualitycarts.com

**WEST HILLS INDUSTRIES
(ACCESSORIES)**
555 Alter St., Suite 19-B,
Broomfield
303-466-2644
westhillsind.net

Golf Charities

COLORADO PGA FOUNDATION
12323 E. Cornell Ave., Aurora
303-745-3697
pgafoundation.com

FIRST TEE, THE
Denver: City Park Golf Course, 2500
York St., 303-370-1556
Denver: Willis Case Golf Course,
4999 Vrain St., 303-455-9801
Pueblo: YMCA Community Campus
Golf Course, 700 N. Albany Ave.,
719-543-5151
thefirsttee.org

OPEN FAIRWAYS
744 Syracuse St., Denver
303-341-4160
openfairways.org

Golf Course Builders/Developers/Financiers/Management Companies

American Civil Constructors
4901 S. Windermere St., Littleton
303-795-2582

COUNTRY CLUB SERVICES INC.
8400 E. Prentice Ave., Suite 325,
Englewood
303-773-1188
countryclubservices.com

**ENHANCED PERFORMANCE
MANAGEMENT**
3225 S. Garrison St., No. 25,
Lakewood
303-763-9300

FAIRWAY SYSTEMS
6 Inverness Court E., Suite 120,
Englewood
303-790-4727

LANDSCAPES UNLIMITED
2820 E. Main St., Cañon City
719-276-2075
landscapesunlimited.com

M.J. MASTALIR
Real Estate Capital Corp.
6950 E. Belleview Ave., Greenwood
Village
303-290-9710

NIEBUR GOLF
830 Tenderfoot Hills Road, Colorado
Springs
719-527-0313
nieburgolf.com

TPS GOLF
2525 16th St., Suite 225, Denver
303-477-4504
golftax.com

Golf Fitness
BODY BALANCE FOR PERFORMANCE
Aurora: 22978 E. Smoky Hill Road,
720-870-1910
Colorado Springs: 1612 S. 8th St.,
719-477-1411
Highlands Ranch: 9655 S. Quebec,
303-437-6387
Loveland: 295 29th St., 970-663-6142

COMPLETE PERFORMANCE
6059 S. Quebec St., Suite 103,
Centennial
303-221-0162
completeperformance.net

NEW DIRECTIONS PERSONAL TRAINING
5774 S. Killarney Way, Centennial
303-898-5945
newdirectionspt.com

PHYSICAL GOLF
5801 S. Quebec St., Englewood
303-770-2582 (ext. 372)
physicalgolf.com

PILATES IN THE PINES
590 Happy Canyon Trail, Castle
Rock
720-733-9307

GPS/Golf Software Development
EGOLFTOURNEY
1822 Blake St., Suite C, Denver
303-395-3123
egolftourney.com

ITINERATIONS
4510 Lee Hill Dr., Boulder
303-619-7441
tothepin.com

PAR 4 COMMUNICATIONS
845 S Geneva St., Denver
303-667-8899
golflogix.com

Home Putting Greens
INTERNATIONAL SURFACING
4615 Spring Canyon Heights Suite
102, Colorado Springs
719-392-1029
internationalsurfacing.com

PRO GREEN SYNTHETIC GRASS
5562 Gray St., Arvada
303-464-7888
progreen.com

PUTTING GREENS PLUS
2160 E. Eastman Ave., Englewood
303-806-9279
puttinggreensplus.com

INSTRUCTION
Bogart Golf Colorado
Broomfield: 265 E. Flatiron Circle,
720-887-3543
Denver: 405 16th St., 720-274-0203
Englewood: 9617 E. County Line
Road, 303-708-0787
bogartgolf.com

CRAFT-ZAVICHAS GOLF SCHOOL
600 Dittmer Ave., Pueblo
800-858-9633
czgolfschool.com

D'LANCE GOLF
151 W. Mineral Ave., Littleton
303-730-2717
dlancegolf.com

ENGLEWOOD LEARNING CENTER
2101 W. Oxford Ave., Englewood
303-762-2674
ci.englewood.co.us/recreation/golf

GOLF ACADEMY OF NORTHERN COLORADO
Collindale Golf Course
1441 E. Horsetooth Rd., Fort Collins
970-266-8552
golfacademynortherncolorado.com

GOLFIX
3234 S. Wadsworth Blvd., Suite G,
Lakewood
303-984-8585

GOLFTEC
Cherry Creek: 201 University Blvd.,
Suite 212, 303-388-4832
Denver: 8101 E. Belleview Ave.,
303-770-5951
Westminster: 9053 Harlan St., 303-426-6600
golftec.com

JOHN JACOBS GOLF SCHOOL
2579 County Road 894, Granby
970-887-2709
jacobsgolf.com

McGETRICK GOLF ACADEMY
4900 Himalaya Road, Denver
303-799-0870
mcgetrickgolf.com

MERIDIAN GOLF LEARNING CENTER
9742 S. Meridian Blvd., Englewood
303-645-8000

NIKE GOLF LEARNING CENTER
Denver: Park Hill Golf Course, 4141
E. 35th Ave., 303-333-5411
Golden: Applewood Golf Course,
14001 W. 32nd Ave., 303-279-3003
Thornton: Thorncreek Golf Course,
13555 N. Washington St., 303-450-7055

PELZ GOLF—3-DAY SCORING GAME SCHOOL
76 Kensington Dr., Edwards
800-833-7370
pelzgolf.com/schools/cordillera.aspx

RICK SMITH GOLF INSTITUTE
800 Eldorado Blvd., Broomfield
303-466-6129
ricksmithgolf.com

Mental Game Training
WINQUEST
Littleton: 7400 W. Coal Mine Ave., 303-932-9020
Greeley: 1032 49th Ave., 970-336-9056
winquest.net

Novelties and Promotional Items
BRASS TACTICS MARKETING
700 33rd St., Boulder
800-822-7308
newgolfgifts.com

CASTRIOTA GOLF SPECIALTIES
P.O. Box 398, Morrison
303-975-1121
golfspecialties.com

CORPORATE GRAPHICS LLLP
1332 S. Cherokee St., Denver
303-722-6420
cglllp.com

GL SPECIALTIES
P.O. Box 2321, Arvada
303-456-9035
glspecialties.com/golf.html

GOLF WHOLESALE CO. INC., THE
1514 Teller St., Lakewood
888-456-7888
golfwholesale.com

PRIME TIME MARKETING
1531 Wazee St., Suite 1531, Denver
303-689-0383

Organizations
COLORADO GOLF ASSOCIATION
7645 E. 1st Ave., Suite C, Denver
303-366-4653
golfhousecolorado.org/cga

COLORADO JUNIOR GOLF ASSOCIATION
7465 E. 1st Ave., Suite C, Denver
golfhousecolorado.org/cjga

COLORADO SECTION PGA
12323 E. Cornell Ave., Aurora
303-745-3697
pga.com/sections

COLORADO WOMEN'S GOLF ASSOCIATION
7465 E. 1st Ave., Suite C, Denver
303-366-7888
golfhousecolorado.org/cwga
Founded in 1916, the association is designed to promote women in the game of golf.

EXECUTIVE WOMEN'S GOLF ASSOCIATION
Denver chapter hotline: 303-938-5771
Northern Colorado chapter hotline: 800-407-1477
ewga.com/chapters/colorado.htm
A national non-profit organization formed in 1991 to promote and foster a spirit of acceptance, dignity and respect for career-oriented women interested in golf.

MILE-HI GOLF ASSOCIATION
303-365-2528
golf-host.com/mhga.htm
Association members receive easy access to week-end tee times, handicap tracking, as well as a number of tournaments to participate in through-out the year.

ROCKY MOUNTAIN GOLF ASSOCIATION
3879 E. 120th St., Thornton
303-840-2673
rmgagolf.com
Part of the American Amateur Golf Tour, the association was formed to provide amateur golfers with a schedule of twelve to fifteen professionally run golf tournaments, plus a season's-end tour championship.

Retailers

2ND SWING GOLF
Lakewood: 1370 Denver W. Blvd.,
303-278-7887
Lone Tree: 8331 S. Willow St.,
Unit D, 303-792-5070
2ndswing.com

ASPEN GOLF SHOP
39551 W. Highway 82, Aspen
970-925-2145

BOULDER GOLF CO.
1780 55th St., Unit B, Boulder
303-938-0900

CHAMPIONS GOLF & GAMES
777 Vondelpark Dr., Colorado
Springs
719-593-9844
championsgolf.net

COLORADO GOLF & TENNIS
4950 S. College Ave., Fort Collins
970-266 -1967

COLORADO SKI & GOLF
Arvada: 7715 Wadsworth,
303-420-0885
Aurora: 2650 South Havana,
303-337-1734
Littleton: 9086 W. Bowles, 303-948-7550

D'LANCE GOLF
151 W. Mineral Ave., Littleton
303-730-2717
dlancegolf.com

GALYAN'S
Broomfield: 31 W. Flatiron Circle,
720-887-0900
Colorado Springs: 3133 Cinema
Point, 719-638-3400
Littleton: 8435 Park Meadows
Center Dr., 720-479-0600
galyans.com

GART SPORTS
25 stores across Colorado.
See gartsports.com for locations

GOLF CONNECTION, THE
506 Main St., Cañon City
719-275-7007

GOLF FOR HER
5435 Boatworks Dr., Littleton
303-770-0406

GOLF PERFECTION INC.
9655 S. Quebec St.,
Littleton
303-470-9300

GOLF SHOP, THE
967 Highway 50 W.,
Pueblo
719-545-2590

GOLF USA
Centennial: 12201 E. Arapahoe
Road, Unit A-10, 303-792-5799
Edwards: 0429 Edwards Access Road,
Suite A209, 970-926-3868

GOLFERY
5809 S. Broadway, Littleton
303-730-8533

GOLF'N GALS
5880 S. Forest St., Littleton
303-741-6272
golfngals.com

GOLFSMITH
Englewood: 9667 E. County Line
Road, 303-708-1858
Westminster: 9440 Sheridan Road,
303-426-7775
golfsmith.com

GREELEY GOLF & TENNIS
965 59th Ave., Greeley
970-353-4653

HANSEN BROS. GOLF & HOCKEY
2464 U.S. Highway 6 & 50, Suite
118, Grand Junction
970-245-0500

LENNY'S GOLF SHOP
2601 S. Parker Road, Aurora
303-369-5900

MAIN STREET GOLF
2460 W. Main, Littleton
303-738-9690

MARTY HUTTS GOLF HEADQUARTERS:
Boulder: 2490 Arapahoe Ave., 303-
440-3444
Lakewood: 850 Wadsworth,
303-233-4935
Littleton: 8430 W. Cross,
303-973-4580
Park Meadows: 9140 E. Westview
Rd. 303-759-9783
huttsgolf.com

OUTBOUND GOLF
8500 W. Crestline Ave.
Littleton
303-904-8710

PAPPY'S GOLF SHOP
3970 N. Stinton Road
Colorado Springs
719-633-2064

PRO GOLF DISCOUNT:
Colorado Springs: 5783 N. Academy
Blvd., 719-260-7193
Colorado Springs: 1670 E. Cheyenne
Mountain Blvd., 719-302-0054
Montrose: 16367 S. Townsend
970-240-8726

PRO GREEN INTERNATIONAL INC.
9940 W. 59th Place, #3, Arvada
303-431-1502

ROCKY MOUNTAIN GOLF
Castle Rock: 5050 Factory Shops
Blvd., Suite 455, 303-706-9200
Denver: 5091 South Quebec, 720-
482-6611
rockymountaingolf.com

ROCKY MOUNTAIN PRO GOLF
4223 S. Mason, Fort Collins
970-229-9022

SPORTS HER WAY
549 Flatirons Blvd. Suite F,
Broomfield
303-465-0065

STEFAN KAELIN PRO SHOP
516 E. Durant, Aspen
970-925-7266
stefankaelin.com

Tour Companies
CLASSIC GOLF TOURS
3045 S. Parker Road, Suite 201,
Aurora
303-751-7200
classicgolftours.com

MILE-HI TOURS
2160 S. Clermont St., Denver
303-758-8246
milehitours.com

Tournament Planners
AMERICAN GOLF CORP.
4141 E. 35th Ave., Denver
303-399-2333
americangolf.com

COLORADO GOLF SERVICES
406 1/2 Pintail, Grand Junction
970-210-0165

GOLF TOURNAMENTS INC.
5301 Quebec St., Commerce City
303-288-1979

HOFFMAN WEST
3327 S. Dunkirk Way, Aurora
303-693-5575
hoffmanwest.com

Web Sites

afgs.com
America's Favorite Golf School combines instruction with a vacation.

coloradogolflinks.com
Links you to various Web sites related to golf in Colorado—from tee times to golf-course real-estate.

e-golf.net
Online tee-time booking for more than 30 courses in Colorado.

frontrangegolfclub.com
Traveling golf club for men and women in the Denver area. Offers more than twenty events throughout the year at different locations on Saturdays.

golfcolorado.com
Provides information on golfing in Colorado–planning a vacation, golf schools, course locations, etc.

leftysonlinegolf.com
Great site for left-handed golfers. Includes a message board as well as plentiful research resources.

mygolf.com/golf/courses/co
Allows you to browse all courses in Colorado and purchase a wide variety of golf equipment and apparel.

rockiesgolf.com
Provides intriguing, blunt analysis of courses and their ratings.

shegolfs.com
Site devoted to women with information to help them improve their golf game.

uskidsgolf.com
Equipment, competition and a junior golf program for kids.

Radio Shows

In the Fairway radio show, hosted by Jerry Walters and Jon Lawrence, KOA 850 AM in Denver, Sundays, 8 to 10 a.m.

The chimney of a brick kiln impacts the second shot on Golden's Fossil Trace Golf Club hole No. 1.

Colorado Golf Courses by City

Colorado Golf Courses Alphabetical

About the author

David R. Holland is an award-winning, veteran journalist of more than 30 years and a journalism graduate of Texas Tech University in Lubbock, Texas. He's been on the sports staff of *The Dallas Morning News* and the *Waco-Tribune Herald* in Texas. As a freelancer for *The Dallas Cowboys Weekly* and *United Press International*, he covered the Texas Rangers and the Dallas Mavericks. He founded and published *Dallas-Fort Worth Metroplex Football Magazine* for almost 20 years and co-hosted a radio talk show on the Texas State Network about the frenzy that is Texas high school football.

But one career wasn't enough for Holland. After serving on active duty in the Air Force during the Vietnam era, he finished a 28-year career in the reserves, achieving the rank of Lieutenant Colonel. In Colorado, he worked at the Air Force Academy. As a member of the Texas Air National Guard he volunteered for Desert Storm and concluded his service in the Air Force Reserve with two years active duty in Monterey, California, working on a special Pentagon project that deterred fraud in the Department of Defense.

Holland's military stint in one of the world's greatest golf locations got him thinking about his next career move – travel golf writing. Over the past six years, Holland, a Colorado resident for 20 years, has probably published more travel golf stories than any other writer in the industry as a senior writer for *TravelGolf.com* and a contributing editor for *Colorado AvidGolfer Magazine*.